NEVADA STATE LIBRARY AND ARCHIVES

3 1428 00276 8527

COMMUNITY, COLLABORATION, AND COLLECTIONS

The Writings of Ross Atkinson

Robert Alan and Bonnie MacEwan, editors

with an introduction by Sarah Thomas

PROCESSED

NOV 1 5 2006

NEVADA STATE LIBRARY & ARCHIVES
CARSON CITY NEVADA

Association for Library Coll
American Libra
Chicago

Published by ALCTS, a division of the American Library Association
50 E. Huron St.
Chicago, IL 60611
www.ala.org

© 2005 by the American Library Association. All rights reserved except those which may be granted by Sections 107 and 108 of the Copyright Revision act of 1976.

08 07 06 05 - 4 3 2 1

Library of Congress Cataloging-in-Publication Data

Atkinson, Ross.
  Community, collaboration, and collections : the writings of Ross
  Atkinson / Robert Alan and Bonnie MacEwan, editors ; with an
  introduction by Sarah Thomas.
      p. cm.
  Includes bibliographical references.
  ISBN 0-8389-8361-8
  1.   Collection management (Libraries) 2.   Libraries--Aims and
objectives. I. Alan, Robert. II. MacEwan, Bonnie. III. Title.
  Z687.A85 2005
  025.2'1--dc22
                                                    2005029882

Printed in the United States of America
Cover and text design by ALA Production Services

CONTENTS

Acknowledgments   v

Ross Atkinson's Remarks   vi

Introduction   vii

1   Uses and Abuses of Cooperation in a Digital Age   1

2   Toward a Rationale for Future Event-Based Information Services   13

3   Contingency and Contradiction: The Place(s) of the Library at the Dawn of the New Millennium   27

4   A Rationale for the Redesign of Scholarly Information Exchange   43

5   Toward a Redefinition of Library Services   57

6   Managing Traditional Materials in an Online Environment: Some Definitions and Distinctions for a Future Collection Management   71

7   Library Functions, Scholarly Communication, and the Foundations of the Digital Library: Laying Claim to the Control Zone   85

8   Humanities Scholarship and the Research Library   103

9   Access, Ownership, and the Future of Collection Development   109

10   The Academic Library Collection in an Online Environment   121

11   Crisis and Opportunity: Reevaluating Acquisitions Budgeting in an Age of Transition   139

12   The Coming Contest   153

13   Networks, Hypertext, and Academic Information Services: Some Longer-Range Implications   155

14 Mass Deacidification in the Context of Access Time Reduction   **171**

15 In Defense of Relativism   **181**

16 The Acquisitions Librarian as Change Agent in the Transition
to the Electronic Library   **185**

17 The Conditions of Collection Development   **199**

18 Text Mutability and Collection Administration   **215**

19 Preservation and Collection Development:
Toward a Political Synthesis   **219**

20 The Role of Abstraction in Bibliography and Collection Development   **229**

21 Old Forms, New Forms: The Challenge of Collection Development   **241**

22 Preparation for Privation: The Year's Work in Collection
Management, 1987   **255**

23 Selection for Preservation: A Materialistic Approach   **275**

24 The Language of the Levels: Reflections on the Communication of
Collection Development Policy   **287**

25 The Citation as Intertext: Toward a Theory of the Selection Process   **299**

ACKNOWLEDGEMENTS

The inspiration for this collection grew out of a telephone meeting called by Peggy Johnson to discuss honoring our friend and colleague Ross Atkinson. After talking over several ideas, Brian Schottlaender, Pamela Bluh, Olivia Madison, and Bonnie MacEwan quickly settled on compiling a selection of Ross' publications.

This volume is a labor of love and a truly collaborative effort. First and foremost, we owe a debt of gratitude to Ross Atkinson, Associate Librarian at Cornell University, who has written tirelessly, brilliantly, clearly, and creatively for more than 20 years. His articles and presentations have shaped our careers and the careers of many of our colleagues. His work is required reading and his presentations provide continuing food for thought. The practice of collection development and acquisitions, indeed librarianship, would be much different today without his insightful ideas.

The contributions were assembled by Bonnie and the copyright clearances were handled by Pamela. Additional assistance with permissions came from Christopher McKenzie at Wiley; *LCATS* editor, Jim Mouw, helped with the Elsevier clearances; and Mark Johnson quickly secured permission for us from the University of Michigan. Bob Alan joined the project to assist with the editing. Sarah Thomas found time in a very busy schedule to write an introduction that captures Ross so well that we can sense his presence as we read it.

Emily Forwood conducted the initial searches to locate the articles. Peggy, Mark Sandler, and Edward Shreeves found electronic copies in their computer files while staff at The Pennsylvania State University Libraries prepared the rest of the articles for scanning.

The digitization unit at Penn State, led by Larry Wentzel, digitized the articles. Heather Solimini, Curt Krebs, Julia Allis, Sarah Allis, Bill Fabinich, Dax Finley and Becky Spitler skillfully scanned and converted the files using optical character recognition software. They brought the same care and love for the beauty of the written word to their work that Ross brought to the original creation of the articles.

A team of experienced librarians including Peggy, Pamela, Bob, as well as Linda Musser, Susan Hamburger, John Attig, Daniel Mack, Amy Paster, Gary White, Greg Crawford, Diane Zabel, Rebecca Mugridge, Rebecca Albitz, and Emily Forwood (a librarian-to-be) read the edited scans to correct any errors. They all found time in crowded work and research schedules to help with this project.

Amy Seachrist kept the editors on track and provided able clerical assistance. Sue Kellerman provided constant support and guidance. The ALCTS Staff, Charles Wilt and Kirsten Ahlen in particular, have been a constant source of help and encouragement.

We also thank our friends and families who once again were patient as we dedicated time and energy to this project. It has been an honor to collaborate with everyone who contributed to bringing this book together and a pleasure to re-read and learn once again from Ross Atkinson's contributions to our profession.—*Robert Alan and Bonnie MacEwan*

[This compilation really makes] me feel like all of my work over the years has been worthwhile. If that work will get folks to stop for a moment, and to consider what they are doing and why, that would be for me the ultimate success.
—Ross Atkinson
December 30, 2004

INTRODUCTION

Ross Atkinson is a runner. A spare, intense man, Atkinson is reserved about his personal life, although he is by no means misanthropic. Indeed, he's the kind of person who will quietly visit hospitalized colleagues or provide a listening ear to a troubled friend. The personal details of his experience remain in the shadow, even to those who have known him for decades. A few facts are shared here, although they are hardly relevant to the body of work that follows.

Deconstructing Ross Atkinson does not depend on biography. Growing up in California in the '40s and '50s, Ross Willard Atkinson Jr. attended the University of the Pacific in Stockton, California, graduating with a degree in German in 1967. Entering Harvard as a graduate student in Germanic Languages and Literature Studies that same year, he pursued a Masters degree. For the next four years, from 1969–1973, he served in the U.S. Army, engaged in military intelligence. Returning to Cambridge, Atkinson completed the requirements for and was awarded a Ph.D. in German from Harvard University. I personally cataloged his thesis "The Textual Conditions of the Early Works of Gerhard Hauptmann" for the Harvard archives in 1976. Ross's training in the close reading of a text has no doubt influenced his analysis and writing in the field of librarianship and information science. Enrolling at Simmons College, Ross completed his Master of Science in Library Science in 1977.

A new chapter in his life began. Ross, his wife Carole, and their infant son Andy moved to Evanston, Illinois, where Ross began his illustrious career in librarianship at Northwestern University. From October 1977 to August 1980, he participated in the Scholar-Librarian Program, where he was responsible for developing methods to integrate the library more fully into the teaching and research activities of the university. He made occasional recommendations for additions to the collection, a responsibility that was the precursor to the role where he has made his greatest mark, building outstanding collections. For two-and-a-half years he served as humanities bibliographer in the Northwestern University Library, before moving up to be Associate University Librarian for Collection Development at the University of Iowa in April 1983.

It was at this phase in his career that Atkinson began an influential course of writing, presenting, and publishing. Atkinson's body of work is characterized by tight definition, linguistic precision, and a combination of abstract reasoning that is frequently reduced to a simple predictive statement or recommendation. He often exhorts practitioners to higher ideals of community, collaboration, and, of course, collections. The abstract for his 1984 publication "The Citation as Intertext: Toward a Theory of the Selection Process," an article based on a presentation he made in 1983 at a Resources and Technical Services Division (RTSD) Collection Management and Development Institute, employs a rich vocabulary with a unique stamp. Drawing on the work of French critic Roland Barthes, Atkinson uses the explication of three categories: the syntagmatic contexts, the contexts of supplementation, and the contexts of resolution. The interrelationships among the categories are presented in a figure, another hallmark of Atkinson's writing, in which he often diagrams his ideas. Atkinson concludes the article that launched his career as one of the profession's most original thinkers with the observation: "for every citation remains from the standpoint of every individual a single intertext in a vast network of personal and constantly evolving contexts that influence decisively the citation's meaning and significance."[1] Its brilliance and originality captured the attention of many, and the Resources and Technical Services Division of the American Library Association bestowed on Ross Atkinson the 1985 RTSD

Blackwell North America/Resources Section Scholarship Award in recognition of its excellence. Atkinson developed a pace of publishing that resulted in an average of one to two solid, often provocative articles per year, sustained over two decades.

Atkinson continued his career at the University of Iowa Libraries as Assistant University Librarian for Collection Development, where he worked from April 1983 through August 1988. At the end of summer 1988, he moved to assume the position of Assistant University Librarian for Collection Development and Preservation at Cornell, now Associate University Librarian for Collections. During the past sixteen years Ross Atkinson has led the development of selection policy at Cornell and has served as a guiding light for generations of librarians. Among his more distinguished publications during this era are "The Acquisitions Librarian As Change Agent in the Electronic Library,"[2] which was awarded the "Best of *LRTS* Award" in 1992, "Networks, Hypertext and Academic Information Services: Some Longer-Range Implications,"[3] awarded the K. G. Saur Award for best *College & Research Libraries* article of 1993, and "Managing Traditional Materials in an Online Environment: Some Definitions and Distinctions for a Future Collection Management,"[4] awarded the 1999 ALCTS Blackwell's Scholarship Award. Bill Schenck, chair of the Best of *LRTS* Award Committee, described "The Acquisitions Librarian As Change Agent in the Electronic Library" as a visionary call to action.[5] Addressing an important issue, the article presents a scholarly and well-reasoned approach to how libraries, in general, and acquisitions librarians, specifically, can facilitate and promote scholarly communications. Jim Williams, chair of the Saur Committee, said of Atkinson's article "Networks, Hypertext and Academic Information Services":

> The Atkinson article is well-written, extremely relevant, and exceptionally well-informed. It has wide appeal and is likely to have a lasting impact, especially in its philosophical implications. It is thoughtful and deals with some of our most important issues.[6]

Jean Padway, Chair of the ALCTS Blackwell Award Committee, in announcing Ross Atkinson as the recipient of the 1999 award for his article "Managing Traditional Materials," declared:

> The committee unanimously agreed that Atkinson's article met and exceeded the criteria for this award. Through his description of a future collection management, he brings together a realistic approach for management of all materials and their necessary coexistence in library collections. His article discusses the increasing role that digital materials play within the library and blends the management of these with traditional materials. While recognizing the growing presence of digital resources, he discusses the importance of management over the total collection's materials, in all formats.[7]

Ross's dedication to his work is legendary, and his accomplishments are prodigious. In addition to managing the process of building a collection which is a resource for international scholarship, Ross unstintingly gives his time and thought to deconstructing the serious challenges that face librarians as they strive to connect authors and readers in their quest to advance knowledge. On Saturday mornings at five-fifteen, Ross routinely logs his signature into the security sheet of Olin Library, eager to work undisturbed on a paper or presentation. He is thorough and methodical about his approach, reading voraciously from a wide range of philosophers, librarians, and other creative thinkers. His methodology may be orthodox, but the result of his examination is far from that. He is prized as a contributor to discussions and his articles are must-reads for all because he combines careful research with visionary and original thinking.

Ross Atkinson's service to the profession extends far beyond his publications. He recently completed a second term on ALA Council, serving as ALCTS divisional member, and he previously was a member of ALA Council from 1991–1995. He has chaired or served on more than a dozen ACRL committees between 1979 and the present, including membership in the ACRL Publications Committee, 1995–99, chairing the Section Review Committee of the Western European Specialists Section, 1985–86, and chairing WESS in 1984–85. He has been a distinguished member of the Chief Collection Development Officers of Large Research Libraries for more than twenty years, joining the group first in 1983. Over the years he has been an active participant in many RLG committees and taskforces. He was a critical member of the Digital Library Federation Task Force during its formative years from 1995–98, and he has been a valued representative to ARL, CNI, and CIC groups and task forces. In 2001 he spent several weeks at the Center for Research Libraries, where he chaired the Task Force on Collection Assessment. His work during that period contributed substantially to the strategic direction of that organization.

Ross Atkinson is a highly principled librarian with passion about freedom of access to information. His integrity, his conviction that we must work together to achieve open access to the documents of civilization, and his commitment to share his thoughts and knowledge with the profession made him a superb candidate for ACRL Academic/Research Librarian of the Year, an award that he received in 2003.

Atkinson continues to stretch our thinking with his presentations and publications, most recently "Uses and Abuses of Cooperation in a Digital Age," in which he urges librarians to eschew competitive actions in favor of constructive cooperation.[8]

In a presentation to Cornell's librarians a few years ago, Ross, speaking on the way in which he prepared himself for a talk, described the period between invitation and delivery as one that began with the notation of his basic ideas and their links, followed by intense immersion in the brew of reading that would ferment his thinking, succeeded by drafting and redrafting his own thoughts and statements, hammering them out in many iterations. He revealed the many months of effort that the polished presentations, delivered with the eloquence and passion of a preacher, required. With this insight into his method, in which hard work and genius come together to create a work of art and meaning, I often find myself picturing the wiry runner, pounding the rolling terrain of Ithaca, beating out a phrase, rhythmically counting out the conditions of cooperation. A runner, apart, cresting the hill, with the future spread out before him.

The articles that follow bring together Ross Atkinson's publications over the period of two decades. They provide the reader with an expansive view of the field of collection development. Throughout his career Ross Atkinson has been a man of vision. We are privileged to have this collection of his writings assembled for our inspiration.—*Sarah E. Thomas, Carl A. Kroch University Librarian, Cornell University*

REFERENCE NOTES

1. Ross Atkinson, "The Citation As Intertext: Toward a Theory of the Selection Process," *Library Resources & Technical Services* 28 (Apr./June 1984): 118

2. Ross Atkinson, "The Acquisitions Librarian As Change Agent in the Electronic Library," *Library Resources & Technical Services* 36 (Jan. 1992): 7–20.

3. Ross Atkinson, "Networks, Hypertext and Academic Information Services: Some Longer-Range Implications," *College & Research Libraries* 54 (May 1993): 199–215.

4. Ross Atkinson, "Managing Traditional Materials in an Online Environment: Some Definitions and Distinctions for a Future Collection Management," *Library Resources & Technical Services* 42 (Jan. 1998): 7–20.

5. "Best of *LRTS* Award Recipient Named," *ALCTS Network News* 5 (Apr. 26,1993). www. infomotions.com/serials/ann/ann-v5n21.txt.

6. "ACRL K.G. Saur Award recipient named,"*ALANEWS* (Apr. 21, 1994). www.infomotions. com/serials/alanews/alanews-940421.txt.

7. "ALCTS Awards Highlight Outstanding Contributions: Blackwell's Scholarship Award," *ALCTS Online Newsletter* 10, no. 4 (July 1999).

8. Ross Atkinson, "Uses and Abuses of Cooperation in a Digital Age," in *The New Dynamics and Economics of Cooperative Collection Development,* ed. Edward Shreeves (Binghamton, N.Y.: Haworth, 2003), 3–22.

1 USES AND ABUSES OF COOPERATION IN A DIGITAL AGE

This article reviews some of the standard issues relating to cooperative collection development, first with respect to traditional materials, and then from the standpoint of an environment increasingly dependent upon licensed electronic resources. Some options for cooperation in a licensed environment are suggested. A few issues relating to a shift from collection management to knowledge management are explored, and some further suggestions are presented as to how services based upon some concepts of knowledge management might be improved through inter-institutional cooperation. The article concludes with a recommendation to replace some of the current competition among libraries with a more competitive stance toward other information intermediaries.

This article is yet another addition to the seemingly interminable discussion of cooperative collection development. Many collection development officers of a certain age no doubt feel, as I do, that they have been reading and talking about cooperation for most of their adult lives. Oceans of ink have been spilled in arguments over the rationale and practicability of cooperation—how future cooperative agreements might work, and why past ones have not. What is in fact so fascinating about cooperative collection development is why it is so plausible in theory—and yet so problematic to implement in practice. Times are now changing so rapidly and so radically, however, that one more examination of a few key issues would seem warranted. Let us fan again, therefore, some of these old embers, and see if they can yet shed some light on this new age.

CONVENTION AND COMPETITION

If the "classic and traditional" purpose of cooperative collection development is primarily to improve local library services, then we must ask at the outset what scales libraries use, such that they can gauge the qualities of those services and determine whether they are in fact improving.[1] Clearly there are many such scales—use and user studies, collection evaluations—but there are two especially important methods of assessing effectiveness that are rarely discussed. First, there are management conventions, by which I mean values and precepts that condition how library administrators perceive the quality of library services. Operations that conform to these conventions are viewed as functioning well, while those that do not are suspected of deficiencies. I want to emphasize that these are not management principles, which would imply a kind of eternal validity, but rather conventions, i.e., concepts of purpose and effectiveness that change over time, depending upon consensus and fashion. We must try to identify such conventions whenever considering such complex

This article first appeared simultaneously in *Collection Management* 28, no. 1/2 (2003): 3–20 and in *The New Dynamics and Economics of Cooperative Collection Development,* ed. Edward Shreeves (Binghamton, N.Y.: Haworth Pr., 2003), 3–20.

management issues as cooperation, therefore, to help us understand why certain decisions are made and certain attitudes prevail.

The other seldom-discussed but unquestionably powerful method libraries use to assess the quality of their services is to look at each other. Libraries need each other—because without each other, they cannot tell what they are. The identity and individuality of any library is understandable only as a relation to every other one. How well I think my library is doing depends to a substantial degree on my perception of how yours is doing. Such comparison is, needless to say, highly selective and subjective, but its effect is undeniably real. There is a fundamental, encompassing, essential and inevitable competition among libraries—although it is considered gauche in the current environment to dwell upon these competitive relationships publicly. The exact opposite situation obtains with respect to cooperation: to discuss inter-institutional cooperation, frequently and at length, is much encouraged—and some might even say that the primary purpose of cooperation is in fact to provide libraries with something to talk with each other about. The problem is that the present custom of ignoring or concealing underlying competition greatly impairs the ability of libraries to set (let alone achieve) cooperative goals, because cooperation is only practicable—indeed, only conceivable—within the context of competition. This is because true cooperation, the kind of cooperation that produces clear and mutually beneficial results, is always necessarily a kind of temporary suspension of competition among near equals within jointly defined rules or parameters.

If there is one convention most central to cooperative collection development, it is surely what we can call the *Law of Local Access Optimization*. Every service a library develops, every action it takes, every dollar it spends, has but one purpose—and that is to enhance local access to and use of relevant information. Any library resource used for any other purpose than the enhancement of local access and utility is *mis*used. The library receives local funding to create local programs that meet local needs. No library would or could spend local funding to meet regional or national needs—unless, in so doing, it could more effectively and demonstrably meet local needs. That is the reality of our situation, and it is from that point that any discussion of cooperation must proceed.

There are of course many implications of the Law of Local Access Optimization, but we should note two in particular. The first is what we can call the rule of *value over cost*. Cooperation entails my expenditure of some of my resources to meet the needs of your users, and vice-versa—but the value of the services my users receive must exceed what I am investing in the cooperation, otherwise I would simply use my resources to meet the needs of my users. The second implication of the Law of Local Access Optimization is the requirement for *relational equilibrium*. A cooperative program, if successful, is indeed a tide that raises all boats—but it does not change the size, wealth, or power of those individual boats in relation to each other. Cooperation can and should result in increased effectiveness for participating libraries, when measured against libraries outside of the cooperative group—but cooperation may not significantly change the relationship of those libraries within the cooperative group to each other. The purpose of cooperation will and can never be to make all libraries within the cooperative group equal: their differential relationship to each other must be maintained, for cooperation to be possible.

TRADITIONAL COOPERATION

With these realities in mind, let us focus on a few characteristics of traditional cooperative collection development. We can begin by resuscitating an old dichotomy: *synergism* and *complementarity.*[2] Synergistic cooperation entails a conscious change in behavior on the part of each participant, such that all participants together create a sense of a consortial collection that meets some of the needs of all members. Complementarity, on the other hand, is the more passive form of cooperation, which focuses mainly on ensuring that effective methods for interlibrary lending are in place—and it might indeed be objected that complementarity does not really qualify as cooperation at all, at least from the standpoint of collection development. Complementarity means that each partner buys what its local users need. This does, of course, result in substantial overlap—but it also permits the acquisition of some unique items; if pursued on a sufficiently broad scale, complementarity may ultimately result in a cumulative collection that contains many materials that might be needed by most members. From the complementary perspective, therefore, there is no need to invest in the (often considerable) expense of synergism: the simple pursuit of self-interest will be sufficient to produce the desired "cooperative" result. Members of the Research Libraries Group did in fact struggle mightily and nobly for more than a decade, trying to put into effect a large scale program of synergistic cooperation—only finally to move more toward complementarity in the early 1990s. This is not to say, of course, that synergism is never successful. Synergistic programs have indeed been very effectively implemented—but they are normally restricted, operating mainly at the regional level. (Two of the most successful examples are the Triangle University Libraries and OhioLINK.[3])

What types of synergism are in fact possible? Let us try to lay out an abstract typology in figure 1. *Prospective synergism,* we can say, is the division of responsibilities in advance for the acquisition of designated categories of materials, while *retrospective synergism* involves dividing responsibility for maintaining materials already acquired. We should also think in terms of proactive and reactive methods of cooperation. We can then refer to *prospective/proactive,* which is indeed the most standard notion of cooperation, such as the Farmington Plan: each institution takes responsibility for a different category of material, so that each member can support some of the needs of the other members with respect to that category. (In order to achieve this kind of cooperation, of course, there must be a relatively clear understanding and agreement among the partnering institutions at the outset as to the parameters of the subjects and the definitions of the collection levels.) *Prospective/reactive,* on the other hand, would be a matter of each institution collecting independently for a predetermined period—and then pausing at some point to divide responsibility for some subset of the materials that remain. All members could, for example, define Harrassowitz slips as the cooperative universe; then, after a period of selection, the group could create a list of the titles that no member of the group had so far acquired, and then divide responsibility for purchasing some or all of those.

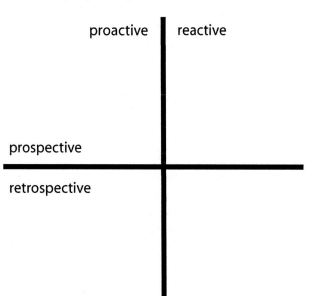

FIGURE 1. Types of Synergistic Cooperation

For *retrospective/proactive* cooperation, each member institution would assume responsibility in advance for maintaining (preferably indefinitely) a particular category of its collection. If one institution in the group agreed, for example, to retain all of the materials it held on a particular subject, all other members would have the option to discard any of those materials and to depend in future upon the holdings of the designated institution. (The library assuming this responsibility might also need to agree to accept the transfer from partner institutions of any materials on the subject that it does not already hold.) The *retrospective/reactive* approach, finally, could be highly chaotic, if not very carefully controlled. As I see it, this method in its basic form would be primarily a matter of any member having the opportunity to withdraw any title held by any other member of the group. One way to provide some control over such an arrangement would be to give all members the option of annotating each others catalog records, so that an institution would know when it has been given responsibility by another member for maintaining a particular title for the partnership. The understanding might be that no member could withdraw an item that another member is depending upon that institution for—unless, of course, the member wanting to withdraw could find yet another member of the partnership holding that item. Needless to say, without carefully crafted rules, the race would be to the swift—and such an arrangement could quickly get out of hand, were many of the partners suddenly compelled for some reason to undertake serious weeding.

Most cooperative collection development focuses on the prospective approach. We can try to model the basic mode of prospective cooperation as seen in figure 2. The entire pyramid represents what I prefer to call the "anti-collection," i.e., those materials that are not in the local collection, and are therefore candidates for selection. As a selector, I should be able to prioritize the objects in this anti-collection according to their relative value to my local users, at least at the time of selection. There is no question that I am going to purchase what I consider to be the very most important material, i.e., down to Level A. Publications below Level A are a somewhat lower priority, so I set some citations aside, see how my budget holds up, and compare materials published over time—but by the end of the year, I know that I will have selected down to Level B. Prospective synergism, at its most rudimentary, is simply a matter of spending initially only down to Level C—and using what funding is saved (by not buying down to Level B), to contribute to the purchase of materials below Level C (and, indeed, below Level B, otherwise such cooperation would not be worthwhile, by virtue of the value over cost rule described previously). Since the anti-collection has no per-

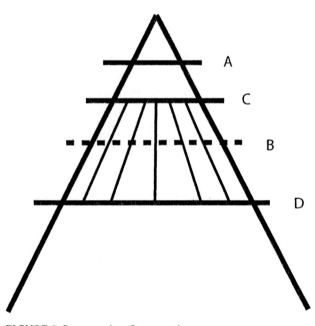

FIGURE 2. Prospective Cooperation

ceivable bottom, the partnership needs to define a base for cooperation, which we can call Level D. The consortial agreement would be to divide responsibility among the members for purchasing materials between C and D. Since no one wants to buy exclusively down toward Level D, and everyone wants to buy up toward Level C—and since selection responsibilities need to be distributed clearly and systematically—the C-D area is usually divided into vertical segments by designated categories, such as subject, publisher, geographical area, or language, so that each member can assume responsibility for one or more segments.

While some refinements and special agreements are, of course, invariably needed, this is, to a great extent, all there is to prospective cooperation. Why, then, we must ask—this concept being so straight forward—is it so insurmountably difficult to put into practice? Ask any selector, and you will quickly find out. The fact is that this clean, neat, abstract model may in fact bear little resemblance to the concrete reality of day-to-day collection building. For a selector to define such levels for himself or herself is difficult enough; for a group of selectors at different institutions to agree upon such divisions can be very problematic. It is for this reason that selectors and collection development officers may often conclude that such a division of responsibilities would be a clear transgression of the value over cost rule, i.e., that the resource expense of trying to define such levels in the real world would likely exceed what would actually be saved through the resulting cooperative program.

This negative perception of cooperation, however, is also driven, at least in part, by what we might call the *tactical fallacy,* which is something to which all of us who work in organizations are unavoidably prone. It is the assumption that the purpose of the organization is equivalent to the operations it performs, e.g., cataloging, or reference, or, in our case, selection. As collection development officers, we may well feel, therefore, that the primary purpose of the library is to build and maintain collections. The fact is, of course, that none of those functions, including collection building, are the library's actual purpose. All such operations are rather always a means to an end—and that end is local user access. We who build collections may often make the mistake, therefore, of reification: the assumption that reality consists of things or relationships among them. The purpose of collection development, we may feel, is to create a thing—the perfect (within resource constraints) collection. The time has now finally arrived, however, to begin to refocus our sense of purpose, to stop regarding the collection as a thing, and to acknowledge that the local collection, as beautiful as it may be, is rather primarily a method or means—increasingly only one among several—to provide effective access to locally needed information.

Another inexorably evolving trend that has impaired cooperation in some ways is what we can call the denigration, repudiation, or demise of the *completeness syndrome.* (This is another one of the management conventions mentioned earlier that condition so profoundly our views of service quality.) By this, I mean the partial disappearance of the sense that managing well is equivalent to doing a complete job. In the span of my own career, I subjectively date the true beginning of the demise of the completeness syndrome from the decision made by Richard Dougherty, the Director at the University of Michigan, to eliminate the Michigan cataloging backlog by having Michigan catalogers create brief (read: less complete) records.[4] As I well recall, this was felt at the time, of course, by some members of the library profession, to border on treason. The best record is the most complete record, and the whole point of cataloging was to create the best possible records. The completeness of the record *was* the service. But Dougherty presumably felt otherwise. He presumably felt that to leave some information out of Michigan catalog records was a reasonable price to pay to get the materials, to which those records referred, on to the Michigan shelves. Over the years, of course, that view for many reasons has gradually become the more prevailing one—but that was the first starkly visible example, for me, at least, of the demise of the completeness syndrome, which we now see manifested wherever we look. To take an abstract example relating to collection development, a library could subscribe to a certain number of monographic series, making certain that it acquires every number in those series; alternatively, the library could use some of the funding it spends on ensuring completeness to purchase yet more series, giving up in return its ability to ensure that it receives every number. Which approach should a library take? Twenty years ago, there would have been, I think, little question: what would be the point of subscribing to a series, one would have asked back then, if some numbers were going to be missed? Good management, good service, was measured and defined by having assembled a complete set. But we now operate in a new age, which no longer views completeness as the ideal. We are in general now much more inclined to purchase access to greater numbers of resources at the expense of completeness in records or collections. There can be no doubt, moreover, that the final nail in the coffin of the completeness syndrome has been the World-Wide Web—where undeniably significant publications come into being, change, and then disappear, without libraries (at least so far) being able effectively to capture and maintain their evolving content. Such circumstances rule out entirely the prospect of ever developing a truly complete collection.

This demise of the completeness syndrome damaged synergism. If we read publications on cooperative collection development from the 1980s, we note that the primary rationale for cooperation was that no library could collect comprehensively.[5] Today, on the other hand, not only do we accept that not even a consortium can collect comprehensively—we feel in many cases that, generally speaking, no consortium should try to. Such an effort would not be cost-effective: it would not be good management or good service, and would be an irresponsible use of resources. This position leads directly therefore to complementarity. Since we cannot acquire everything, each library should simply acquire what it needs; all libraries together will therefore acquire most of what is important—and if a few important materials are not acquired, that is acceptable.

THE ONLINE ENVIRONMENT

Cooperation in the traditional environment is a matter of sharing. One library decides not to purchase something, with the understanding that it can rely on another library for access to that item. Now that we are moving increasingly into an online environment, however, such a method of cooperation is no longer an option for many of the most important materials. If my library cannot afford the *Web of Science,* my users are obviously not going to be able to rely on your "copy." From the standpoint of cooperation, therefore, the single most important development in the new era is the adoption of licenses that prohibit cooperation and define sharing as theft.

Publishers have been obliged in the traditional environment to allow libraries to share materials within strict, legal parameters. In the online environment, publishers have argued, technology would allow users to share everything, which would obviously be entirely impractical from the commercial perspective. The answer for publishers, therefore, has been to create licenses that in many cases allow libraries to share nothing—and libraries have for the most part accepted such restrictions and signed such licenses. While we recognize only too well that these licenses are highly problematic, we do need electronic access to high-use materials, and we have been prepared to accept these restrictions as part of the price of that access. We do need to continue to protest and oppose such licenses, therefore, as part of the broader battle against third-party ownership of scholarly information—but the prosecution of that battle will doubtless take some time.

Even when forced to submit to the oppression of licenses, there are still a variety of opportunities for libraries to cooperate. To begin with, we can still effect cooperative programs for traditional materials. We are still at liberty in the traditional environment to apply any of the methods we have developed over the years for cooperative collection development. While these methods have not worked nearly as effectively as we had hoped in the past, there may be a new willingness to try them now. Because libraries seldom receive additional funding to acquire new and needed electronic materials, for example, we might consider freeing up such funding by cooperating on the acquisition of traditional materials. The major problem, I hasten to note, in taking such an approach (aside from the obvious perversity of increasing cooperation in order to move more rapidly into an environment in which cooperation is prohibited) is that, while the literature of some subjects is becoming increasingly digital, the publications of other disciplines remain primarily traditional. That being the case, the transfer of funding from traditional to digital materials could in effect shift support from some subjects to others. At the present time, the humanities could be severely damaged in such an arrangement, therefore, were effective safeguards not taken.

A second opportunity for cooperation in the new environment might take the form of information exchange in what we might call the "regressive mode." Some publishers, in other words, will permit interlibrary loan (ILL) operations to print articles from electronic journals and fax them to other libraries. We need to work to retain that capacity in our licenses.

Another opportunity for cooperation in a restrictive licensing environment could be the sharing of auxiliary resources (by which I mean resources other than information resources). Such auxiliary resources come in three basic forms: money, space and time. We have traditionally concentrated on sharing information resources, or indirectly the money that purchases them—but we can certainly also share other resources, such as storage and even disk space. Above all, however, we can share what may be our scarcest resource, time—specifically, selector time. The greatest redundancy among research libraries may be in the area of human resources. We do need to ask at some point whether every institution must have a selector for every subject—and to consider whether some (parts of) local collections might be built by selectors at other institutions.

We can, finally, also engage in cooperation through joint buying and negotiation of license agreements, although labeling this activity "cooperative" is admittedly questionable. Cooperation (at least in its synergistic form) should mean that each partner changes its behavior somewhat in order to contribute to the creation of the consortial whole. Cooperative buying often entails no such change of behavior, nor any such sense of a whole. It would be different, of course, if more consortia were prepared to negotiate as a cohesive group; all members would agree, for example, to purchase an item at a particular, fair price—and if a higher price were offered, all members would agree not to purchase it. That would indeed be synergistic cooperation. Whether it would also be restraint of trade is something that needs to be tested.

KNOWLEDGE MANAGEMENT

Joe Branin has recently observed that, in the same way that collection development shifted to collection management some 15 or 20 years ago, collection management now needs to transform into knowledge management.[6] I must note, to begin with, that I do disagree that collection development did in fact evolve into collection management in the 1980s—despite the heralding of that transformation with great fanfare in the library literature. Collection development, we must remember, involves primarily looking outside of the collection at the anti-collection. The purpose and practice of collection management, on the other hand, is to apply the same skills and values used for collection development to the maintenance and improvement of the collection already in place—through, e.g., preservation, weeding, or advice on cataloging. Collection management is indeed now a standard practice—but this has come about, I believe, only relatively recently, as a result of the significantly increased dependence on offsite storage: it is that new requirement to transfer substantial parts of our collections off campus, creating a bifurcation of the collection (a spatial core and periphery), that has forced collection development to turn its attention back to its own collections, and to move finally into an era of true collection management.

What, then, is knowledge management, as it relates to libraries? There is, to be sure, a vast quantity of published information on the subject of knowledge management—but most of that literature relates to business. The purpose of knowledge management, as explained in the business literature, is to assist commercial organizations in making use of their knowledge as a strategic asset, to enhance productivity and competitiveness. Knowledge, in the knowledge management literature, is often divided into two categories: *explicit knowledge* (e.g., in files and databases), and *tacit knowledge* (in the minds of staff and consultants).[7] In some cases, applying knowledge management to libraries may be viewed primarily as emulating such business practices, in the sense of developing methods to move information among library staff more effectively.[8] In other cases, I infer that knowledge management may entail an expansion of the content for which libraries should be responsible, to include more informal materials (e.g., Web sites, working papers, technical reports, lecture notes, data sets). This may be manifested most clearly in the rapidly developing interest in local repositories.[9]

We must ask, however, whether either of these paths is sufficiently transformative to warrant the level of effort that would be needed to bring it about. One way to achieve a deeper transformation might be to apply some version of the so-called cognitive model of information services.[10] To do that, we might stipulate for this discussion that knowledge is something you have, while information is something you exchange. Knowledge, let us say, cannot be shared: it is private and constantly changing, based in part upon new information received. Information takes the form of sign (symbol) strings—which people exchange, in order to enhance their knowledge.

What concepts might be needed, then, to set out on a course of effective transformation? Perhaps at least one further stipulation. We noted above the problem of the tactical fallacy, i.e., the false assumption that the library's purpose is its operations—while in fact that purpose is access, and library operations are merely a means to bring about that end. Let us now move that concept up one more level, and define what we can call a *strategic fallacy,* which is the false assumption that the library's purpose is access. The real purpose of the library is in fact the production of information by local users—and access is only a means to that end. We can then stipulate that the primary rationale for the library is to improve the capacity of local users to produce new and significant information.

This being the case, we must bear in mind the information production cycle. For our purposes, we can use the model in figure 3. Information is identified in the universe, it is retrieved, it is understood, used, and applied as knowledge—and then new information is produced and inserted into the universe, so that the cycle can continue. The library, if it is serious about moving into knowledge management, must be prepared to provide services not only at the information level (identification, retrieval), but also at the knowledge level (understanding, application, production).

If this is—if this be—library knowledge management, how then could cooperation further such a service? Let me make three suggestions.

1. *Amplification of Local Production.* Academic libraries know very little about the information being produced on their local campuses. There is, to be sure, a general understanding about who is doing research in which areas, but I suspect we know very little detail about local research, especially at larger institutions. If libraries seriously intend to effect a system of knowledge management services, they must now find a way to acquaint themselves with that detail. Libraries need to assemble dynamic information databases that summarize and track local research-and those databases should be shared with other institutions. Needless to say, issues of privacy would have to be taken very carefully into account-and some of this work may best be done in consultation and cooperation with scholarly societies. The main point, however, is that synergism, in a knowledge management environment, may be not so much a matter of libraries working together, as the creation by libraries of some kind of connecting services that will allow scholars at separate institutions to work much more effectively with each other.[11]

A further facet of such a goal of amplification should be an increased willingness by libraries to take more responsibility for the information produced at their institutions. That information may have been formally published, but the library should still be ultimately responsible for ensuring that it remains accessible one way or another over time. The library also has a responsibility at the citation level—ideally ensuring that all information cited in local publications remains accessible. This should be the case especially for electronic information: if Web pages, for example, are cited in publications produced at a library's institution, then that library should be responsible for ensuring that those Web pages remain accessible indefinitely—preferably in the form they took at the time of the publication.

2. *Boundary Definition.* Research libraries as a group should define those objects of information that are essential for research on each subject: they need in effect to circumscribe core materials, which is to say they need to agree that any library supporting research on a particular subject should provide access at minimum to particular objects. Cooperation is not merely a matter of ensuring access to unique materials, therefore, but also of defining those standard materials needed by all researchers. Core definition can be, of course, highly problematic—for the same reason it is so difficult to define the levels in figure 2. It is time now, however, to make an attempt at core definition, because values and conventions have changed—including especially the completeness syndrome. Some specialists will inevitably believe that some items should not be included in such a core, while others will certainly feel that some items not in the core should be; but the core boundary can be agreed upon anyway, if perfection or completeness is no longer a prerequisite.

Research libraries must also ensure, needless to say, sustained access to materials beyond the core. In order to do that, we need to decouple selection from acquisition. To select something should no longer be understood as necessarily equivalent to buying it. To select something should rather be to acknowledge that the item is (or will likely be) needed to do research on a particular subject. The job of selection, therefore, does not end with the local budget.

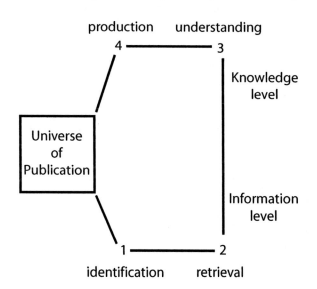

production   understanding
4 ——————— 3

Universe of Publication

Knowledge level

Information level

1 ——————— 2

identification   retrieval

FIGURE 3. Information Production Cycle

Merely because a library cannot afford to purchase particular objects needed by local users does not mean that the library is not responsible for ensuring access to them. Libraries must not succumb to the siren-song of complementarity. We must not imagine that, when we each run out of money, we have done all we can—and that we must each then simply trust to the invisible hand of collection development that needed but unaffordable information will be accessible somehow, someplace, in the future. The building of local collections in all formats must be coordinated. This is the job of large and small libraries alike, because scholars at smaller institutions will need the same information for research as scholars at larger ones. The only difference is that larger institutions will be able to provide better (in the sense of faster) access than smaller ones, because larger institutions can afford to purchase more materials for immediate access.

3. *Differentiating the Means of Production.* In a knowledge management environment, the library (information services) is a means for the production of information. In discussing the means of production, Marx drew one particularly useful distinction between the tools of production (*Arbeitsmittel*) and the materials of production (*Arbeitsgegenstand*).[12] If you

are going to build a wooden box, you need (a) a hammer, saw and nails, and you need (b) some wood. These are two very different categories from the standpoint of economics and production. It is the same with the use of information objects for knowledge production. There is a difference between objects you work with, and those you work on. Those you work with may be defined as secondary literature, while those you work on are primary literature. There is a danger that research libraries may begin to lose their grasp on the concept of primary literature—mainly because, as libraries race to put in place an effective digital library, they are working most closely with those disciplines that have significant portions of their materials in digital form, and most of those disciplines are in the sciences. The problem, of course, is that the sciences, regardless of their terminology, do not have primary literature. Scientific literature is not something you work on, but rather something you work with. The main purpose of scientific literature is for scientists to communicate with each other about the work they are doing. And the work they are doing is not *on* literature, not on information objects, but is rather for the most part on natural (or social) objects, that they then describe *in* the literature. We need to find a means, therefore, to protect primary literature in an increasingly online environment, because there are many disciplines that need primary literature for their practitioners to engage in the production cycle. (Some of this work has, to be sure, already begun, most notably in the Early English Books Online project.[13]) Primary and secondary literature require different treatment and different service options. Format, for example, can play a key role in primary literature, and needs therefore to be protected when possible. The format of secondary literature, on the other hand, is often relatively unimportant. Above all, however, there is a difference in the use and value of primary and secondary information. We are rapidly beginning to build collections that are mainly use-driven. This works well for secondary literature, such as science serials. Libraries must acquire high-use secondary materials, because those materials are where the action, the essential conversation, is; indeed, the more used a secondary object is, the more valuable it is. The opposite is sometimes the case, however, with primary literature: the less used it has been, the more valuable it can sometimes be. We need, therefore, to find a way to accommodate and safeguard access to very low use materials, and the only effective means to that end is likely to be retrospective synergistic cooperation.

CONCLUSION

Previously I have suggested four areas in which libraries might cooperate in an online environment, even when forced to bear the yoke of highly restrictive licensing. I have furthermore suggested a simple concept of knowledge management, and I have identified three opportunities for cooperation, by applying such a concept. What then are the chances, we must ask in conclusion, that libraries will actually take advantage of these or similar cooperative opportunities in the near future? Frankly, if nothing changes, practically zero. There is no evidence (that I can see) that libraries are any more prepared at this time than in the past to engage in cooperative collection efforts. The reason is that traditional axes of competition remain in play.

Assume each point on the horizontal axis, in figure 4, is a library, and each point on the vertical axis is another kind of information intermediary (e.g., publishers, printers, booksellers, database providers, software programmers). It has been and remains the custom and practice of libraries, especially research libraries, to cooperate with the intermediaries on the vertical axis, in order to compete more effectively with other libraries on the horizontal axis.

Why then should we assume this will change? Libraries certainly have not hesitated to sign licenses prohibiting cooperation—probably primarily as a result of what we have defined above as the Law of Local Access Optimization: I need those databases and electronic journals on my campus, because others have them on their campuses—and if my users do not have electronic access to those materials, then my users will not be competitive. I am therefore prepared to pay whatever price I must, to provide such local access—and if part of that price is not to share those materials, then so be it.

There are, of course, other, related reasons that libraries have been so willing to sign such licenses. One of those reasons may be that licenses tend to reinforce the relational equilibrium. Licensing, by prohibiting cooperation, effectively freezes all institutions in their present positions in relation to each other; this ensures, among other things, that the large and the small, the rich and the poor, remain in their respective places. The most powerful reason, however, that libraries have been so ready to sign licenses prohibiting cooperation, may be that such licenses provide us in collection development with something to say to our libraries, to our users, to our institutions, and above all to each other, as to why we are not cooperating. It is not our fault, we can say: the reason we are not cooperating does not have to do with the library, let alone with collection development. The reason, we can say, is external and beyond our control. It is the publishers who are responsible for our lack of cooperation: we in libraries are merely the victims of the avarice of capitalism.

These are the excuses that licenses allow us to make to each other—but are we indeed that self-deceiving? Are we really possessed by such timidity, such impotence? If we are, then there is no reason that libraries, or at least their collection development components, should not and will not become increasingly subordinated to other information service providers, the further we move into an online environment. But if we are now prepared to accept full responsibility for providing the best possible local services, then the library community in general and collection development in particular have only one choice: it is to shift the action on the axis of competition from the horizontal to the vertical. Libraries have the ability to cooperate with each other very effectively—if they want to—while the businesses on the vertical axis are for the most part incapable of doing so. Cooperation is, somewhat paradoxically, one of the few competitive advantages libraries have. Such cooperation does indeed entail significant risks for those libraries bold enough to engage in it—but those risks are in fact negligible, in comparison with the dangers libraries will surely encounter by continuing to insist that they should each face the future alone.

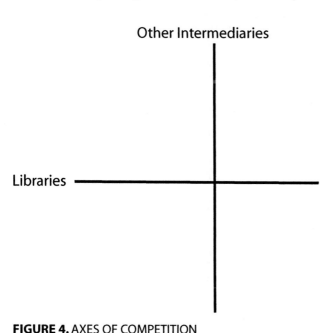

FIGURE 4. AXES OF COMPETITION

REFERENCE NOTES

1. Edward Shreeves, "Is There a Future for Cooperative Collection Development in the Digital Age?" *Library Trends* 45, no. 3 (1997): 373–90.

2. Ross Atkinson, "Preservation and Collection Development: Toward a Political Synthesis," *Journal of Academic Librarianship* 16, no. 2 (1990): 98–103.

3. Patricia Buck Dominguez and Luke Swindler, "Cooperative Collection Development at the Research Triangle University Libraries: A Model for the Nation," *College & Research Libraries* 54, no. 6 (1993): 470–96; Gay N. Dannelly, "Cooperation is the Future of Collection Management and Development: OhioLINK and CIC," in *Collection Management for the 21st Century: A Handbook for Librarians,* ed. G. E. Gorman and Ruth H. Miller (Westport, Conn.: Greenwood, 1997), 249–62.

4. Lynn Marko and Barbara von Wahlde, "BRC (Brief Record Cataloging) at Michigan," *The Journal of Academic Librarianship* 11, no. 6 (1986): 339–40.

5. Paul H. Mosher, "A National Scheme for Collaboration in Collection Development: The RLG-NCIP Effort," *Resource Sharing & Information Networks* 2, nos. 3/4 (1985): 21–35.

6. Ross Atkinson, "ARL Conference on Collections and Access for the 21st Century Scholar: A Forum to Explore the Roles of the Research Library: A Brief Report," *Library Collections, Acquisitions, & Technical Services* 26, no. 2 (2002): 161–65; Joseph Branin, Frances Groen, and Suzanne Thorin, "The Changing Nature of Collection Management in Research Libraries," *Library Resources & Technical Services* 44, no. 1 (2000): 23–32;

7. Ikujiro Nonaka and Noboru Konno, "A Knowledge Management Ecology: The Concept of 'Ba': Building a Foundation for Knowledge Creation," in *The Knowledge Management Yearbook 1999–2000* (Boston: Butterworth-Heinemann, 1999), 37–51.

8. Ronald C. Jantz, "Knowledge Management in Academic Libraries: Special Tools and Processes to Support Information Professionals," *Reference Services Review* 29, no. 1 (2001): 33–39.

9. Raym Crow, *The Case for Institutional Repositories: A SPARC Position Paper* (Washington, D.C.: The Scholarly Publishing & Academic Resource Coalition, 2002). www.arl.org/sparc/IRlir.html.

10. Penelope Yates-Mercer and David Bawden, "Managing the Paradox: The Valuation of Knowledge and Knowledge Management," *Journal of Information Science* 28, no.1 (2002): 19–29.

11. Wendy Pradt Lougee, *Diffuse Libraries: Emergent Roles for the Research Library in the Digital Age* (Washington, D.C.: Council on Library and Information Resources, 2002).

12. William H. Shaw, *Marx's Theory of History* (Stanford, Calif.: Stanford Univ. Pr., 1978).

13. Mark Sandler, "Academic and Commerical Roles in Building 'The Digital Library,'" *Collection Management* 28, no.1/2 (2003): 107–19.

2 TOWARD A RATIONALE FOR FUTURE EVENT-BASED INFORMATION SERVICES

Everything in the world is composed of "events."
—Bertrand Russell (*An Outline of Philosophy*)

Good, bhikkhus. I too do not see any possession
that is permanent, everlasting, eternal,
not subject to change, and that might
endure as long as eternity.
—The Buddha (*Majjhima Nikaya*, 22,22)

Change, we are told, is accelerating.[1] What we need now in the information professions, therefore, is not so much passive prediction about where we might end up—but rather active discussion about where we should want to go. In order to do this, we will need to re-examine and agree upon the very foundations of what we do. The following paper consists of some assertions about the nature of knowledge and information—as well as an initial attempt to apply some of those concepts to a few suggestions about future information services. These are, needless to say, very broad issues, and obviously no one can ever discuss them with any real authority. Progress in considering such vast topics can only be made through dialogue and collegial debate. My hope therefore is that the issues I am raising here will so interest (or exasperate) the readers of this paper that they will want to respond, and that further discussions of this kind will result.

UTILITY

The purpose of information services is to make objects of information useful for the production of new knowledge. For our purposes here, we will define new knowledge as something not previously known to the individual. New information, on the other hand, is something not previously published or formally communicated. Knowledge is something an individual "has"—it is private and cannot be communicated. Information is a set of signs or symbols created by people (or machines) for purposes of communication. The aim of information services is to enable individual users to make use of information in order to expand their knowledge and to apply that knowledge to their own purposes, one of which may be the production of new information.[2]

Utility and access are, of course, inseparable. In one sense, they can even be viewed as synonymous, in that something may be seen as being truly accessible only when it is applicable to a particular need or situation. But access can also be understood as a necessary but insufficient condition for utility. A relevant object of information may be accessible, and yet it may for a variety of reasons lack utility. Its relevance may not be evident, either because the user cannot

This article first appeared in Patricia Hodges et al., eds., *Digital Libraries: A Vision for the 21st Century* (Ann Arbor, Mich.: Univ. of Michigan Library Scholarly Publishing Office, 2003), 154–75.

decipher the object, or because the user does not perceive the relationship between the object and the task at hand. Information services malfunction whenever the user is unable, for whatever reason, to apply a relevant object to the production of new knowledge.

The information professions need therefore to temper somewhat their preoccupation with information-seeking behavior. Helping users discover information is only one, increasingly shrinking part of the responsibility of information services, and that responsibility does not end once the user has access to the object sought. Merely to ensure that the user and the relevant information, the subject and the object, come into contact with each other no longer justifies the existence of information services if it ever did. We are, moreover, rapidly entering an era in which discovery can be carried out, to a large extent, increasingly mechanically. Brute force computing, moreover, while it may not be as subtle or precise as human-produced metadata, is unquestionably faster and cheaper for purposes of discovery; and in the new age we are entering, faster and cheaper may be sufficient in many cases.[3] If libraries continue to imagine that their purpose is to boost access, rather than to enhance utility, then their future role in information services and knowledge production will become increasingly peripheral and perhaps eventually even superfluous.

INSIGHT

Knowledge, at least as we have defined it above, is personal and private. Information requirements—and the ability to understand information and create new knowledge—necessarily vary therefore from one individual to the next. Everyone creates his or her own intellectual world, and the potential to share aspects of that world through communication is relatively limited. Making effective use of information for purposes of knowledge production depends therefore upon the individual user having precise insight into his or her own abilities and needs. Services intended to increase the awareness and utility of information objects require special provisions to accommodate the different skills and values of individual users—and the user must learn or be taught to take advantage of these individualized and individualizing options.

Libraries have, to be sure, always recognized the importance of tailoring services to meet the differing needs of particular disciplines and individuals. The move from traditional to online services has allowed libraries now to extend service much more effectively to the individual—moving in effect from customized to personalized services. Current efforts at personalization remain still in the early stages—but progress is being made toward the goal of empowering the user to make increasingly complex and individual decisions, based upon personal awareness of individual values and needs.[4]

A true personalization of services, to be sure, unavoidably entails some reduction in the role of the intermediary, because the aim is to place users in a position to make more decisions on information selection and use for themselves. This does not mean, however, that the intermediary function could ever be eliminated. This is linguistically and epistemologically impossible. Some system of shared codes, conventions and technologies must be in operation for users to discover, decipher and apply what creators of information are seeking to convey. Information services, in some form, must remain indefinitely in place. The question is how to ensure that such services will continue to meet user needs, when these are changing so rapidly and becoming so increasingly specialized.

DIFFERENCE

Knowledge is difference—in the simple sense that knowledge is (let us say) fundamentally the capacity to distinguish and relate things.[5] The function of information is therefore to define, create, and refer to differences. All information is consequently and unavoidably relational, in the sense that any element of information is understandable (and useful) only within a context, as part of a relationship with other such elements.

As we consider this, it is of course essential always to bear in mind that information is, as we have already noted, an aggregation of signs that stand for things; there is obviously a difference therefore between a sign and its referent (i.e., the thing it stands for). Whether we can in fact perceive and understand anything but signs (whether not only information but also knowledge consists of signs) is certainly not an issue we want to get entangled in here. All we need to agree upon is: to look at information is always to look at signs that stand for things, rather than to look at those things themselves. If to know is to understand the differences among things, then to make use of information is to perceive and apply the differences among representations of things.

Perhaps the cardinal quality of reality, recognized since the dawn of human thought, is that it (reality) constantly changes. Some of the most fundamental areas of knowledge have to do therefore with the perception and explanation of change. In order to discuss change, let us apply some further concepts provided by Saussurian linguistics.[6] Let us say that all differences, which is to say in effect all knowledge, can be divided into two broad categories—synchronic and diachronic. Synchronic knowledge is the (realization of the) difference between different things at the same time. Diachronic knowledge is the (realization of the) difference between different manifestations of the same thing as it has existed at different times. Imagining the diachronic to be the horizontal axis and the synchronic to be the vertical, all of one's knowledge could theoretically be plotted or defined on that single matrix. To understand (and make use of) anything would be to locate it at the convergence of those two axes. We can then say that information, as a sign object, created by a person or a machine, is therefore intended to engender perception of such differences (the point of convergence) on the part of another person (or machine). Understanding (learning, applying) is therefore never ending—not because the matrix itself is necessarily infinite, but because its use certainly is; any point on the matrix requires for knowledge production a comparison or relationship with another point—and that point in turn can only be understood by comparing it to other points, and so on indefinitely. Thus learning—the attainment of knowledge, the creation of differences—never ends.

This simple model of knowledge only works, of course, if we assume that the user, the subject making use of such a matrix, is not strictly speaking part of it. In other words, the user must somehow occupy a kind of separate, Archimedean position external to the matrix, in order to observe or operate it. Another point we should notice is that the user engaging in such operation is always only here now. His or her work with such a matrix can only happen at one time, in the present. Both the diachronic and the synchronic are therefore necessarily present differences, in the sense of differences recognized—understood, created—by the user at the present time.

METADATA

Let us define metadata as any sign (or set of signs) that has another sign (or set of signs) as its referent. Metadata are therefore twice removed from the world, so to speak—in that, if information refers to (represents) the world, metadata refers to information. There are, of course, many kinds of metadata, but let us for our purposes divide all metadata into two broad categories: iterative and explicative.[7] Iterative metadata repeat and thus privilege language or other signs that occur in the referent (as, e.g., in the case of a citation). Explicative metadata, on the other hand, provide information about the referent that is not directly contained or expressed in it. Iterative metadata play therefore primarily the role of the surrogate, accelerating access to the referent. In the case of electronic data, some of its iterative metadata can be produced automatically, assuming a standardized mark-up system—and it is essential that all traditional formats (e.g., books), for as long as they continue to be produced, be designed in such a way that iterative metadata can in future be automatically derived from them. Explicative metadata, on the other hand, add new information about the referent. This is not to imply that explicative metadata can never be automatically generated. Some explicative metadata for information in online form can certainly be created through calculation or reference to other sources or scales. Most explicative metadata, including especially evaluation and analysis relating to the referent, must necessarily be created by people. One of the major administrative and political challenges of information services in the future will be to agree upon how the responsibility and authority for creating explicative metadata will be distributed and shared.

Like all data, metadata are created for purposes of communication across space and time, i.e., they are intended to be viewed or used again by someone or (in the case of computers) by some thing—otherwise there would obviously be no point whatsoever producing them in the first place. Being a form of communication, metadata are a way for their creator to inform, talk to, other people. This means that the creator's own capabilities, values, biases and insight will be unavoidably reflected in the metadata. While this is the case even with iterative metadata (because their creation entails the selection or privileging of certain signs over others), it is especially true of explicative metadata. It is, moreover, not unlikely that more and more of the reading humans do in the future, especially for professional purposes, will be of metadata, with increasingly selective consultation of the referent. This is one reason it is essential that some of the explicative metadata be created by the referent's author, since that metadata will in fact form not only the pathway but also the introduction to the referent; it is equally important that some explicative metadata be created by users of the same referent, to advise each other on its utility for purposes of knowledge production.

Although it would be fun to argue to the contrary, we must assume that the referent can and does exist separately from its metadata. This is not to say, however, that the metadata does not profoundly affect the (perception of the) referent. Just one example is the fact that all metadata engage in an act of what we can call "primacy instantiation"—i.e., the creation of primary literature. An object becomes "primary" only by virtue of the fact that it is being referred to in a particular way. This is not a trivial point. Primacy instantiation is a quality of the reflexivity of language, and harkens back to the infinite nature of understanding—in that metadata can and does become primary itself, when referred to by yet further metadata. Such primary instantiation, moreover, holds true for all disciplines. It is only by defining and accepting all secondary literature as a form of metadata that we can reconcile the use of the terms "primary" and "secondary" with respect to information in both the sciences and the humanities. In the sciences, the predominant form of metadata is iterative (e.g., indexes), while in the humanities, secondary literature is most frequently explicative, such as history and commentary.

ONTOLOGY

In philosophy, ontology is a branch of metaphysics concerned with the theory of being.[8] To speak of an ontology, therefore, is to refer to a (description of a) system intended to allow or assist someone to view, make sense of, talk about being, existence, the world. Computer science appropriated the term "ontology" in the 1970s, and now uses it to mean, according to one definition, a "specification of a conceptualization."[9] There is, however, not as great a difference as one might expect in the way computer science and philosophy use the term. In both disciplines, ontology can be understood as referring to an abstract, systematic construct intended to enable understanding of and work with (some aspects of) the world. It is also worth noting that ontology has always been in a way a core function of information services, even if the term has not been used. The purpose of information services since antiquity has been to present users with an access system of some kind, and that system has necessarily been based upon a shared set of values, assumptions and definitions about the nature of reality. Such systems are in effect installed by information services "on top" of the available aggregation of information objects, in order to facilitate their access and use.

Computer and information sciences have created many kinds of ontologies, but I want to focus, as a non-specialist, on a recent one, called the ABC Ontology—because it is one of the few I have tried to understand, and because it seems to me to be especially illustrative of the abstract issues I have tried to outline previously.[10] The ABC Ontology is a product of the Harmony Project, which is a joint Australian, UK, and U.S. effort to study and develop methods that will contribute to the greater unification of the universe of digital information.[11] The Harmony Project is especially interested in creating options for interoperability among different metadata packages that serve different disciplines, constituencies and purposes. By highlighting some of the Project's efforts to achieve this goal through the ABC Ontology, I want to draw some further conclusions about the nature of information. I will then use those conclusions to lead into some final suggestions about the possible future shape of information services. My intent therefore—and this cannot be overemphasized— is not to explain or interpret (let alone criticize or defend) the ABC Ontology, for which I have neither the knowledge nor the license, but rather to use my own efforts to understand parts of ABC (as I will hereafter call it) as a way to think about information use and future services to support that use.

Work on ABC has progressed through several stages, beginning with an initial "strawman" document, proceeding through an essay on an "Event-Aware Model," and arriving at the most recent iteration, which provides a very rigorous description.[12] I would recommend the middle document, the "Event-Aware Model," as probably the best place for the non-specialist to begin. Let us look carefully at one formulation of the rationale for ABC, as it is defined in that middle document. We can call this the *ABC core argument*—and the italics are mine.

Briefly stated, our argument is as follows. Understanding the relationship among multiple metadata descriptions (and ultimately the vocabularies on which they are based) begins by understanding the entities (resources) they purport to describe. Understanding these entities entails a comprehension of their lifecycle and the events, and corresponding transitions and transformations, that make up this lifecycle.[13]

The first thing we note is that ABC is above all a system designed specifically to track change. As explained in the most recent iteration, its primary purpose is to provide "the ability to model the creation, evolution, and transition of objects over time." In their effort to create a kind of super-metadata system, therefore, the authors have fashioned an ontology that succeeds in placing diachronic difference on an equal footing with synchronic. This means that the system allows the representation not only of differences that separate things, but also of differences that separate the same thing from itself at different times. In speaking to the Library of Congress, Carl Lagoze, one of the ABC authors, emphasized that such attention to changes of entities over time is essential, as information becomes increasingly available in online form.[14] Because digital objects are inherently unstable—easily changed not only by design but also by accident—some of the most important and useful information about such objects is precisely how they evolve. The catalog record, Lagoze argues, "should model a digital document as a series of transition events, and should describe the nature of the events, the agents responsible for the events, and the times and places of those change events."

The concept of the event is indeed the key to understanding the whole ABC endeavor. The different publications on ABC, however, define events in slightly different ways. In the original "strawman" document, we read: "Events are enacted upon resources and produce other resources. Properties of events include the agent(s) associated with the event and the time and place at which the event was enacted." So, an event is something done by someone (or some thing) to a resource, such that a new resource is produced. In the "Event-Aware Model," we read that an "event is an action or occurrence. Every event has a Context (Time and/or Place) associated with it (although it may not always be explicit)."[15] In both of these documents, some examples of types of events are given; these include (but are certainly not limited to) modification, compilation, extraction, reformatting, translation, and derivation.

On the basis of my description so far, it may be assumed that the primary focus of ABC is information objects—such as the digital documents Lagoze discussed in his Library of Congress presentation. Certainly ABC is a very powerful system for representing how information objects are altered and move through various formats and versions over time. In its effort to connect different metadata systems, however, ABC does in fact not focus exclusively on situations in which information objects are the primary entities of interest. The Harmony Project has collaborated from the outset extensively with the museum information consortium CIMI, and has tried therefore to ensure that the model can accommodate not only information objects, but also museum objects—what we in libraries would call realia.[16] This effort to create an ontology that will serve the needs of both areas has been a major challenge for ABC—and a series of workshops were held in 2001 and 2002 to work on integrating ABC and the International Committee for Documentation of the International Council of Museums (CIDOC) Core Reference Model into a "core ontology."[17] Many points of overlap and difference were identified in those workshops—but it remains clear that the work to bring about such a coalescence will continue. It is in fact precisely the effort and the persistence of the ABC authors to build a system that is useful in both domains that makes, I think, trying to follow and understand their work so challenging and worthwhile.

Let us look again at the ABC core argument. There we read that in order to understand "entities," we must understand "their lifecycle and the events, and corresponding transitions and transformations, that make up this lifecycle." We note that "transitions and transformations" are not directly equivalent to or synonymous with "events," but rather correspond with them. We will need to bear this in mind and consider what it means as we proceed. We should also note the pairing of "transitions and transformations." This is not a mere rhetorical flourish, but is, as we will see, a key to understanding some of ABC's most important features.

In order to illustrate the potential use of ABC, its authors provide a number of examples. In the most recent iteration, they boldly include a human baby as one such "entity" that ABC could describe (and for which the system is in fact singularly well suited—since the baby obviously grows and changes over time). But for our purposes, two of their examples are particularly instructive. One is, of course, a book, *Charlie and the Chocolate Factory,* which evolved through various editions and manifestations (including an audiocassette). The second example of interest is a dinosaur bone, which was discovered, moved to a museum, classified, photographed, and the photographic image then mounted on a Web page. It is clear that the evolution of the book through various editions and formats corresponds well to the definition of an "event" in the original "strawman" document (i.e., something enacted upon a resource that produces another resource). But what about the dinosaur bone? Its move to the museum and its classification are also defined as events in the most recent iteration—and yet the results were hardly "another resource," as the "strawman" definition stipulates: the bone that was dug up was the same one after being transferred to the museum that it was before.

We can start to answer this question by noting that the definition of an event has been refined and generalized in the most recent iteration where these examples are provided. In the most recent iteration, an event is something "that marks a transition between Situations." A Situation "is a context for making time-dependent . . . assertions."[18] So, an event is something that represents ("marks") the change of an entity from one context to another. Events are, in other words, not only changes in the form or content of an entity—as in the case of the book moving through various editions and manifestations—but events are also actions done to the object (moving it, classifying it), without changing its form or content. I am admittedly simplifying the system in describing it in this way, but I believe I am fairly representing its intent. Returning to the core argument in the Event-Aware Model, we see now the significance of the pairing of the terms "transition and transformation." ABC is intended to describe not only things that are transformed from one state to another, but also things that move from one situation to another.[19] Both are in fact changes in context—one emphasizing what we have been calling the synchronic, and the other the diachronic.

To consider this further, we need to note two (of many) further categories of the most recent iteration—namely the dichotomous "actuality" and "abstraction." An actuality is any entity that is sensible, i.e., accessible to the senses. An abstraction, on the other hand, is a concept or an idea. Quite reasonably, the model prohibits reference to an abstraction, except as realized in an actuality. The main purpose of the abstraction, the authors note, is to accommodate the concept, so familiar to catalogers, of a "work," e.g., the work Hamlet, as manifested and expressed in different forms.[20] But what exactly is an abstraction? Are we to assume, for example, that the abstraction of the book remains changeless—and that only its actualities change?

That would be a mistake, because the abstraction and its actualities are inseparable. The abstraction, we can say, is somewhat akin to our description above of knowledge. The actuality, on the other hand, is an information object. As actualities are perceived to come into existence, change, and go out of existence, the perception of the abstraction necessarily changes as well.

Obviously what we are moving toward is the realization that the dinosaur bone, as it sits in the museum, is in fact a kind of abstraction that "exists" only to the extent that it is described, i.e., only when data of some kind about it are created. The bone "is," in the sense of being understandable and useful, only by virtue of difference, which is to say contextual representation. ABC functions therefore as a system that permits the generation of information (and therefore the building of knowledge) by locating an entity at the convergence of diachronic and synchronic axes—in any present moment. At different places on the diachronic axis, the entity's relationship with other entities differs. Because understanding is a product of such differences, and because the entity "is" as it is understood, the entity must necessarily change, become different, as it progresses (as it is represented to be at different points) along the axis.

At the risk of complicating things still further, another approach might be to distinguish between intrinsic and extrinsic context. In the former, we understand the entity as being composed of elements, so that information (difference) is produced, i.e., the entity changes, by virtue of the fact that some (although never all) of its composite elements are (perceived as) different, in relationship to each other, at different times. In the case of extrinsic context, on the other hand, the entity is viewed as an information element within a larger aggregate—so that information is produced as a result of the other elements, with which the entity is contrasted, being different at different times. Sometimes change can be conceived therefore to be within the boundary of the entity—and sometimes it is conceivable within a larger boundary that encompasses the entity.

What, we must now ask, does ABC seek to enable its users to refer to? Because of its inclusive purpose, just about anything. In the original "strawman" document, we find that

"Everything in ABC is . . . modeled as a 'resource.' Resources include real-world entities—physical and digital—as well as intangible entities such as concepts, performances or relationships . . ." (In the ABC core argument above from the "Event-Aware Model," we find that the objects referred to are "entities (resources);" and by the time we reach the most recent iteration, the more general term "entity" is used exclusively.) Note that the authors do not say that everything in ABC is a resource, but rather that everything is modeled as a resource. It is easy to lose sight of this. ABC is based in part upon, or is heavily influenced by, the Resource Description Framework, which defines a "resource" as anything that can have a Uniform Resource Identifier.[21] The fact is, of course, that a dinosaur bone cannot have a URA. Only a model of or reference to a dinosaur bone, i.e., only an information object, can have a URI. Nor can metadata—at least as we have defined it above—refer to a dinosaur bone, but only to data about a dinosaur bone, i.e., only to an information object. An ontology is a means to define, describe, model, think about the world. An event is not the transition or transformation of an object—but rather is something that signifies or refers to (or "marks") that transition and transformation. This may in fact be what the ABC authors were implying in the ABC core argument, when they stated that transitions and transformations "correspond" to events.

It could, of course, be objected, and quite rightly, that I am very selectively reading a few parts of the ABC documents with excessive attention. The ABC documents are essays—efforts to express new ideas—and not lyric poems that should be submitted to a microscopic, close reading. But on the other hand, there is indeed something very lyrical about the ABC documents—at least in the sense that lyric poetry is often thought of as a use of language, in which the form reflects and amplifies the content; poems, it is well known, "do" what they say. And that is in fact precisely what one experiences in working on the ABC documents: they not only speak of events, but they provide a demonstration of them, because they refine their ideas through successive iterations. Because ABC has been a work in progress, the views of the ABC authors about how things change over time have changed over time. For anyone trying to track the evolving concept of the "event" in the ABC documents, the need for a metadata that would track events could not be more obvious.

I do want to raise one final issue about ABC, before moving at long last to the subject of future information services. If an entity changes as a result of its changing relationships to other entities, where is the person who is making those changes? Does that person—the subject, the user—belong somehow in the model? Certainly ABC does include agents as a category—people doing things to entities and thus changing them—but is not the user also somehow making changes in order to understand and use the system? We have noted above the central role of insight in knowledge production, and the drive for an increased personalization of information services. There would seem to be no place in an ontology such as ABC for the user of the model to take into account his or her own use of it—and there probably needs to be.

SERVICES

On the basis of the assertions and definitions provided so far, we might envision two broad forms of future information services, one that emphasizes work with objects, and the other that provides support for the development of individual user insight.

An Objective Program

We can subdivide an objective program into two general service groups, one that allows users to track and work with individual objects of information, and one that helps users to traverse and ignore object boundaries.

The Analytical Service. We need first to ensure that users have above all the ability to determine that particular information was created by particular individuals at particular times. This is of course the central capacity and purpose of event-based services, and we have seen that ABC provides very useful concepts for understanding such services. It is in part inevitably an historical service, allowing the user to trace the background of a publication, including in some cases its detailed evolution over time. This service should be one that provides the user with the ability to access and use products of individually identified authors. It should also protect the author, ensuring as much as possible that his or her intentions are honored and maintained. It should track changes or emendations in the publication, and should place primary emphasis on most recent versions or states. This kind of service requires stable objects, periodically harvested and stored. Multiple objects can be pursued along their diachronic axes, compared at different points, and influences through direct and implied citations could also be plotted. The evolution of particular concepts could be traced, and sets of concepts that characterize or affect different historical periods could be inferred.

This service should also obviously allow the user to trace a particular object, or some component of it, back to its origins. Here we find a meeting of the oldest form of scholarship with the newest technology. The primary purpose of scholarship used to be understood as determining the correct text.[22] This was necessary when dealing with the information products of a period that depended on handwritten manuscripts for communication over time, since each new act of copying unavoidably (or sometimes purposefully) introduced new variations to the text. Tracing the origins of the extant manuscripts and relating them to each other in order to determine the true form of the original (the "archetype") was what scholarship was about.[23] It is interesting that we have now come full circle. All such changes in the evolution of manuscripts are equivalent to what we are now calling events. We had to some extent lost this demand to track and study such events, i.e., textual criticism, during the machine press period, in which the text was to a great extent relatively stabilized. Now in the online environment, we face a condition much more similar to the manuscript period, in which works have the potential to change with some frequency, so that tracking the work back to its origins and confirming its veracity become once again of paramount importance. Events-based services provide the functionality needed in the online environment to track such variations, to account for their origins and purposes, and thus to trace the evolving history of the text.[24]

In order to support such analytic services, the library will need to ensure the stability of individual objects, so that the user can return to them regardless of the changes they undergo.[25] For some selected texts, intermediate versions between the original and the most recent or most used version, will need to be retained as well. While maintaining intermediate versions is obviously a formidable challenge, it should be possible, within reason, provided that libraries are more willing than they have been to divide such responsibilities among themselves. Bearing in mind, furthermore, the distinction made above between intrinsic and extrinsic context, the analytical service should be not only a matter of providing the user with the ability to trace the evolution of an object from one state to another, but must also supply the capacity to plot the evolution of a concept (information element) from one object to another over time.

The Synthetic Service. The purpose of the analytical service is to identify (and protect the integrity of) individual objects—and in some cases selected states of individual objects—so that their history and the history of their contents can be understood. The synthetic service, on the other hand, should be designed to allow the user to combine the contents of different objects, without necessarily taking their historical evolution into account. The objective should rather be to understand how concepts change in different contexts—not by tracing them through their evolving historical contexts (which is a function of the analytical service), but by creating new contexts for them.

The synthetic service is therefore in some ways the exact opposite of the analytical one. The analytical service is more observational, seeking not to disturb objects, but to observe them, so to speak, in their natural habitat—rather like a delicate archaeological dig. The synthetic service, on the other hand, has the potential to pull objects to pieces, recombining parts of them into new forms, disregarding in some cases even the intentions of their original creators. In the synthetic service, the purpose of objects is to serve as building blocks for new user creations.

A certain amount of "damage" to a personal database could be done in the course of the kind of recontextualization made possible by such a synthetic service. One role the library plays, therefore, is the same as that for the analytical service—to serve as the protected space to which the user can always return to find the original intact. It should also be the library's responsibility in such circumstances to ensure proper protocol and citation, so that despite the chaos and fragmentation that will necessarily result from such a synthetic service, the user will still be able to give proper credit to the originators of different concepts used.

In the analytical service, utility is dependent upon—and in some cases even synonymous with—understanding. The aim is to understand the object ever better by seeing how it relates to its traditional contexts. In the synthetic service, on the other hand, understanding is not the ultimate aim—but rather use. Here we must be careful, of course, to avoid the pitfalls (and accusations) of relativism—but we must also note that the use of an information element to create new knowledge—and new information products—does not depend upon "fully" understanding that information element. In fact, the synthetic service (again, within reason) will and should actually promote a kind of misunderstanding, because it is providing the user with the ability to pull elements out of context, and it is only on the basis of such context that things are understandable. On the other hand, it is also worth bearing in mind that, because of the infinity of understanding—the endless movement about the matrix, in which one thing can only be understood in relation to another, and so on forever—no one can ever "fully" understand anything anyway. The difference between the analytical and the synthetic service is, in that sense, really only a matter of degree (i.e., the analytical service takes original context somewhat more into account)—but the aim of the synthetic service should be, in any case, to exploit that infinity of understanding and to allow and encourage the user to produce ever new knowledge by disregarding old contexts and creating new ones.

A Subjective Program

We noted above that, in order to conceive of the use of a system, such as the model of the knowledge matrix, we must assume that the user occupies a position separate from it. This is, however, exactly what makes such a model so simplistic—because from a production standpoint, the user of course is always in some way an intimate part of it. The inability to find a place for the user in the system was also one of the things that arose in trying to understand the implications of ABC.

If an ontology is a set of rules or methods that permit an abstract, systematic description of (some aspect of) the world, then it is the case that everyone is in effect working with a kind of personal ontology all of the time—and real understanding must include an awareness of that personal ontology. Such a personal system is, however, often obscure—at best, visible only sporadically, at the very edges of consciousness. It consists of what one already knows, which necessarily forms the context for producing any new knowledge—and it includes the values, assumptions, biases and perspectives that condition how knowledge is extended. The ultimate personalization of information services, the ultimate empowerment of the user, should therefore be to place the user in a position to observe and track his or her own thought and learning.

Individual understanding and application of information are, in other words, very real events in themselves—and the agent of such events is the user. A system needs to be designed and made easily accessible therefore that allows the user to witness, store, and retrieve those ultimate events over time. Such a service should somehow provide immediate access to what is already accepted—to what conclusions have already been drawn that inform and make possible the next step in knowledge production. The user must be given the ability to confront herself, as in a mirror, to trace what she is learning, to note the parameters of her knowledge, to model her own thinking, and to explain to herself how she understands new information by relating it to the context of what she already knows.

I have, needless to say, no idea of what such a Subjective Program would actually look like—but I suspect its primary function would be to provide the user with the ability to create, apply and expand a highly personalized form of metadata. (Each of us is, after all, producing a kind of unsystematic metadata all of the time. The very act of reading is to create a form of fleeting metadata.) Such personalized metadata would be used primarily to trace the context changes, the events, that define and drive the user's intellectual life. The conscious articulation of such changes would not only enhance and focus knowledge production, but it would also improve substantially the ability to formulate and articulate new information, so that it could be shared more effectively with others.[26]

Unitary objects of information are useless for purposes of knowledge production. In order for them to be made useful, they must be related to other objects, including in some cases other states of themselves. Such a relationship is not so much something that "is," as it is rather something that the user does. The creation or perception of that relationship is an event, and the production of knowledge is a consequence of such event experiences. Ensuring that such experiences are possible, and that users have the ability to record, apply and communicate the results of those events, must form the abstract foundation, in my opinion, for any truly effective information services in the future.

REFERENCE NOTES

1. Ray Kurzweil, *The Age of Spiritual Machines* (New York: Penguin, 1999), 3.

2. I believe I am taking a position here somewhat related to the so-called "cognitive" perspective. See Nicholas J. Belkin, "The Cognitive Viewpoint in Information Science," *Journal of Information Science* 16 (1990): 111–15.

3. See William Y. Arms, "Automated Digital Libraries: How Effectively Can Computers Be Used for the Skilled Tasks of Professional Librarianship?" *DLib Magazine* 6 (July/Aug 2000): 2–4. www.dlib.org/dlib/july00/arms/07arms.html.

4. For a recent discussion on the benefits and pitfalls of personalization, see Cass R. Sunstein, "MyUniversity.Com?" *EDUCAUSE Review* 37 (Sept./Oct. 2002): 32–40. www.educause.edu/ir/library/pdf/erm0252.pdf.

5. Difference is a key concept in continental philosophy. For a recent study, see Jeffrey A. Bell, *The Problem of Difference: Phenomenology and Poststructuralism* (Toronto: University of Toronto Press, 1998). For a recent anthology of essential writings, see *The Theory of Difference: Readings in Contemporary Continental Thought,* ed. Douglas L. Donkel (Albany: State Univ. of New York Press, 2001). My own views on difference are admittedly much more rudimentary, stemming mainly from Ferdinand de Saussure's seminal *Course in General Linguistics,* trans. Wade Baskin (New York: Philosophical Library, 1959), 111–22 (on "Linguistic Value").

6. Saussure, *Course in General Linguistics,* 81–83 ("Inner Duality and the History of Linguistics").

7. See the Library of Congress' "Core Metadata Elements," http://lcweb.loc.gov/standards/metadata.html#types.

8. See Edward Craig, "Ontology," in *Routledge Encyclopedia of Philosophy,* vol. 7 (London and New York: Routledge, 1998), 117–18.

9. Thomas R. Gruber, "A Translation Approach to Portable Ontology Specifications," *Knowledge Acquisition* 5 (June 1993): 199. See also Gruber's Web site "What Is an Ontology?" www-ksl. stanford.edu/kst/what-is-an-ontology.html.

10. For a good place to start investigating ontologies, see Peter Clark's "Some Ongoing KBS/ Ontology Projects and Groups," www.cs.utexas.edu/users/mfkb/related.html.

11. The homepage of the Harmony Project is www.cs.utexas.edu/users/mfkb/related.html.

12. Dan Brickley, Jane Hunter, and Carl Lagoze, "ABC: A Logical Model for Metadata Interoperability," Harmony discussion note 19991019, www.ilrt.bris.ac.uk/discovery/harmony/ docs/abc/abc draft.html. Hereafter cited in the text as "strawman"; Carl Lagoze, Jane Hunter, and Dan Brickley, "An Event-Aware Model for Metadata Interoperability," in *Research and Advanced Technology for Digital Libraries: 4th European Conference, ECDLI 2000, Lecture Notes in Computer Science, 1923* (Berlin: Springer, 2000), 103–16. http://link.springer.de/ link/service/series/0558/bibs/1923/19230103.htm. Also available at http://techreports.library. cornell.edu:8081/Dienst/UI/1.0/Display/cul.cs/TR2000-1800. Hereafter cited in the text as "Event-Aware Model"; Carl Lagoze and Jane Hunter, "The ABC Ontology and Model," *Journal of Digital Information* 2 (Nov. 2001). http://jodi.tamu.edu/Articles/v02/i02/Lagoze. Hereafter cited in the text as "most recent iteration."

13. Lagoze and Hunter, "The ABC Ontology and Model," 104.

14. Carl Lagoze, "Business Unusual: How 'Event-Awareness' May Breathe Life into the Catalog?" paper delivered at the Bicentennial Conference on Bibliographic Control for the New Millennium, Library of Congress, Nov. 15–17, 2000. http://lcweb.loc.gov/catdir/bibcontrol/lagoze.html.

15. Ibid., 110.

16. The CIMA Homepage is www.cimi.org.

17. See Martin Doerr, Jane Hunter, and Carl Lagoze, "Towards a Core Ontology for Information Integration" at http://archive.dstc.edu.au/RDU/staff/janehunter/JODI_Oct2002.pdf and www. cs.cornell.edu/lagoze/papers/Core_Ontology.pdf.

18. This is not to imply that the concept of an event was not meant from the beginning to include work on museum objects. The "strawman" document makes clear that many different communities, including museums and businesses, are concerned with events, and that ABC is intended to serve all of them.

19. An "Towards a Core Ontology," it is noted that the ABC authors, in working toward closer compatibility with the museum CRM ontology, changed certain "concept definitions." "For example, the ABC concept 'State' was transformed and clarified to 'Situation.'"

20. For information on the history of this complicated concept, see Martha Yee, "What Is a Work?: Part 1" *Cataloging & Classification Quarterly* 19, no. 1 (1994): 9–8; "Part 2" *Cataloging & Classification Quarterly* 19, no. 2 (1994), 5–22; "Part 3" *Cataloging & Classification Quarterly* 20, no. 1 (1995) 25–46; "Part 4" *Cataloging & Classification Quarterly* 20, no. 2 (1995), 3–24. See also Elaine Svenonius, *The Intellectual Foundation of Information Organization* (Cambridge, Mass.: The MIT Pr., 2000), 35–38.

21. "Resource Description Framework (RDF) Model and Syntax Specification," www.w3.org/ TR/REC-rdf-syntax. See also Eric Miller, "An Introduction to the Resource Description Framework," *D-Lib Magazine* 4 (May 1998), www.dlib.org/dlib/maY98/miller/05miller.html.

22. See Rudolf Pfeiffer, *History of Classical Scholarship from the Beginning to the End of the Hellenistic Age* (Oxford: Clarendon, 1968), 3.

25. For a current introduction, see D. C. Greetham, *Textual Scholarship: An Introduction* (New York and London: Garland, 1992).

26. Jerome J. McGann has recently made the point that humanities scholars will also need to relearn the techniques of textual editing, because "the entirety of our inherited archive of cultural works will have to be re-edited within a network of digital storage, access, and dissemination." "Literary Scholarship in the Digital Future," *The Chronicle of Higher Education* 49 (Dec. 13, 2002): B7.

27. This is also Lagoze's advice for the future of library services in his "Business Unusual."

28. This service of personalized metadata may be related to or benefit from the concept of reification (another old philosophical term appropriated and enlivened by computer science). In RDF,

statements are made about Web resources. Such a statement can also be "reified," i.e., modeled as a resource itself, such that further statements can then be made about it. (And then presumably those statements can be reified, so that further statements could be made about them, etc.) See the RDF "Model and Syntax Specification," Section 4.1. I am grateful to Carl Lagoze for referring me to this feature of RDF.

3 CONTINGENCY AND CONTRADICTION

THE PLACE(S) OF THE LIBRARY AT THE DAWN OF THE NEW MILLENNIUM

*Ne pas choisir, en effet, c'est
choisir de ne pas choisir.*
—Sartre

Librarianship has become preoccupied, perhaps to a point of obsession, with its own future. There seems to be a growing sense that change is now moving at such a rate that steering may have ceased to be an option. But that is all the more reason to stop now for a moment—balanced, as we are, on the cusp between millennia—to reaffirm, or redefine, the core values of information services, and to consider how those values can be most effectively fulfilled in the intermediate future.

The aim of this article will be to suggest answers to two questions. First, what should be the primary purpose of information services in general and libraries in particular as we enter the new millennium? Second, assuming such a purpose, what array of services should the library be prepared to provide? While these questions will be approached mainly from the academic library perspective, much of what is said should be applicable to all types of libraries. The division in any case between certain types of libraries—especially public and academic—is becoming increasingly problematic and questionable from both the service and the economic perspectives. Although initial efforts to combine public and academic libraries have predictably experienced major political and methodological challenges, we should, nevertheless, persist in those efforts eventually to bring about such a merger.[1]

STIPULATIONS

Let us begin by setting the stage (or stacking the deck) with four definitions or stipulations, which will inform this inquiry.

1. Information, we will say, consists of material information objects that exist independently in time and space. These objects can be stored, retrieved, moved, named, counted, hoarded, bought, sold, and owned. All such objects have primary encoding, i.e., they are composed of signifiers, which users can decrypt, interpret, or otherwise attribute meaning to. Some objects have secondary encoding, in the sense that the primary codes are further encoded for purposes of machine storage and transfer. As opposed to information, let us say that knowledge is always private and personal. It cannot be

This article first appeared in *Journal of the American Society for Information Science and Technology* 52, no. 1 (2001): 3–11. Reprinted with permission of John Wiley & Sons, Inc.

effectively shared with anyone else, and is continuously evolving. Knowledge is a kind of personal competency; it is through the use of that competency that information is (encrypted and) decrypted, and it is partially through the decryption or interpretation of information that knowledge increases. To confuse information and knowledge is to succumb to the positivist fallacy.

2. Information services assist individual users in locating and making use of (understanding, applying) information objects. Every formal information service is designed and intended to meet the specific needs of a particular community or society at a particular time. The service is perceived, assessed, maintained, and adjusted in accordance with the prevalent values of that particular society or community. Every formal information service is, therefore, at once both a political institution operating within its community, and an epistemological instrumentality intended to meet individual knowledge needs or to solve specific problems of the community it serves.

3. There are different kinds of information service agencies, one of which is libraries. Although there are many differences between libraries and the other institutionalized information service providers, the most important differences are economic (and, therefore, ideological): libraries (let us stipulate) are created and intended for public or collective benefit, and are maintained by public or collectively created support. Libraries are by their nature nonprofit institutions, in the sense that their end purpose is to provide services rather than to generate revenues. (A commercial library is an oxymoron.)

4. In planning for the future, the primary responsibility of libraries is not prognosis, in the sense of projecting what user needs and information technologies are likely to evolve. The primary planning responsibility of libraries should rather be to determine what institutionalized information services ought to be provided in future for particular communities, and then to work with those communities to ensure that the process and technologies necessary to provide those services are created as rapidly as possible.

CONTINGENCY

It will be noted that there is a potential contradiction between stipulation 2, which implies that libraries are mainly reactive, responding to the needs and values of the community, and stipulation 4, which states that libraries must be proactive, creating or at least affecting the needs of the communities they support. This is, I should admit, the first of several such "loopy" contradictions we will encounter in this inquiry, and it is in part by confronting or resolving such loops that we will make progress. The fact is (and this is perhaps a fifth stipulation) that we can never effectively or fully escape the confines of our own community, in the sense of the values and presuppositions that drive our community at any particular time, because our knowledge is in many ways a product of that community, conditioned by the information the community has privileged and validated. (In fact, to continue looping, the position I am taking here—i.e., that our perspectives and understandings are significantly conditioned by, situated in, the society of which we are members—is, as will be evident below, *itself* unavoidably informed by or derived from the present values of the society we are part of.) The library is, therefore, inextricably woven into the fabric of the society it serves—(in)forming that society, while at the same time being (in)formed by it. That being the case, the library has not only the right but also the responsibility to contribute actively to the vision and design of the community's future information services.

What then is the purpose of information services in this particular society at this particular time? Or, more precisely, what do we assume at this time that information objects are for, such that we should create public or collectively supported institutions, libraries, to assist members of society in locating and using those objects? Drawing on stipulation 2 above, we will approach this question from two directions: from the political or social point of view on the one hand, and from the epistemological perspective on the other.

From a political standpoint, modern libraries are motivated for the most part by a *liberal ideal*, by which I mean a core conviction that individual needs and views should be tolerated and supported. "Every individual is to be equally free to propose and to live by whatever conception of the good he or she pleases, derived from whatever theory or tradition he or she may adhere to, unless that conception of the good involves reshaping the life of the rest of the community in accordance with it."[2] The right of the individual to make decisions for himself or herself is among our highest values, and the library as a political institution is designed specifically to promote and assist that individuality of decision making. This particular bias toward being unbiased (another contradiction, to which we will return later) lies at the core of many library values, as embodied most formally perhaps in the ALA Library Bill of Rights. The ideals of equity of service and privacy of access are, therefore, fundamental to our present understanding of the library mission. Perhaps most indicative of this liberal perspective, however, is the basic library value of impartial or neutral service.

Although it is no doubt true, as Gary Radford has argued, that one purpose of neutrality is to provide library services with a semblance of objectivity as a basic tenet of positivism, the main origin of the high premium placed upon service neutrality is contemporary society's, and therefore the library's, liberal political disposition.[3] One of liberalism's central concerns is to ensure fairness or justice, and the library is, therefore, intent upon providing a "just" service. As defined by John Rawls, the ideal person to engage in such a just interchange would be someone who is entirely without bias or predilection—someone who views the world through a "veil of ignorance" with respect to his or her own needs, preferences or place in society.[4] Only, we imagine, by totally ignoring our own personal histories can we avoid prejudicing the user's search: we want always to connect the user directly to the information without getting in the way ourselves. Although such total neutrality is, of course, impossible, this value is relevant to any debate about the advancing automation of information services.[5] Our interest in replacing human services with mechanical ones derives not simply from the fact that machines are faster, more accurate, more comprehensive, and above all cheaper than people—but also from the expectation that machines can avoid all human bias, and thus treat all users impartially.

We must now also consider the future function of the library from the epistemological perspective. That function or purpose will always depend upon how the society views the nature and utility of knowledge at that particular time. Perhaps the most prevalent ontological trend at the turn of the millennium—one that has, to be sure, been building throughout the 20th century—is a general loosening of the sense that there is a valid and verifiable external truth—an objective world "out there," separate from our perception of it, that we can know and study and agree upon; instead, there has evolved a sense in all fields of human thought that reality is always necessarily conditioned and contingent. This "postmodern" perspective has gradually gained momentum in the second half of the 20th century, and we can assume its influence will broaden yet further as we move into the new millennium. This multifaceted trend has certainly not gone unnoticed in the library literature, and there have been several excellent essays that consider different aspects of its effect upon library services.[6] There are countless varieties and applications of this new perspective, from the deconstruction of Jacques Derrida to the spatial theory of Fredric Jameson, but perhaps the most accessible and appropriate for our purposes here will be found in the philosophy, or antiphilosophy, of Richard Rorty:

> If we see knowing not as having an essence, to be described by scientists or phi-
> losophers, but rather as a right, by current standards, to believe, then we are well

on the way to seeing conversation as the ultimate context within which knowledge is to be understood. Our focus shifts from the relation between human beings and the objects of their inquiry to the relation between alternative standards of justification, and from there to actual changes in those standards which make up intellectual history.[7]

This is a primary component of Rorty's concept of pragmatism. One of the most persistent themes in Rorty's writings has been that pragmatism, at least as he has defined it, should not be construed as relativism.

> Except for the occasional cooperative freshman, one cannot find anybody who says that two incompatible opinions on an important topic are equally good. The philosophers who get called "relativists" are those who say that the grounds for choosing between such opinions are less algorithmic than had been thought.[8]

As Rorty says repeatedly, simple relativism is self-contradictory, and cannot be used as a rational argument. (I cannot, for example, reasonably assert that there are no absolutes, without making that absolute assertion.) Liberalism has, of course, a closely related problem: how can one take the position that any position is acceptable and should be tolerated, and that no one position should therefore be privileged? Is that not to privilege a position, i.e., that no position should be privileged? In fact, it is indeed a contradiction, but that should not stop us from adopting precisely that position.

The point, of course, is that all knowledge is at one level situational or contingent. One does not advance society or create individual knowledge except through dialectic or dialogue, which is to say except by taking a position. We can call this for our purposes the *positional imperative*. This does not mean that such a position need ever be viewed as the only possible or final position, or even necessarily as the right position, but rather one that is a prerequisite for continuing the inquiry. What counts is not so much what the position is, but rather that one takes a position—and, equally or more important, that one recognizes and acknowledges that a position is being taken. The library is unavoidably part of the universal discussion by which knowledge is advanced—and, therefore, must always take a position, regardless of how much we try to insinuate a "veil of ignorance" into our services. This being the case, then what generally should the library's position be? For libraries serving societies that have embraced basic liberal views and the (admittedly sometimes tacit) acceptance of contingency, taking no position (to play on Sartre) is unquestionably the best position to take—as long as we bear in mind that such a position is all-encompassing and totally uncompromising. We will brook no challenge to our view that all views should be challenged—and we must learn to be comfortable with that.

The same will inevitably be true, of course, of the machines we program. It will even be true, if machines begin to program themselves, because to communicate at all, to understand at all, entails perspective. The real value in this respect of using machines for information services is not that they can somehow achieve some value-free level of presentation, but rather that they have the capacity (providing they are properly and creatively programmed) to provide the human end-user with a much greater ability to perceive and to trace the biases and underlying assumptions that inevitably inform any communication.

What then are the implications for information transfer and services of the (post)modern value of situationalism or contingency, in particular Rorty's formulation of the ongoing conversation, coupled with the political tendency toward liberalism? If progress or discovery ultimately derive from an ongoing, never-ending dialogue, then the primary purpose of information services should be to sustain and contribute to that conversation, mainly by assisting its participants. Because of the positional imperative, the individual participant will always necessarily be intent upon adopting or fashioning a point of view, which he or she plans or hopes to place in competition with other positions.

PERSUASION

Rhetoric, the use of language for the purpose of persuasion, evolved in antiquity, and was an especially critical skill in those Greek democratic states, where every (male) citizen was not only his own lawyer, but also was expected to take part in debates on public policy.[9] The earliest purveyors of systematic rhetoric were the Sophists—itinerant teachers who traveled around Greece in the fifth century BCE, teaching young men the skills of public speaking in return for payment. The Sophists were for any number of reasons sometimes very unpopular—but mainly, one assumes, because they provided young men with the verbal tools to challenge authority. Rhetoric and philosophy grew from the same soil, but their relationship was sometimes uneasy, and they frequently came into conflict.[10] Plato clearly despised the Sophists, seeing them as opportunists who placed argumentation above the search for truth. Aristotle, on the other hand, recognized the value and place of rhetoric, and wrote what is probably the most famous treatise on the subject. In this work, Aristotle views rhetoric and dialectic (i.e., philosophical disputation) as being separate but related. Unlike dialectic, Aristotle says, rhetoric can appeal to character and emotion; and while dialectic must use induction and the syllogism, rhetoric can apply more flexible methods of argument.[11] We must admit, however, that on the practical level, most serious conversation is really a combination of what Aristotle labeled rhetoric and dialectic, and—if Plato's dialogues are anything to go by—this was equally the case in antiquity.

In recent decades, there has been a resurgence in the status and the study of rhetoric.[12] The Sophists especially have been approached anew, and have been found (i.e., can be viewed) as representing perspectives that resonate deeply with us 2,500 years later:[13]

> Sophistical rhetoric maintains that the world of discourse consists not of a singular, real logos awaiting to be discovered and distinguished from its apparent counterpart, but of *dissoi logoi*–human linguistic creations in unceasing contest with one another. . . . its aim is to displace or overcome an uttered logos temporarily, not to eliminate it once and for all. Such elimination would short-circuit its claim to make the weaker argument stronger, and negate its faith in the unending flow and constant circulation of discourse. . . . sophistical rhetoric . . . points out that the established order of things does not represent the manifestation of *a priori* truths but rather reflects human choices that people have forgotten were choices. In this sense, rhetoric suggests that if a given order is at all legitimate, it is so not inherently or permanently but only for as long as its heirs reaffirm the choices that have gone into its making.[14]

In a culture such as ours at this time, suspicious of (most) absolutes, which sees truth increasingly as a continually evolving product of discussion, and which tries hard to believe that all positions deserve a proper hearing, the centrality of rhetoric for human progress is gradually if belatedly becoming apparent. The primary purpose of information services in general, and library services in particular, therefore, as we now move into the 21st century, is to provide citizen users with the intellectual resources to persuade their fellow citizens to accept particular perspectives, adopt particular values, take particular action. Because the purpose and result of absorbing information is always finally to produce further information, i.e., to continue the conversation, the function of the library must be understood as one that assists members of the community both in taking particular positions and in recognizing and assessing the positions taken by others.

If we are prepared to accept this role of the library at this time, then how should we go about designing specific library services? That is clearly the next question to be answered in this inquiry. Before we confront those issues, however, we must indulge in a very brief detour, to consider some practical applications of the positional imperative in the institutional context.

EXCURSUS: INSTITUTIONAL EXIGENCIES

We noted above in stipulation 2 that every formal information service is at once a political institution and an epistemological instrumentality. In the preceding discussion, I have done my best to link and reconcile a few aspects of two key trends or values—the modern political position of liberalism, and the postmodern sense that all knowledge is ultimately contingent. There are many areas that I am admittedly ignoring where liberalism (which stems ultimately from the Enlightenment) and postmodernism (elements of which are based specifically upon the rejection of Enlightenment tenets) come into conflict. At a more practical operating level, however, there remains a potential for conflict that I cannot ignore between the library's institutional objectives and its more apolitical responsibilities as an epistemological instrument. Before we can proceed further, therefore, I need briefly to consider this divergence, and to try to resolve it.

We must admit up front, as distasteful as it may be, that the ultimate goal of most institutions is to compete and to survive—and the library is an institution. Each library's primary competitors are other libraries, and other information service providers—including especially publishers, who, if they have their wits about them (and many of them do) are now laying plans to disintermediate libraries, even as many of us academic librarians are urging the academy to disintermediate publishers. Academic libraries and scholarly publishers will soon bring their carefully contrived arguments before the collective decision makers of the academy to make their cases. The outcome of this real or inferred debate will determine who will be primarily responsible for creating and providing academic information services in the near future—nonprofit libraries, or for-profit entrepreneurs.

At first glance, of course, we seem to have bumped into yet another contradiction. We have already implied that libraries are never ends in themselves: they are rather always a means to an end, and that end is to assist local users to engage effectively with the other members of their community. This, in turn, implies that if some other information service provider (say a commercial publisher or aggregator) could fulfill that service better than libraries, then libraries, not being ends in themselves, should immediately go out of business and hand over responsibility for local information services to that other provider. But never fear, for we librarians have set the rules of this game ourselves. We have defined the terms such that only a library can, in fact, provide the "right" services—for the right services are by definition the kind of services that distinguish libraries from other providers.

The ideological cornerstone of the modern library position is that information access is a right of all citizens, and not a privilege of the few who can afford it (see, e.g., Principle One of the Keystone Principles.[15] Therefore, only agencies that are publicly or at least collectively funded can provide the right services—for to allow for-profit providers to enter the game would surely be to jeopardize access, and we can point to the so-called serials crisis in the print environment as evidence. The perception should therefore be that libraries (not being ends in themselves) are not, in fact, arguing in their own interest, but rather in the broader interest of society and human progress. Only publicly or collectively supported agencies can provide and safeguard the necessary services that will ensure such progress, and libraries are by definition the formal information agencies that embody such support.

Although it is unavoidably the case, therefore, that aspects of the institutional and the instrumental identities of libraries do come into conflict, that conflict, once acknowledged, can for all practical purposes be effectively set aside. Certainly each member of the library profession can and should consider which of these identities is more central to his or her service vision. Is the institution the base, and the instrumentality the superstructure, or vice versa? Do we fight to maintain the institution to provide the (in our view) best possible instrumentality—or do we fight to provide the best possible instrumentality to guarantee the future of the institution? How each of us answers that question for himself or herself will reveal much about us as individuals and professionals. But from a practical position, the answer to that question is, in fact, irrelevant, because the final outcome, i.e., the continuation and prevalence of libraries and the services they provide in the new millennium, is the same in either case.

FUTURE SERVICES

Bearing these values in mind, let us turn now to a definition of what the library should be—in the sense of the kinds of services the library should be prepared to provide—in the intermediate future. What should be the key components of the library function? As a basis for this definition or description, I will use the concept of *place*— partially because place is simply a convenient way to visualize and describe relationships, partially because one kind of place (the topos) is a central concept of rhetoric, but also because the place of place in information services is clearly changing as we move into an increasingly networked environment.

Let us posit three service levels for the future of the library, each characterized by or based upon a different kind or concept of place. We can further divide our definitions of place into two broad categories: (a) place viewed from the objective perspective, which is primarily concerned with relationships among information objects, and (b) place understood from what we will call the subjective perspective, which focuses mainly on the relationships between people and information objects. See figure 1.

	objective	subjective
geographical	archive	agora
topical	description	evaluation
situational	author bias	reader bias

FIGURE 1. Places of Service

Service Level 1: Geographical

We can begin with the most standard sense of place, the local or geographical. Here we can consider the design and use of physical space.

Geographical Objective. The ubiquity of information in an online environment has become a cliché. Such ubiquity is, of course, an illusion: it is not that information is everywhere, on every desktop, but rather that information can now be moved practically anywhere at such speed that it looks like it is everywhere. This has resulted in a healthy disregard for geographical location on the part of the library's user community: the sense is that the object is located "at" a particular address in cyberspace, rather than in a particular physical place elsewhere.[16] But the less important the geographical dispersal and location of objects are for the user, the more important the network of locations becomes for the library. Such a "placeless" culture of research is only possible if someone behind the scenes is paying a great deal of attention to the geographical places where objects are kept.

One central responsibility of information services must, therefore, be to ensure that digital information is properly stored, so that it can be effectively identified and transported. Probably the key issue in fulfilling this responsibility will be interoperability, both synchronically, which is to say among different places (systems, platforms) at the same time, but also diachronically, i.e., between different versions, generations, formats of systems in use at different times. Because of secondary encoding, we sometimes have the sensation that digital information is (unlike, e.g., a book) somehow immaterial—but it is, of course, wholly material, being merely composed of very small pieces moving very fast. Acknowledging the materiality of digital information in all of its aspects, taking into account all of its physical properties, ensuring that there are physical places where digital information can be effectively stored and from which it can be transmitted across space and time—that remains at least as important a responsibility for libraries in the online environment as it has been in the traditional library setting.

The greatest challenge academic libraries will face in taking up this responsibility of objective geographical place will not be technical, however, but rather inevitably political—because, much more than in the traditional environment, fulfilling that responsibility will entail systematic coordination and communication among individual institutions. This will be especially the case for academic libraries. Either the level of competition among institutions will need to subside, therefore, or some arrangements will need to be created whereby selected library services are explicitly excluded from interinstitutional competition. The most troubling cloud on the horizon in this respect is the rapid advent of highly competitive distance learning programs in some institutions. If academic institutions and their libraries do not make a conscious effort to avoid it, such programs could severely impair library cooperation, and could conceivably even undermine the nonprofit ideology of the academy as a whole.

Geographical Subjective. In the same way that the future library will need to continue to concern itself with providing (and connecting) places for digital objects, the future library will also want to continue to provide a central, local place for reader-users. Precisely because of the increased role of computer-mediated communication, each academic institution, and presumably each civic community, will need an agora of some kind—a central place where people can meet face to face and can work together, using digital and other information objects. Students especially must have a place where they can come together and share ideas as they explore digital resources. As interdisciplinarity inevitably increases, scholars will also need neutral spaces outside of their respective departments, where they can exchange ideas and evaluate information with colleagues from other disciplines.

By creating such a central digital information commons that occupies a real geographical place, interactions among people could actually be increased, with one result being more informal learning through the sharing of ideas and mutual access to the same information. In the traditional environment, this has not been the library's responsibility, aside from providing a few group study rooms. In the new environment, on the other hand, the purpose of the library as a geographical place must change, so that it is no longer intended primarily for people to work quietly in isolation from each other. In the digital environment, such isolated study is what people do outside of the library—in their dorm rooms or studies or homes. The new library must be mainly a social gathering place, somewhat noisy, with plenty of coffee. Some of the people who will be making such noise should continue to be, of course, public service librarians. One assumes further that the library should also be the place one goes not only for personal assistance but also to use hardware and software that is more advanced than one is likely to own personally.

The more the academy accepts and develops programs of distance learning, as I have previously noted, the more significant this social function of the library will become.[17] We must expect some colleges and universities to contract with each other for courses, so that some courses will be taught by faculty at remote institutions. (Disintermediation will be something experienced not only by information service providers, but also by faculty— perhaps revealing that teaching faculty are ultimately to some extent information service providers themselves.) Student interaction is an essential prerequisite for learning, so that students will need a place to come together, even when the professor is professing from elsewhere. At the same time, such remote instruction will be greatly enhanced by having access to interactive networked resources, which the (remote) professor and the students can use together. Providing that social space, for both formal instruction and informal inter- action, must, therefore, also be an essential library responsibility in the new era.

Service Level 2: Topical

The Greek word "topos," from which we derive our word "topic," means place (cf. topog- raphy). In rhetoric, the term topos has a special meaning with a very complicated lineage— and in some ways the whole history of rhetoric since antiquity can be traced by the changes in the meaning of that term, which continues to be pondered today.[18] A topos meant initially a standard argument for a particular situation, and it was probably again the Sophists who began the practice of collecting arguments on specific subjects. It may be that the term referred originally to a place in a manual where one could find the standard argument for a particular need. Aristotle devoted considerable space in his treatise considering rhetorical (vs. dialectical) topics.[19] Two and a half centuries later, Cicerone wrote his own *Topica,* in which he famously describes the topics as *sedes*, i.e., seats, regions, homes: stable places in which arguments can be stored.[20] One kind of topic Cicero included was the reference to authority. As Ann Moss explains it:

> Another kind of place, very subordinate in the *Topica* . . . was also to become very familiar. This is testimony by quotation, quotation from the sayings and writ- ings of respected experts, orators, philosophers, poets, and historians. A process of reflexivity has already begun to operate. For Aristotle, places were grounds of inference for arguing from the generally accepted opinions of the wise and famous. In the *Topica* the specific opinions of respected authors have, in a self- authenticating way, become constituent elements, proof-places of such argument. They are called *auctoritates*.[21]

In late antiquity, Boethius took up the subject once again, and created a much advanced classification scheme (*differentiae*) to categorize the topics.[22] This system of topoi created by Boethius served as a standard source for teaching and study throughout the Middle Ages.

It becomes clear, then, that the topos, or topic in this special sense, has features that relate closely to our modern and rapidly moving view of information and bibliographical services. The topic is a generally or consensually agreed upon item of information which a person uses, draws upon, cites as a basis or authority for saying something—making an assertion—about a particular subject. It is one component of a codified system, all segments of which might be understood as theoretically fitting together to make up the current, agreed-upon state of the subject area; each component has its place so that it can be found and related to the others.

Topical Objective. One of the most basic responsibilities of all information services is certainly the topical service. The library has always been and will always be a kind of super handbook, which contains places (objects) where one goes to find arguments or issues that can be used as a basis for making a persuasive contribution oneself to the conversation. These places or objects must be arranged and linked or related in such a way as to promote their discovery, use, and evaluation. From the objective perspective, therefore, the topical service is a matter of in-depth indexing, abstracting and cross-referencing of (at the least) all formal publications. (It should be left to individual disciplines to decide on their own certification processes, and to define what constitutes a publication in their disciplines.) In most cases, the user will be looking for specific information (arguments, issues) *within* publications, and will then use the remainder of the publication as context for the application and understanding of the specific information needed. Ensuring that there are links between the specific information and the publication containing it will be a key topical responsibility in the online environment. The user-reader will certainly want to take into account direct citations in the publication by the author, if there are any, but the main topical job of the library will be to provide indirect citations, in the sense of access to other places that refer to similar or related issues.

From a bibliographical or topical perspective, then, the extent of a discipline is the defined parameter of its public information, which (as long as we do not confuse it with knowledge) can always be identified and circumscribed. Defining those disciplinary parameters, linking their contents, connecting all such disciplinary information to the totality of what is collectively "comprehended," in the strict sense of what has been publicly presented, should, therefore, be another key service of libraries.

Topical Subjective. Libraries should not only describe and link objects of information, but should also openly evaluate information and pass those evaluations on to users as a method of assisting access and use. Libraries in the traditional environment are constantly evaluating information (by way of selection, cataloging, referring, and instructing users), and acting on that evaluation. However—as we have discussed previously—whether out of the misguided sense of maintaining an unbiased impartiality (the unattainable "veil of ignorance") or out of a wish to appear objective as dictated by an innate positivist ideal, libraries often seem to try to conceal or deny such ongoing acts of evaluation, to the ultimate detriment of information services. Because of the library's feigned impartiality and detachment, users cannot easily recognize the extent to which evaluation is part of the services being provided—and yet, how one approaches information, attributes meaning to it, and uses it to further one's knowledge depends in part upon one's perception of the bias or values from which such information is inevitably derived. It is time now for libraries to abandon the neutrality sham. Libraries must do more evaluation of the utility (i.e., persuasiveness) of different objects for different purposes and then libraries must ensure, probably through some new forms of metadata, that users are aware of the basis for such evaluation, so that they can accept or reject that service according to their own needs and values.

What should be the basis for such library evaluation? For scholarly information, the most obvious basis will be certification, which is to say successful peer review in the new environment. A trusted group of scholars in each discipline, probably working on a rotating basis, need to consider all new information produced, and decide whether each item makes a true contribution to the field. Whether an item has or has not been certified should be used as a primary basis for evaluation; a library should relay such certification status to the user, and should encourage the user to accept that an item that has been certified has a greater value from the standpoint of the discipline than something that has not been: for a discipline to certify something is to vouch for its validity and utility in that discipline. On the other hand, there will be many information objects that have not been certified, either because they were never submitted for certification or because their application for certification was denied. In the new environment, these objects should also definitely be available to users, but with the understanding that they have not been endorsed by representative members of the discipline. Only by making such uncertified materials accessible can the library ensure that unorthodox or revolutionary information is not silenced or obscured by the dominant community.

Libraries need more sophisticated mechanisms for tracking the use of library resources and services, and can provide evaluative information to users on the basis of such use tracking. (Users need, e.g., to be especially aware of uncertified items that have received significant use.) As an extension of this service, direct citations by authors of particular publications, as we have already noted, can also be used. Citation analysis has, of course, been a bibliographic service available for decades, but with the advent of online citation, we need a much more sophisticated form of tracking, which will require better coordination with and within the scholarly community. Why certain works are cited and others are not remains obscure, because there are so many different motives for citation.[23] The current conventions of citation are disparate, and vary not only among but even within disciplines. While citations have a range of purposes, each is invariably a kind of topos, intended to add legitimacy in one form or another to the publication's argument. If citations are to be truly useful, however, conventions must be established in scholarly writing, and some method of tagging must be developed for authors, to distinguish and identify different purposes of citation.

Service Level 3: Situational

The third service level we should consider is, on the one hand, significantly different from traditional library services, but it is also at the same time merely the logical extension of Service Level 2. If we assume that all knowledge is based mainly upon relationships of one kind or another, that something is presented or understood mainly in relation to something else, that all cognition is inevitably contextual—then a primary bibliographical service should be to make such contexts as transparent to the user as possible. This can, of course, admittedly only succeed up to a particular point, for if situation or context is an inescapable prerequisite for understanding, then we are faced with an infinite regress: there must be a context for the understanding of a context . . . for the understanding of a context, etc. Once again, however, we should not allow ourselves to be intimidated by this kind of circularity or loopy logic, which is an inevitable byproduct of contingency. Of course there are limits to how deeply context can be analyzed and understood, but this should not discourage us from envisioning and creating services or bibliographical mechanisms to highlight context—or each revelation of context enhances understanding of the object's position, and thus supports the user''s further interaction with the object.

Situational Objective. Assuming that context is in a way a sophisticated or obscure form of citation, creating services that reveal such contexts is a proper and advanced bibliographical responsibility. From the objective perspective, such an advanced service should permit the reader to move beyond direct or indirect citation and to identify underlying assumptions or antecedents. Marx speaks, for example, of the "ruling *intellectual force*" in a society. ("The class which has the means of material production at its disposal, consequently also controls the means of mental production."[24]) A truly effective bibliographical service would be one that reveals such ideological contingencies of a particular target text; it would show through indirect citation how such "ruling" ideas affected and effected the content, and perhaps how other ideologies would have resulted in different contents. Or Foucault, to take another example, posits a "regime of truth" for any particular society, i.e., "the types of discourse which it [the society] accepts and makes function as true."[25] Could we not somehow make apparent through some advanced form of citation this regime of truth underlying a particular text so that the reader would be more specifically conscious of the beliefs the writer is necessarily embracing, perhaps by revealing alternative beliefs? Or consider Kuhn's view of "normal science," which presumes a common paradigm, upon which all science done at a certain time is based.[26] Should not the library be providing a service that makes that paradigm more visible behind any particular scientific text, so that the user would be more aware of the disciplinary presuppositions upon which the assertions in the text are based? Such a service would present the reader with a multidimensional perspective on the text—and with the ability to challenge the text, to argue with it, to pull at its seams, and to consider alternatives. Instead of only providing the user with topics to be used to take a particular position, therefore, the library would also present the user with the capacity and the opportunity to see through and to challenge whatever is asserted from any perspective: the ultimate Sophistic ideal.

We should also take care not to overlook the political dimensions of such a third level service, at least in the academic community. That service would be, in a way, a highly subversive contribution—one that the conservative academy might not necessarily welcome. It could in some ways be viewed as forming a kind of competitive service to teaching, because it would put the student in a position always to look behind the views presented in the classroom, to challenge any statement, and to assess alternatives. If tenure survives in the academy into the next century, providing such a third-level service (or even trying to) would require that librarians be awarded tenure in the same way that faculty now receive it—and for similar reasons: librarians might well need job protection before they could provide students and others with the ability to challenge prevalent disciplinary doctrines.

Situational Subjective. To move from the objective to the subjective perspective at the third level is perhaps to take a step into something bordering on science fiction—but we must nevertheless consider it in the abstract. If we can imagine a bibliographic service that would reveal conceptual antecedents for any target object, can we not also conceive of some service that would make the user herself aware of those personal presuppositions and prejudices that serve as the basis for her particular understanding of that object? As I approach a text, as I try to understand and apply it, what values or assumptions am I basing that understanding upon? The text does not sit on the screen meaning something all by itself: I make it mean based on my own history and perspectives. But what exactly are those perspectives? What assumptions am I making to create this meaning? Those presuppositions or prejudgments are, again, understandable at least on one level as a kind of complex, obscure network of citations or references. But such citations are admittedly hidden and personal—indeed, they fall into the realm of knowledge, as we have defined it, rather than information. Nevertheless, we should at least consider, debate, whether there is any possibility of providing library services that would allow users to capture and maintain more effectively aspects of what they have already read, in such a way as to clarify how that which they already know affects their understanding of texts they are newly approaching. A personal library that would organize and trigger one's personal presuppositions, a set of key personal references ("uncommonplaces"?) would be in some ways the ultimate bibliographical service. Only by providing such services could the contingency of understanding be brought into sharper focus as the coalescence of the presumptions of the writer and the reader.

CONCLUSION

What form the kinds of services suggested above might finally take would depend, of course, on the special demands of the community the library is serving—but such services in general are, I believe, what society will expect and deserve early in the new millennium. One primary syndrome emerging from our discussion of service levels for the future of libraries should, in conclusion, not be overlooked. If we observe each level, especially from the subjective perspective, we note a recurring implication. In each case—whether we are considering the service that helps the user understand his or her own understanding (situational), or the service that provides overt content evaluation and challenges the user to accept or reject it (topical), or the service that creates a physical space for users, especially students, to come together to learn and possibly to interact with remote instruction (geographical)—the boundary between learning in the classroom and learning in the library begins to dissolve. It is not that some things now done in the classroom should in future be done in the library, and vice versa, but rather that the distinction between the library and the classroom may well ultimately begin to become obstructive, and may need finally to be minimized or even removed.

Eliminating distinctions between the classroom and the library, like reducing or removing the distinction between the academic and the public library, is a direction that libraries should be prepared to embrace and to champion. The long-term goal for the new millennium must be nothing less than to make the digital library a new learning place for all citizens of the society—and ultimately for all human residents of the planet. Such an extension of responsibilities and eradication of boundaries may admittedly diminish the independence and specialization that have characterized libraries throughout the traditional era. Although the need for public services and for what we have called above the topical services will certainly persist and likely increase, some of the work now done by librarians may be appropriated by others—machines, technicians, teaching faculty, and within very carefully set limits perhaps even publishers. At the same time, however, some responsibilities previously belonging to others will doubtless also be assumed by libraries. The ultimate benefits of all these changes for society will, in any case, easily justify whatever political compromises individual information service professions may be finally called upon to make.

REFERENCE NOTES

1. Gordon Flagg, "Share and Share Alike?" *American Libraries* 30 (1999): 40–44.

2. Alasdair MacIntyre, *Whose Justice? Which Rationality?* (Notre Dame, Ind.: Univ. of Notre Dame Pr., 1988), 336.

3. G. P. Radford, "Positivism, Foucault, and the Fantasia of the Library: Conceptions of Knowledge and the Modern Library Experience," *Library Quarterly* 65 (1992): 412.

4. J. Rawls, *A Theory of Justice* (Cambridge, Mass.: Harvard Univ. Pr., 1971), 137.

5. MacIntyre, *Whose Justice?* 346.

6. See especially J. M. Budd, "An Epistemological Foundation for Library and Information Science," *Library Quarterly* 65 (1995): 295–318; C. Martell, "The Disembodied Librarian in the Digital Age," *College & Research Libraries* 61 (2000): 10–28; Radford, "Positivism, Foucault, and the Fantasia," 408–24.

7. R. Rorty, *Philosophy and the Mirror of Nature* (Princeton, N.J.: Princeton Univ. Pr., 1979), 389–90.

8. R. Rorty, *Consequences of Pragmatism* (Minneapolis, Minn.: Univ. of Minnesota Pr., 1982), 166. See also Rorty, *Philosophy and the Mirror of Nature, 373–79,* and R. Rorty, "Science as Solidarity," in *The Rhetoric of Human Sciences: Language and Argument in Scholarship and Public Affairs* (Madison, Wisc.: Univ. of Wisconsin Pr., 1978), 42.

9. The current, standard history is G. A. Kennedy, *A New History of Classical Rhetoric* (Princeton, N.J.: Princeton Univ. Pr., 1994).

10. S. Ijsseling, *Rhetoric and Philosophy in Conflict: An Historical Survey* (The Hague: Martinus Nijhoff, 1976).

11. Aristotle, *On Rhetoric: A Theory of Civil Discourse,* trans. by G. A. Kennedy (New York: Oxford Univ. Pr., 1991), 38–40.

12. Ijsseling, *Rhetoric and Philosophy in Conflict,* 1–6.

13. K. E. Welch, *Electric Rhetoric: Classical Rhetoric, Oralism, and a New Literacy* (Cambridge, Mass.: MIT Pr., 1999), 13.

14. J. Poulakos, Sophistical Rhetoric in Classical Greece (Columbia, S.C.: Univ. of South Carolina Pr., 1995), 190–91.

15. Association of Research Libraries, "The Keystone Principles," in *ARL: A Bimonthly Report* 207 (Dec. 1999): 8–9.

16. P. Berthon and C. Katsikeas, "Essai: Weaving Postmodernism," *Internet Research* 8 (1998): 152.

17. Ross Atkinson, "A Rationale for the Redesign of Scholarly Information Exchange," *Library Resources & Technical Services* 44 (2000): 59–69.

18. For a good example see L. Hunter, "From Cliché to Archetype" in *Toward a Definition of Topos: Approaches to Analogical Reasoning,* ed. by L. Hunter (Basingstoke, Hampshire: Macmillan, 1991), 199–227.

19. Aristotle, *On Rhetoric,* 45, 190–204.

20. Cicero, *De Inventione. De Optimo Genere Oratorum. Topica,* trans. by H. M. Hubbell, Loeb Classical Library (London: Heinemann, 1949), 386.

21. A. Moss, *Printed Commonplace-Books and the Structuring of Renaissance Thought* (Oxford: Clarendon Pr., 1996), 6.

22. Boethius, *De Topicis Differentiis,* trans. and ed. by E. Stump (Ithaca, N.Y.: Cornell Univ. Pr., 1978).

23. L. Egghe and R. Rousseau, *Introduction to Infometrics: Quantitative Methods in Library, Documentation, and Information Science* (Amsterdam: Elsevier Science, 1990), 211–14.

24. K. Marx and F. Engels, "The German Ideology," in *Collected Works,* vol. v, trans. by C. Dutt, W. Lough, and C. P. Magill (New York: International Publishers, 1976), 59.

25. M. Foucault, *Power/Knowledge: Selected Interviews and Other Writings, 1972–1977,* ed. by C. Gordon (New York: Pantheon, 1980), 131.

26. T. S. Kuhn, *The Structure of Scientific Revolutions* (Chicago: Univ. of Chicago Pr., 1962), 10.

BIBLIOGRAPHY

Aristotle. *On Rhetoric: A Theory of Civil Discourse.* trans. and ed. G. A. Kennedy. New York: Oxford Univ. Pr., 1991.

Association of Research Libraries. "The Keystone Principles." *ARL: A Bimonthly Report* 207 (Dec. 1999): 8–9.

Atkinson, R. "A Rationale for the Redesign of Scholarly Information Exchange." *Library Resources & Technical Services* 44 (2000): 59–69.

Berthon, P., and Katsikeas, C. "Essai: Weaving Postmodernism." *Internet Research* 8 (1998): 149–

55.

Boethius. "De topicis differentiis." Trans. and ed. E. Stump. Ithaca, N.Y.: Cornell Univ. Pr., 1978.

Budd, J. M. "An Epistemological Foundation for Library and Information Science." *Library Quarterly* 65 (1995): 295–318.

Cicero. *De inventione; De optimo genere oratorum; Topica.* trans. H. M. Hubbell. Loeb Classical Library.London: Heinemann, 1949.

Egghe, L., and Rousseau, R. *Introduction to Infometrics: Quantitative Methods in Library, Documentation, and Information Science.* Amsterdam: Elsevier Science, 1990.

Flagg, G. "Share and Share Alike?" *American Libraries* 30 (1999): 40–44.

Foucault, M. *Power/Knowledge: Selected Interviews and Other Writings 1972–1977.* ed. C. Gordon. New York: Pantheon, 1980.

Hunter, L. "From Cliché to Archetype." In *Toward a definition of topos: Approaches to Analogical Reasoning.* ed. L. Hunter. Basingstoke, Hampshire: Macmillan, 1991, 199–227.

Ijsseling, S. *Rhetoric and Philosophy in Conflict: An Historical Survey.* The Hague: Martinus Nijhoff, 1976.

Kennedy, G. A. *A New History of Classical Rhetoric.* Princeton, N.J.: Princeton Univ. Pr., 1994.

Kuhn, T. S. *The Structure of Scientific Revolutions.* Chicago: Univ. of Chicago Pr., 1962.

MacIntyre, A. *Whose Justice? Which Rationality?* Notre Dame, Ind.: Univ. of Notre Dame Pr. 1988.

Martell, C. "The Disembodied Librarian in the Digital Age." *College & Research Libraries* 61 (2000): 10–28.

Marx, K., and Engels, F. The German Ideology. In *Collected Works,* vol. v. trans. C. Dutt, W. Lough, & C. P. Magill. New York: International Publishers, 1976.

Moss, A. *Printed Commonplace-books and the Structuring of Renaissance Thought.* Oxford: Clarendon Pr., 1996.

Poulakos, J. *Sophistical Rhetoric in Classical Greece.* Columbia, S.C.: Univ. of South Carolina Pr., 1995.

Rawls, J. *A Theory of Justice.* Cambridge, Mass.: Harvard Univ. Pr., 1971.

Radford, G. P. "Positivism, Foucault, and the Fantasia of the Library: Conceptions of Knowledge and the Modern Library Experience." *Library Quarterly* 65 (1992): 408–24.

Rorty, R. *Philosophy and the Mirror of Nature.* Princeton, N.J.: Princeton Univ. Pr., 1979.

Rorty, R. *Consequences of Pragmatism.* Minneapolis, Minn.: Univ. of Minnesota Pr., 1982.

Rorty, R. "Science as Solidarity." In *The Rhetoric of Human Sciences: Language and Argument in Scholarship and Public Affairs.* Madison, Wisc.: Univ. of Wisconsin Pr., 1987, 38–52.

Welch, K. E. *Electric Rhetoric: Classical Rhetoric, Oralism, and a New Literacy.* Cambridge, Mass.: MIT Pr., 1999.

4 A RATIONALE FOR THE REDESIGN OF SCHOLARLY INFORMATION EXCHANGE

The disintermediation that will inevitably result from the increased electronic publication of specialized scholarly information affords an excellent opportunity for one of the traditional intermediaries (e.g., libraries, publishers) to assume responsibilities previously held by other intermediaries. Members of the academy should use this opportunity to take back the responsibility for a significant portion of the specialized scholarly publishing that has, in the traditional environment, been placed in the hands of external publishers. The most imposing impediment to such a reappropriation by the academy derives from the inability of institutions to cooperate with each other. If new attitudes could be created within the academy to circumvent that obstruction, then an academy-based process of scholarly information exchange would finally be feasible. One effective model for such a new form of scholarly publishing would be to establish separate domains, or designated channels, for individual disciplines.

It has been more than a decade since Thompson issued his energetic call for academic librarians to consider the possibility of displacing and assuming the role of specialized scholarly publishers.[1] Since that time, there has been a variety of efforts to increase the participation of libraries in scholarly publishing, probably the most visible and successful being Stanford's High Wire Press (http://highwire.stanford.edu/intro.dtl) and the ARL SPARC Project (www.arl.org/sparc).[2] Still, we must admit that the most significant challenge to scholarly trade publishing in the 1990s has come not from libraries but rather from the scholars themselves in the form of Ginsparg's server for preprints of articles on high-energy physics and related subjects (http://xxx.lanl.gov).[3] This innovation has demonstrated beyond a doubt that the formal exchange of specialized scholarly information can thrive outside of traditional publishing channels.

The Ginsparg server at Los Alamos is in some ways a practical manifestation of a theory that some scholars—most notably and effectively Stevan Harnad—have been advocating for much of the decade: the view that computer-mediated communication can and should be used to make specialized scholarly information, properly refereed, freely available via the Internet.[4] This "subversive" position assumes that most scholarly communication will shift to electronic form in the relatively near future—which is a very reasonable expectation. Although different disciplines will, to be sure, move to electronic publishing at different rates, the bibliographic and economic advantages of online communication far outweigh the liabilities. While some paper and microform publishing will no doubt continue for some time, mainly for archival purposes, there can be little doubt that most of the action of scholarly information exchange will migrate to online form in the short-term future.[5]

This article first appeared in *Library Resources & Technical Services* 44, no. 2 (2000): 59–69. Earlier versions of parts of this article were presented at several public meetings, including the ALCTS Business of Acquisitions preconference on June 25, 1999, and the Library Research Committee Forum at the University of Virginia on October 28, 1999.

Whether or not the academic library community is prepared to play a truly formative role in the reenvisioning and redesign of scholarly information exchange depends not only upon whether academic librarians have the will to take concerted action, but also upon their having a clear and unified position as to what is ultimately in the best interest of scholarship and higher education. It will be my purpose in this essay to consider, in mainly abstract terms, why the academy must move to reappropriate (i.e., take back from external publishers) at least some responsibility for specialized scholarly publishing, why the academy has been so slow to accept this responsibility, how an academy-controlled system for specialized scholarly publishing might be designed, and what function the academic library should be prepared to assume in that process.

THE FUTURE OF INTERMEDIATION

The transfer of information across space and time entails intermediation. Someone, some agency, some mechanism must conduct the information from sender to receiver, from writer to reader. For scholarly information exchange, the two principal intermediaries are publishers (mainly working with writers) and libraries (mainly assisting readers). There are obviously many other intermediaries—editors, printers, programmers, vendors—who are indispensable for the formal transfer of scholarly information in the traditional environment. As we move increasingly online, however, the need for such traditional intermediation will surely diminish—if for no other reason than that some of the work traditionally performed by intermediaries can be automated and managed by writers and readers for themselves. Our sense is that the metaphorical space between the writer and the reader will contract, and that there will be less room online for the range of intermediaries now needed in the traditional environment. The realization that some disintermediation is inevitable in the new environment is already engendering considerable competition for Lebensraum in the intermediary space. Intermediaries are eyeing each other suspiciously, recognizing that opportunities for traditional intermediation will decline and that survival may depend upon the ability of one intermediary to assume responsibilities that have traditionally belonged to others.

The unavoidable and inexorable decline in the need for traditional intermediation does not mean, however, that intermediation *per se* will be generally less important for information exchange in the new environment. Quite the contrary. While it is true, as already noted, that information technology will empower writers and readers to do some things for themselves that intermediaries did for them in the traditional environment, it is also equally likely that intermediaries will provide some services for writers and readers in online circumstances that writers and readers now provide for themselves in the traditional environment. The more we move online, in fact, the *more* intermediation (admittedly of a very different kind than in the traditional environment) will likely be needed to transfer information from writers to readers.[6] We might label this syndrome *hyperintermediation*. Much of this new service will admittedly be transparent to the user and will take the form of technology and network maintenance, but some of the new intermediation will be highly visible and will derive from the special quality of digital information, which consists of both a content—the database—and a highly flexible modality, let us call it the software, which provides access to and manipulation of the content.

That flexible modality is one of the key differences between traditional and online information exchange: it enhances but also necessarily complicates the exchange process. One obviously does not open an electronic publication as simply as one opens a book. The whole concept of "opening" changes—different databases necessarily "open" differently—and there may be several ways to access or apply a single database, depending upon what one wants to do with it. While more can be done therefore with information in digital form, more intermediary assistance will likely be needed to do it. All intermediaries in the new environment, including libraries, will compete with each other to provide that new assistance.

The distinction between the content and the modality, the database and the software, is one that demands much more consideration. All information services can in a way be reduced to those two elements: (1) building and maintaining the database, and (2) providing the ability to find and manipulate what has been built and maintained. Libraries supply the same or similar services in the traditional environment—collection development and preservation on the one hand, organization (cataloging) and access assistance on the other—and to some extent, society no doubt expects libraries to continue to provide those same services, after much currently needed information shifts online. But will librarians—or, more to the point, *should* librarians—take up that responsibility in support of scholarly information exchange?

Disintermediation is not merely an inevitability of the new environment and a challenge to traditional intermediaries, it is also an unprecedented opportunity to reconfigure information services. From the standpoint of academic libraries, such disintermediation can be used as a tool to improve information exchange by promoting the redesign and streamlining of the process by which scholarly information moves from writer to reader. This effort will entail in part working to reduce or eliminate those aspects of the traditional process that have severely hampered such exchange. Because one of the most significant impediments to scholarly information exchange in the traditional environment has been the outsourcing of some major segments of scholarly publishing to for-profit publishers, the academy needs to use disintermediation as a tool to reappropriate responsibility for formal scholarly communication that in the past has been the exclusive domain of scholarly publishers.[7] Such reappropriation is in effect a form of vertical integration—the assumption of responsibility by one producer for multiple stages of the production process—that displaces other producers previously responsible for those other stages. In this case, it will be a matter of one intermediary exploiting the process of disintermediation to displace and assume the function of other intermediaries.

But which intermediaries will (and should) do the displacing, and which will be displaced? We must not be so naive as to expect that librarians will naturally or automatically prevail in this inevitable contest. Publishers—or at least those wise enough to realize that no intermediary is likely to survive the transition to the new environment intact—are doubtless also examining the same process from their own perspective. At the moment, publishers depend upon libraries for the effective dissemination of their products. Such dependence need not last much longer, however, and as soon as publishers see opportunities to maintain or increase revenue by selling directly to users rather than through libraries (or as soon as libraries become more trouble than they are worth to publishers for whatever reason), publishers will initiate such direct services. This direct selling would work particularly well in the academic community. The chances that publishers would be willing, as Gherman has recently advocated, to relinquish their ownership of scholarship and serve as editorial bureaus are therefore very remote.[8] Publishers will necessarily and understandably work to increase their role in scholarly information exchange.

Odlyzko has argued skillfully that, in the competition for survival between publishers and librarians, it will be the publishers who prevail. They will do this by convincing the academy that the unnecessary costs of moving information from writer to reader are not those of publishing but rather those of libraries:

> What keeps the publishers' situation from being hopeless is the tremendous inertia
> of the scholarly community, which impedes the transition to free or inexpensive

electronic journals. Another factor in the publishers' favor is that there are other unnecessary costs that can be squeezed, namely those of the libraries. Moreover, the unnecessary library costs are far greater than those of publishers, which creates an opportunity for the latter to exploit and thereby to retain their positions.[9]

Odlyzko, like many scholars and academic administrators, apparently sees the library mainly as a big box of books, and the library's budget as being devoted primarily to tending them. If publication moves entirely online, the cost of maintaining a paper collection, which is to say (from this perspective) the cost of running the library, can be eliminated, or at least substantially reduced, and the savings can go to the publishers—or can be divided between the publishers and the institutional administration.

Many research librarians may well naively assume that this will never happen—that as long as they continue to provide (*mutatis mutandis* in the new environment) the same excellent services they always have, their presence on campus will be needed and sustained. This is, of course, absurd. If the academic institutional administration could be convinced that it would be economically advantageous to outsource library services to publishers or other information entrepreneurs, then institutions would likely move—with some justification—to eliminate libraries altogether (beyond presumably a vestigial warehousing function). Institutions might take such action, not realizing the implications of outsourcing many library services, because librarians have never succeeded in explaining those implications effectively. Or, more problematically, institutions could conceivably take such a step, if the academic community were to conclude that the economic advantages of substantially disintermediating academic libraries outweigh the pedagogical and research liabilities. Librarians must move now therefore to understand and confront both of these prospects.

THE RATIONALE FOR LIBRARIES IN THE NEW ENVIRONMENT

Technology and Ideology

We have noted that, in the traditional environment, intermediaries are distinguished from each other for the most part by their place in the production process, i.e., their role in the transfer of information from the writer to the reader. Publishers work with writers, editors, printers, and distributors, in order to bring the work of the writer to market. Librarians work with readers and vendors, in order to ensure that needed information is rapidly available to local users. While we can perhaps anticipate that some aspects of this division of labor will continue as we move increasingly online, it is nevertheless the case that the new technology and the resulting hyperintermediation afford a single intermediary or intermediary group the ability to assume responsibility for ever broader ranges of the transfer process.

As efforts at such vertical integration increase, and all intermediaries—librarians, publishers, booksellers, and others—scramble to assume an ever more comprehensive role in moving information from writers to readers, they will all likely begin to adopt similar processes and to make use of the same basic technology. This means that many, if not most, intermediaries may ultimately become for a time in the course of the transition technologically similar—perhaps even indistinguishable: they may well all be competing, including librarians, to offer the same general set of services. What will then, under such circumstances, distinguish one intermediary from another? It will be not merely the services provided and their costs, for these may all be very similar, but rather the values that drive and inform that provision of those services—in short, the service ideology. Librarians have a very special service ideology, and as librarians now begin their journey into the new online environment with all of its complexities and uncertainties, they must take care to bring with them above all else that defining ideological perspective.

It is for this reason that we are now entering such a critically significant juncture in the history of scholarship. While publishers and librarians may in the new environment compete and end up offering similar or identical services, the long term evolution and nature of information services will depend finally upon the intermediary ideology that ultimately prevails. In the case of academic information services, the fundamental ideological question is quite simply whether specialized academic information should be understood as a commodity, intended primarily for (and judged in each case by the extent to which it succeeds in generating) revenue—or whether access to scholarly information is a social good that must be freely available. The defining quality of modern academic (and public) libraries is not that they provide access to certain types of information using particular service methods, but rather that such access, facilitated by such methods, is available to the individual without significant financial charge and is supported for the most part by public or collective funding. What characterizes the modern library is above all else its assumption that access to information, like access to other key social goods and services, is a right of all citizens and not a privilege of the few. It is that cardinal assumption, that ideological position, rather than any technical or bibliographical skills or facilities, that separates librarians from most other information service providers, including especially many publishers of specialized scholarly information. If there were no ideological differences between publishers and librarians, then there would be in fact very little sense in trying to continue to distinguish them in the new environment.

In many respects, therefore, the ideology of the library is the service. The only problem, of course, is that we live in an age in which choices are seldom viewed in primarily ideological terms. Even academic institutions, which should and do serve as a key source of ideological definition and debate, are obliged to base many of their essential decisions on a range of considerations beyond the purely ideological. It is unlikely at the present time, therefore, that either society at large or the academy in particular will be persuaded to take a course of action on the basis of ideology alone. Is there then a more functional argument that could be used effectively to support the position that librarians should continue to operate and prevail in the new information environment?

Agency

All information service providers are agents of some kind. Ross states: "We will say that an agency relationship has arisen between two (or more) parties when one, designated as the agent, acts for, on behalf of, or as representative for the other, designated the principal, in a particular domain of decision problems."[10] In order to define or understand agency better, let us posit a universe of resource—the set of all extant resources at any point in time. See figure 1. Let us say that a resource is anything that will facilitate action. It is stored labor, raw material, power, potential, energy—the capacity to do work. It takes a great many forms. It can have exchange value, or it can have use value. It can be money. It can be information. It can be some kind of formative or base material. It can even be some person's, or some group's, attention. But what all resources have in common is their scarcity—for to be scarce (let us stipulate) is a quality of a resource.

Because resources are scarce, individuals or groups needing resources often contract with specialists for assistance in obtaining access to such resources. Those specialists then become the agents of those principals or clients for whom the resources are being obtained. Such agents are hired by clients, therefore, to compete with other agents representing other clients. Agents are expected to act always in the best interest of their clients, and their success is measured by the extent to which they succeed in supplying their clients with the resources that have been targeted. The only complication is the classic and natural tendency for agencies to prefer themselves to their clients: if it occasionally comes to a decision between doing something of value for the client and doing something of value for themselves, agents tend sometimes understandably and predictably to select the latter. One manifestation of this problem—let us call it the agency delusion—is the false assumption on the part of the agent that whatever is beneficial to the agent is necessarily beneficial to the client. No agent is immune to this delusion, no matter how pure its goals—and this includes librarians. The best we can do is to be aware of it and try to circumvent it in our decision making whenever possible.

Let us further posit a distinction between *primary* and *ancillary* resources, clientele and competitors. The primary resource is the one the client has contracted with the agent to obtain. An ancillary resource is one that is used (e.g., for purposes of exchange) as part of the process in obtaining the primary resource. Money is therefore a frequent ancillary resource—although money can certainly also be, and often is, a primary resource. For librarians, information is the primary resource, while money is the ancillary resource; in the case of for-profit publishers, the opposite is true.

We should also distinguish between primary and ancillary clientele. Ancillary clientele often evolve as a result of agents contracting with each other. If, in figure 1, Agent 2 believes Agent 3 can provide access to some resources more effectively, then Agent 2 can contract with Agent 3 to provide access—through Agent 2—to Client 2. In that case, Client 3 remains Agent 3's primary client, while Client 2 becomes Agent 3's ancillary client. The danger for Agent 2 in such a process is, of course, disintermediation: Agent 3 might at some point move to provide resources directly to Client 2, without any longer involving Agent 2. In many respects, librarians are in the situation of Agent 2, contracting with Agent 3, the publisher, to provide users (Client 2) with access to needed scholarly resources.

Finally, there can also be primary and ancillary competitors. Primary competitors are those agents that are competing for essentially identical resources, in order to pass those resources to different (or in some cases conceivably even the same) clientele. Ancillary competitors are those agents that are competing only for similar resources. Ancillary competitors can therefore occasionally join forces temporarily, if such partnerships will enhance the capacity of each to compete with its primary competitor.

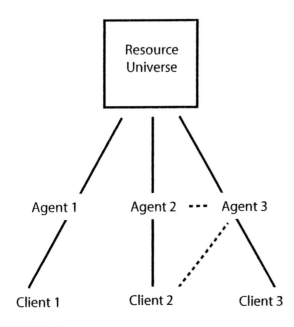

FIGURE 1. Agency

With this very simple model in mind, we can return to our original question: why should (academic) librarians, aside from ideological reasons, not simply step aside, as information moves increasingly online, and urge academic institutions to outsource their information services? Are not businesses often more efficient than public institutions and their supporting information services? Are not academic librarians falling victim to the agent's delusion by insisting that their continued existence is in the best interest of scholarship and higher education? Would librarians serve students and scholars best by simply getting out of the way and turning over all information services to publisher-aggregators or other commercial information entrepreneurs?

No, of course not. To outsource most information resources to commercial agents would be a substantial, strategic error for the academy—mainly because of the distinction between primary and ancillary clientele. The primary clientele of academic libraries are local scholars and students. The primary clientele of publishers are their owners—often their shareholders. When it comes to making decisions between the two, publishers will inevitably, understandably, and justifiably make those decisions that are in the best interest of their primary clientele. We are used to this, of course, in the traditional environment—its chief manifestation being the so-called serials crisis; but the difficulty caused by this syndrome in the traditional environment, the extent to which it impedes scholars and students from being able to access the information they need for their work, is surely minor when compared to what we must expect to happen in an online environment. Those who own information control access to it. Information technology greatly enhances that control. If it is in the primary client's best interest for the publisher to use that control to restrict access to needed information as much as possible, in order to make such information scarce and to drive up its price, then that is exactly what will happen—and there is certainly no evidence in the behavior of specialized scholarly publishers in the traditional environment to lead us to believe that anything other than this will occur, when the majority of scholarly communication shifts online.

There is only one solution therefore to this problem, which we must keep repeating: it is the reappropriation of (at least a substantial portion of) specialized scholarly publishing by the academy. That there is really no other answer has been clear for many years. Despite a few notable but still limited attempts, however, success in achieving such reappropriation continues to elude us. Why is it that academic librarians are having such difficulty promoting this crucial decision in the academy?

One reason for the delay is certainly the difficulty librarians have experienced in explaining the issues to working scholars, and it is those scholars who must ultimately endorse and effect such changes. Reappropriation will require, to be sure, deep-seated cultural adjustments within the academy—redefinitions, in effect, of what scholarship is, how it is done, how it is evaluated, and even what it means to be a scholar. The heavy dependence of the academy upon convention makes any such broad, cultural, or behavioral adjustment controversial and problematic.

Another reason for the academic library community's difficulty in leading the way toward reappropriation may be the naiveté that librarians occasionally exhibit with respect to publishing. Some librarians may tend to assume that the primary, if not only, purpose of publishing is information transfer—but there are in fact many reasons academic information is written and read, not all of which have directly to do with the topical information conveyed.[11]

Librarians may also overlook or underestimate the real role played by publishers. Contrary to what we may sometimes be inclined to think, the primary function of the scholarly publisher is not to provide access to content—that is not the value that publishers add and sell. We do not really pay for *what* is in their publications; what we pay for is rather *that* what is in their publications acquires a certain status and attracts a certain attention by virtue of its location in those publications. Attention, as noted above, is an important resource—and that capacity to draw attention is what is being sold and what we are buying. Drawing attention to a writing by virtue of its location in a particular journal or in a book published by a particular publisher is of enormous value both to the writer, because it brings prestige and notoriety, and to the reader, because it answers the reader's most important question: what to read, in what order. If therefore the academy in general and academic librarians in particular are truly interested in reappropriating some significant responsibility for specialized scholarly publishing, then the system created to replace the current publisher-based method must add the same or similar values for both writers and readers that publishers add now. Until methods are devised for adding such values, the goal of reappropriation will remain unfulfilled.

These then are a few reasons why librarians have not yet succeeded in bringing about the changes in the ownership of scholarly information that must take place if scholarship and higher education are to continue to flourish in an online environment. But even if such impediments were to be overcome—even if we could create an academy-based process of scholarly information exchange that provided similar compensations to writers and similar services to readers as those offered by the current publisher-based process—is reappropriation of scholarly publishing by the academy a realistic and practical objective from the institutional perspective?

THE ACADEMY AND THE POLITICS OF IMPLEMENTATION

The modern academy is, of course, many things—but certainly one of its key, defining dynamics is the tension or dichotomy between the institution and the scholarly disciplines. This dichotomy is most clearly manifested in the dual role of faculty as teachers, an institutional responsibility, and scholars, an activity undertaken normally within a discipline. While most scholars are certainly loyal to their institutions, it is probably the disciplines that generally have the higher status and attention. The discipline determines what the scholar does—and what he or she is: one is first and foremost a mathematician, an historian, a sociologist. The institution determines mainly *where* such scholarship is practiced.

On the other hand, there can be no question that the institution serves as the primary economic base for the whole academic enterprise. The individual institution markets a service: higher education. The compensation the institution receives, often from multiple sources, for that service normally exceeds the cost of providing it—and it is that surplus that forms a major part of the support for disciplinary research. From this purely economic perspective, therefore, the institution is always the base, and the disciplines are the superstructure. See figure 2.

	place	interaction	transfer	medium	focus
institution	local	subjective	instruction	oral	external
discipline	topical	objective	publication	graphic	object

FIGURE 2. Attributes of Institutions and Disciplines

What distinguishes institutions from disciplines? One of the basic qualities of the institution is its locale. It is situated in one or more physical, i.e., geographical, spaces where people come together. The discipline, on the other hand, is not local, but is rather topical—which is to say that it also resides in places, but those places are bibliographical rather than geographical. They are places in the literature—in bibliographical resources. To be a scholar in the discipline is to be recognized as one who knows such places, who defers to them as authorities, and who participates in their continued evolution. The institution, therefore, with its emphasis on instruction as primary service and its nature as a geographical location where people gather, can be viewed as a more subjective entity with a strong emphasis (even despite the advent of e-mail) on oral communication.

Orality provides a much more intense and active form of expression than graphic communication. It is far preferable for many forms of information exchange, especially instruction. The discipline, on the other hand, is primarily objective, in the sense that it is focused primarily upon the topic that resides in a bibliographic place; and while disciplines certainly engage in some oral exchange, their primary means of formal communication is graphic, because graphic communication is most conducive to study, archiving, and "objective" analysis. Ong writes: "Writing separates the knower from the known and thus sets up conditions for 'objectivity,' in the sense of personal disengagement or distancing."[12]

One further distinction that might be drawn between the institution and the discipline is what could be called focus. Because the institution is essentially a nonprofit business with a primary service (higher education) to market, its success depends upon its ability to focus a great deal of its attention outside of itself. This is not to deny that there is much internal action in the institution (the political competition for scarce resources inside any institution can certainly be consuming and contentious), but the successful institution must and does make many of its key decisions based upon an assessment of things outside of itself: its potential clientele, its funding sources and prospects, and especially its competitors. By contrast, the discipline is for better or worse much more internally focused. It looks mainly at itself. There is, to be sure, always a certain evolving interdisciplinarity, but the view of the topical place as authority, as starting point for all discussion and research, means that the discipline, unlike the institution, is concerned mainly with its own values and objectives.

Having noted some of the characteristics of this dichotomy between institution and disciplines, we must also concede that the inexorable transition from the traditional to the online environment is markedly changing at least some aspects of this defining distinction. Geographical location as a fundamental feature of the institution is certainly challenged by the increasing shift toward distance education—for this is a form of education bounded less by geographical location than by something more closely resembling topical or bibliographical space. The atmosphere or tone of distance education may therefore be rather more objective than subjective.

Another change, as formal disciplinary communication moves increasingly online, may well be a substantial decline in the disciplinary preference for graphic communication. If it is indeed true that oral, or audio-visual, communication is a richer and more potent method of conveying information, then we should expect more use of audio-visual communication for serious scholarly publication. Graphic language, writing, evolved almost certainly because oral language could not be transferred across space and time. Information technology has now to a great extent solved that problem, so that we can transfer audio-visual or multimedia communication across space and time as easily as graphic language—providing it with equal potential for storing and analysis. This does not mean that graphic language will have no place in formal, scholarly communication, of course—only that its dominance will likely subside. This trend will certainly be hastened by advances in information technology, because we must assume that voice activated computers—that both hear and speak to the user—will soon become common. Typing is very likely a twentieth-century skill.[13] Information services, moreover, will also need to respond to this new multimedia communication with appropriate metadata—and this means not only better metadata to describe multimedia objects, but also probably the creation of multimedia metadata.

Despite all of these probable changes, however, it is highly unlikely that the educational institution as geographical entity is in any real jeopardy, despite the increasing significance of distance learning. Education requires a geographical location for people to gather—not only for students to interact with scholars but also for students to interact with each other. Effective education is always in part a peer social experience—and the support of that experience is likely a primary future purpose of libraries as well. The future function of libraries as geographical places, in other words, will presumably not be so much to connect people with resources—subjects with objects—as is the case in the traditional environment, for that can be done virtually anywhere in a networked society. The main purpose of the library as geographical place may rather be to serve as a location for students to gather and to interact as groups with information objects.

The concept of "simultaneous users" will change, therefore, from individuals using the same database in separate places to individuals using the same database together in the same place and learning from each other. Perhaps the most important implication of such a scenario is that if this does indeed happen, the distinction between the library and the classroom must necessarily begin to blur. In some distance- learning situations, students will come together in a place—the library/classroom—to work with distant scholars and with interactive information objects, and we must expect that their ability to shift back and forth between these will be enhanced by the continued evolution of information technology.

Will the outward focus of institutions (and the inward focus of disciplines) be altered by the electronic revolution? Probably not. Institutions remain fundamentally economic entities, so that their continued success requires an external focus. It is precisely this unavoidably outward perspective, however, which has perhaps the most serious implications for the long-term future of scholarship and higher education and their supporting information services. Institutions are externally focused in part because they recognize correctly that they are in competition with each other—for students, faculty, funding, prestige. Institutions use many of their available resources to engage in such competition and their libraries are certainly one of their most visible and comparable resources. It is essential that we recognize, however, that some actions or positions taken by the institution—which make complete sense for purposes of interinstitutional competition—can be antithetical and even detrimental to the broader mission of the academy, scholarship, and higher education. This problem is in fact one institutional manifestation of the agency delusion: it is the occasional assumption by the institution that anything that benefits the institution also benefits its scholars and students and even the academy as a whole. But that is not always the case.

One of the most striking, recent examples of this contradiction from the library perspective can be found in the adoption of new integrated library management systems by academic libraries around the country. There are a number of such systems commercially available—and there are at least six different commercial systems at this particular time that two or more prominent ARL libraries have purchased and installed.

The problem, of course, is that the market for such large library management systems is relatively small, even if expanded internationally—probably too small, in fact, to support so many different commercial systems. If that is indeed the case, then there can be no doubt that some of these systems may well soon go out of business, and the institutions that have invested in them may well lose millions of dollars. Librarians at each research library know, therefore, that the survival of the system that has been chosen depends in effect on the demise of other systems selected elsewhere. But why is this happening? To use large research libraries as an example, let us suppose that each ARL library ends up spending on average $2 million to implement its new system fully.

If that assumption is correct, it means that all ARL libraries together may well end up spending nearly a quarter of a billion dollars. One cannot help thinking what a fine library management system ARL libraries, working together, could have built for that amount. Such a system, designed jointly by all of the ARL libraries, would not be subject to the extreme vicissitudes of the marketplace, as all commercial systems are now and will continue to be in future. And for that kind of money, the system could have been designed with sufficient flexibility that each institution could have undertaken the substantial customization needed to fit its particular local requirements. There are no doubt many reasons why research libraries have not pooled their resources to design a single, optimal system, but surely the most fundamental reason is that research libraries cannot in fact cooperate to any meaningful extent, because the institutions those libraries represent are engaged in a profound competition with one another, and libraries are key components of that competitive process.

Returning to figure 1, we must now acknowledge that, from an institutional standpoint, it is academic institutions that are the primary competitors. The primary competition is not between the academic institution and the commercial service provider, but rather, between one academic institution and another. Commercial information service providers function at most as ancillary competitors. What this means is that institutions, rather than partnering with each other in order to counter the detrimental practices of some external service providers such as specialized commercial scholarly publishers, are instead choosing in effect to partner with such external providers, in order to compete more effectively with each other. It is this institutional competition, therefore, that likely forms the single most significant impediment to the reappropriation of scholarly publishing by the academy.

One of the most pressing questions facing academic librarians at this time is how to relate to such a situation ideologically. If it is indeed ideology that will in future distinguish libraries from other services, such as commercial publishing, and if one of the library's most basic ideological tenets is the position that access to information should be a right and not a privilege, and if academic institutions use such access as a tool for competition with each other, then how should academic librarians respond?

Certainly librarians should not be opposed generally to interinstitutional competition—for to try to eliminate such competition would surely tear the very fabric of the academy and would ultimately result in a severe decline in the potential for disciplinary research. But we must at the same time somehow urge that the damage deriving from such a culture be acknowledged and that some restrictions be placed on the objects of interinstitutional competition.

If some forms of competition are ultimately injurious to scholarship and higher education, as is the case in the competition for access to scholarly information, then librarians must be prepared (if they are ideologically committed) to do whatever is necessary to create a structure in which information access is not counted as a tool in the competitive struggle among institutions. We must aim to create an academic culture in which the availability of needed information is guaranteed—so that interinstitutional competition centers not, as it does now, on access to information, but rather exclusively upon the use to which such equitably accessible information is put. In order to promote action that will achieve this objective, the academy must move to redesign the process by which scholarly information is exchanged.

AN EXAMPLE OF ONE RATIONAL PROCESS: THE DESIGNATED CHANNEL

Suppose we had the opportunity to design from scratch the primary means of scholarly communication in an online environment: what would it look like? Because of the disciplinary culture that dominates the academy, and because of the essentially inward focus of the disciplines, the most effective approach would be to create a designated channel or domain for each discipline. One large channel encompassing all disciplines, such as a National Electronic Article Repository as advocated by Schulenberg might serve as a place to start, but such a megachannel would still need to be organized into disciplinary subdivisions.[14] Such channels would have both a political and a bibliographical value.

Politically the channels would serve to separate information access from the institution—although it would clearly be essential for institutions, as the economic base for scholarship, to provide financial support in some kind of membership capacity. To be a member—and all academic institutions would need to be members—would be to support full public access to all contents of the channels. Institutions would be able to provide the financial support necessary for such a network of channels, because institutions would no longer be compelled to purchase publications written by academic scholars.

A primary bibliographic value of the channel would be to provide the long sought one-stop shopping. Any reader wanting to understand what is known (in the sense of what is being published, what is being said publicly) in a discipline would consult the content of that channel. And if a scholar has a formal contribution to make about some aspect of the discipline, that is where he or she would place it. Far from impeding interdisciplinarity, such a system could promote borrowing from one discipline by another—especially if the kind of interoperability now being proposed by the Open Archives Initiative is achieved (www.openarchives.org).

The key requirement for publication in any such channel would remain, as in the traditional environment, quality control. That is presently provided through peer review—a practice that works well for scholarly communication and which should be maintained and protected in the online environment. A trusted group of scholars in the discipline should take responsibility, probably on a rotating basis, for deciding which materials inserted into the designated channel should be certified. Certification should have two implications. First, it should mean that reputed scholars have decided that the item does indeed add substantial knowledge to the discipline. Second, certification should mean that academic information services, the library community, will take responsibility for the item, and will guarantee its access over time.

The organization, software, metadata, and archiving of such a designated channel should be the responsibility of academic information services. If an item submitted is not certified, that does not mean it would not be accessible through the channel, but only that it is not viewed as significant by the current peer reviewers, and that means it would not become the responsibility of information services.

If a writing is not certified, therefore, its maintenance remains the responsibility of the author. Certification of a publication should define it as a "core" item, in the sense that users should normally be encouraged to read it before uncertified materials. Normative metadata, informing the reader that certain items are currently viewed as being more important than others, should lead the reader to certified materials. While the uncertified publication might be found through keyword searching, the certified publication should be subject to indexing based upon a carefully controlled vocabulary, preferably arrived at in consultation with the author.

In all likelihood, most scholars today would admittedly object to such a process of publication, because it purposefully eliminates individual journals and publishers. The objection would derive from the fact that every discipline, as noted above, has a hierarchy of journals and publishers well known to all members of the discipline—and that hierarchy is presently used by writers to gain prestige and by readers to decide what to read in what order. How, then, could the designated channel replace (from the standpoint of both writers and readers) that service now provided by the separation and hierarchy of journals and publishers? The answer must be use-tracking.

We need to convince scholars that the quality of their work should be judged not by whether a few editors decide it is worth publishing in a particular journal—but rather by the extent and quality of its use by the scholarly community once it is published. To provide this level of use-tracking, the channel manager—academic information services—will need to create a method of tracking and computing the degree to which different publications are used in different ways. While privacy would obviously need to be protected, a use-tracking system should be designed to allow an author and all members of the discipline to know the extent to which other scholars in the discipline (or scholars in other disciplines, students, and members of the general public) access the publication. Metadata describing various aspects of the use of a particular certified publication should probably include citation data, so that together such information can be used to estimate (or define) the publication's current and continued utility—although there is admittedly still much work to be done on how such user information is to be evaluated, for mere quantity of use does not necessarily indicate value.[15]

While the author may provide an abstract of the uncertified publication, the library, in assuming responsibility for making the publication accessible, should perform what may possibly be its most important bibliographical function, the creation of a *synopsis*—although we must supply this term with a special meaning. By synopsis I mean a description of how the certified publication fits into or relates to all of the other publications that have been certified in the channel, i.e., the certified whole. See figure 3. The purpose of the synopsis should be in effect to stipulate what is new or unique in the publication.

As the designated channel grows in size, its use will become more complicated and congested. Information services will inevitably need to produce a new form of cumulative metadata, which we can call the surrogate whole. This surrogate whole provides a summary of the discipline, in effect presenting the user with an overview of all aspects of the discipline and permitting the user to move selectively from the surrogate whole into the certified whole to read particular publications. One primary function of synopses should be, therefore, to merge together in such a way as to form in their aggregate the surrogate whole. The base or model bibliographical format must shift under such circumstances from the catalog or bibliography, which dominates in the traditional environment, to the encyclopedia. The primary purpose of information services must be not to list publications by name, but rather to provide a narrative context for their content, while at the same time ensuring direct access to those publications at the user's discretion.

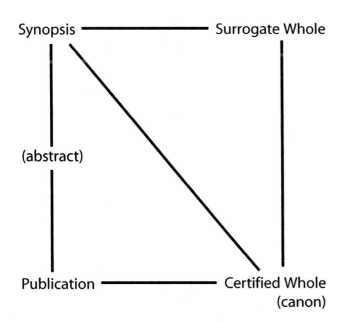

FIGURE 3. Designated Channel Model

In the same way that we must expect the library and the classroom to merge in an increasingly online, distance education environment, we must also work to link more effectively the work of the scholar and information services. While it should be the work of information services in the future to define the discipline and its parameters (including the creation of such synoptic resources as textbooks), the work of the scholar should focus on extending such disciplinary parameters through the certification and creation of new publications.

Were the academy to decide to create such a network of designated channels, librarians would need to take the lead in partnering above all with university presses and probably unavoidably with scholarly societies. While some scholarly societies at the present time may not be interested in such partnerships, we should bear in mind that the "shareholders" of such societies are often mainly scholars in academic institutions. Here, as elsewhere, success will depend directly upon the academic library community's ability to explain the options and the vision to individual working scholars.

This concept of the designated channel is, needless to say, only one simple model of an academy-based process for scholarly information exchange in a primarily online environment. Which model is ultimately selected is of less importance. What matters, regardless of the method eventually chosen, is that scholarly information in the future be freely and openly accessible to all who need and want it, and that the natural competition among institutions be based upon the application of that information rather than access to it. It is only by such a refocusing of the processes and priorities of scholarly information exchange that the academy will be able to ensure that its primary clientele will continue to have in future the specialized information that it needs and deserves.

REFERENCE NOTES

1. James C. Thompson, "Journal Costs: Perception and Reality in the Dialogue," *College & Research Libraries* 49 (1988): 481–82; Sharon J. Rogers and Charlene S. Hurt, "How Scholarly Communication Should Work in the 21st Century," *Chronicle of Higher Education* (Oct. 18, 1989): A56; reprinted in *College & Research Libraries* 51 (1990): 5–8.

2. Association of Research Libraries et al., "To Publish and Perish," *Policy Perspectives* 7 (Mar. 1998), 1–12. Also at www.arl.org/scomm/pew/pewrept.html; Kenneth Frazier, "Liberating Scholarship," *Library Journal* 123 (Oct. 15, 1998): 40–41.

3. Paul Ginsparg, "Electronic Research Archives for Physics," in *The Impact of Electronic Publishing on the Academic Community*, I. Butterworth, ed. (London: Portland Pr., 1998), 32–43. Also at http://tiepac.portlandpress.co.uk/books/online/tiepac/sessionl/ch7.htm.

4. Ann Shumelda Okerson and James J. O'Donnell, eds. *Scholarly Journals at the Crossroads: A Subversive Proposal for Electronic Publishing* (Washington, D.C.: Association of Research Libraries, 1995). Also at www.arl.org/scomm/subversive/sub0l.html.

5. Chad Buckley et al., "Electronic Publishing of Scholarly Journals: A Bibliographic Essay of Current Issues," *Issues in Science and Technology Librarianship* (spring 1999). Accessed Dec. 15, 1999, www.library.ucsb.edu/istl/99-spring/article4.html.

6. Franklin Allen and Anthony M. Santomero, "The Theory of Financial Intermediation," *Journal of Banking and Finance* 21 (1997): 1461–85.

7. ARL, "To Publish and Perish."

8. Paul M. Gherman, "Electronic Publishing: A New Financial Model," *SPARC E-News* (Sept. 1999). Accessed Dec. 15, 1999, www.arl.org/sparc/enews/0999.html.

9. Andrew Odlyzko, "Competition and Cooperation: Libraries and Publishers in the Transition to Electronic Scholarly Journals," *The Journal of Electronic Publishing* 4 (June 1999). Accessed Dec. 15, 1999, www.press.umich.edu/jep/04-04/odlyzko0404.html

10. Stephen A. Ross, "The Economic Theory of Agency: The Principal's Problem," *The American Economic Review* 63, no. 2 (1973): 134–39.

11. Faytton Rowland, "Print Journals: Fit for the Future?" *Ariadne* 7 (Jan. 1997). Accessed Dec. 15, 1999, www.ariaedne.ac.uk/issue7/fytton.

12. Walter J. Ong, *Orality and Literacy: The Technologizing of the Word* (London: Methuen, 1982).

13. Daniel Akst, "The Sound of No Hands Tapping," *Technology Review* 101, no. 6 (1998): 88–90.

14. David Schulenberg, "Moving with Dispatch to Resolve the Scholarly Communication Crisis: From Here to Near," in *Confronting the Challenges of the Digital Era*: Association of Research Libraries proceedings of the 133d annual meeting, 1998. Accessed Dec. 15, 1999, www.arl.org/arl/proceedings/133/shulenburger.html.

15. Blaise Cronin, "The Warholian Moment and Other Protoindicators of Scholarly Salience," *Journal of the American Society for Information Science* 50 (1999): 953–55.

5 TOWARD A REDEFINITION OF LIBRARY SERVICES

Building two libraries simultaneously, a digital one and a traditional one, is highly problematic, especially in the absence of a major funding increase—but most libraries today have decided quite rightly to try to accept that challenge. Most libraries have made the commitment to bring about the transition from traditional to digital services. We who manage libraries are not therefore merely reacting to changes in the environment, but are rather acknowledging potential opportunities for change, which will greatly enhance access. It is important always to bear in mind, therefore, that this transition is not something being done to us, but is rather something we have chosen to do in fulfillment of our most basic service mission. Such a transformation will necessarily entail an enhancement and redefinition of library services. My purpose in this chapter is to provide some suggestions or discussion points for that redefinition. As an academic librarian, I approach these issues primarily from the standpoint of library support to higher education and research, but I am hopeful that most of the points I make will be applicable to all types of libraries.

PARAMETERS

We must consider at the outset the parameters of any such reassessment of library services. How far should we be prepared to go in re-visioning our purpose and operation? Should we set parameters at all? I think we must—but we should also be willing to extend such boundaries as widely as possible. I would draw the line—seriously—at the mystical-religious. On the mystical plane, the practitioner encounters the ultimate knowledge-experience: the unio-mystica, the intimate blending of the individual with the cosmos. It is the *kensho* of Zen Buddhism: the direct and unalloyed apprehension of reality. We can begin by acknowledging, therefore, that access to such a level of knowledge is obviously out of scope for information services.

At the same time, however, we must also assert that every form of knowledge up to that level of the mystical-religious does fall within the bounds of information services. This is a worthwhile distinction, because what apparently separates mystical from nonmystical knowledge is that the experience of knowledge on the nonmystical plane entails some form of mediation: there must always be something between the perceiver and the perceived. The individual never knows reality directly, but rather unavoidably perceives it always through some intermediary faculty or agent.

DISINTERMEDIATION

Such dependence upon mediation nevertheless generally is distrusted and even disliked. One hankers always for direct knowledge of reality—hence the temptation and ubiquity

---

This article first appeared in *Virtually Yours: Models for Managing Electronic Resources and Services,* eds. Peggy Johnson and Bonnie MacEwan (Chicago: ALA, 1999) 3–21.

of mysticism. One may hanker for *disintermediation*, which is the removal or reduction of the role of librarians in linking the user and information. Disintermediation did not originate in information services with the advent of computer technology—and it is precisely because of this general preference to avoid or reduce reliance upon mediation whenever possible that it is only natural for users to be interested in circumventing the library, for example, to connect more directly to information whenever practicable. At the same time, we (and certainly our users) recognize that mediation takes many forms. Some of those forms are, to be sure, positive or even essential, providing enhancement, amplification, clarification—while other forms can be intrusive. We must continuously review library services, therefore, to identify and mitigate instances of intrusive mediation.

It would be a serious error for libraries to dismiss or denigrate the trend toward disintermediation. It should not be viewed as some kind of threat or hobgoblin pursuing the library profession. We must rather understand and accept it as part of that very transition we are trying to bring about. Disintermediation is, after all, one of the primary goals of education in general. The teacher does not intend to interpose herself or himself indefinitely between the student and the subject. The aim always is to bring the student to a level at which he or she can be delivered over to the subject, in order to know and interact with it more directly. The library, as a primary vehicle of education, must come to hold similar views of disintermediation. The danger for libraries, therefore, is not that, if we do things wrong, a certain amount of disintermediation will result—but rather that a certain amount of disintermediation will not evolve, for that absence of disintermediation would ultimately prove detrimental to our users' interests. In short, we must be prepared to make disintermediation a goal of library services—but always with the understanding that, on the nonmystical plane, total disintermediation is never possible. This means that disintermediation is, in fact, always a form of re-mediation. New forms of mediation will be needed and will develop. If we in library services have the foresight and the agility—if we can move quickly enough—we can create and offer such new services.

TIME

Speed is indeed the operative term, for all information services are ultimately understandable only in terms of time. Time is the currency of access: how long it takes for the user to gain access to needed materials; how long an item remains needed or relevant; how long an item can survive in its present physical form; how the time of the user can be expanded through an investment of the time of library staff—and above all, how much time the user has available to achieve a particular research goal. Users probably spend, in any event, too much time finding information—time that they should spend reading (or otherwise absorbing) it; and they probably spend too much time reading things—when they should instead be thinking. There is notoriously too much information to be read and digested effectively—and the next generation of computers, to be truly applicable to real information needs, should somehow be able to read for the user. That is not an unreasonable demand—although we must at the same time take care not to distinguish too sharply the activities of finding information, reading it, and thinking about it, for these are surely in many ways merely separate stages or methods of a single process.

CONTEXT

One of the most essential time-reduction tools provided by library services is the local collection. For purposes of this chapter, let us adopt as broad a definition of the collection as possible. Let us define a collection as any set of linked information objects. The purpose of collection development in the most traditional sense is in fact always to link specific objects—documents, publications—by moving them into proximity to each other; or perhaps more exactly, it is to put the user into a position to establish such links by moving such materials into closer proximity to the user.

Why are such links important? Because all understanding, all knowledge necessarily entails context. On the nonmystical plane, there is no unitary reality. A thing is understandable, knowable, only in relation to another thing. We are now entering an era of revolutionary change precisely because information technology is providing us with new methods of linking objects that exist in widely dispersed environments—the ability to establish radically new contexts.

If a collection is a set of linked objects, then how should we conceive of an object? Let us, for our purposes here, view an object as a *text* in the broadest sense—i.e., a closed set of signs or symbols that have meaning to any user who has the ability to decode them. In the traditional environment, the user normally brings the code (e.g., the natural language) to the text. We must, in any case, take care to distinguish the code from the context, for both are fundamental prerequisites for understanding. The context is rather a relationship among texts. We should also recognize, moreover, that every document consists of a multiplicity of contexts—its constituent parts—which is to say a multiplicity of texts.

Using this definition, then, a document is, to be sure, an object—but we must also admit that a part of a document can be an object as well. In fact, several parts of a document can be an object. Several parts of several documents can together constitute an object. Several documents can be an object. Every collection, then, is in effect an object—and most objects can be viewed as collections of objects. The significance of this phenomenon—let us call it for our purposes *object embedment*—for the future of information services should not be underestimated. We have always understood object embedment in the abstract—but information technology is providing us with the ability to work with it in reality. It is perhaps related to the concept of "granularity." There are, for example, large-grained and small-grained databases. A large-grained database is presumably one which, using our definitions, contains objects that themselves contain objects, and so forth. In a way, therefore, the traditional library collection is a kind of large-grained object—or even a kind of large grained document, which has been written or authored by bibliographers. One can read that document—or parts of that document, or the surrogates of that document—in a catalog. It is for this reason that finding and reading and thinking—and even writing—are really all variations of a single activity: context building, the creation of collections of objects. It is this object creation and manipulation—which is to say this collection development and management (done, to the extent possible, directly by the user)—which must form the basis of any future information services.

THE THREE TIERS

In the library we have traditionally distinguished among three collection tiers. See figure 1. The upper tier is the universe of publication—all of the documents to which someone could gain access, with an adequate investment of time. This universe is, of course, a mess—in the sense that it is fundamentally uncontrolled; while parts of it are, to be sure, subject to some bibliographical control, those instances of control are not coordinated, so that this universe ultimately lacks any real system. A second collection tier is the personal collection, i.e., all objects used by a particular user to do a particular kind of work at a particular time. The objects that comprise the personal collection may derive from many sources, exist in different formats, and be the property of various owners. This collection tier is constantly changing, as the work and perspectives of the individual user change.

In order to facilitate the creation of the personal collection from the universe of publication, the library creates an intermediate set of documents, the local collection, that serves as a representation of the universe of publication. This intermediate set is very carefully selected and controlled to meet the perceived and projected needs of local users; its purpose is to function in part as a substitute for the universe of publication, which is not effectively or easily accessible because of its uncontrolled, chaotic nature.

- universe of publication   (total document set)
- intermediate set   (local document set)
- personal collection   (private text set)

FIGURE 1. Traditional Collection Tiers

When we speak of disintermediation in the context of collection services, therefore, we mean the reduction—gradually over time—of the significance of the intermediate set for the purposes of the local user. Our aim must be—when the technology and the culture permit—to apply some of the resources that we now use to select and control the intermediate set to the increased control of the universe of publication. If all research libraries could engage cooperatively in this effort, then perhaps our combined resources could provide a substantial segment of the universe of publication with sufficient organization and transparency that our users could draw directly on that universe for the creation of their personal collections, rather than being obliged to work always through the mediating agency of the intermediate set. Why should we want to do this in the long term? Because there are aspects of the intermediate set, as a mediation service, that are—without question—intrusive. Our goal must be, therefore, a condition in which the user, as much as possible, makes his or her own selection decisions. It is admittedly difficult to say at this time whether that will ever be possible, but our hope must be that technology and bibliographical organization will allow us eventually to empower the user by reducing the level of mediation.

ORGANIZATION

Our traditional organization in libraries is divided into a subjective and an objective service orientation. See figure 2.

The objective side of the operation views the needs of the user community as a given and tries to add value to specific information objects in order to increase the capacity of such objects to meet those local information needs. The subjective side takes the objective collection—intermediate set, universe of publication—as a given and works with local users to increase their capacity to make use of available objects to meet their evolving information needs. The weakness of the subjective side is the potentially inadequate understanding about how objects relate to each other and how their relations change over time; the liability on the objective side is the failure to understand in sufficient depth the continuously evolving needs of the user community. On the objective side, the focus is always on potential utility, while on the subjective side the emphasis is usually on actual use. The objective orientation tends therefore to be the more abstract and the subjective orientation the more practical.

At the same time, library operations can and should be viewed increasingly as falling into two main categories, which I have written about often before: delivery and mediation.[1] Mediation services are focused on content and are mainly concerned with the distinctions between individual information objects. Delivery services, on the other hand, are the more technical, engine-like side of the operation. This technical aspect is an essential component of library operations—and has been since Alexandria; it did not suddenly evolve with the advent of computer technology. Delivery services form the machine that keeps the operation running. (Information technology, library systems, should be understood as also belonging in general to the delivery side of the operation.) It focuses more on form, on the naming of objects rather than their distinguishing relationships, and does not easily brook differences. Perhaps the strongest inclination of delivery services is, in fact, to treat every object as much (as possible) the same, because differences impair efficiency—and the purpose of delivery services is to strive continuously to create a more efficient operating process.

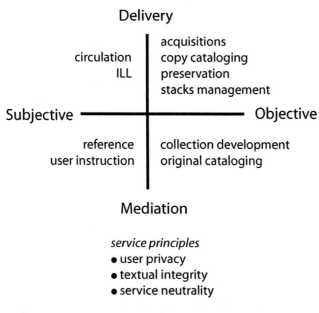

Delivery

circulation
ILL

acquisitions
copy cataloging
preservation
stacks management

Subjective ———————— Objective

reference
user instruction

collection development
original cataloging

Mediation

service principles
● user privacy
● textual integrity
● service neutrality

FIGURE 2. Organization and Principles

Mediation services have more prestige—it is there that we employ most of our professionals (although that is also slowly changing)—but delivery services have ultimately the higher priority, because without effective delivery services the library cannot function, regardless of the level of mediation it provides. (If the engine does not run—if you don't pay your bills, if receipts go unprocessed, if materials do not get back on the shelf, if books cannot circulate—then the library is effectively out of business.) Most of the real crises in library operations happen in delivery. When they happen, libraries routinely—sometimes blatantly, sometimes covertly—shift resources, temporarily or permanently, from mediation into delivery.

We have traditionally organized operations in the library on the basis of the service sequence: (a) the object is selected, (b) it is acquired and processed, (c) it is presented to the user, and (d) the user is assisted in its location and use. Then, if all goes as it should, the experience from that work directly with the user informs the selection of new material—thus completing the circuit. Operations that are adjacent in that sequence are, therefore, often and quite reasonably linked in the organizational structure. We consequently have tried to connect acquisitions and cataloging as closely as we can, as we have circulation and reference.

Linking operations across the vertical and horizontal divisions in figure 2 is probably the primary organizational challenge for library management. The division between the subjective and objective sides of mediation is often, in my experience, less contentious; the purpose of both sides is, in a way, to help people think, so that the private and relatively informal nature of those operations reduces the level of friction between the subjective and objective sides. In delivery services, on the other hand, if the subjective and objective sides get "out of sync," the gnashing of gears throughout the library system can be deafening—because these are two technical components of the same engine. If they do not run in unison, one will inevitably interrupt or destabilize the other.

A range of fundamental service principles derives from these operations. Let us select three more obvious examples. From the subjective side, one of the most obvious principles is user privacy. The library must protect the user's right to free and open access without the knowledge or interaction of other users. The objective equivalent is perhaps textual integrity. The library is expected to protect the original composition of the text from any intrusion, so that the text is, as much as possible, exactly as the writer intended. The subjective side aims to protect the reader, while the objective side is concerned also with the rights of the author. Both the subjective and the objective combine in the third fundamental principle, service neutrality. The library must avoid entering too obtrusively into the information process, lest it influence or skew the judgment or decisions of its users. This third principle is the source of much of the confusion and soul-searching that pervades the library profession—because most librarians do believe unreservedly in this fundamental principle, while at the same time spending most of their working day refuting it in practice—constantly steering the user to one source rather than another, in effect guiding (if not actually participating in the making of) user decisions at every level.

As we move increasingly into an online environment, we must consider how this organizational structure should evolve. If we succeed in our quest for disintermediation (which is, of course, nothing other than an effort to fulfill more effectively the principle of service neutrality), how should this structure change? In order to answer this question, we must give some thought to the nature of research.

THE RESEARCH PROCESS

In considering the research process in the abstract, we must begin with the notion of "primacy," by which I mean the designation of a particular text upon which the research will focus. This text serves as the core of the personal collection. Once primacy is defined, all other texts become potential contexts, although obviously only a subset of those other texts finally plays that role. See figure 3.

While it is clear that scholars in humanities disciplines concentrate their work on primary texts, what about the scholars of the natural and social sciences, whose focus is on nature and society rather than primarily on texts? Let us posit tentatively that those disciplines do in fact focus on texts—that the primary focus of such scholars is in fact not on the natural or social worlds, but rather always on the core literature, which (in)forms their understanding of the natural or social world. Such scholars are therefore (let us say) always working first with a set of information objects, and only secondarily (through the medium of those objects) with the natural and social world. There is, therefore, no difference between the term "primary literature" in the sciences and in the humanities. The central activity in all cases is work with the information object.

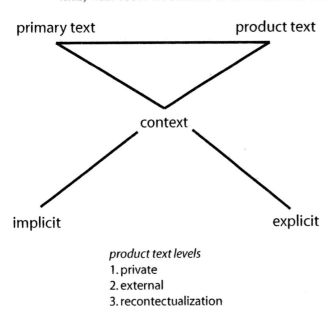

product text levels
1. private
2. external
3. recontectualization

FIGURE 3. Research Components

The primary text is analyzed, understood, made to mean, on the basis of its relationship with other texts, i.e., through context. We can therefore stipulate two broad categories of context. Implicit context provides background for the work with the primary text, while explicit context is that text (those other writings) which refers specifically to the primary text. We also should note that the availability or existence of a library is not necessary for this model to function: this abstract process is taking place all the time. All analysis focuses on some kind of primary text, which can be understood only by virtue of a context. The function of the library is always precisely to increase or boost the extent and capacity of the context so that understanding can be enhanced.

In every act of research—or textual understanding—the researcher necessarily creates a *product text*. We can distinguish at least three levels of such product texts. The first is the private level, in the sense that anyone reading anything necessarily creates a mental text, separate from the text read; but that product text is entirely private—the personal product (text) of understanding. At a second level, the researcher may externalize that product text—i.e., pass it on in some form to other people. The third product text level is an expansion of the second, in which the product text becomes a formal part of the explicit context, to be taken into account in any future analysis of the primary text.

No one legitimately enters an academic library except to create a level two or level three product text. One can enter a public library with the intention of creating a level one product text (although many people also use public libraries for level two or three), but to enter an academic library to create a level one product text is to be a nonproductive consumer—someone who draws from but fails to replenish the total store of knowledge. One is expected to use an academic library either to create term papers or reports, or to write tests or lectures (level two), or to create articles, books, or databases that will ultimately be published and form part of the new context (level three).

This simple model can be applied, of course, to all forms of intellectual work—including all library operations. Cataloging, for example, views the item in hand as the primary text and, on the basis of classification tools (implicit context) and knowledge about the subject (explicit context), creates a product text in the form of the catalog record. (Collection development perhaps views the universe of publication as its primary text and the local collection as a product text.) The central mission of information services is always to ensure that this cycle of knowledge production continues to operate effectively. How does the library do this and how should it proceed with that work in the future age of transition? The answer is to be found in two fundamental library functions: archiving and metadata.

ARCHIVING AND METADATA

The first of these functions is archiving. For some information service experts, this is an exceedingly dull activity. Few rewards and little money will probably derive from large scale archiving—which is why the rest of the information services community is expecting libraries to take care of it. And we will. Some aspects of archiving, to be sure, have received much attention. One of the more prominent is certainly "backwards compatibility"—the capacity to access information originally created with now obsolete hardware and software. This will require an ongoing program of "refreshing" or migration as part of a national archiving process. One imagines that all electronic information ultimately will be in a more or less continuous state of being copied—not only to ensure its longevity, but also to make certain that it is upgraded, so that it remains accessible by way of contemporary technology.

The belief that libraries should assume responsibility for the future of archiving is, of course, not shared by everyone. See, for example, Brewster Kahle's current effort to archive large segments of the content of the World-Wide Web.[2] Certainly he is of the opinion that there will be a market for such long-term historical content. However, one wonders—perhaps somewhat naively—whether such automatic and total archiving will eventually bring us to a point at which, by virtue of the finitude of natural language vocabulary, any search, regardless of what filter is used, will still result in too much information to be useful for any purpose (except perhaps counting hits); again, if the function of information services is to reduce the amount of time required by the user to locate needed information, will not the indiscriminate archiving of all Web content ultimately undermine that fundamental objective? Not only do we need, therefore, to create more effective selection mechanisms for what is archived, but we must also consider any options available to increase or augment the facility of natural language for purposes of searching and retrieval.

This whole problem of archiving is, of course, merely one of the latest manifestations of the eternal dilemma of preservation. On the one hand, one goal of preservation always must be to protect the future from the present. The present is exceedingly selfish and is fully prepared to expend all of its resources in satisfying its own needs. Some authority must intervene, therefore, to ensure that some of those resources are diverted to meet the needs of the future—so that the future will have at least some of the information it will require. At the same time, however, preservation also must be prepared to protect the present from the past, because the sheer weight of the past can immobilize the present. We are moving now into an era in which very significant portions of our present resources must be diverted to retaining past information—so that the cost of maintaining what we already have is beginning to impair our ability to acquire new materials, to continue to grow. One of the biggest questions today confronting preservation, and information services at large, is what price history? One of the most serious challenges we face is to create systems to help us decide (to put it bluntly) what to lose, what to forget.

Preservation selection, however, is no longer simply a matter of deciding what gets preserved and what does not. The revolution in information services—especially that quality we have referred to as object embedment—does provide preservation selection with some expanded options. See figure 4.

All preservation selection must start with the identification of specific items as being of key significance. We must make certain that these are immediately accessible indefinitely and in their totality. At the same time, some materials, while deserving of maintenance in their entirety, may not be required for such immediate access—so that we can maintain them offline. Still others may need to be rapidly accessible, but may not need to be totally accurate—in the sense that we may not need to expend resources to ensure their total accuracy. This is admittedly a somewhat radical perspective—but ensuring totally accurate transmission over time can be expensive. In some cases we may want to pass only parts of larger objects on to the future or we may find that it is most cost effective not to invest the level of quality control that may be necessary to ensure 100 percent accuracy.

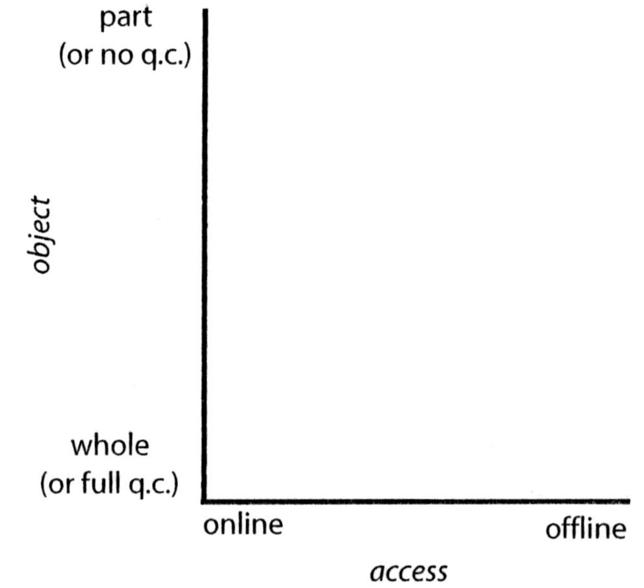

FIGURE 4. Archiving

The other major responsibility or focus of information services in the future must be metadata. The term metadata—data about data—is an important one that the discipline of bibliography has greatly needed for some time. (The prefix "meta-" means next to, outside of, behind, related but separate.) The most important work done on metadata standards for online resources is certainly the Dublin Core. (I would recommend

Warwick Cathro's summary as one good place for the less initiated to begin learning about this subject.[3])

The purpose of metadata is to facilitate the creation of object contexts. We can therefore divide metadata into two broad categories, nominal and relational. See figure 5.

I make this distinction partially because it also supports the organizational distinction between mediation and delivery. The delivery services operation is more concerned with nominal metadata, in that delivery services requires identifiers for all objects, but prefers to treat them as much the same as possible. Mediation services, on the other hand, is more focused on relational metadata, in that its aim is to distinguish and compare the content of information objects. We can further divide relational metadata into two broad categories. One is descriptive metadata, which can take at least two forms. There is discrete description, which identifies different qualities that are essentially equal in value (e.g., formats, genres). There is also what we might label taxonomic metadata, which entails some hierarchical system of relationships—the most obvious example being controlled subject categories.

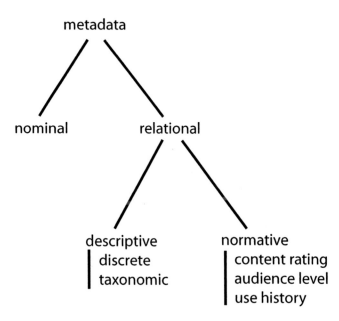

FIGURE 5. Metadata Categories

We also must distinguish a second kind of relational metadata—one to which we will need to devote increasing attention in the future—which we will designate as normative metadata. This is information that evaluates other information, mainly as a basis for information selection—for deciding what to read. One form of metadata must be content rating, which is roughly equivalent to editorial decision making, except that it is made subsequent to publication. This is a change in the publishing sequence that we must expect and welcome in the future. Rather than someone submitting something for publication, which editors then decide whether to publish, the writer can put something up on the network, in effect publishing it. Subsequent to that act of publication, scholars in the field can then determine the significance of that publication and can communicate that significance to others. (We are seeing now an early version of this process in the posting of pre-prints, the most notable example being the pre-print service for physics articles at Los Alamos.[4]) In the case of scholarly information, that responsibility should be delegated in the future to designated, trusted experts. The conclusions of those experts, the content rating, should take the form of metadata, which then can be used for searching.

Content rating is one of the metadata elements identified as part of the Warwick Framework, which is a suggested expansion of the Dublin Core. Carl Lagoze, in a report on the Warwick Framework, lists, as one example of content rating, the Platform for Internet Content Selection, which rates the suitability of different Web pages for access by children.[5] As Carl Lagoze has noted, however, that same rating software could be used for any kind of rating—including presumably that done by experts in specialized scholarly disciplines.

Another form of normative metadata should be some indication of the target audience: for whom is this publication intended? What background must the reader have in order to understand the publication? Is the publication intended for the lay reader? For undergraduates? If intended for advanced readers, how much of the previous literature must be known in order to understand it? This relates also perhaps to a concept I have discussed previously, which I have called "concentric stratification."[6] The revolution in information services provides us with the opportunity and the necessity to develop less linear methods of graphic communication. Although information objects in the paper environment are of a totally linear construction (a codex is conceptually simply a folded scroll), writers do not write from front to back, nor do readers usually read that way (except for very short works, or certain kinds of material like belles lettres). We need therefore more realistic and effective methods of writing and reading in the online environment. A (virtual) stack of increasingly larger discs is one model. On the smallest, top stratum is the citation or, possibly, an abstract. The next disc contains that same information, further expanded to include the most significant points in the writing. The next stratum contains that same information, plus further, more detailed and enhanced information—and so forth.

If some kind of nonlinear approach like concentric stratification were to evolve, standards could be created for specific strata in any scholarly publication. One aspect of such standardization would be to define different strata for different audiences. A reader would know which stratum of a particular publication to enter and read, depending upon how acquainted the reader assumes herself to be with the topic. The object itself, moreover, then becomes a kind of teaching or learning mechanism, in that the reader can teach herself by reading vertically—i.e., one stratum at a time. Each stratum thus provides a context for the stratum preceding it—and the most significant information is repeated and is developed through each stratum.

While the reader or editor is responsible for content rating, and while the writer is primarily responsible for the definition of audience level, there is also a third category of normative metadata that can be generated more automatically and can be used to supplement the first two: use history. We should be able to capture and make public what specific groups of users are reading. This will require that we begin as soon as possible to "catalog" users into categories. In order to decide what to read, the user could take into account what other categories of users are reading. What are other scholars in the field reading? What are undergraduates reading? What are experts in discipline A reading in discipline B? Or what are they not reading in discipline B, so that I, an expert in discipline A, can see what my colleagues are overlooking?

We also should bear in mind that the author can achieve a result somewhat similar to normative metadata by making a more extended or creative use of tagging within the document. Certainly the writer can link to other information beyond the publication—that is the future of hypertext citation. But if some new mode of writing like concentric stratification proves not to be an option, the author still can engage in a kind of internal linking to add new dimensions to the reading experience. Tagging should be learned and used, therefore, as part of the writing process—and it may be that such tagging will eventually provide us with some opportunity to increase the capacity of natural language to permit more effective archiving and retrieval. If vertical reading and writing, which allow the "core" of the document to be repeated and developed, are not a possibility, the writer at least can link parts of the publication internally. Different parts of the publication could be connected to other parts. Or, to approach the same problem slightly differently, tagging could be used by the writer to differentiate or define the significance of different parts of the publication—a kind of internal content rating.

We began by expressing a hope that the next generation of computers would have the capacity to do some of the reading for the reader. It now becomes clear that we have, in a way, always had that capacity—we have always provided that service—it has always been the fundamental purpose of information services or bibliography or cataloging. It is the service that provides the reader-user with the capacity to create new contexts. Our goal now must be to enhance that service by exploiting advances in information technology.

Assuming the service structure posited earlier, based on the division between delivery and mediation, we can now conclude that delivery services should focus increasingly on archiving, while mediation services should concentrate more on the fast expanding area of the creation and use of metadata. We also must aim, however, to use this increased emphasis on archiving and metadata to bring about a greater administrative and cultural synthesis between delivery and mediation services for library management purposes. We must close the gap between these two cultures, because archiving and metadata will be fully effective only to the extent that they are mutually supporting. Backwards compatibility, to take one example that we have already mentioned, is not simply a delivery/archiving problem. It does not simply entail the ability to regenerate a set of signs that were originally produced by a now obsolete hardware/software configuration. Backwards compatibility also must ensure the ability of readers to understand those signs. That understanding derives from codes and contexts—so that we must concentrate (as we always have in collection development) not on the archiving of documents but rather on the creation and maintenance of collections. Some fundamental concepts of collection development, therefore, come in a way to their fruition in the activity of long-term archiving—although the collection developer likely will play a very different role in that future archiving work.

BEYOND DOCUMENTATION

Is, finally, the provision of access to the universe of publication enough? Is it possible to expand the concept of library services even beyond that universe (without colliding with the mystical plane)? If so, the answer is perhaps to be found in the previously mentioned concept of "primacy." I took the position earlier that all science and social science research, like the humanities, ultimately starts from a text written by someone else—a set of information objects. But perhaps that is too narrow a perspective. Robert Losee has recently argued that information science needs to expand its scope beyond information objects produced by human beings—to include the study of all information production and transfer, including signals of nonhuman origin.[7] For more assistance along this line, we can reach back twenty years, and resuscitate yet again the many faceted concept of "textuality." In a classic article published in 1976, Frederic Jameson defined textuality as "a methodological hypothesis whereby the objects of study of the human sciences (but not only the human ones: witness the genetic 'code' of DNA!) are considered to constitute so many texts which we *decipher* and *interpret*, as distinguished from the older views of those objects as realities or existants or substances which we in one way or another attempt to *know*."[8] The world is, therefore, ultimately a text, which one interprets rather than knows—in the same way perhaps that one never attains the direct knowledge of the nonmystical plane, but rather only deciphers or interprets by way of mediation and context.

Perhaps we can expand the concept of information services, therefore, finally beyond the traditional library and into all research of the natural and social worlds. The real purpose of information services thus is to provide the context for understanding all perceived objects— not just information objects in the traditional sense, but all objects from which learning can be derived. Only through such an expansion of information services can we hope to achieve the long sought functional coalescence of the library, the laboratory, and the classroom.

CONCLUSION

To summarize, disintermediation should be a goal for all information services. We should aim to connect the user more directly to the universe of publication whenever possible.

This can be accomplished only by significantly improving delivery and mediation services—or specifically by providing more effective archiving constructs and more incisive metadata, including especially normative metadata. That normative metadata, however, should not have its origins in the mediator (i.e., in the library)—but should rather be supplied by the reading experts (content rating), by the writer (e.g., defining audience level), and automatically (by, e.g., use history). We also have said that we must try to integrate information services into the broader research activity at large. Such changes will be wrenching for ourselves and our users, but to overturn long held, cherished principles is a quality of revolution.

Returning to our fundamental service principles (figure 2), we can see now that privacy will need to be compromised somewhat, if we are to apply the history of use as a basis for searching and evaluation. Textual integrity will not survive object embedment, nor should it. We must be prepared to compromise here, as well—and to accept that the integrity of some texts may be unavoidably violated. Service neutrality has always been a charade and a source of acute emotional tension in library services—mainly because we enter so deliberately and intrusively into the research process, while at the same time self-righteously disparaging such intrusion. If we can reduce that intrusion somewhat, especially through such agencies as normative bibliography, then we can more easily acknowledge such guidance as one of the library's truly core functions.

On the other hand, we must also realize, however, that privacy, textual integrity, and service neutrality are, on the whole, only surface values. There are, at the same time, more fundamental values—an underlying ideology—that we must take every precaution not to deny or abandon. Indeed, the more we move into the online environment, the more essential it is that we remain strong advocates of that ideology. For that reason, any truly effective redefinition of the traditional service paradigm must include a very real and visible political action component.

The commercial information business is growing rapidly—and we live in an age that is fascinated by business to a point of obsession. Business is contemporary society's highest ideal. Our understanding of management in general is defined for us by business. We read books written by business managers for business managers and we try to apply those same methods and principles to our own work. We make the mistake above all of assuming that we are in the service business—but this cannot be the case, because our primary purpose is service. The primary purpose of the service business, on the other hand, is not service, but business. It is revenue generation—not the use of funding to increase access, but the use of access to increase revenue. This is an ideology that is fundamentally antithetical to our own and, if that ideology is allowed to grow unchecked, it will ultimately impair and degrade access to some kinds of information—most notably the specialized scholarly variety.

The most significant threat to access on the horizon is therefore without question the galloping commercialization of information. It is the capacity provided by information technology for publishers to limit radically access to the information under their control. Anyone who imagines we are entering an era of increased access is destined to be greatly disappointed. There is, in fact, a good chance we are entering an era of effectively reduced access to information as compared to the traditional paper era—because information technology provides the proprietors of information with a much greater capacity to reduce access. Some publishers will no doubt use that capacity to make needed information scarce, in order to drive up its value and price. Anyone who thinks this will not happen is blind to what has been going on in the paper environment. Small libraries especially may be operating on the assumption that they are entering a new and better era, in which they will finally be able to provide remote access for their users to all kinds of information they do not own. That probably will not happen. If current trends continue, there is a very good chance that smaller libraries will have inadequate access in the future, for the same reason they have inadequate access in the present—they do not have enough money. For that is what will be required for access in the future—a great deal of money. Unlike the present, there will be no alternative avenue of access in the future. If things continue to proceed in their present direction, there will be no equivalent of interlibrary loan in an online environment. Libraries will either pay what publishers demand for access or they will not have such access.

Everything I have said in this chapter—and much of what was said at the conference—is just so much self-indulgent fantasy and wishful thinking if the current relationships of information ownership and production remain in place. Some of those relationships will have to be overturned if information services are to move forward. A new service paradigm cannot possibly be achieved, in other words, without the decommercialization of significant parts of the publication process, without the disintermediation of the traditional methods of specialized scholarly publishing *per se*, and without the reappropriation of at least some of the responsibility for scholarly information exchange by the academy itself.

That can be achieved in only two ways. First, we must develop concepts—methods, theories, experiments, testbeds—that will provide practicable alternatives to the current methods of information exchange (practicable in the sense that they will provide writers with the same rewards, and they will provide readers with equivalent or superior methods of access and control, as is the case in the traditional environment). Second, we must use direct action—which is to say that we must galvanize our college and university administrations. We must explain exactly what is going on and why it is that we may end up spending more and more money to provide access to less and less information. We must work above all with the faculty, to help them learn how they can use other, more effective methods to exchange information than relying on traditional publishers. We must help faculty to understand the fact that if we continue to exchange information in the traditional manner, it will lead ultimately to a severe degradation of scholarly information exchange and possibly of scholarship itself.

This revolution upon which we are embarking, therefore, is not simply technical or bibliographic—but is rather, like all real revolutions, fundamentally political. Its realization will require political skills and commitment. It will require a clarity of vision, an assertiveness, an audacity—and, above all, courage—for these are career-threatening issues that we raise in a career threatening time.

We are now rapidly approaching a point at which we as a profession will need to make a choice. Either we step back—admitting, in effect, that these are not our affairs—but that these issues of access and commercialization must rather be the concerns of the producers and the proprietors of information, that we are only the mediators, the public servants, the helpers. Or we stand up and accept the moral responsibility that is being offered to us at this very special time in the history of libraries and scholarship. For those of us who, at this time at the end of the twentieth century, are still proud to call ourselves librarians, the right choice is clear—and there is no doubt in my mind that we will ultimately make it.

REFERENCE NOTES

1. Ross Atkinson, "Access, Ownership, and the Future of Collection Development," in *Collection Management and Development: Issues in an Electronic Era*, ed. Peggy Johnson and Bonnie MacEwan (Chicago: ALA, 1994), 94–96.

2. "The Internet Archive," www.archive.org.

3. "Metadata: An Overview," www.nla.gov.au/nla/staffpaper/cathro3.html.

4. "e-Print archive," http://xxx.lanl.gov.

5. Carl Lagoze, "The Warwick Framework: A Container Architecture for Diverse Sets of Metadata,"

D-Lib Magazine (July/August 1996), www.dlib.org/july96/lagoze/ 071agoze.html; "Platform for Content Internet Selection," www.w3.org/PICS.

6. Ross Atkinson, "Networks, Hypertext, and Academic Information Services: Some Longer-Range Implications," *College & Research Libraries* 54 (May 1993): 208.

7. Robert M. Losee, "A Discipline Independent Definition of Information," *Journal of the American Society for Information Science* 48 (Mar. 1997): 254–69.

8. Frederic Jameson, "The Ideology of the Text," *Salmagundi* 31/32 (1975/76): 205.

6 MANAGING TRADITIONAL MATERIALS IN AN ONLINE ENVIRONMENT

SOME DEFINITIONS AND DISTINCTIONS FOR A FUTURE COLLECTION MANAGEMENT

Collection management (as opposed to collection development) should be understood as the activity of adding value to—or deleting value from—objects of information subsequent to their selection. The management of materials in traditional formats will become increasingly problematic the more we move into an online environment. Although digital resources will sooner or later come to dominate scholarly communication, the effective management of traditional materials will remain essential. While a central goal of libraries must be to manage traditional and digital resources as two aspects of a single service, we must also recognize that all information services will eventually be conditioned by a digital mentality. In order to start planning now for collection management to play a more prominent role in the future of information services, we must begin to define with as much precision as possible the abstract values collection management adds to and deletes from selected information objects.

In every age, humankind imagines itself to be moving through a period of transition so acute that the effect borders on the dysfunctional. Our own age is no exception. We long for a simpler past, or for a more focused future, but the fact is that every era is one of profound change, and it is now our turn. Because we have come to understand ourselves mainly in technical terms, we necessarily and correctly view our transition as a consequence of technology, and those of us in academic libraries see our main objective as the transformation of academic information services from a primarily paper-based activity to an increasingly electronic one.

If we had our druthers, we would probably opt to build two libraries—one traditional and one digital; we could then gradually shift resources from the traditional to the digital as needed. Fortunately for academic libraries and higher education, we do not have anything approaching the means that would be required to create such a schism—because if we did, those two libraries would inevitably become politically disaffected and veer apart, and the library as an institution might well under such circumstances become associated primarily with the traditional side. As a result, the library would forfeit much of its political influence, academic information services would be severely impaired, and much time would be lost trying to effect a reconciliation and reunification. Our primary strategy in academic

This article first appeared in *Library Resources & Technical Services* 42, no. 1 (Jan. 1998): 7–20. An earlier version of this article was presented at the 4th Annual University of Minnesota Collection Development Symposium on May 5, 1997.

libraries must be, therefore, to bring about this transition through a synthesis of the traditional and the digital and we will no doubt be obliged to do this using the same amount or less funding than we presently have.

In pursuing this objective, one of the most immediate and obvious challenges we must confront will be the management of traditional materials in a world where information is conveyed increasingly in electronic form. Because we are aiming for synthesis, we must accept that our planning for the place of traditional materials in a digital environment can only be undertaken and understood as a relationship to the role of digital materials in a digital environment—because the traditional and the digital must together form the basis for a single, systematic service. At the same time, we must accept the fact that the more we enter an environment in which most scholarly communication is accomplished in electronic form, the more a digital mentality—conditioned by the qualities of digital sources and methods—will come to dominate and define information services. In the course of this essay, some of the main components of such a mentality will be identified, because it is on the basis of that mentality that we will view and build future services.

In considering dichotomies such as that of the traditional and the digital, we would also do well, at the outset at least, to note what is perhaps the most fundamental dichotomy of information services—that of subject and object. The purpose of information services is and always will be to ensure that local users have access to the right information objects (as defined as those that are needed) within the right time frame. That responsibility can be viewed from either a subjective or an objective perspective. From a subjective position, the goal of information services is—given a particular set of information objects—to provide local users with the tools and skills they need to make the most effective uses of those objects. But the service can also be approached from the objective perspective: assuming a particular group of local users with clearly defined needs, the goal of the service is to add selected values to specific information objects, such that those objects can be used more effectively to respond to those local needs. While the subjective perspective is most often assumed by reference services, the objective viewpoint is typically that of collection management and development, preservation and cataloging. Much of the political tension in the modem library derives directly and unavoidably from the differences between these two positions. Since my aim in this essay is to approach the problems of the transition from a primarily objective position, we should always bear in mind that a view from the subjective perspective could conceivably lead to different conclusions.

THE OBJECT

As befits an approach to information services from the objective direction, let us begin with a description of the current state of the information object. The division between the traditional and digital object is the source (objectively speaking) of the current hybridity of information services. The term "traditional" is now often used for nondigital services, so it seems reasonable to extend its use to nondigital objects.[1] It is a conspicuously time-dependent term that tends to be used in the midst of a fundamental transition before the vocabulary has caught up; because we do not seem to have an accepted term for nondigital services or objects, we can call them "traditional," by which we mean "of a kind we have worked with until now." The transition will progress much more effectively once we have agreed to replace the term "traditional' with one referring to some quality of the object rather than one that refers to our present temporal relationship with the object.

From traditional originals are created traditional derivatives, which include photocopy and microform—but we are now also able to create digital derivatives. Such digital derivatives can be subdivided into the categories of image and text (e.g., ASCII). Digital objects can be divided into the two broad categories of digitized (i.e., derived from a traditional original) and "natively digital"—also a tentative term—meaning materials that have been produced originally in digital form. On the one hand, therefore, we are working with a hierarchy of concepts (vertically in the diagram), but at the same time we perceive a kind of formal or

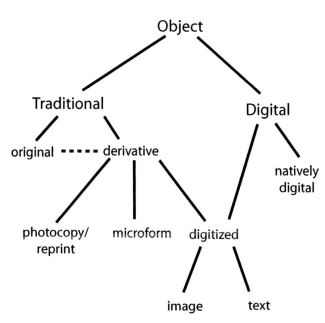

FIGURE 1. Relationships among Information Objects

temporal progression—that is, the more one moves horizontally in the diagram from left to right, the further removed one becomes from the concept of the traditional original.

While there are clearly derivatives of digital objects, these are not the same as traditional derivatives. Digital derivatives are more clones than copies, because there is no apparent loss of physical information: digital objects are characterized, therefore, by what we might call derivative parity. In the case of traditional objects, on the other hand, the creation of the derivative necessarily entails some loss of physical content.

We must take care always to distinguish physical from intellectual content. Physical content is information that is found in the physical construction of the object. Historical bibliography is the study of the history of such physical construction. Analytical bibliography is the study of the relationship of physical and intellectual content. Textual criticism uses historical and analytical bibliography, along with other techniques, to trace the history of the intellectual content of specific texts back to their original archetypes.[2] We must wonder what will happen to these disciplines, especially textual criticism, as we move into an increasingly online environment, one of the primary characteristics of which will be derivative parity.

In the traditional environment, we have been willing to accept a certain level of loss of physical content in return for other (usually preservation) advantages. That is the basis for our current traditional derivative decisions. Microforms, photocopies, and reprints eliminate much of the physical content (notably the original format), but retain the typeface; the same is true of digitized images. In the case of the digitized text, on the other hand, all of the physical content is lost, including the typeface, leaving only an encoded symbol string. Both the library preservation profession and the scholarly community remain perhaps still unprepared for the trauma of the loss of the typeface—and there may well even be some resistance to designating text-only digitization as a legitimate form of preservation.

Such questions as to how much loss is acceptable stem from a deeply held cultural value in the library, which we might call the warranty syndrome. Librarians in the modern library often seem to assume that one of the most fundamental (objective) responsibilities is to guarantee that an object with which they have been entrusted will remain continuously accessible in all of its parts. This warranty syndrome has certainly contributed to the failure of librarians to achieve effective levels of interinstitutional cooperation in the areas of collection, development or remote storage. For one institution to withdraw a title and then depend upon the availability of that title at another institution can require (as a consequence of the warranty syndrome) a level of negotiation and formal interinstitutional commitment that may only be achieved at considerable administrative cost.[3] If we insist on guaranteeing access—in other words, eliminating any chances of loss then it is much more cost-effective to store materials in a local offsite facility than to engage in formal negotiations with other institutions.

The effect of the warranty syndrome on the library's readiness to disregard original physical content (e.g., text-only digitization)—especially with the subsequent withdrawal of the original—remains unclear. What is clear, however, is that the warranty syndrome prohibits the conscious loss of any intellectual content whatsoever. Regardless of whether the loss of all physical content might eventually be acceptable, therefore, the loss of any intellectual content remains generally abhorrent to the traditional library culture. The digital culture, on the other hand, while assuming derivative parity, i.e., no apparent loss of physical content, is rather more habituated to, and accepting of, some loss of intellectual content. The digital culture is characterized by information extracted from remote sites, of which the local user has little knowledge and even less control; it is a culture of Web sites that change every day without warning. Some loss—or "lossiness" as an object attribute—while obviously avoided whenever possible, is nevertheless becoming increasingly understood as part of the price of digital access. This tolerance for some loss of intellectual content conflicts sharply, therefore, with the traditional library culture.

COLLECTION MANAGEMENT OVERVIEW

Let us now proceed to a simplified overview of the collection development and management process. While the exact definition of collection management remains somewhat obscure, it has often been assumed that collection management should be understood as an expansion of the concept of collection development.[4] Collection management then becomes an umbrella term under which collection development is subsumed. However, we need terms that separate policies and actions that drive selection (collection development) from policies and actions that affect the access status of an object subsequent to its selection. The programs and processes by which library materials are selected, therefore, should be termed "collection development, while the process of adding value to objects subsequent to their selection should be considered "collection management." Collection development and management, thus defined, operate on the basis of somewhat different values, and those values must be separated and contrasted in order to be understood and effected.

The activities and concepts of collection development and management should be kept separate also for strategic reasons. There is a chance, perhaps a very good one, that aspects of collection development will not survive the transition to a primarily online environment, because the responsibility for selection in such an environment might be reappropriated by users. When all forms of publication, including monographs, are routinely network accessible, and if an effective level of cataloging can be achieved for those networked resources, then it might well be the user rather than the bibliographer who selects material. In that case, some of the knowledge and creativity that have evolved over decades in collection development will need to be transferred to collection management. If, moreover, collection development ceases to be a primary library operation, then the materials budget will no doubt be reclaimed by the institution and somehow apportioned among its users. Should that happen, libraries could lose the funding needed for collection management, if library managers have not previously separated collection development and collection management funding into distinct budgets.

Returning to the present condition, in which the librarian retains responsibility for selection, let us use the term "anti-collection" for all objects that do not reside in the local collection, or are not made accessible to local users by the library.[5] See figure 2. The "anti-collection" is, of course, an abstraction: the set of all objects not in the local collection.

We will assume that offsite and onsite locations (quadrants b and c in figure 2) contain objects owned by the library in all traditional formats, including traditional derivatives. In the past thirty years, the great majority of our efforts have been centered in traditional collection development (the movement of objects from a to c). More recently, however,

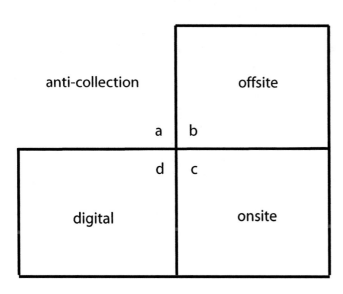

increasing amounts of our attention have shifted to the selection of digital materials (moving natively digital materials from a to d), digitizing materials (i.e., moving information from c to d), or offsite selection (c to b). While most librarians at research libraries have, to be sure, always done some offsite selection, there has been a rapid growth in such selection for remote storage in more recent years—as if all large collections had crossed some kind of line beyond which the transfer of traditional materials offsite has become more politically and bibliographically acceptable. It is as if traditional collections had finally become so large that the central retention of all materials might actually be seen as a potential impediment to access.

object space

FIGURE 2. General Model of Objects in a Collection

This increase in the significance of offsite and digital selection calls for a rejuvenation and redefinition of collection management.

Using figure 2, we can then define collection development more exactly as the movement of an information object from the open quadrant (a) into any one of the closed quadrants (b, c, d). Collection management, as we are defining it here, is the movement of an object from any one of the closed quadrants into any other quadrant (including the open quadrant a—that is, weeding).

Pitschmann has suggested that, in order to facilitate the transition from traditional to digital services, we might consider replacing the term "collection management" with "resource management."[6] On one hand, this suggestion could be problematic because it obscures the significance of object relationships as implied by the term "collection." On the other hand, it is an enticing suggestion because the term "resource" can be applied to both information and economic conditions. The purpose of much of the librarian's activity, after all, is to convert economic resources into (access to) information resources—so that the term "resource management" is a provocative one in that sense. In some cases, moreover, there can also be a conversion of (access to) information resources into (savings of) economic resources.

Collection development is, to be sure, unidirectional: it only converts economic resources into information resources. Collection management also moves in that same direction: it uses economic resources to boost access to information objects that have already been selected. However, one of the most important functions of collection management is that it, unlike collection development, also routinely operates in the opposite direction saving or increasing economic resources by reducing or eliminating (access to) information resources. Thus, in figure 2, collection management either increases access at the expense of economic resources (moving objects clockwise, b to c, c to d, b to d), or it reduces access, saving economic resources (moving objects counterclockwise, c to b, b to a, c to sand perhaps eventually d to c, or d to a). The criteria for the decisions made by both collection development (in one direction) and collection management (in both directions) are always ultimately based on some application of the prime criterion of potential local utility—i.e., how useful the target object will likely be for the work of current and future local users.

GOAL VALUES

This description of collection development and management is, needless to say, greatly oversimplified. For one thing, each of the three closed quadrants contains a whole range of service gradations, which are so extensive that it is even possible in some cases to move an object into a higher access quadrant, but actually to reduce its accessibility (as, for example, if one digitized an object—moving it from c to d—but neglected the index or interface). Rather than relying on the metaphor of object space, therefore, it would be more accurate to define the (objective) work of information services on the basis of the distinguishable values added to information objects. These values added might be divided into two broad categories: (a) functionality—i.e., values that improve the user's ability to manipulate and work within the object, and (b) maintenance—i.e., values ensuring that the object remains stable and available overtime. See figure 3.

These two value categories might each be further broken down into two broad goal values (i.e., values, which it is the goal of information services to add to objects). Functionality can be divided into (a) transferability, the capacity to move an object from one location to another, and (b) analyticity, the ability to be analyzed, in the sense of breaking down an object into smaller parts for more effective access. Indexing is the main service manifestation of analyticity In the case of maintenance, the two main goal values would probably be (a) integrity—i.e., ensuring that the content of the object remains stable and uncorrupted as the author intended (what Graham has called "intellectual preservation"), and (b) longevity, ensuring the object's long-term survival.[7]

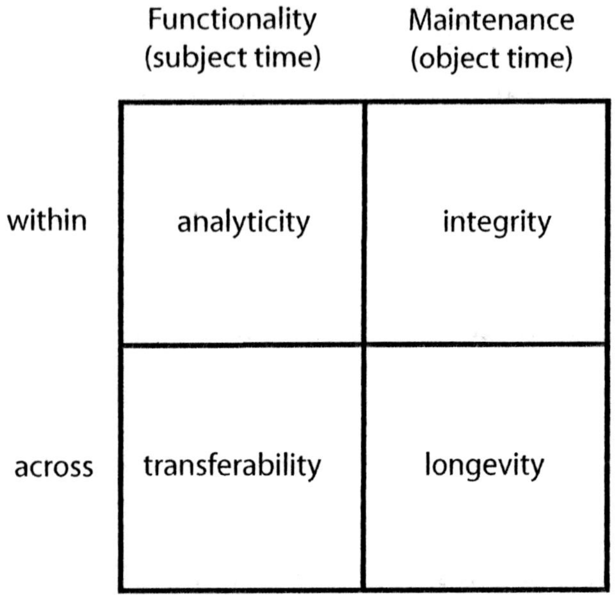

The goal values of functionality are concerned with subject-time; they are intended to reduce the amount of time required for the user to gain access to, or to make use of, the object. The goal values of maintenance are concerned with object-time, or the time the object remains extant and intact. The goal values of analyticity and integrity are intended to enhance users' ability to work within an object, while the purposes of transferability and longevity are to move the object across space or time. All of the goal values, therefore, derive from a sense of *embedment* or context: transferability and longevity entail or presume a larger universe of space and time, just as analyticity and integrity imply the use or quality of the components of an object embedded within its whole.

	Functionality (subject time)	Maintenance (object time)
within	analyticity	integrity
across	transferability	longevity

FIGURE 3. Goal Values

But despite such conceptual relationships and mutual support among the four goal values, it is nevertheless the case that each of these is operationally and economically distinct; each is independently applicable, so that the addition of one does not entail or require the addition of any other. Because, moreover, the addition (or boosting) of each of these does require an expenditure of economic resources, each is in effect engaged in continuous competition with the others for the library's increasingly scarce economic resources. This competition is the basis (at least from the objective perspective) for the whole economics of information services; all of the library's economic resources (e.g., funding, staff time, staff skill, space, equipment) exist for only one purpose, and that is to add these goal values—individually or in combination to selected objects. The main criteria for that selection—for deciding which objects should have value added to them, and which values should be added to which objects—will normally be (a) the prime criterion of projected utility, (b) the initial economic value of the object itself, (c) the information philosophy of the library or institution (i.e., an institutional bias for some values over others), and (d) available economic resources.

In making such decisions, the format of the target object is, on the one hand, irrelevant: the librarian should and does aim to add such values to selected objects regardless of format. On the other hand, such decisions will also necessarily be affected by format conduciveness: some formats are more receptive than others for adding or boosting certain values. In general, digital objects are more conducive to functionality. They can be moved across space at nearly the speed of light, and (if in textual form, rather than images) they can be rapidly searched or analyzed. Digital objects are, however, far less conducive (at least at this point in time) to maintenance: they can be easily corrupted, and no standards exist for their long-term archiving and migration.[8] Traditional objects are the opposite of digital objects in this regard: traditional objects are not nearly as conducive to transferability and to analyticity (cataloging and indexing cannot be supplemented with automatic text searching)—but traditional objects are much more conducive (at this time) to maintenance than are digital objects.

THE POLITICAL DIMENSION

If competition among goal values forms the basis for the economics of information services, then we must expect a political superstructure that reflects that competition—and there is indeed a fundamental ideological or political division that is a manifestation of the dichotomy of the two broad value categories, and that is probably as old as the library itself. It is the dichotomy of the information service agency as purveyor on the one hand, and as repository on the other. Drawing on the distinction made by Waters and Garrett, we can use the term "library" for the former, and "archive" for the latter.[9] This ideological division is further reflected—and will likely be heightened by the fundamental dialectic in the digital culture of the search engine and the database. See figure 4.

The library side of information services, as opposed to the archive, has vastly greater political power, not only because it is much more associated with the digital culture, but also because its primary user community is present; librarians can rely upon those users to influence current decision-making in the institution. The archival side of information services, on the other hand, views the present in some respects mainly as a conduit through which to move objects from the past into the future. The primary user groups of this side have not yet arrived on the scene, so they have no real political influence. But the archival side has, at the same time, a far greater existential responsibility than the library side, because "life and death" decisions about objects are made; they determine whether objects will survive into the future, while the library side is concerned more about increasing access (reducing access time) to objects that are presently extant. This side increases the availability of objects that are for the most part already available, while the archival side decides whether objects will remain available at all. On the archival side, there is less concern about subject time and more for object time: from the purely archival perspective, it does not really matter how long it will take to gain access to an object, provided that access per se remains possible. From the extreme library side, on the other hand, if an object requires too much time to access, it might as well not exist at all, and any economic resources spent on its maintenance are wasted. On the value distinctions between librarians and archivists, see McCarthy.[10]

Library	Archive
functionality	maintenance
subject time	object time
short-term	long-term
present	past or future
synchronic	diachronic
flexibility	stability
reader	writers
sciences	humanities

FIGURE 4. Comparison of Library and Archive Attributes

The library perspective is focused mainly on the needs of readers. The archival perspective is also concerned about reader requirements, but at the same time it represents the writer by ensuring that the object creation remains intact as the writer intended. Also, the library side represents more of a scientific approach, in the sense that it is less concerned about maintaining dated information (which is not to imply that all scientific information necessarily becomes less useful over time), and is well disposed to summary. The archival side, on the other hand, with its concern for history and its focus upon the artifact, might perhaps be more associated with the values of the humanities.

It might sometimes be assumed that the territory of collection development is the library, while collection management is more the concern of the archive. That should not be the case, however, and we must take care not to allow such a political schism to debilitate collection services. Collection management must take into account the needs and goals of both the library and the archive sides—and it should be the main political function and rationale of collection management to connect and synthesize these two fundamentally and historically divergent aspects of library operations.

TRADITIONAL OBJECTS

The options we have for providing access to traditional objects in future will depend upon both economic and political factors. See figure 5. From the archival perspective, maintaining the original object in a protected form (as in a special collection) is the ideal. Under such conditions, the integrity and longevity of both the physical and intellectual content are assured. The cost of providing objects in their original form with a high level of protection, however, can be significant. (The relative costs for these different operations are only assumptions based on experience; they are not a result of any empirical study.) Less preferable from the archival perspective, but presumably somewhat less expensive, is to maintain a reformatted version only, in which the typeface is retained. Because of the reduced costs and the more ready accessibility, this is also a much preferable solution from the library perspective—and even more so, if the reformatting is digital. Less preferable from the archival position, but probably even less expensive, is the maintenance of the original in unprotected form, e.g., offsite; seen from the archival position, this is a deferral of necessary action, but it does mean at least that all physical content is maintained for the moment. From the library position, the unprotected original is somewhat more accessible than some forms of typeface-only reformatting (notably microform), although it is obviously far less preferable than digitization.

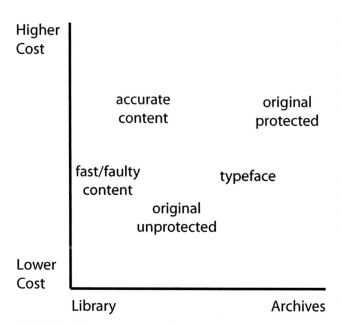

FIGURE 5. Economic and Political Factors for Providing Access to Objects

Much more acceptable from the library viewpoint would be a total digitization of the text only, which would render the entire document keyword searchable. This could be, of course, a very expensive undertaking, since unevaluated optical character recognition (OCR) would not provide full accuracy; such an undertaking would require very costly quality control. From the archival standpoint, such a step is even less preferable because it entails a loss of all physical content—but at least the symbol string of the original, representing the intellectual content, is kept intact. Totally unacceptable from the archival side would be fast but not entirely accurate digitization (uncorrected or "dirty" OCR), for this would inevitably entail some loss of intellectual content. From the library perspective, such rapid digitization would be—in some cases—an ideal solution, because it would provide access to (pound for pound) more information at a much reduced cost. (Needless to say, however, in those instances requiring totally accurate content, even the library position would support fully accurate digitization.)

For more important (potentially higher use) traditional objects, combinations of one option from the library side and one from the archival side are the preferable action. The combination of fast but inaccurate OCR with typeface digitization, for example, is an especially effective option, because it allows the user to search the OCR, but view an image of the typeface; both processes can be done relatively automatically, as opposed to fully accurate OCR, which entails much expensive human intervention. (The current JSTOR project, for instance, uses both OCR and images; the OCR done for JSTOR, however, is subject to quality control, and the project feels it has achieved 99.95 percent accuracy as a result. See www.jstor.org/about/production.html.)

Well after much of the action in academic scholarship has shifted online, institutions will doubtless remain custodians of large quantities of paper materials—unprotected originals. The reason for this will be partially economic (it costs less, we assume, to put such originals someplace on a shelf, rather than to convert them). However, the maintenance of unprotected originals will also have political motivations: the unprotected original is a compromise between the library and the archival value directions, and as such will be acceptable to the broadest range of libraries and users.

THE FUTURE MODEL

As we noted earlier, the movement of objects from the anti-collection to the onsite library has been the primary and dominant focus of academic information services for centuries. As we move more into a digital environment, however, we must now expect the centrality of the onsite library for information services gradually to dissolve. The onsite collection, (quadrant c in figure 2), will and should eventually disappear as an independent conceptual entity, and its basic functions will be divided and drawn into the other two quadrants, b (offsite) and d (digital). This does not mean that the onsite library will cease to exist, but rather only that users (and information service providers) will probably come gradually to view any library that is not desktop accessible as being a remote storage facility, even if it is on a central campus. The offsite storage facility is merely more remote than the onsite facility, while traditional objects maintained in collections at other institutions are simply more remote still.

The three closed quadrants—onsite, offsite, digital—in our general model (figure 2), therefore, will ultimately contract into two: online and offline. See figure 6. Given the significance of transferability in the functional value system, we should begin to define objects in the online collection as those that are network accessible at the local institution—that is, not objects that have only the capacity to be network accessible, but rather those that are locally network accessible at the present time.

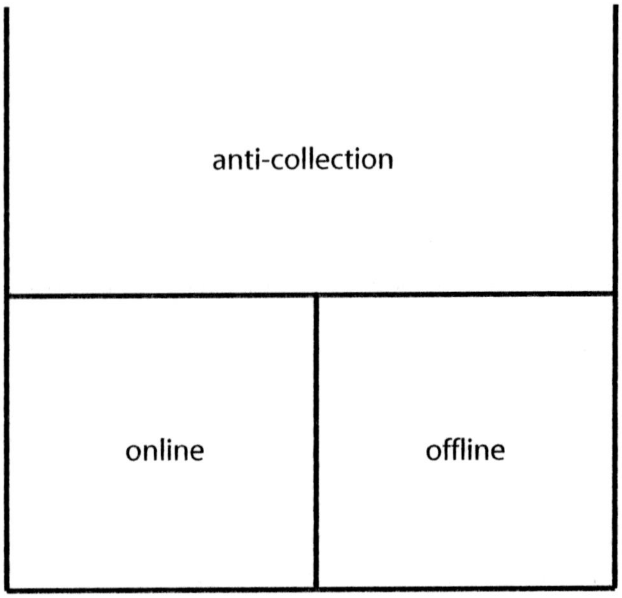

It is this dialectic of online and offline that should become the operative dichotomy, ultimately replacing the transitional dichotomy of traditional and digital. It is not that the concepts of traditional and digital objects should lose their relevance, but rather that they should be subsumed within this operative dichotomy. While online object space contains only digital objects, offline object space should be seen as holding both digital and traditional objects. Digital objects that are maintained offline are those that are not network accessible, such as stand-alone CD-ROMs. There are

FIGURE 6. Modified Model for Objects in Collections

also different gradations of offline (and online) access; the more offline the object is, the less accessible it becomes as an information resource—but also, in general, the lower the cost in economic terms of its maintenance and functionality.

We can expect three broad categories of objects to reside offline:

1. The most obvious (and possibly largest) category will be objects of low potential use. These will consist mainly of large collections of unprotected traditional objects, although we must assume some digital materials will also fall into this category. Such digital objects will be kept offline because they do not promise high potential utility; this category will include some objects that were once online, but that have now been moved offline for storage purposes, because their local utility has declined.

2. While there will be some objects kept offline because they are considered less important, there will be a second category of objects kept offline because they are more important. These will include all of the protected traditional originals (although some of these might have been digitized as well); most of these will presumably reside in special collections. We must also expect to create and maintain offline backup copies of particularly important digital objects for archival or historical purposes.

3. A third category of materials maintained offline will be those that are either technically unsuitable for online access as well as, more importantly, those for which there are legal impediments to digitization. We do well to remember that libraries do not own the intellectual content of many of the objects they maintain—but rather only, so to speak, the physical content of the copies they have purchased. The owners of the intellectual content—individual publishers—presently have the right and responsibility to decide whether such objects may be digitized for online access, and we must expect that a certain amount of material that is legitimately, needed online for scholarly purposes will be kept offline by publishers to protect their investments. If the academy continues to outsource its publishing to (especially commercial) publishers, then it is possible that access to such information will be increasingly restricted, the more we move online. Re-appropriating at least some of the responsibility for specialized scholarly publishing must therefore be one of the highest priorities for the academic community.

THE ROLE OF COLLECTION MANAGEMENT

What are the responsibilities of collection management in an evolving digital environment? To answer this question, we must return to the fundamental values added (depicted in figure 3), bearing especially in mind the factor of format conduciveness. We should recognize that the acts of selection and acquisition add to the selected object all four goal values—transferability, analyticity, integrity, longevity—to a limited degree; we could, in fact, define selection and acquisition as the modest addition of these values to particular objects. If the object is considered to be especially important, collection management can then boost access to the object by increasing one or some combination of those values. This can be done by increasing further those values to which the object by virtue of its format is already conducive: digital objects can be made more transferable or analyzable, or the integrity and longevity of traditional objects can be further improved. Alternatively, or in addition, collection management can move to compensate for values that are less prevalent because of format: the integrity or longevity of digital objects can be boosted by, for example, creating offline back-up copies, or the transferability and analyticity of traditional objects can be increased through digitization.

If the object is determined to be of less importance, the collection management decision maybe simply to do nothing, i.e., to leave in place the values added by selection, but not to boost those values in any way. On the other hand, if an object is determined to be of less potential utility to local users than at the time of its selection, then collection management can move in the opposite direction, reducing access in order to increase or maintain economic resources. In those cases, for example, digital objects might be moved offline, or traditional objects could be digitized, and their originals discarded. In many (but certainly not all) cases, such adding or subtracting of value—the primary work of collection management will be increasingly accomplished by moving objects online and offline.

THE DIGITAL MENTALITY

We noted at the outset that as the work of scholarship becomes increasingly available in digital form, our thinking about information services in general will be informed by a digital mentality that is conditioned by the special qualities and capabilities of digital objects. We have already drawn some conclusions about that mentality. We have seen, for example, that the old tension in the library culture between the library and the archival value directions is likely to be heightened in future by the fundamental division in the digital mentality between the search engine and the database. We have also speculated that the operative dichotomy for information services (online or offline) should be based upon network accessibility, because transferability appears to be a primary (perhaps dominant) value of functionality, which is more conducive to digital objects. We have also remarked in passing on two other aspects of the digital mentality that are likely to have wide ranging effects on the transformation of information services-loss tolerance and embedment. Let us conclude by considering these attributes more carefully.

As both the library community and its users become increasingly accustomed to some forms of information loss in some circumstances (not only of physical but also intellectual content), we must expect the iron grip of the warranty syndrome to loosen: librarians will no longer be inclined to see as an essential function the provision of total access forever to every object for which they assume responsibility. We can perhaps begin to develop levels of responsibility or warranty connected to or derived from the standard collection levels, which are defined by Bryant.[11] This change in culture and philosophy will have a number of important implications. It will mean, for one thing, that we should be able to put in place much more effective programs of cooperative collection management, which will become increasingly necessary for unprotected originals. If we can avoid the high levels of negotiation and item tracking that have sometimes appeared as necessary prerequisites for cooperation in the past, then we can begin to rely more regularly on each other—with the understanding that such reliance will necessarily entail a certain amount of loss. The dissolution of the warranty syndrome should also increase our willingness and ability to make macrodecisions. Such macro-decisions will become more necessary as we are compelled to move more materials offsite. As that work can rarely be done on an item by item basis, the ability to make broad decisions on large groups of objects is essential, but these decisions will unavoidably engender some loss of information for the local user community. The greater tolerance for lossiness, and the concomitant reduction of the warranty syndrome, should also mean that we will be prepared to engage in much more fast-but-less-accurate conversion, e.g., uncorrected OCR. If the choice is between digitizing ten items very accurately and digitizing several hundred items less accurately, we should have the option of choosing the latter in some cases.

We may also conclude that there is indeed an important future for textual criticism in an increasingly online environment. Because of such contrivances as uncorrected OCR, we are perhaps entering an era in which we will see a real renaissance of textual criticism. For economic reasons, librarians will create poor digital copies of objects—and then we will inevitably lose the originals in some instances. If a later age then decides those objects were important, much highly specialized scholarly work will be needed to reconstruct the archetypes of those objects.

The decline of the warranty syndrome should also contribute to the final elimination of the myth of comprehensiveness. To collect comprehensively on a subject, or to provide comprehensive access, has always been a highly questionable concept.[12] The fact is that all research and bibliographic searching, no matter how systematic and sophisticated, is necessarily a form of browsing—but it has taken Web browsers to remind scholars (and even some librarians) of that reality. We need, therefore, not only to condone browsing, but to search for ways to improve it. Because of offsite storage, as well as the increasing use of more streamlined cataloging methods, there has probably never been a time in the history of modern libraries when main stacks browsing has been more difficult and unproductive. We need to replace what was lost in the stacks with a new ability to browse online—albeit with the understanding that online browsing is something very different from traditional browsing.[13]

Equally important for the future of information services will be the heightened sensibility for embedment. Both transferability and analyticity entail embedment. Transferability is the potential to move objects within a wider universe, while analyticity is the capacity for the user to move within the object. Thus while every database is an object, we must also recognize that every object is a database. We should anticipate, therefore, a loosening or broadening of the concept of the object. Presently we feel that we have a firm grasp in the traditional environment on the nature or definition of the object. We think of it as a document. It is a book or a journal—but we know an object is also a chapter of a book, or an article within a journal. But does that mean that several articles in the same journal might also conceivably together constitute an object? Would it be possible to think of several journals on the same subject area as an object? How about all of the publications of a single author? The separate publications of a group of associated authors? A number of items in different formats on the same subject areas? A collection of items in the same place? A collection of items in different places that are administratively linked? A collection of items in the same geographic region?

It is by asking such questions that we begin perhaps to gain some insight into the novelty and complexity of the collection management environment we are now entering. It is a highly volatile environment, in which information services will be called upon as never before to balance the library and the archival sides, the capacity for reformulation and the prerequisite for stability. New objects can and will be created increasingly from previously extant objects, but the traces and components of those extant objects will need also to be safeguarded in some cases. It will be neither loss tolerance nor embedment that paves the way to the new information environment, but rather their dynamic combination—because each implies the other.

The digital mentality, with its heightened sensitivity to embedment, will cause us to realize more than ever that the collection is itself an information object. Collection development has always had the potential to be viewed and practiced as a form of authorship; because, if every text is to some extent a compilation of previous texts, then the collection is a kind of text—and the building of the collection is a kind of authorship. Opportunities and requirements for that same creativity will now be found through collection management, as we move increasingly online, and as technology provides us with abilities for text manipulation and object definition. Even if the responsibility for selection is partially or totally transferred to users in the online environment, so that collection development ceases to be a key responsibility of the academic librarian, the creative skills and knowledge of collection management—the ability to change the relationships of objects to each other, and of users to objects, by adding values to (or deleting values from) objects already selected—will remain a fundamental information service.

REFERENCE NOTES

1. M. Keith Ewing and Robert Hauptmann, "Is Traditional Reference Service Obsolete?" *Journal of Academic Librarianship* 21 (1995): 3–6; Mary Beth Fecko and Linda Langschied, "The Impact of Electronic Journals on Traditional Library Services," *The Serials Librarian* 21 (1991): 185–87.

2. D. C. Greetham, *TextualSscholarship: An Introduction* (New York: Garland, 1994).

3. Dan C. Hazen, "Cooperative Collection Development: Compelling Theory, Inconsequential Results?" in *Collection Management for the 21st Century: A Handbook for Librarians,* eds. G. E. Gorman and Ruth H. Miller (Westport, Conn.: Greenwood, 1997), 263–83.

4. Charles B. Osburn, "Collection Development and Management," in *Academic Libraries: Research Perspectives,* ed. Mary Jo Lynch (Chicago: ALA, 1990), 1–37.

5. Ross Atkinson, "Access, Ownership, and the Future of Collection Development," in *Collection Management and Development: Issues in an Electronic Era,* eds. Peggy Johnson and Bonnie MacEwan (Chicago: ALA, 1994), 92–109.

6. Louis A. Pitschmann, "Organization and Staffing," in *Collection Management: A New Treatise,* eds. Charles B. Osburn and Ross Atkinson (Greenwich, Conn.: JAI Pr., 1991), 141.

7. Peter S. Graham, *Intellectual Preservation: Electronic Preservation of the Third Kind* (Washington, D.C.: Commission on Preservation and Access, 1994).

8. Donald Waters and John Garrett, *Preserving Digital Information: Report of the Task Force on Archiving Digital Information* (Washington, D.C.: Commission on Preservation and Access, 1994), 41.

9. Ibid.

10. Paul H. McCarthy, "Archives under Library Administration: Points of Convergence and Conflict," *Journal of Library Administration* 7 (1986): 17–34.

11. Bonita Bryant, ed., *Guide for Written Collection Policy Statements,* Collection Management and Development Guides, no. 3. (Chicago: ALA, 1989).

12. F. C. A. Exon and Keith F. Punch, "The Self-sufficient Library Collection: A Test of Assumptions," *Journal of the American Society for Information Science* 48 (1997): 11–16.

13. Michael Heim, *The Metaphysics of Virtual Reality* (New York: Oxford Univ. Press, 1993), 24–27.

7 LIBRARY FUNCTIONS, SCHOLARLY COMMUNICATION, AND THE FOUNDATIONS OF THE DIGITAL LIBRARY

LAYING CLAIM TO THE CONTROL ZONE

As libraries prepare to convert an increasing proportion of their services to online form, it is essential that they pause to review and define the core qualities of those services; only in that way can the systematic and conscious transfer of such services to an online environment be assured. This definition of core services is especially important for academic libraries, which face special economic and political challenges. Some of the most fundamental aspects of library operations entail the existence of a border, across which objects of information are transferred and maintained. Such a parameter, demarcating a single, distributed digital library (the "control zone"), needs to be created and managed by the academic library community at the earliest opportunity. One basic objective of such a single digital research library should be to serve as an alternative publishing mechanism for specialized scholarly communication. In order to achieve that combination of the collection and the publication functions in the coming online environment, some responsibilities now performed by academic library collection development will probably need to be transferred to the faculty.

There can be little doubt by now that inexorable advances in information technology will—for reasons of economics, access, and convention—ultimately transform many aspects of information exchange, including especially the role of traditional information services such as libraries. Much work has been devoted in recent years to determining and proposing the qualities that need to characterize digital library services.[1] In its effort to focus so intently upon what the library will become, however, the library community must take care not to lose sight of what the library has been and should remain—the qualities and values of the traditional library that constitute the service itself—for it must be a primary task of libraries at this time to ensure that those basic services provided in the traditional environment are effectively transferred to the digital library.

This article first appeared in *Library Quarterly* 66, no. 3 (July 1996): 239–65. Earlier versions of different parts of this article have been read in a variety of presentations, most notably at the Research Libraries Group "Symposium on Scholarship in the New Information Environment" on May 3, 1995, and at the Association of Library Collections and Technical Services preconference titled, "The Business of Acquisitions" on June 22, 1995.

Identifying such core elements of library services, and making certain that these are taken into account in the ongoing transformation of information services, will not be easy—primarily because it is not always apparent which service methods or concepts now in place are simply responses to the technical requirements of the traditional, paper environment (and can therefore be abandoned or replaced in the new environment) and which of those methods and concepts form the basis for needed services that must be retained and somehow replicated in the digital library. Plans and speculations about the future of library services, therefore, need to devote more attention to defining and agreeing upon those most basic and abstract library functions in order to ensure their continued availability, regardless of changes in technology.

Academic libraries have special responsibilities and face unique challenges in preparing for and participating in the transition, not only because of the specialized nature of scholarly information but also because of the complicated culture and politics of scholarship. The role of the publisher, especially the commercial publisher, in scholarly information exchange, has become increasingly problematic in the planning and operation of academic libraries, a situation further complicated by the fact that information technology is already causing the line between these two traditional intermediary services—libraries and publishers—to blur. No planning for the academic library of the future is possible, therefore, without taking the complex and increasingly strained relationships of scholars, publishers, and libraries fully into account. While there is little question that information technology has the potential to bring substantial improvements to higher education and scholarly communication, the ability of the academic library community to achieve such gains for its students and scholars will depend directly upon its willingness to take unusually high risks and to assume radically new responsibilities. The purpose of this article will be to define some fundamental functions or abstract qualities of library services that must be transferred to the digital environment and then to relate those basic functions to some of the main challenges facing academic libraries as more of the information needed by academic client-users becomes accessible online.

BASIC LIBRARY FUNCTIONS

The purpose of information services, including especially libraries, is to add value to specific objects (that is, sources) of information from the perspective of (usually local) clientele. That value added is access value and is best understood temporally, in terms of access time: to increase or improve access is always to reduce access time, and the fundamental purpose of all information services has always been, and will always be, to reduce the time needed by individual client-users to gain access to that information they need to accomplish their personal or institutional work objectives.

Access value should be distinguished from content value or relevance, the relationship between an object of information and the client-user's work or interest at the moment.[2] For any user, at any point in time, we might posit therefore a single, user-specific, content-value continuum. Let us further imagine along that continuum all extant objects of information, arrayed in the order of their relative content value for that user's work or interest at that particular moment. At the front of the continuum would be that object, the content of which would best or most respond to the information needs of that user at that specific time, followed by the item nearly as much needed, and so forth—on down the continuum.

The aim of information services is always to add access value to those objects of higher content value from the perspective of the individual client-user. The most effective information services operation is the one that is able to vary access enhancement such that the more toward the front of the content-value continuum an item is located, the better will be its accessibility (which is to say, the shorter will be the amount of time the user will require to gain access to it). The order of items on any individual content-value continuum is, of course, constantly changing, as the user's knowledge evolves and as his or her work progresses. Because it would be difficult to plot the content-value continuum for any individual, and because the library must normally serve the needs of many individuals, the library must generally operate on the basis of a more generic content-value continuum for (usually groups of) its particular clientele.

While content value is therefore a subjective perception of relevance from the perspective of the individual client-user, access value is always the result of some objective action by information services—something done to a particular object—in order to make it more (rapidly) accessible. The aggregate value of an object of information is always a combination of content value and access value, which, like yang and yin, continually affect and define each other. Not only does the high content value (however determined) of particular objects impel the library to add access value to those objects, but the library also boosts content value, makes sources more needed, and moves them more toward the front of the continuum by reducing the time required to gain access to them. To render a source more accessible to a user is to create a relationship that would not otherwise exist between that source and that user's work. The service—adding access value, reducing access time—does not simply respond to user needs and directions but also necessarily and unavoidably generates and conditions them.[3]

In considering these issues, care must always be taken not to confuse such information services with their enabling technologies.[4] The function of the technology is to create the potential to add access value to any and all information to which that technology is applicable. The function of the service, on the other hand, is to use that technology to enhance aggregate value by adding access value to those specific objects that are inferred to exhibit high content value from the standpoint of particular client-users.

Integral to the function of information services in general, and of libraries in particular, therefore, is the fact that value is not added to all objects of information but, rather, only to a subset of objects, namely, those located (or in need of being located) toward the front of the (usually generic) content-value continuum. This situation is a reflection or consequence of the very nature of value—at least in the "value-added" sense that I am using the term here—for such value is always relative or differential: to add value (for example, accessibility) to something is always concurrently to reduce the value of some other related thing. It is therefore never possible, in the kind of situation we are considering, to add value to all (related) things (that is, to all objects of information), for to do so does not change the relationship of those things to each other—and it is primarily on the basis of that relationship that value is gauged. To add value to everything, in other words, would be, in this particular sense, to add value to nothing, because it would leave unchanged the relationship of all the objects to each other. To add value to certain objects of information, therefore, always necessarily entails a reduction in the value of other objects. Therein lies the dynamic of selection, which is the core operation of all information services.

Essential to the conduct and definition of information services, therefore, is the concept of a boundary. Information services entail the transfer of an object of information, usually through the application of some form of technology, across a boundary, by which action that object is distinguished or "privileged" (that is, given a special status) with respect to other objects. The service is defined, in other words, on the basis of the opposition between what is inside and outside that boundary. All information services, including especially library services, are subject to—and comprehensible only in terms of—this imperative of circumscription.

As the enabling technologies used to provide information services become increasingly based on computer-mediated telecommunications, it is essential not to lose sight of this defining imperative. In the traditional paper environment, libraries have used location—the movement of information objects across the physical boundary of the local library—as a primary means to add value to such targeted (usually paper) objects. This emphasis on location has been possible because the amount of time required to transport information from one location to another has significantly affected access. In an electronic environment, storage location is to a great extent eliminated as an access factor: all (online) objects of information are in general equally accessible (accessible at the same speed, in the same perceptible time), regardless of where those units are stored. This removes the temporal differentiation that in the traditional paper environment has served as the principal mechanism for access value enhancement. While electronic information technology has, to be sure, added significant gross access value to all online objects of information in relation to all objects in traditional formats, such technology also, when applied without mediation, effectively "devalues" information in online form, in the sense that it subtracts rather than adds differences: it has the potential to move everything—which, as we have noted, is equivalent to nothing—across the service boundary. (To move all objects across the boundary, in other words, is to leave the access relationship among all objects unaffected, so that the accessibility of all objects in relation to each other remains the same.) In order to consider whether and how library services should respond to this evolving condition, and to examine the difficulties academic libraries face in making the transition to the online era at a more practical level, I will draw some conclusions about the traditional methods and motivations of information services in more detail.

SERVICE OPERATIONS AND RATIONALE

The Process of Importation

The first phase of access-value enhancement is necessarily importation: the movement of an object across the service boundary so that the attention of client-users can be focused on it. Let us stipulate that this process of importation normally consists of three phases: decision, negotiation, and transfer. In the decision phase, the determination is made to import; this decision is always based on some form of acknowledged expert judgment; while such a decision can be made by the individual user, it is more usually (and probably more effectively) made by some agent of the user. In the traditional library this function is carried out by collection development staff; selectors, acting as agents for local clientele, scan the information universe and decide on the basis of their knowledge of subject trends and client needs which information objects are more potentially valuable for local use and should therefore have their accessibility enhanced through physical proximity. The second phase of the process of importation involves negotiation with the information proprietor, which usually includes some form of payment. The third phase is the physical transfer of the item across the boundary, which, in the traditional environment, is usually the local library building. Once imported, the objects can then be acted upon in various ways within the library (for example, referred to by cataloging and reference, stored systematically) in order to distinguish them from each other and to boost further their local utility or attraction. We should draw a fundamental distinction, therefore, between the process of importation, which moves the item across the boundary, and the "postimportation" action subsequently taken by the library once the object has crossed the boundary. In terms of the online environment, importation may be understood as being somewhat equivalent to the creation of the database (which may, of course, also include remotely located objects), while postimportation services might be viewed as something more akin to the design and application of the manipulating software or search engine.

For most information services, this process of importation is generally the same. Publication provides a further example. Publication is the transfer of the object from outside to inside the parameter of the document.[5] It is by the inclusion of certain information (or by the exclusion of other information) that user attention is focused, access value added, access time reduced. As in the library, the process of importation consists of the same three phases. The decision phase is the responsibility of the editorial board or staff: on the basis of their expert judgment, certain objects are determined to have potentially greater content value and their access is therefore enhanced through publication. By relying on such expert judgment, the time needed by the user to separate objects with higher content value from objects inferred by experts acting as agents for client-users to have less value is substantially reduced. In the negotiation phase, the publisher then deals with the proprietor, who is usually the author. The third phase, the physical transfer, may be seen to consist, in traditional publishing, of printing and distribution.

The Social Ethic

Information services are defined and distinguished not only by their operations but also by their social goals and motivating values. At least since Jose Ortega y Gasset presented his controversial paper on the future function of libraries in 1934, the library profession has been frequently uneasy and occasionally confused about some of the political and ethical implications of its core operation, selection.[6] Ortega, it will be recalled, not only took the position that "there are too many books" but was also of the opinion that many of these "are useless and stupid." Librarians of the future, therefore, should be "held responsible by society for the regulation of the production of books." The future role of the librarian must be "as a filter interposed between man and the torrent of books." Ortega also foresaw—and clearly had little patience with—charges of censorship: "Let no one offer me the foolish objection that such an organization [of book production] would be an attack upon liberty. Liberty has not come upon the face of the earth to wring the neck of common sense. . . . The collective organization of book production has nothing to do with the subject of liberty."[7]

This position naturally clashed with the modern American library's view of itself as the ultimate guarantor of intellectual freedom. Perhaps the most energetic attempt to reconcile Ortega's radical views with the library's traditional opposition to censorship in any conceivable form was Lester Asheim's 1982 essay "Ortega Revisited."[8] In that essay, which has been called with some justification "one of the most tortured pieces of writing in library literature," Asheim concluded after long and intricate argumentation that, while librarians must select in order to counteract information overload, they should never "prescribe."[9] The fallacy of Asheim's position is obvious: because importation always and necessarily entails exclusion, selection is inevitably a form of "prescription." Selection renders some information more accessible than other information and, thus, biases the user's perceptions. Selection effectively shifts certain objects to the front of the content-value continuum. It is in fact impossible to enhance access without influencing user perceptions and research directions and, indeed, exercising such influence is precisely the key service that libraries—and all information services—have to offer.

A much more modern, sophisticated, and applicable discussion of the significance of exclusion is to be found in Richard Lanham's book *The Electronic Word*. There Lanham argues that, because economics is the optimization of scarce resources, and since information—in the electronic age especially—is no longer scarce but is rather overabundant to a point of excess, what we need is not an economics of information but, rather, an economics of attention.[10] The future of education (of which information services may be viewed as a central part) must therefore be to assist the client-user to focus his or her attention on those objects of information most needed at any particular time. The function of the service is in fact to intervene in the search process in whatever capacity is required to ensure that the scarce resource of the client-user's attention is put to the best possible use. A primary purpose of the boundary, across which objects are (or are not) imported, is to facilitate that service. The client-user must and normally does trust the expert judgment that drives the decision phase of that importation and effectively excludes vast portions of the universe of information from the client-user's view. Selection—filtering, to use Ortega's word—far from being an ethical transgression, therefore, is (and always has been) the core service; indeed, the greatest ethical transgression the library could ever commit would be to avoid selection—that is, not to prescribe.[11]

The real ethical question we must ask, therefore, is not whether someone other than the user should effect selection, and thus affect what the user reads and learns—for that must always be the case (even if that "someone" is the designer or programmer of some mechanism operated by the user); what we must ask, rather, is what the basis or motivation for such selection *ought* to be. It is only in the answering of that question that the social ethic of the library is clarified, for it is through that ethic that the library must continue to distinguish itself, regardless of changes in the technical environment, from other information services.

The answer should be, and is, fairly simple. If the motivation for selection is entirely (or at least primarily) in the client-user's interest—if the true goal of the selection is bibliographical, or pedagogical, or in some sense epistemological—then such selection should always be ethically acceptable and justifiable from the library perspective. In the same way that the teacher in the classroom steers the student to particular knowledge, the information service has the responsibility for guiding the user to certain information. But if the selection is undertaken primarily in the interest of someone other than the client—in the interest of the proprietor of the information, or in the interest of the intermediary, agent, or selector—if the selection is done for political reasons or for reasons of personal or corporate financial gain—then such selection must be considered ethically unacceptable to the library and should be disparaged and resisted.

One key to the library's ability to uphold social ethics is the library's normally nonprofit status. Regardless of changes in the technical or economic environment, the library's purpose must remain not commerce but service, and its objective not revenue production but access enhancement. The basis for any fees levied by the library on the client community must be not what the market will bear but, rather, what the services cost—and it must be a primary goal of the business side of the library operation to keep those costs to an absolute minimum. Costs are, to be sure, always limiting; but if and when those costs become a substantial impediment to access, then it is without question one of the library's highest ethical responsibilities to find or to create the means to reduce those costs in order to ensure that public access to information can be safeguarded and enhanced.

In the process of importation, the ethically proper place for exclusion is therefore always in the decision phase, for it is in that first phase that expert judgment, however defined or assigned, is brought to bear. In the academic library context, what is needed to support local teaching and research is assessed or represented by that expert judgment; while one may disagree with individual selection decisions, one cannot disagree with the necessity that such judgments be made and, therefore, that certain materials be excluded. That is different, however, from the kind of exclusion that takes place in the second or third phases of the process of importation: when material defined by expert judgment as needed by the client community cannot be made accessible because the stipulations—often in the form of prices—by the proprietor in the negotiation phase are consistently beyond the resources of the information service provider, then that form of exclusion becomes in effect an ethical challenge to the nonprofit provider working for the public good.

APPROACHING CONFLICTS

As information services move increasingly online, libraries must expect to encounter several areas of friction, some of which are likely to have significant implications for the future of information services. I want to define two general types of these coming conflicts, which I will call the minor and major contentions.

The Minor Contention

As I have suggested elsewhere, it behooves libraries to accept or adopt a fundamental distinction in information service structure between delivery and mediation.[12] While delivery is that service responsible for the transport and maintenance of information objects without respect to their content (in the paper environment, the main library delivery services are acquisition, circulation, interlibrary loan, preservation, and many systems functions), mediation is that service intended to assist the client-user in gaining access to objects of information with a specific content needed for a specific purpose (in the paper environment, mediation services are mainly cataloging, reference, and collection development). All of these functions will doubtless merge and recombine into new functions as libraries proceed into the online age, but the fundamental distinction between delivery and mediation will remain.

By the "minor contention," I mean to refer to those conflicts that will take place within particular types of information services, such as libraries. Library administrators must be conscious of and prepared for the corrosive potential of these conflicts, because they can seriously impair the ability of libraries to achieve their broader objectives. The minor contention will be as a rule a direct consequence of some form of disintermediation—which is, we should always bear in mind, inevitably a special form of mediation; this is because disintermediation often requires someone or something to enter into the space between the sender and receiver (writer and reader) in order to create or provide some mechanism or procedure that will allow the sender and receiver to link more directly than has been possible in the past.[13] Often disintermediation entails the creation of a mechanical link, empowering the receiver to establish connections that could previously be done only through the assistance of human mediation, which was more costly for the institution and more confining for the receiver. (Some reference services now performed by staff, for example, will very probably be performed in the future by expert systems.)

Much of the responsibility for creating such mechanisms that permit disintermediation belongs to delivery services. The difficulty that will inevitably arise will be that some of the functions that could be circumvented or potentially marginalized through such disintermediation will be essential mediation services (such as reference or cataloging). Delivery services, in other words, will through disintermediation begin to assume or replace some of the key operations of mediation services. If library management does not aggressively intervene, delivery services will almost certainly eventually come to view their primary objective in the library as the reduction or elimination of mediation services, while mediation services will understand their main function (always, of course, in the interest of the user) to defend themselves—and to counterattack. The result could well be a political and functional schism that has the potential to impair or even to paralyze library operations—at precisely what could be the most critical period in the whole history of library services. If allowed to run its course, this "minor" contention will cause the library to become so preoccupied with its own internal relationships that it will lose the ability to look beyond itself and to compete in broader arenas with other information services.

Mediation services must be protected, therefore, in an increasingly online environment, for they not only link the library to its primary clientele, they also provide—or facilitate the application of—the essential expertise needed for postimportation services. At the same time, however, as services move increasingly online, some forms of disintermediation, especially in the area of collection development, should be anticipated and even supported: academic libraries should be prepared to take the risky step of increasingly relinquishing to their expert users significant aspects of the core service function of selection. For reasons that will become clearer below, therefore, one of the most far-reaching manifestations of disintermediation—at least for academic (and special) libraries—should be the return to the user community of what once was a user function, namely, the decision-making authority for the creation of the collection. It is important also to bear in mind, however, that this assumption of major selection responsibilities by the user community (in the case of academic libraries, by the faculty) will render the maintenance of links with those faculty through the agency of mediation services all the more essential.

The Major Contention

The other category of conflict in an increasingly online environment, what I will call the "major contention," will have even wider implications for the future of information services and knowledge production because its outcome will determine the effectiveness, competitiveness, and perhaps even the continued existence of some forms of information services, including key aspects of library operations. Unlike the minor contention, which pits different operations in the same information service organization against each other, the major contention takes place between different information service agencies that have fundamentally the same clientele but that operate on the basis of different service goals. Certainly one of the most visible and critical arenas of the major contention will be the conflict that must necessarily and unavoidably arise in an online environment between academic libraries and those commercial publishers that concentrate on the publication of highly specialized, scholarly information.

Readers of the professional library literature are, of course, long accustomed to the heated but still relatively civil disagreement between academic libraries and commercial publishers in the paper environment.[14] Such conflicts are the source of many of the more problematic forms of exclusion noted above, namely, those that take place not in the first ("decision") phase but rather in the second ("negotiation") phase of the process of importation. Academic libraries sense that they are paying more and more to acquire less and less—an especially troublesome circumstance, considering that much of the specialized material they purchase is a product of the labor of their own faculty.

In wrestling with these problems, academic libraries are perhaps gradually coming to understand that there are values other than access enhancement that can be added to objects of information—values that most libraries, however, would not consider contributions to the aggregate value of any information object. Such values are confusing to libraries because they serve not the reader but the writer; their purpose, in other words, is not so much to promote scholarship as it is to enhance the reputation of the scholar. While libraries, because of their identification with the reader, naively assume that the subject of a work is its topic, publishers survive and flourish by recognizing that the true subject or reference of any work is, at least in part, its author—and that a primary function of the publication is to facilitate the competition for scholarly status among individuals and institutions. The chief mechanism of such value added is the hierarchy of publishing vehicles that obtains in every discipline.[15] To publish in a certain journal (or in a certain series or with a certain publisher) that is relatively high in that hierarchy brings to the author a kind of proactive prestige, not because of any intrinsic quality of the item itself but, rather, because of the known value of items previously published by that same journal (series, publisher). In the highly competitive life of the academy, such status by association is of inestimable value—it is what much success is defined by and what many careers are made of. Because the worth of an item cannot be easily or quickly assessed at the time of its publication and because the evaluation of highly specialized scholarship is difficult in any event, even for specialists in the field, the value of the publication is at least partially inferred from the reputed value or utility of other items previously accepted and published through the same editorial process.

The successful publisher understands this mechanism and invests consciously over time in a journal or series in order to build up the reputation required to bestow such status by association—and for that investment the publisher expects a significant return.

In recent years, however, the prices of such specialized scholarly publications have become in some cases so excessive that they now certainly constitute the single most substantial impediment to scholarly communication: academic libraries can no longer provide access, in the paper environment, to the materials many of their client-users must have in order to do their work, because libraries' (reasonably increased) budgets cannot keep pace with the escalating prices charged—especially by a few key commercial publishers.[16] The plain fact is, therefore, that the current system of scholarly information exchange is no longer working—and the scholarly community is approaching a major information crisis.

Why does the academy, which is the primary producer and consumer of scholarly information, find itself in this position? Clearly there are many reasons, but one of the most critical is that, for reasons having little if anything to do with either content or access value, but everything to do with individual and institutional status, the academic community insists on treating every published item generally the same—regardless of its potential use level. Highly specialized, low-use materials (that is, having relatively few readers) are published in more or less the same way as potentially high-use items: the methods used to produce and exchange scholarly publications, in other words, are fundamentally the same as those used to disseminate the latest bestseller. It may be, in fact, that one of the key rewards that scholars seek and receive for their (often highly specialized, low-use) work is for that work to appear and to be exchanged like every other work—to be treated as if it were in effect heavily used—and such treatment forms perhaps the essence of the elusive value added by scholarly publishers. Because the true content value of the highly specialized publication is difficult to ascertain, that value is implied by treating it and making it appear externally identical to previous works of accepted value or utility.

One of the most serious errors academic libraries could make at this time would be to assume that advances in information technology will change any of these relationships or solve any of these problems—or to imagine that the advent of electronic publication will not only bring down publishing production costs but also that such savings will then be passed on to customers in the form of lower prices. To begin with, it must be understood that prices will not decrease simply because publications move online. While publishing costs may indeed decline by moving publication online, commercial publishers have no incentive whatever to pass those savings on to library consumers in the form of reduced prices.

Information technology, we must always bear in mind, does not promote access: it rather promotes control. That control can be used, of course, to promote access, but it can also be used to constrict access, and we would have to be blind indeed to what has occurred in commercial scholarly publishing over the past twenty years to imagine that technology will be used by commercial information proprietors for any purpose other than to increase revenue as rapidly as possible. If, moreover, such increases in revenue can best be achieved through a decrease in access, if demand can best be enhanced by making needed information scarce, then there can be no question that the commercial proprietors of that information will begin to make use of the new technology to do just that.

Reappropriation

Libraries have recently become much enamored of the potentials of outsourcing, that is, hiring agencies outside the library to perform operations previously performed by the library. Although relatively few opportunities to outsource yet exist, more outsourcing services will doubtless evolve as demands increase, and libraries will rely increasingly on such outsourcing, whenever it is cost effective to do so. If an individual library were to realize, however, once having outsourced a particular operation, that it would be significantly more cost effective for the library to perform such work again itself, then the library would, needless to say, resume that responsibility immediately. It is time now to recognize—that specialized scholarly publication has been one of the most longstanding instances of outsourcing in the academic community. The excessive prices that academic libraries are now experiencing, mainly at the hands of commercial publishers, should be sufficient to convince libraries that such outsourcing is no longer cost effective and that the time has come to take whatever steps are necessary to reappropriate that function.

Technology will provide libraries with the ability to exchange scholarly publications much more effectively. But, as already noted, if institutions, led by libraries, do not use such advances in information technology to achieve that reappropriation, then that same technology may well be used (by publishers) to restrict access in the interests of a different service ethic. One of the primary objectives of the academic library community must be, therefore, to provide effective leadership and to develop practicable business plans to bring about what amounts to a new form of disintermediation, in which scholars are more acceptably able to exchange information and to establish reputations without the mediation of large commercial publishers. Only by accepting that goal explicitly and aggressively at the outset of the online revolution can the academic library continue to play a prominent and beneficial role in research information services—for in a primarily online environment, either the library or specialized publishers will provide that fundamental service, but not both. The only questions that remain to be answered, therefore, are, (a) How do libraries identify that specialized scholarly information—that material at the low end of the use spectrum—for which the academy should assume publishing responsibility, and (b) How can the major value added by publishers, that is, the prospective status by association, deriving from the relative reputation of individual journals, series, or publishers, be replaced?

CONTROL ZONE

This discussion has led us to two clusters of potential problems, the resolution of which will be a prerequisite for the successful insertion of library services into an increasingly online environment. At the more abstract level, the capacity of the network to supply almost anyone with almost any online object, at almost any time, in almost any place, at almost the speed of light is at odds with fundamental precepts of library services embodied in what we have labeled the imperative of circumscription. This disparity has not been readily recognized, partially because there is a tendency to confuse the network, which is a technology, with the digital library, which is a service. The network is not a digital library. We cannot sit back and imagine that what is on the network is in the digital library.[17] A library, digital or otherwise, is always a highly selective subset of available information objects, segregated and favored, to which access is enhanced and to which the attention of client users is drawn in opposition to objects excluded.[18]

In addition to these more abstract issues, it must also be concluded that, from the practical standpoint of the academic library community, the publishing practices and objectives that significantly impede scholarly information exchange in the traditional environment have the potential to become even more damaging to scholarship and higher education in the online environment. The more key information becomes available online, moreover, the less need there will be for some forms of mediation. The chances are, therefore, that the need for two separate mediation service categories—libraries and publishing—in highly specialized areas of scholarship will diminish so that only one will eventually prevail. For these reasons, it is essential for the academy to reappropriate responsibility for formal scholarly information exchange.

Both of these basic problem clusters have a single solution: it is time—past time—for the academic library community to begin work on the creation and management of a single, virtual, distributed, international digital library, a library that has (conceptual, virtual) boundaries, that defines its service operationally on the basis of the opposition between what is inside and outside those boundaries, and that bases that service on the traditional social ethic that has motivated all library operations in modern times. The academic community must consider, in other words, the creation of a control zone. Such a control zone should be understood as something that is technically and conceptually separate from the open zone. The open zone, the network at large, should remain free and unfettered as much as possible by standards and structure—the wild frontier of cyberspace, so highly prized and closely protected by those rugged individualists who work and roam there, where one can do what one wants, say what one wants, change what one wants. Creativity is indeed at least partially dependent upon such an absence of constraint. But when an object of information is moved across the boundary from the open zone into the control zone, then that should be done with the understanding that the library community takes certain responsibilities—and makes certain guarantees—for the quality and accessibility of that object indefinitely."[19]

The most fundamental and far-reaching implication of the imperative of circumscription is that the universe of information has never been and should never be considered the library's responsibility. To be sure, intelligent electronic agents need to be developed and should be used by individuals to explore that universe—the open zone. But the basic, ongoing responsibility of the library must be to assume control of a systematically selected subset of that universe and to ensure that such a subset remains stable and accessible over time. That epistemologically and ethically essential function of the library in the world of primarily paper information must be retained and strengthened as society moves increasingly into the online information environment.[20]

Components

One of the most pressing responsibilities of library services, therefore, must be to begin to consider and define the characteristics of such a control zone—or more generally to identify those qualities of, or relationships among, information objects that the user can depend upon when the library community has taken responsibility for them. If it is the case, in other words, that to move an item into the control zone is to add value to it, what exactly is that value added?

Core definition.—As already noted, the library does not simply respond to the need for core material (objects at the front of the content-value continuum) but also actually creates core material by boosting its accessibility. This value enhancement is even more effective in the online environment. If the control zone functions successfully, objects moved into it will be defined as core—in the (as always, temporal) sense that they will be read before other information is read, so that such other information will be understood on the basis or from the standpoint of that core information. Communication and understanding require a commonality of knowledge. Agreement about significance or novelty depends on such common understanding. Far from discouraging exploration of the wild frontier of the open zone, therefore, the control zone will encourage such searching by providing a basis for assessing information found in the open zone—and ultimately perhaps for determining and endorsing the admissibility of some of that information to the control zone.

Particularization.—For purposes of evaluation and retrieval, units of information need to be differentiated or particularized. The author, when available, should take responsibility for highlighting certain parts of the text, so that the reader or searcher will know that, at least from the standpoint of the writer, the publication is intended to add to the knowledge of those subjects. Beyond the kind of tagging that can be done increasingly automatically, and which we must expect will eventually take the place of routine cataloging, some kinds of special cataloging action—the creation of metadata that refers to the object without highlighting selected parts of its content—will remain necessary. At least two new forms of metadata, in my opinion, will need to be included in any pointers or surrogates referring to objects in the control zone. The first is use level. In the same way that libraries can now track circulation, it must be possible to track the history of the use of information units in the control zone. In an online environment, the use of all objects can be tracked, regardless of their location, and such use can even be differentiated by user group. It should be possible to ascertain which items have been read (or at least retrieved) by experts (for example, members of academic departments in the field), which have been read by scholars in other fields, which have been read by students, which by the public at large, and so forth. This feature is a key component of the economics of attention: deciding what to read, and in what sequence, should be at least partially a response to the relative "significance" of objects, as defined by the number and type of readers who have previously accessed them.

The other new identifier that should be considered for inclusion in any records of objects in the control zone should be the work level. This identifier should differentiate information objects by their level of difficulty or specialization and should indicate to the reader in effect how much he or she needs to know about the topic in order to make use of that particular object. The audience at which an object is aimed needs to be designated, in other words, so that the user, who is deciding what to access, can make that decision based on his or her own level of knowledge. This identifier as well is an essential function of the economics of attention. Working with writers to identify accurately the work level should become an essential responsibility of the library.

It is now possible to return to the questions posed above in our discussion about the institutional role in online publication: (a) How should the academy determine which types of publications it should reappropriate responsibility for publishing, and (b) How can the proactive status now supplied by the reputation of individual journals, services, or publishers of specialized information be replaced in an online environment?

The first question can be at least partially answered through the declaration of the work level. If the acknowledged work level is strictly scholarly—if the publication is written by a scholar for other scholars, and its understanding depends on highly specialized knowledge—then that work should be considered for publication by the academy. Scholarly communication and progress depend, as noted above, on the favored treatment of highly specialized, scholarly publication; if such scholarship does not receive special support—if it is allowed to compete in the open market with other works for publication—then its low potential use either deters its publication entirely or substantially increases the cost of that publication, as is now happening in the paper environment. Research libraries, after all, already significantly support scholarly works in the paper environment; because the research library acts for the user, often without consulting the user directly, and makes its selection decisions on the basis of potential rather than actual utility, the research library community creates what is in effect an artificial demand for scholarly publications. If the publication of scholarly information depended on real demand—on direct purchase by individuals—much truly scholarly publication (that is, refereed) would probably be too expensive to appear at all. In creating a control zone, the academy would therefore merely be extending that practice of special support to its logical conclusion by assuming direct responsibility for the publication process itself. The institution should take full responsibility for moving specialized scholarly publications into the control zone and maintaining them according to standards agreed on by the scholarly community. Anything not specifically intended for an exclusively scholarly audience should remain the responsibility of the commercial sector, which is and will continue to be much better equipped to publish higher-use information than the academy.[21]

And now the second question: how to compensate for the loss of that prospective prestige—status by association—that derives from publishing in individual journals or series. If, through the creation of a control zone, many individual specialized journals or series are successfully eliminated, how is that prestige to be supplied and measured?[22] The answer to that question is to work with scholars to replace such prospective status with much more retrospective tracking of actual use by different user communities, which would be a primary purpose of use-level metadata. This arrangement would be admittedly a kind of marketplace approach to status—an extension of the practice of assessing the value of publications through citation—but it can be done in an online environment much more quickly and accurately. All publications moved into the control zone should enter with equal status and potential and should then compete in the control zone for the reader's attention. Those publications that have higher use will also have greater prestige, and it will be that higher use, rather than the reputation of previous by other authors, that should serve to gauge the relative status of objects in the control zone. Actual use will of course condition subsequent use: since users will decide what to read at least partially on the basis of previous use, it will be the readers—especially expert readers—who appropriately create status and prestige for specialized scholarly publications.

Maintenance.—Once an item is installed in the control zone, the user must expect to be able to locate it there indefinitely. Since certainly not all information in the control zone will be published by the academy, effective contracts with the information proprietors will be needed. On the technical side, retention will require continuous recopying (what we now call "refreshing") of the online information, to ensure that its access is not impaired as a result of degradation over time or as a consequence of hardware or software upgrades. Such maintenance will be a major responsibility of our future preservation programs.[23] And finally, from a bibliographical perspective, systematic methods for moving information into less accessible locations—perhaps even offline into paper archives—must evolve in order to avoid what would otherwise inevitably become serious congestion; if the control zone is to function efficiently, the library community will need to concern itself, in other words, with the creation of the online equivalent of weeding or remote storage, the purpose of which must be to make some units of information less (that is, more slowly) accessible than others.

Another important responsibility of maintenance is authentication. Much has been written, especially by Peter Graham, on this requirement.[24] Once an object is admitted to the control zone, the user must be able to depend that the content of the object is, to the extent possible, exactly as the author intended it to be, that is, "authorized." While an item encountered in the open zone may have been subject to any manner of influences or alterations, an item maintained in the control zone must always be, by definition, the unaltered original. Any citation of an object therefore should always be to that copy or version that resides in the control zone. Needless to say, this requirement would not prohibit the author of the original work from producing new editions, but it does mean that each edition must be defined by the author as finished before it can be admitted to the control zone.

Certification.—I considered earlier the essential role of expert judgment as the basis for the first phase of the process of importation. In research libraries, the responsibility for exercising such judgment currently resides with collection development, and in the case of publication the equivalent function is performed by editorial boards. One of the most important conceptual goals that academic libraries need to pursue as information becomes increasingly available online should be the elimination of the distinction between academic library collection building and specialized scholarly publication. A primary rationale for the creation of the control zone must be to bring about the fusion of those two traditional acts of expert judgment—editing and collection building. To move an object into the digital library that is the control zone must be equivalent to publishing it. Any object in the control zone should be by definition published. Anyone reading anything that has been admitted to the control zone must be able to do so with the understanding that the item has been subject to editorial scrutiny—and, at least in the case of specialized scholarly information, that it has been accepted by peer review.

This fusion of collection development and some forms of publication is one of the main reasons the academic library needs to begin to return responsibility for collection building to the faculty as more and more scholarly information becomes available online. Because admission to the control zone will be a new form of publishing, that admission must be in the hands of some network of editorial boards—and those editorial boards must consist of the scholars who, for the most part, make up college and university faculty. This requirement will lead unavoidably to an array of management and coordination questions, because structures will need to be established for scholars to assume expanded editorial responsibilities around the country and around the world. To assist this work, scholarly societies should probably receive and assume a much broader range of responsibility than they have had in the traditional environment. The academic community will need to develop detailed procedures and criteria for decisions on importation (and possibly also on excision or electronic remote storage), but the benefits deriving from this work will be well worth the effort invested in it, for it will transform the role of the scholar and the communication of scholarship.

What agencies will assist the academic library in working with scholars to achieve these goals? To be sure, academic computer centers must play a key role, for nothing can be accomplished without their technical expertise and political support. Academic libraries must also link much more effectively with library schools because radical changes in library operations and values can be achieved only through radical adjustments in training, indoctrination, and research. But academic libraries must also and above all work ever more closely with their university presses. Indeed, in the case of the presses, our links must go beyond mere alignment. The sooner that libraries can, in fact, convince the university administration (not to mention the university presses themselves) that the presses and the library are in fundamentally the same business of scholarly information exchange—and the sooner the library and the press can be amalgamated into a single administrative unit—the sooner the academy can get about its business of moving academic information services into the online era. Many universities have committed a major error in trying to force their university presses to become self-supporting. This policy has resulted in the presses identifying increasingly with—and adopting the values of—commercial publishers. University presses need to be subsidized by universities because scholarly communication must be the responsibility of the scholarly community. And the funding for such subsidy should probably come in the long run, at least in part, from what has been the academic library's acquisitions budget.

Standardization and coordination.—Everything in the control zone needs to be presented and accessed according to the same protocols. This requirement, too, will entail significant administrative and technical coordination. Such standardization must be a major responsibility of and prerequisite for the control zone—as it has always been ultimately of all information services. Only through standardization, moreover, can virtuality be achieved, so that the entire digital collection occupying the control zone appears to the end user as a single database. It is unlikely that the academic community, or even the international library community, would be able to manage such extensive coordination on its own. Some intermediary agencies or businesses will need to develop in order to facilitate such an exchange. It is in this area that we find at least one online equivalent of the vendor, linking a multiplicity of organizations—in this case academic institutions; such vendors would admittedly look less like Yankee Book Peddler than like the Research Libraries Group, but the fundamental function of interconnection remains the same.

The publication of specialized scholarly research—the composition of the control zone—should ideally be carried out without any money changing hands among institutions. With the assistance of university presses as part of the library system, each institution needs to use some of that funding now used for the purchase of library materials to mount certified, specialized scholarly publications on its own servers. It could be, for example, that the responsibility of the institution should be to mount the publications of its own faculty (once those publications have been accepted through the standard national or international refereeing process), or it may be that the institution would provide access to publications on a particular subject for which that institution has assumed responsibility, or the selection of publications may be based upon some other division of responsibility that has been negotiated among institutions. In return for an institution mounting and maintaining that database of specialized scholarly publication and making it accessible to all other institutions, the users at the institution should have free access to similar servers at all other institutions. This goal is admittedly an ideal, which would no doubt be difficult to achieve in the real world, but it is to my mind the only reasonable and responsible method to exchange specialized, low-use, scholarly information in a primarily online environment.

The Compromise of Regionalism

While future access to scholarly information will depend directly on the academic library community's resourcefulness and willingness to provide the leadership necessary for the academy to assume—or reappropriate—responsibility for specialized scholarly publication, it is essential also to bear in mind that such publication will remain only a subset (albeit an important one for the academic library) of the total publication output. Even if the academy succeeds, therefore, in its quest for reappropriation, there will remain a large publishing industry in the online environment that will continue to flourish by publishing higher-use materials of all kinds—and it is conceivable that some of those publications might also be candidates for the control zone. I have been envisioning the control zone as if it were to be a single, monolithic, international, virtual library, and indeed such an open and omni-accessible database should be the academy's ideal objective. But it is also clear that, from a business perspective, such an objective is probably impractical—and if libraries set their sights so unrealistically high, they stand to undermine from the outset any effort to create such a single, coordinated digital library as the control zone. Some form of "regionalism," that is, the creation of private regions in the control zone, will therefore probably be unavoidable—because some commercial publishers will continue to own the content of some publications and will survive and prosper through the sale of that content. Some higher-use publications will need to compete with each other in the open market—unlike specialized scholarly publications—if publishers are to remain willing to invest the capital needed to bring such publications into existence. Although the sale of one copy of such a publication to the entire control zone may be an occasional option, with all libraries paying a share, the chances of such arrangements are probably small in all but a few cases. Such publication will depend, therefore, on some kind of regionalism in the control zone, so that publishers can sell to more than one customer.

There will be other reasons as well for building into the control zone a capacity for private regions—most notably the fact that different academic institutions have different levels of resources (or apply their resources in different ways) and use those differing resource levels and decisions as a means to compete with each other. Some institutions will inevitably provide their users with more or superior information services than other institutions, in order to attract better faculty, students, and funding support. If that is to happen, private regions will be unavoidable. These regions, however, must still be part of, or directly linked to, the control zone, using the same access protocols, so that the local user will not need to distinguish between private and public regions. One would hope, however, that in the long term, the real arena of competition among institutions could shift from the importation process—that is, what data are made available to local users—to the postimportation process—that is, how such data, once made available, are accessible and manipulable by local users. Let academic institutions compete, in other words, by developing increasingly sophisticated search engines and software; that would be a much more equitable and effective method than the denial of access to the information itself.

CONCLUSIONS

If the optimum information service consists of equal and undifferentiated access to all extant objects of information, then libraries will indeed rapidly become antiquated and superfluous as information becomes increasingly available online. But if the walls that have enclosed libraries for millennia have served not merely to keep the rain off the books but have also responded to an elemental bibliographical and epistemological need, what I have been calling circumscription, then the bounded, systematically selected collection will remain the ultimate and quintessential research instrument. The creation of a single, vast and virtual, digital library along the lines of the control zone would facilitate the coordinated access that libraries have for so long sought in the traditional environment but would retain the structure and function of the bounded collection. As long as the client-user, moreover, continues to have access to the open zone, and as long as libraries do not fall into the trap of imagining that providing access to that open zone is somehow their responsibility, then the library will succeed in transferring its fundamental service functions into the electronic environment—despite the current network user community's general aversion to control in any form. There is, in any event, little alternative. Either the academic library community agrees on its core contributions, and then takes whatever steps are necessary to ensure that it is able to continue to make such contributions in online circumstances, or the academic library needs to accept and resign itself to the fact that it is primarily a product of a waning information environment and should neither expect nor prepare to continue to play a major role in higher education and scholarly information exchange.

REFERENCE NOTES

1. Two recent and well-reasoned overviews of the probable components of the digital library have been written by Shaw and Graham: Debora Shaw, "Libraries of the Future: Glimpses of a Networked, Distributed, Collaborative, Hyper, Virtual World," *Libri* 44 (Sept. 1994): 206–23; Peter Graham, "Requirements for the Digital Research Library," *College & Research Libraries* 56 (July 1995): 331–39. For a literature review of publications relating to the digital library, see Karen M. Drabenstott, *Analytical Review of the Library of the Future* (Washington, D.C.: Council on Library Resources, 1994).

2. Taemin Kim Park, "The Nature of Relevance in Information Retrieval: An Empirical Study," *Library Quarterly* 63 (July 1993): 318–51.

3. I have previously referred to this syndrome as the "utility loop": Ross Atkinson, "Access, Ownership and the Future of Collection Development," in *Collection Management and Development: Issues in an Electronic Era*, eds. Peggy Johnson and Bonnie MacEwan (Chicago: ALA, 1994), 96.

4. For an extended philosophical discussion of the relationship between technology and the work it does, see Ihde's treatise, especially chapters two through four, on the "phenomenology of instrumentation." Don Ihde, *Technics and Praxis,* Synthese Library, vol. 130 (Dordrecht: Reidel, 1979).

5. For some original ideas on the relationships between the concept of the book and that of the library, see Chartier's investigation of the term *bibliotheque.* Roger Chartier, *The Order of Books,* trans. Lydia G. Cochrane (Stanford, Calif.: Stanford Univ. Pr., 1994). The same translation of the pertinent chapter, "Libraries without Walls," will be found in *Representations* 42 (spring 1993): 38–52.

6. For a discussion of the standard ethical issues relation to selection, see Robert Hauptmann, *Ethical Challenges in Librarianship* (Phoenix, Ariz.: Oryx, 1988), 23–25 and 67–70.

7. Jose Ortega y Gasset, "The Mission of the Librarian," trans. James Lewis and Roy Carpenter, *Antioch Review* 21 (summer 1961): 133–54. The original paper, which was presented in 1934 at a conference in Paris, appeared as "Mission du Bibliothecaire," *Archives et Bibliothkque* 1 (1935): 65–86.

8. Lester Asheim, "Ortega Revisited," *Library Quarterly* 52 (July 1983): 215–26.

9. Jorge F. Sosa and Michael H. Harris, "Jose Ortega y Gasset and the Role of the Librarian in Post-Industrial America," *Libri* 41 (March 1991): 3–21.

10. Richard A. Lanham, *The Electronic Word: Democracy, Technology, and the Arts* (Chicago: Univ. of Chicago Pr., 1993), 227–57.

11. The resourceful user can, after all, always search the broader universe also and make, in effect, his or her own selection decisions—and it is indeed one responsibility of the library to provide such a side door to that universe, which in the traditional library is a primary purpose of interlibrary loan.

12. Ross Atkinson, "The Acquisitions Librarian as Change Agent in the Transition to the Electronic Library," *Library Resources & Technical Services* 36 (Jan. 1992): 7–20 and "Access, Ownership and the Future of Collection Development," in *Collection Management and Development.*

13. The fact that disintermediation is a special form of mediation is perhaps what has led to the optimistic view that, as "we disintermediate information transactions, the idea of [and presumably the need for] the information intermediary, paradoxically enough, expands." Philip Doty and Ann P. Bishop, "The National Information Infrastructure and Electronic Publishing: A Reflective Essay," *Journal of the American Society of Information Science* 45 (Dec. 1994): 785–99.

14. The best summary of the current situation remains Anthony Cummings et al., *University Libraries and Scholarly Communication,* (Washington, D.C.: Association of Research Libraries, 1992), especially pt. 1. The most important effort to combat these conditions to date is certainly the joint work of the Association of American Universities and the Association of Research Libraries *Reports of the AAU Task Forces on Acquisition and Distribution of Foreign Language and Area Studies Materials: A National Strategy for Managing Scientific and Technological Information, Intellectual Property Rights in an Electronic Environment* (Washington, D.C.: Association of Research Libraries, 1994). These reports are currently also accessible at http://arl.cni.org/aau/Frontmatter.html. For more detailed discussions, see the electronic *Newsletter on Serials Pricing Issues,* back issues of which are archived at www.library.uwa.edu.au/libweb/sers/serprice.html.

15. Hierarchies are clearest and probably most relevant among scholarly journals. For a review of methods used in establishing such hierarchies, see Ralph Weisheit and Robert Regoli, "Ranking Journals," *Scholarly Publishing* 18 (July 1984): 313–25. The extent to which articles in a journal are cited has, of course, much to do with the journal's perceived place in the hierarchy. For the sciences, annual citation frequencies are provided by the Institute for Scientific Information in their journal impact" reports. *Science Citation Index Journal Citation Reports* (Philadelphia: Institute for Scientific Information, 1989).

16. Martha Kyrillidou and Kendon Stubbs, "Introduction," in *ARL Statistics, 1993–94,* eds. Martha Kyrillidou, Kaylyn E. Hipps, and Kendon Stubbs (Washington, D.C.: Association of Research Libraries, 1995), 5–13. The ARL statistics, with other applicable documentation can currently also be found at http://viva.lib.virginia.edu:80/arlstats.

17. David M. Levy, and Catherine C. Marshall, "Going Digital: A Look at Assumptions Underlying Digital Libraries," *Communications of the ACM* 58 (April 1995): 77–83.

18. To be sure, all information on the network—most electronic information generally—is divided into files and databases, which have some parallels to discrete library collections, but the tendency, culture, and objective of the network is, in a sense, to ignore just such divisions or to view them at most as inconveniences to be overcome technically whenever possible. That is perhaps one of the primary considerations of the Networked Information Delivery and Retrieval (NIDR) project of the Coalition for Networked Information. Because the work of this group is at this time still underway, it is risky and improper to draw conclusions about the group's purpose, but it does appear that such work presumes that network users want to view the entire content of the network as a kind of single, giant, digital library, the complete content of which can be ideally searched simultaneously. The authors of the NIDR report also clearly acknowledge and understand, however, the threat of massive information overload, so that balancing those two potentially contradictory concepts is perhaps one core challenge to that project: on the one hand, everyone seems to want to see everything, and on the other, there is far too much for anyone to see. At the time of the writing of this article, the draft of the first chapter of the NIDR report is available by ftp from ftp.cni.org/CNI/projects/NIDR.

19. L. Costers, building on the experience of Dutch research libraries, has come to somewhat similar conclusions. He describes a three-layered digital library structure: the first layer consists of objects the particular library maintains itself, the second layer refers to objects maintained by cooperative partners, and the third layer is viewed to be the uncontrolled network at large. L. Costers, "The Electronic Library and Its Organizational Management," *Libri* 44 (Dec. 1994): 317.

20. Some projects are already underway to create a digital library by amalgamating the digital work of several libraries. One of the broadest of these is the National Digital Library Federation (NDLF), a consortium now being hosted by the Commission on Preservation and Access. This group will develop different digital collections on aspects of U.S. history, which are intended ultimately to fit together into a single, linked, distributed collection. The hope is that such linkages created by the NDLF will eventually be used by other groups and enterprises to create a growing library of digital materials. Guy Lamolinara, "A New Federation," *Library of Congress Information Bulletin* 54 (June 12, 1995): 251.

21. Since my writing of this article, the Association of Research has published a discussion on electronic publishing that took place on the Internet, in which some similar ideas were presented. See especially Stevan Harnad's emphasis on the distinction between specialized (which he calls "esoteric") publishing and more general publications. Ann Shumelda Okerson and James J. O'Donnell, eds., *Scholarly Journals at the Crossroads: A Subversive Proposal for Electronic Publishing* (Washington, D.C.: Association of Research Libraries, 1995), 11 and 26.

22. The alternative view is that journals will simply shift online and that the hierarchies now in place will remain. This would appear to be an earlier position taken by Stevan Harnad, "Implementing Peer Review on the Net: Scientific Quality Control in Scholarly Electronic Journals," in *Proceedings of the 1993 International Conference on Refereed Electronic Journals* (Winnipeg: Univ. of Manitoba Libraries, 1994), 8.1–8.14. Needless to say, that would leave intact most of the problematic economic and cultural relationships that obtain in the paper environment and is something very different from the idea of a control zone.

23. A paper titled "Preserving Digital Information," written by the Task Force on Digital Archiving of the Commission on Preservation and Access and the Research Libraries Group, distinguishes between "digital libraries" and "digital archives" and proposes a "national archival system"—which does bear some resemblance to aspects of the proposed control zone. An initial draft of this paper is presently (Sept. 1995) available at www.rlg.stanford.edu/ArchTF/Draft-Report.

24. Peter S. Graham, "Electronic Information and Research Library Technical Services," *College & Research Libraries* 51 (May 1990): 241–50; Peter S. Graham, *Intellectual Preservation: Electronic Preservation of the Third Kind* (Washington, D.C.: Commission on Preservation and Access, 1994).

8 HUMANITIES SCHOLARSHIP AND THE RESEARCH LIBRARY

The purpose of this article is to provide a simple definition of humanities scholarship from the library perspective, and then to comment on the ability of the research library to support such scholarship. There is no aspiration to present a developed theory or argument; rather the intention is only to draw attention to some current issues and relationships that might warrant further discussion.

To what extent will research libraries remain able to support humanities scholarship in the immediate future? In order to answer this question, we need first a quick definition of humanities scholarship from the library perspective.[1] Because it is the function of the library to provide access to that information needed by local users to do their work, and because the primary unit of information (at least from the library's point of view) is the publication, we should look to the publication as a form for our definition.

Let us consider, therefore, scholarly publications, of the type produced by the faculty users of research libraries; one can draw a single, simple distinction in such publications between (a) reference and (b) citation. Reference is what the publication "does," i.e., the verbal pointing to concepts; the referent is what the text is "about":

> Traditionally, the term reference designates the relation oriented from a semiotic entity toward a non-semiotic entity (the referent) belonging, for instance, to the extra-linguistic context.[2]

Citation, on the other hand, is a very specialized form of reference: it is a verbal pointer to another publication—or, pushing that concept a bit further, let us say it is a pointer to another symbolic artifact, i.e., to another human product intended to convey information.

Applying this simple distinction between the general reference and the specific citation, let us divide all scholarly publication into two gigantic sets. The first set, which we will call scientific publication, consists of documents in which the references and the citations are to two different object categories: the reference is to some physical or social ("extra-linguistic") reality or phenomenon, while the citation is to documentation (which, no doubt, refers in turn to that same physical or social reality). The author intends that the work cited be looked "through"—to the physical or social reality to which it refers. The other huge set of scholarly publications, which we will call humanities publication, consists of materials in which the primary reference is, very generally speaking, to the citation; or more exactly, the reference and the citation are to fundamentally the same category of objects, i.e., to particular symbolic artifacts. The objective of the publication is to look not only "through" the texts cited (i.e., what they refer to), but also, and more importantly, "at" them. (On the dichotomy of "through" and "at," see Lanham.[3]) As librarians, then, let us define the humanities as that scholarship, the constituent docu-

This article first appeared in *Library Resources & Technical Services* 39, no. 1 (1995): 79–84. It is derived from a presentation made at a program of the Library Research Round Table on the topic of "The Humanistic Research Perspective in a Technological Age," held at the ALA Annual Conference, June 25, 1994.

mentation of which is characterized by a general coincidence of the reference and the citation, while the sciences (both natural and behavioral) are those forms of scholarship producing documentation that exhibits a difference or disparity or dissonance between the reference and the citation.

Having made this simple distinction, what can we say briefly about humanities scholarship—and the ability of research libraries to support it?

AUTHORITY

A citation refers to an artifact produced or created by someone—and it is at least partially upon the relationship between the artifact and the individual who produced it that the identification, description, and evaluation of the artifact in humanities scholarship is based. Scholarship characterized by the coincidence of the reference and the citation is therefore greatly concerned with, and highly dependent upon, bibliographical authority. How individual works relate to each other, how they relate to their authors—who wrote (or created) what, and who wrote what else—these are issues that are central to all humanities scholarship.

One of the most difficult—and certainly one of the most expensive—services provided by the modern research library is appropriately authority control, the primary result of which is the production of catalogs that do not simply list holdings, but rather consciously and painstakingly establish relationships among those holdings. The main beneficiary of such work in research libraries is humanities scholarship.[4] (A recent study has revealed that fully half of the subject search terms used by a test group of humanities scholars referred to individuals or characters.[5] Authority control has come to be recognized as a cornerstone of information services, and the need to maintain or increase it, even in (or especially in) times of declining technical services budgets, is becoming broadly accepted by research libraries.

There can be little doubt that the research library will fight hard, therefore, to continue to provide authority control, even though few scholars or institutional administrators (or librarians) understand much about it. More problematic, however, is the fact that we can expect a similar lack of understanding about the nature and importance of authority control on the part of many of the technicians who are now designing some of our online services. Network designers, many of whom have been nourished primarily on a diet of scientific publication, may well assume that, for example, the automatic indexing of full text databases will provide sufficient access for future scholarship. Those of us responsible for library technical services understand that authority work of some kind must be done to information prior to its permanent insertion into the database, if its relationship to other items in that database is to be effectively established. Without that preliminary work, no amount of automatic indexing will track or identify that relationship with any precision. In the interests especially of humanities scholarship, therefore, libraries must persist in their demands that the process of authority control be transferred to the online environment. (Peter Graham, in a presentation to the Cornell University Library on 16 March 1994, noted that authority control maybe one of the major contributions libraries will make to the design of network services.)

Another aspect of bibliographical authority, in which the library must be willing to play an increasing role, is authentication: determining that the work made available to the reader matches as closely as possible the text originally intended by the author. This is an old responsibility of libraries, extending back to antiquity, and one that must now be revitalized. In the online era, changes can be made to works with a few keystrokes; the research library must be prepared to archive materials in an (as nearly as can be determined) authoritative form, therefore, so that users will always have access to a stable and authentic text.[6]

NEUTRALITY

Scholarship in which the reference and the citation are to the same objects, i.e., to symbolic artifacts, is driven by a multiplicity of perspectives and motives. Such scholarship is indeed humanistic—in the sense that it respects and encourages individuality and diversity. No single system of norms governs either how the signs, of which symbolic artifacts are composed, are interpreted and evaluated by the scholar, or which artifacts are selected by the scholar for such interpretation and evaluation. In this sense, then, Thomas Kuhn's assertion is valid: the sciences operate generally under the aegis of a single paradigm, while nonscientific scholarship does not.[7] There is no "normal humanities" equivalent to "normal science": there is no single world view, no universally accepted network of truths that all humanists are working to illuminate and validate. Humanities scholarship assigns different values or qualities to different symbolic artifacts, and much of the work of the humanities consists of defining and redefining those values and qualities. There is no real linear progress. We probably do not really know "more" about Shakespeare's works—in the same way that we know more about, say, DNA—than we knew twenty years ago. What Shakespeare scholarship has provided us that we did not have twenty years ago are new perspectives more consistent with current values and sensibilities from which to assess the quality and wisdom of Shakespeare's works.

The humanities, therefore, while admittedly operating within certain parameters established by tradition and fashion, nevertheless generally subscribe to a kind of methodological neutrality, in which a plurality of values can be used to evaluate symbolic artifacts. The research library, at least in recent decades, has done much to support this neutrality. Perhaps the most important step in this process has been the transfer of collection building responsibility from the faculty to the library: this has led to the development of collections that reflect a range of methods, rather than only those used or favored by the faculty currently active at the institution. As the purchasing power of our budgets diminishes, however, and we shift more to user-driven collection building, we must expect our ability to provide this representation of multiple perspectives gradually to decline. It remains to be seen, moreover, whether the advent of electronic, networked publication will provide new opportunities for the publication of, and access to, a diversity of perspectives.

While research libraries have (so far) managed to respond to the methodological neutrality of the humanities, another kind of neutrality—let us call it object neutrality—is much more problematic. By object neutrality I mean the increasing acceptance among humanities scholars that any consciously created human product, any symbolic artifact, is an acceptable object of study. Partially a manifestation of the retreat from the canon, this inability and unwillingness on the part of some humanities scholars—perhaps an increasing majority of them—to agree upon privileging a specific set of publications has led to the general position that virtually every symbolic creation must be considered equally worthy of study.[8] Because any publication or human creation can have research potential, humanities scholars—and the information service professionals who support them—have become increasingly unwilling and incapable of coming to terms with what should be collected and maintained, and what should not.

This would be less of a problem if the humanities, like the sciences, were capable of endorsing the withdrawal of older secondary materials; or if the humanities were able to summarize effectively earlier publications. But the humanities can do neither. Older secondary materials cannot be discarded because, as we know so well in research libraries, the second a critical work is no longer in fashion, it becomes as valuable—or more valuable—as a primary work, to be used in the study of the history of the field. For this reason alone, history remains probably the most expensive "subject" the library supports—probably much more expensive in the long term than the notoriously costly natural sciences.

Summary is also alien to much humanities scholarship.[9] Unlike the sciences, which are able to summarize their findings in textbooks so that the original publications need no longer be regularly consulted, the humanities generally scorn synopsis. This is, again, an understandable quality of a scholarship characterized by the coincidence of reference and citation, and because of the need of the humanities to look "at," rather than only "through" the text. The focus of the humanities is not upon what the text refers to. (That is more the objective of the sciences, which is the reason the sciences are at ease with summary.) The focus of humanities scholarship is rather upon the text referring—how the text refers, and what must be done to make the text refer. Each scholar, each student, each generation of humanists assumes anew the responsibility for this "working" of the text, to demonstrate its reference repeatedly—and the result of such scholarship is to create variant references over time, that reflect in turn the variant values of the humanities scholars and their times. In order for such work to be done, therefore, the full, authorized text must be maintained in a stable form indefinitely.

Fair enough. Research libraries can and do meticulously provide that essential archival service—but this obviously cannot be done for every text ever produced. Because summary is not an option, relatively stringent selection is unavoidable; but the humanities, mainly by virtue of their methodological and object neutrality, are seldom able to supply a broadly accepted, coherent scale of values upon which to base such selection. This is, of course, especially critical for preservation selection, which, like authentication, is an ancient function of libraries that is becoming ever more vital to scholarship. Selection (what to acquire initially, and what to retain) has always been a fundamental service of libraries—and all of our new and sophisticated information technology does not now, nor will it ever, relieve us of that responsibility. Certainly digitization opens many opportunities for us to preserve more materials and to enhance access, but even digitization provides us with neither the right nor probably even the capacity to assemble and retain everything. The undisciplined, unsystematic collection and retention of materials will necessarily result in a bibliographical congestion that will ultimately retard some branches of humanities scholarship.[10] The desperate urge to hoard and safeguard every graphic utterance because we cannot predict with any precision its future utility must be resisted. The jettisoning of information—disciplinary "forgetting"—must therefore be not only accepted, but endorsed and systematized by humanities scholarship—if for no other reason than we will necessarily lose large quantities of information in the future regardless of what we do. Even if it becomes technically possible some day to retain every human utterance, such a practice will doubtless never be economically justifiable, even if every research library in the country cooperated in the effort. That being the case, the only question remaining is whether we want to sit back and observe the haphazard retention and loss of humanities information, or whether we are willing to make decisions and take control of what future humanities scholars receive from the past.

DERIVATION

Scholarship characterized by the coincidence of the reference and the citation is not highly valued by society—or at least not nearly to the degree that society values either the products of the sciences or even the creative works that serve as the objects of the humanities. Humanities scholarship is not practiced to any extent outside of the academy. This is essential and understandable in a preponderantly capitalist society which views all serious activity from the perspective of the marketplace. While the educational commodity of the humanities (i.e., classroom instruction) remains accepted and valued, advanced humanities scholarship presents a much more difficult marketing challenge. Formal publication is troublesome for humanities scholarship, because the direct market demand for such scholarship is no doubt often insufficient to support the costs of production.

How then is specialized humanities publication possible? A major and indispensable role in this process is played, of course, by the university press—but even the (sometimes) subsidized university press cannot publish scholarship in a totally market-driven economy when there is insufficient demand. Here is where research libraries enter the equation: it has been and will continue to be a primary responsibility of research libraries to serve as an artificial market for humanities scholarship. When a university (or major society) press through its editorial process decides to publish a work of humanities scholarship, the press can count on the fact that most research libraries will purchase that work, regardless of its content. The library will make this decision, not because of a demonstrable demand, but rather because the library is expected by convention to hold precisely this material. The difficulty mentioned earlier of predicting future utility works in this case very much to the advantage of humanities scholarship. If the library could accurately forecast use, and knew for certain that an item would never be used, then probably no such purchase would take place—but the library has no such ability. It is also well understood that the library will sometimes effectively create user demand for materials by adding those materials to the collection.

One reason society may place a low value on the humanities is that scholarship characterized by the coincidence of reference and citation is conspicuously derivative. The humanities always speaks of things already spoken; it says things about things already said:

> More often than not, really important scholarship in the humanities does not consist in the discovery of something entirely new but in presenting what is already there in a pattern of higher significance, so that the "map of knowledge" is substantially changed.[11]

This periodically frustrates the humanities; it causes feelings of inferiority, which sometimes precipitate efforts to escape this curse of derivation by trying to replace the object studied with the study itself. Some of these efforts, notably some of the recent work in literary theory, have tended to alienate society at large still further from humanities scholarship.

While such a concern over derivation is understandable, it is also ultimately unwarranted. Humanities scholarship, even in its most advanced form, always has a direct pedagogical or didactic function; the inseparable link between the humanities and the academy, therefore, makes complete sense. The purpose of the humanities remains to help people understand and apply symbolic artifacts. In ways very different from the sciences, therefore, the humanities are a true service, and the humanities scholar is always, necessarily a public servant.

Which leads to my final point: What is bibliography—what are library and information services—if not reference to the citation? Libraries, all libraries, do humanities work. This work is admittedly in some of its forms at a rather more rudimentary level, to be sure, than that performed by humanities scholars; but the difference between the work of a librarian, who maneuvers a user into a position to work with a particular set of publications, and the work of a humanities scholar, who writes an essay on those publications so that readers can better understand them—that is a difference of level or sophistication, but it is not a difference of kind. They are the same fundamental public services.

The future of the humanities and of research librarianship should therefore necessarily lie in the direction of much greater coordination and ultimately fusion. As we enter the age of information, humanists need to learn more about the discipline of bibliography—the study of the record. And librarians need to learn more about the rich theoretical work of the humanities and its application to bibliography, instead of trying vainly to pattern so much of their work on that of the (social) sciences.

In a way, therefore, the question posed at the outset—about the extent to which the research library will continue to be able to support the humanities—is an unnecessary one. The library is the humanities, or at least an integral component thereof. The humanities will not rise or fall because of library support; rather the fortunes of the humanities and the library are so inextricably interconnected that their future is fundamentally one.

And this includes, I hasten to add, all aspects of librarianship—including especially science librarianship. The physics librarian is not a physicist; she is, without question, a humanist. Her object is not physical reality but rather the citation. The physics scholars at her institution depend upon her as a humanist. The sciences depend upon the humanities, without which the communication of scientific scholarship cannot take place. Society depends upon the humanities, because all real progress, all communal enterprise, rests ultimately upon the maintenance, understanding, and application of the record, of the symbolic artifact. That is indeed the indispensable public service that the humanities, in all of its guises—including especially the bibliographical one—will continue to provide, regardless of any changes that may occur in information technology.

REFERENCE NOTES

1. On previous definitions, see pp. 293–94. Sue Stone, "Humanities Scholars: Information Needs and Uses," *Journal of Documentation* 38 (1982): 292–313.

2. A. J. Greimas and J. Courtes, *Semiotics and Language: An Analytical Dictionary,* trans. Larry Crist et al. (Bloomington, Ind.: Indiana Univ. Pr., 1982), 259.

3. Richard A. Lanham, *The Electronic Word: Democracy, Technology, and the Arts* (Chicago: Univ. of Chicago Pr., 1993).

4. Steven E. Wiberley Jr., "Subject Access in the Humanities and the Precision of the Humanist's Vocabulary," *Library Quarterly* 53 (1983): 420–33.

5. Marcia J. Bates, Deborah N. Wilde, and Susan Siegfried, "An Analysis of Search Terminology Used by Humanities Scholars: The Getty Online Searching Project Report no. 1," *Library Quarterly* 63 (1993): 1–39.

6. Ross Atkinson, "Text Mutability and Collection Administration," *Library Acquisitions: Practice & Theory* 14 (1990): 355–58.

7. Note expecially the remarks in the postscript, pp. 208–209. Thomas S. Kuhn, *The Structure of Scientific Revolutions,* 2d ed. (Chicago: Univ. of Chicago Pr., 1970).

8. Mark Cyzyk, "Canon Formation, Library Collections, and the Dilemma of Collection Development," *College & Research Libraries* 54 (1993): 58–65; Peter Shaw, "The Assault on the Canon," *Sewanee Review* 102 (1993): 257–70.

9. James H. Sweetland, "Humanists, Libraries, Electronic Publishing, and the Future," *Library Trends* 40 (1992): 781–803.

10. On the problem of overabundance of scholarly information, see Charles Perrow, "On Not Using Libraries," in *Humanists at Work: Papers Presented at a Symposium Held at The University of Illinois at Chicago on April 27–28, 1989* (Chicago: Univ. of Illinois at Chicago, 1989), 29–42 and Karl J. Weintraub, "The Humanistic Scholar and the Library," *Library Quarterly* 50 (1980): 22–39.

11. Bernhard Fabian, *The Future of Humanistic Scholarship* (Washington, D.C.: Library of Congress, 1990), 19.

9 ACCESS, OWNERSHIP, AND THE FUTURE OF COLLECTION DEVELOPMENT

Jerry Campbell has recently argued that the academic library must make survival its primary goal. "We have to understand that the only thing that must be saved is our future. We must be willing to turn loose, to let go of everything that belongs to the past. Perhaps we will not have to let go of everything, but we must be willing to do so if necessary."[1] This is, to my mind, a questionable strategy. The primary goal of the library must be not survival but information services. Study the changing information needs of the academic community, design services that will meet those needs more effectively than services offered by other agencies inside or outside of academe, and survival will take care of itself. That is the only practicable and responsible strategy to follow.

At the same time, however, it must be admitted that many academic library functions and values now in place will not survive into the future—nor should they. The longer we try to prop up obsolete processes and philosophies, the more we impede scholarly research, obstruct rather than support higher education, and jeopardize the library's participation in the future evolution of academic information services. While the shift from paper-based to electronic scholarly information exchange doubtless will be gradual and incremental, we must agree with the authors of the recent Mellon study on university libraries and scholarly communication that "it is equally inconceivable that there will not eventually be a more-or-less complete transformation of scholarly communication. The new technologies are too powerful and their advantage too clear for current practices to continue indefinitely."[2] Of all traditional library functions, the future of collection development in this transformation is certainly one of the most problematic. The purpose of this paper is to consider that future within the context of the dichotomy of ownership and access.

I want to establish at the outset three principles or caveats that need to be borne in mind as we approach this topic. The first is that traditional divisions of library operations not only are changing but also are blending into each other, primarily as a result of innovations in information technology. It is not possible, therefore, to discuss the future character and evolution of any single operation, including especially collection development, in isolation from other library operations. The future of collection development can be understood and planned, therefore, only within the total context of academic information services. If we are to consider the nature of collection development functions in an increasingly online environment, that consideration necessarily must include some assessment of other library functions—especially reference and cataloging.

The second principle to which we must adhere in discussing the shift away from ownership as the primary form of access is that we must try to devote as much attention as possible to the process of the transition itself. Where we are going, I think, becomes clearer every day. How we are going to get there, on the other hand, remains in many ways obscure. What we require is not simply discussion about the differences between an

This article first appeared in *Virtually Yours: Models for Managing Electronic Resources and Services,* eds. Peggy Johnson and Bonnie MacEwan (Chicago: ALA, 1999) 92–109.

information environment consisting primarily of paper and one depending mainly upon computer-mediated communication, but also some consideration of the administrative, operational, and political adjustments that will be needed, if the library is to undertake the transition from one environment to the other successfully. We are now in the midst of what may be the most difficult period of this transition, when the changes that will result from the eventual prevalence of online information are evident, but when nearly all of the information our user communities routinely require and use remains in paper form. This entire transition is further complicated by the indisputable fact that scholars working in different disciplines, or in different areas within individual disciplines, or in different institutions, or in different countries, will experience the shift in their information requirements from paper to electronic form at very different rates.[3] We will need to consider, in the course of this article, how this variation will affect the future development of academic information services.

The third principle we need to bear in mind in approaching this topic is that it is unavoidably abstract. This is because the only effective prospect we have for planning the transition of information services is to generalize upon individual operations that are performed in the paper environment, and then to attempt to apply those generalizations to what we imagine will be the conditions and needs in an environment characterized increasingly or primarily by online information sources. Only in this way can we compare services presently provided with services potentially needed under radically different circumstances, and begin to plan for the necessary adjustments to carry out the transition.

MEDIATION AND DELIVERY

I have argued previously that information services in the online environment should be considered in terms of the dichotomy of mediation and delivery.[4] I continue to feel this to be the most reasonable and practicable model. I do not mean to imply, however, that I think we will or should divide all information services administratively into those two basic categories eventually, although that may be an option. Rather I suggest it is helpful to use this fundamental division between delivery and mediation as a basis for planning at this time. The purpose of delivery is to transport information units—e.g., books, articles, electronic files, and datasets—across space; this is a function that is performed specifically without respect to the content of such information units. The object of delivery is, therefore, the effective transportation or transmission of packages or signals rather than the consideration or evaluation of their information content. In the paper environment, delivery includes such functions as acquisitions, circulation, interlibrary loan, preservation, and many current computing operations. I have made some suggestions elsewhere about delivery and about the critical role acquisitions might play in the future of delivery services.[5] I now want to concentrate on mediation services, which in the paper environment consist mainly of collection development, cataloging, and reference.[6] The primary function of mediation services is to add value to individual information units in support of local (educational and research) objectives by distinguishing or differentiating in some way the content of those units from each other.[7]

COLLECTION DEVELOPMENT AS MEDIATION SERVICE

The most fundamental purpose of all information services—both mediation and delivery—always has been and always will be access. The quality of access—how well access is provided or achieved—is best understood or defined in terms of time, so that the objective of information services always is ultimately access time reduction. Access time always is at least partially a function of space. Because the transportation of paper publications requires considerable time, value can be added to paper publications (i.e., their utility can be enhanced) by increasing their proximity to the potential user. The purpose of collection development in the paper environment, therefore, is to gauge the current and future information needs of local users, to determine which publications resident in the environment best would meet those needs, and then to ensure, by installing those publications in close proximity to local users, that less time is needed by those users to gain access to those more needed publications. This goal of proximity is achieved mainly through ownership—the library buys the publication to reduce the space between the user and the medium of information. The library obviously usually does not own the information; instead, the library owns the paper medium and the right of local users to use that medium to gain access to the information.

The Service Sequence

Library operations are conditioned, and at least partially defined and regulated, by their location in the service sequence. In the paper environment, the library service sequence is divided into three mediation-delivery phases:

Mediation	*Delivery*
1. selection	acquisition
2. cataloging	storage/preservation
3. reference	circulation/ILL

In each phase, the objective or fulfillment of the mediation function is—from a process perspective—the subsequent delivery function. There are, of course, many variations on this sequence. In the case of reference, for example, the user can obtain direct (human) assistance from a reference librarian; or, more often, the user can do his or her own reference work, using the reference tools made available by the various mediation services. It is also important at this point to distinguish between selection, which is a standard information service activity, and collection development. For the purposes of this paper, we can define collection development as that administratively separate library operation that coordinates the selection effort throughout the library system, formulates selection policy, and regulates the relationship of collection building and maintenance to other library operations.[8]

The location of an operation in the service sequence determines whether we consider the operation an input or output function.[9] The stored collection forms the center of the sequence; any function preceding storage counts as input, and any following counts as output. (Whether storage itself is input or output—to which library function the stacks "belong"—is often a matter of some confusion and dispute.) Mediation, of course, is intended to link particular (local) users with specific information (i.e., readers to writers). The three mediation services (collection development, cataloging, reference) relate differently to the users on the one hand, and to the universe of publication on the other. The user enters the sequence directly only in the third mediation delivery phase, the preparation of that entry being the purpose of the first two phases. The extent to which access is provided successfully is visible (to the extent it is at all) only in the third phase when the user actually makes use of available information units. The final delivery phase, circulation, not only validates the entire previous process but also serves, at least theoretically, as the basis for the continuation of the process, because mediation services attempt to anticipate and provide for future needs by analyzing past use.

The major logical limitation in this process, however, is what we might label the utility loop. The point of mediation services is to add value to selected items by making them more easily (which always means more quickly) accessible. This adding of value increases utility, on the assumption that such increased utility is justified for the particular items selected. Selection and use are, therefore, mutually conditioning. Every selector recognizes this, although perhaps not necessarily in these terms. Every selector understands that there is always some potential to make an item useful that otherwise would not be used by adding value to it, i.e., by reducing the amount of time required to gain access to it—by adding it to the collection. This means that while it is possible for collection development to rank documents in relation to each other with respect to their potential utility, it is not normally possible to separate the useful from the useless, because utility is at least partially created by information services. This is the reason that collection development cannot easily comprehend uselessness as a category. And it is this inability that contributes in turn to the universal drive for comprehensiveness, a topic to which we will return shortly.

The library service sequence is only part of the full information service sequence: the writing and publication sequence precedes the library service sequence. Since selection stands at the front of the library sequence, it is preceded by functions external to the library. The function immediately preceding selection is, I would stipulate, description.[10] The citation, as well as supplementary information, must be made available by the publisher in order for selection to be done. Such description is a significant part of the writing and publishing process. In the paper environment selection operates sequentially between—and is necessarily conditioned and regulated by—description, on the one hand, and acquisition on the other.

BIFURCATION

Because ownership in the paper environment is by far the most effective method of providing access, collection development perceives the universe of publication as bifurcated into the local collection and what we might call the *anti-collection*, i.e., the set of all publications not held in the local collection. Selection is, therefore, to a great extent, a continuous series of decisions about which items in the anti-collection should be moved into the collection. Once the decision is made to move an information unit from the anti-collection to the collection, that unit ceases to be of concern to collection development. The local collection itself is of interest to collection development mainly as a source of patterns or criteria or needs (lacunae) upon which to base future decisions about what should be moved out of the anti-collection.

In recognition of this preoccupation with the anti-collection, some effort was made several years ago to create the field of collection management. A central purpose of this effort was to draw attention back to the local collection already in place to ensure that collection development staff would have some understanding of—and would provide some input into decisions on—collection maintenance (including especially preservation) and use.[11] That effort has been in my experience only mildly successful. Collection development today remains focused primarily on the continuously evolving anti-collection. Failure to establish large-scale cooperative collection development programs is due partially to this same syndrome: items held in other collections are viewed as belonging to the anti-collection. Value is, to be sure, added to those publications held in collections with which the non-owning library has a cooperative collection agreement—in the sense that access time for those publications may be less than it would be were no such agreement in place. This is not, however, the value that collection development understands itself as being responsible for adding, i.e., proximity of the information unit to the local user is not increased. Proximity in the paper environment can be achieved only through ownership.

For purposes of this discussion, let us divide the selection or collection building process into three phases: first, discovering or defining the anti-collection; second, ranking the content of (some segment of) the anti collection; and, third, the actual selecting (the selection decision "proper.") The selector repeats the entire process, all three phases, continuously. The selector first discovers or defines a segment of the anti-collection represented primarily by citations in that subject for which he or she is responsible. It is always clearly understood that this is only a segment, and that the anti-collection is in a process of continuous evolution—both objectively as new publications are added or deleted, and subjectively as the selector's perception of the anti-collection (and the utility of its content) adjusts. After defining a segment, the selector reviews the citations that compose it. He or she may then rank these first with general categories but ultimately uses a single continuum of potential utility for current and future local users.

The third phase is the selection decision proper, in which the selector proceeds to select items on the continuum, beginning at the top with the items of highest potential use and proceeding downward in the direction of less potential use.[12] The selector stops selecting and starts rejecting at a point on the continuum we can call the *line of acceptance*. At this point resources no longer are available to purchase material on the continuum in addition to materials of equal or greater potential utility that are known or suspected to exist elsewhere in the anti-collection. The process then is repeated on another segment of the anti-collection.

In considering selection from this perspective, we need to bear two points in mind. First, creativity in selection occurs in the ranking on the continuum, not in the selection decision proper. The selection decision proper is relatively simple—indeed, even mechanical because there are only two options: own or don't own (i.e., buy or don't buy). Selection is always a binomial decision because everything above the line of acceptance on the continuum should be purchased and everything below should not be. This is simply an additional manifestation of collection development's fundamental bifurcation of the (paper) information universe into the owned collection and the unowned anti-collection. Selection is very different from the other mediation services/cataloging and reference—that have a range of decision alternatives. Cataloging, for example, has a series of options, ranging from minimal level cataloging (or perhaps even only an acquisitions record) up to the detailed descriptive cataloging usually reserved for rare books. Collection development in the paper environment, therefore, is one of the most wasteful (uneconomical) library operations—performed, because the real creative and professional work of selection, i.e., the evaluative ranking of information items on the continuum, is lost as soon as the selection is made, resulting only in the mechanical decision of own-don't own. Even though the selector has already ranked materials for his or her purposes, those same materials often will be ranked and reranked by other local mediation services subsequent to acquisition.

The second point we need to bear in mind is that the placement of the line of acceptance on the continuum (separating owned from not owned) is primarily an economic decision driven by the individual selector's perception of available library or institutional resources. While those resources may include such capacities as staff time and shelf space, the primary resource influencing the selection decision is the materials budget—or at least that portion of the budget controlled by the selector. It is only the lack or scarcity of resources that forces the placement of any line of acceptance at all. Under most circumstances, I am convinced, every library would opt to own everything ever published in its subject areas of responsibility were resources available to do so. Why? One reason, as already noted, is that utility is at least partially created (the utility loop), and access to all publications in a paper environment therefore can be justifiably improved through ownership.[13] Another reason is because it is the ultimate goal and aspiration of probably every information service agency to provide comprehensive access in those areas of knowledge for which the agency is responsible. Since ownership in the paper environment is the most effective form of access, every library will aspire to comprehensive ownership in its subject areas and is prevented only by inadequate resources from achieving that aspiration.

Like many—perhaps most—service professions, collection development is, in a manner of speaking, suicidal, because its primary objective is to eliminate its own purpose for being. If comprehensiveness, the ultimate (albeit unspoken and fashionably denied) goal of collection development were possible, then collection development would become superfluous. Ranking of publications on the continuum, which is the true professional work of collection development, no longer would be necessary, because there would be no need for a line of acceptance. Individual information units no longer would need to be differentiated by the nature of their content, and the work of collection building would belong not to mediation but to delivery. The position could even be taken that the collection under such circumstances would cease to exist, because the collection is understandable only in terms of the bifurcation between the owned and not owned, between the collection and the anti-collection. In a condition of comprehensive ownership, the anti-collection, and therefore the collection, no longer exists. Inadequate resources are a precondition for collection development, because without inadequate resources, there would be no rationale for selection—no own-don't own bifurcation.

THE ONLINE ENVIRONMENT

It is impossible to determine with any precision how the availability of increasing quantities of information online ultimately will affect information services in general or collection development in particular. Nevertheless we must have the courage to project and speculate. Let us assume, for purposes of discussion, that some kind of mediation services will remain necessary in an online environment. The mere availability of enhanced delivery services, in other words, alone will not suffice, and some value will need, therefore, to be added to individual information units to ensure effective access. While access time necessarily remains a function of space, electronic information can be transported across space with such speed that proximity of the information to the user is not necessary prior to the user's decision to read. What changes in the online environment is not the prerequisite of proximity for use (the user and the information obviously always need to be in the same place at the same time for access to be possible—the computer screen must have something on it), but rather the point in time at which delivery services must effect or create that proximity. What changes, in short, is the service sequence. In a primarily online environment, selection need not be aimed at and immediately followed by acquisition. Acquisition in its online form can be deferred until after the user's decision to read.

If we understand selection as that activity that results in acquisition, then it is the user in the online environment who becomes the selector. If, on the other hand, we are prepared to accept that the objective of selection in online circumstances no longer is acquisition, no longer moving information units from the anti-collection to the local collection, then we must ask what is it? Presumably the purpose of selection will be to continue to engage in activities similar to the first two steps in the paper selection process defined above, namely discovery and utility ranking. The main difference is that the third step, the own-don't own (buy-don't buy) selection decision proper that triggers acquisition, may well disappear as an information services responsibility. Eliminating the selection decision proper, which in the paper environment would eliminate the library function of collection development entirely, brings about a significant service enhancement in online circumstances. Eliminating the selection decision proper leads to or promotes retaining the results of the ranking process. Loss of ranking-results in the paper environment always has made collection development an uneconomical operation. The selection activity in the online environment may consist, therefore, of a continuous ranking and reranking of the potential utility of information units as they relate to local research and instruction. Such ranking would be adjusted continuously in response to changing local information needs and the changing composition of the universe of publication. Selection as a mediation service in a primarily online environment would be more accurately described as *source assessment* and presumably would consist mainly of tagging or organizing bibliographic records or some other surrogates in a way to recommend use to local users in response to individual needs. The selector would search continuously for or learn of new publications online, would assess these in relation to others already available, and would integrate them into a local ranking of some kind. No line of acceptance would be necessary because the own-don't own decision would be eliminated, although some economic constraints obviously still will be required. If there is an equivalent of a line of acceptance, it presumably will be placed by or for the individual user. Since the selector is no longer spending local funds directly on source acquisition, the drive for comprehensiveness can be indulged, and the user can (at least theoretically) be presented with the full array of relevant publications. From a budgeting perspective, therefore, we may revert to a condition similar to what existed before collection development, in which users authorize local expenditures for acquisitions—a procedure that will return the final responsibility to the user for deciding if access to a particular title justifies its cost. That decision will be influenced heavily by the utility ranking done by the library.

We already have noted that mediation services not only change but also coalesce in an online environment. We must, therefore, consider how selection under such circumstances relates to the online equivalents of cataloging and reference. If the purpose of cataloging is to describe information units in such a way that they can be identified easily, and the purpose of reference is to assist local users in identifying those units they need to do their work, what is the unique purpose of selection? What value does selection add that those other two functions do not and cannot? If selection—source assessment—were fundamentally a matter of tagging, how would it differ from cataloging?

Our first inclination may be to assume that cataloging is descriptive, while selection is evaluative, but we also must recognize that all description is ultimately selective and evaluative. Of the many subjects treated in a document, for example, the cataloger must select only a few as being the most prevalent. There is, to be sure, a difference between stating what a document is about and stating how useful a document might be for local research purposes, but that difference is more negligible than we realize, and probably is not alone significant enough to justify the retention of two operationally or professionally distinct functions. What is needed, therefore, and what necessarily will evolve, will be a system of description for use by catalogers that is at once precise and evaluative enough that local users can apply it (presumably most effectively with the assistance of an online accessible reference librarian) to select the items they want to access and the order in which to do so.

We must recall now our distinction between collection development as an administratively separate library operation and selection as an information service activity. Of all the standard, traditional library operations, few are more derivative of or dependent upon the paper medium than collection development. None is more closely bound to the paper service sequence, and none is more conditioned upon ownership being the most effective form of access. The gradual reduction and eventual elimination of the paper collection, and consequently of the distinction between the owned collection and the unowned anti-collection, will not necessarily eliminate the need for selection in the sense of source assessment as an information service. It almost certainly will render obsolete collection development as an operationally separate function. If selection as source assessment remains in demand as an information service in an online environment, that service will and should be absorbed and adequately provided by the online equivalent of the cataloging and reference operations. Collection development as a separate library operation, therefore, probably will not survive the eventual disappearance of paper as the primary and preferred medium of scholarly information exchange. Collection development will have, nevertheless, a critical role to play in the transition from paper to online access.

THE TRANSITION

We have been assuming so far that a need for mediation services will persist in the online era and that libraries should begin to develop strategies that will permit and facilitate the gradual adjustment of these services to online conditions. The user community's perception of the need for continued mediation once an increasing number of relevant sources are available online is likely to be mixed at best. The most immediately visible and revolutionary information services will be in the area of delivery—the digitization and transportation of information packages. We must anticipate, therefore, a growing assumption on the part of many new and influential online information users that enhanced delivery will reduce, and perhaps ultimately eliminate, the need for mediation of any kind, and that the user will be able to satisfy his or her information needs in an online condition by confronting or tapping into the raw information directly. This self-service philosophy probably will be further encouraged and strengthened at least initially by the frontier spirit that reigns on the network. In these early days of network development, total freedom to do anything one wants in any way one wants on the network is highly prized and probably will remain a fundamental value for some time.

The transition to an online environment, in which we now are engaged, is characterized by a rapidly growing body of bibliographic and numeric information in digital form. While the availability of full-text information online also is increasing, full-text information in electronic form necessarily will grow more slowly for some time as a proportion of all essential full-text publications.[14] The assumption may develop that the same kind of searching and retrieval capabilities will be possible in future large-scale, full-text databases that are now possible in large-scale bibliographic and numeric databases and smaller full-text databases. It may be assumed, in other words, that the application of such techniques as contextual and Boolean searching will permit the effective retrieval of information from increasingly large full text databases, and that mediation is for the most part no longer required. This is obviously a naive assumption, but its naiveté may not be apparent to those users in authority until the total full-text database available reaches a certain critical mass. Until that quantity of full-text information is available online, direct rough-and-ready searching of raw information by users may achieve adequate or at least satisfactory results. One must assume that a point eventually will be reached, however, at which the database no longer is penetrable and manipulable using unassisted techniques. For full-text databases of any size to be of value, someone will need to do something to the constituent information—preferably at the point of input—something more than mere descriptive cataloging. Someone is going to have to add value to those constituent information units by evaluating them in some way. This will be a critical and onerous responsibility, since it will have a direct effect on research and education—and knowledge production in general—but it is really no different from, and no more critical and onerous than, information services in the paper environment. The utility loop will remain an omnipresent feature or by-product of information services, regardless of the information medium; it may simply be more apparent in online circumstances. On the whole most input operations of information services are likely to remain at least as invisible as they are in the paper environment. On the output side of library mediation services, some service will remain necessary to assist with the increasingly complicated searching that will be required for work with large-scale, full-text databases, even if—or especially if—there is significant value added at the point of input.

As in the paper environment, the purpose of output mediation services will be to exploit the value added by input mediation services., I would expect output mediation services to be responsible for and knowledgeable of local needs, while input mediation services aim to create and apply a system of evaluative description to all significant information units.

The transition from paper to online information services inevitably also will present many economic challenges, the most obvious one from an administrative perspective being how we manage two services—paper and online—simultaneously, with resources that have become demonstrably inadequate to operate even one.[15] These economic difficulties will create and be driven by political pressures that derive from, among other things, the fact noted above that different subject areas will shift from paper to online instruction and publication at very different rates. However this evolves, an essential role of collection development in this process will be to ensure that those disciplines which lag behind, and which abandon the primarily paper phase more slowly or reluctantly, are adequately serviced. Those disciplines, presumably the humanities and many area studies programs, will be politically and economically weaker than the disciplines that move more quickly online. Those slower moving disciplines must be protected and allowed to advance into the online era at their own pace as much as possible; this must be done not only in the interest of those disciplines, but also in the interest of the future of the academic library.

In my opinion, the major political-economic problem libraries will face will be how to justify and support mediation services—no doubt at the expense of or in competition with rapidly expanding and promising delivery services—until the total full-text database reaches that critical mass at which the need for mediation becomes indisputably apparent. We might postulate three phases in the transition: (1) the primarily paper phase, in which mediation will remain an accepted necessity; (2) the intermediate phase, in which enough material is easily accessible online to make mediation appear increasingly obsolete; and (3) the primarily electronic phase, in which much of the information needed for instruction and research is available online, and there is widespread realization that human intervention in the form of mediation is an essential precondition for database access and use. Viewed from this perspective, the fact that different disciplines will doubtless move from the primarily paper phase into the intermediate phase at different rates is an advantage for the library. If all disciplines were to enter the intermediate phase simultaneously, the library might not be able to protect mediation services from reduction. Depending upon the length of the intermediate phase, however, it may be possible to justify mediation services on the basis of the needs of those disciplines still in the primarily paper phase long enough for those disciplines in the intermediate phase to move into the primarily electronic phase.

THE FUTURE OF COLLECTION DEVELOPMENT

The responsibility for protecting and maintaining mediation services for disciplines that continue to rely on paper will be a critical factor in the transition. This is certainly not the only role collection development will be called upon to play in this process. Let me discuss, in conclusion, three additional essential responsibilities or objectives for collection development in the transition. The first will be full-text retrospective conversion, which will be an enormous undertaking and will form the last major effort of traditional collection development. The further we move into the online era, the more inconvenient paper will become as a storage medium and retrieval device. Large portions of our paper holdings will need to be converted to online form, but it is very unlikely that we will want or that we will be able to convert everything in the intermediate term, regardless of how inexpensive digitization becomes. If we cannot or do not want to convert everything in paper to online form, then we have a classic job for collection development. The paper collections will need to be divided into segments and then ranked on a continuum of potential utility. The position of the line of acceptance on the continuum will be determined by the availability of economic resources, and the result of that action will be a binomial decision of scan-don't scan. There is considerable work to be done in full-text retrospective conversion, but like all recon, it is finally a project and not a profession. It will be completed at some point, after which small, individual conversion jobs gradually will be undertaken, probably only in response to individual user demands.

A second critical responsibility for collection development will be working with acquisitions to design the budgetary procedures for access to online information. Acquisitions and other delivery functions can and must create the mechanisms for payment—primarily, one hopes, among institutions (i.e., if institutions assume more responsibility for publishing)—but also inevitably between institutions and some commercial publishers. Collection development, on the other hand, may assist in the design of the allocation procedures. Even though access in the online age doubtless will become highly individual and decentralized, funding support by institutions for that access still needs to be managed centrally by academic information service units like the library. This is necessary to ensure institution-wide allocation of funding that is not only reasonably equitable, but also flexible enough to take into account different needs of different academic programs at different times. The design of that allocation system and the stipulation of the values that ultimately should drive it are essential jobs for collection development. But they are, again, only jobs, and not full-time occupations. Part of the design challenge will be to include the capacity to make adjustments to the allocation system over time, but the need to make these periodic adjustments would not alone justify a separate library operation.

The third critical responsibility of collection development in the transition, and in some ways the most important, will be to ensure that selectors begin to learn more about, and to form closer administrative links to, what are now the cataloging and reference operations in order to prepare the way for what will be the inevitable fusion of selection with those two operations. As I have implied throughout this paper, I believe we must anticipate a gradual polarization of mediation services that will become increasingly necessary the further we move into an online condition. The input component of mediation services will evolve out of our present cataloging effort, will have evaluative description as its primary function, and will work, I hope, for the most part directly with authors rather than through the agency of publishers. The function of the input component will be, as in the paper environment, to produce descriptive surrogates of information units that readers can use to learn about and to decide whether they want access to those units. The output component of mediation services will evolve out of the current reference function, and will continue, as in the paper environment, to assist readers in locating, evaluating, and gaining access to information units by means of the descriptive surrogates produced at input. Staff responsible for the output component of mediation services will be charged with having a reasonably detailed understanding of the specific information needs of their local clientele. I anticipate that the most economically effective action would be that staff responsible for the input component of mediation services would not be concerned directly with local information requirements, but instead would concentrate on design and use of standard descriptions sufficiently sophisticated and flexible to be applied to all or most local output purposes. In online circumstances, needs obviously will remain local, while collections of information units and the descriptive surrogates that respond to those needs are not necessarily created or maintained in the same locality. Input can be done anyplace, while the output component of mediation services must, on the other hand, remain a local operation.[16] The input component of mediation services will be more like the paper era model of periodical article indexing, rather than that of local library monographic cataloging. The difference is that input work describing current scholarly publications must be done or sponsored by academic institutions rather than commercial bibliographic publishers and will need to be carried out at a much more advanced level bibliographically than current periodical indexing.

This does not mean that description—in the sense of the input component of mediation services—cannot be done at local institutions. It certainly can and may well be. But the descriptions produced need not refer to information units produced locally. Dividing responsibilities for description among institutions by subject might be more sensible in this model. A scholar who has written something on a particular subject will work through the network with the online equivalent of a cataloger at one of those institutions responsible for description in that subject area. Any such process will require considerable coordination, and this kind of coordination probably will become the prevalent form of cooperation in the online era. For the most part, however, our concept of inter-institutional library cooperation is very difficult to separate from the paper medium and culture. Our current views and programs of cooperation presuppose proximity. While we can expect increasing interinstitutional cooperation in the online environment, much of this cooperation will be so automatic and routine that we will not think of it in those terms.

There can be no doubt that the coordination of input and output mediation services will require conscious and careful design. This work will be necessary to counteract the negative effects of the polarization of input and output that is likely because output must be local, but input need not be, and probably will not be. The success of input can be measured only at output, the intentions of input operations must be clear to mediation services staff at output, and the potential needs of current and future readers at output must be understood by those creating the description at input. The basis for this coordination between input and output mediation services must be a common perception of bibliographic value and evaluation, an in-depth understanding of the nature of information utility, and the ability to add value to information units by ranking them in relation to each other.

In short, coordination depends on the skill and knowledge that collection development has defined and acquired over the past thirty years. That skill and knowledge somehow will need to be transferred by and from collection development to both the input and the output components of mediation services. If done correctly, this act should effectively link those two components, thus making what will be collection development's final and perhaps most significant "boundary spanning" contribution to library operations.[17]

REFERENCE NOTES

1. Jerry D. Campbell, "'Changing the Sixty-Forty Split' Revisited," *Library Administration & Management* 6 (summer 1992): 129.

2. Anthony M. Cummings, et al. *University Libraries and Scholarly Communication: A Study Prepared for Andrew W. Mellon Foundation* (Washington, D.C.: Association of Research Libraries, 1992), 165

3. See Dan C. Hazen's discussion of "dependence" in his "Selection: Function, Models, Theory," in *Collection Management: A New Treatise,* ed. Charles B. Osburn and Ross Atkinson (Greenwich, Conn.: JAI Press, 1991), Part B, 273–300.

4. Ross Atkinson, "The Acquisitions Librarian as Change Agent in the Transition to the Electronic Library," *Library Resources & Technical Services* 36 (Jan. 1992): 11–15.

5. Ibid., especially 15–18.

6. For current perspectives on mediation in reference, see "The Reference Librarian and Implications of Mediation," ed. M. Keith Ewing and Robert Hauptman, *The Reference Librarian* 37 (1992).

7. A tendency of delivery, therefore, may be to treat all publications as identically as possible, while the objective of mediation is to highlight or stipulate how each publication differs from any other.

8. Hendrik Edelman, "Selection Methodology in Academic Libraries," *Library Resources &*

Technical Services 23 (winter 1979): 34.

9. The input-output distinction is, of course, always relative, depending among other things upon the scope of the inquiry. Since I am limiting my discussion here to libraries, I am dividing library functions into input-output. If we were to include the information services external to the library, such as publishing (as I did in "The Acquisitions Librarian as Change Agent"), then the input-output distinction would need to be defined more broadly.

10. There is, of course, also an inevitable intermediate delivery operation, by means of which the description is transported in some way (often in the form of publishers' announcements or catalogs) to the selector.

11. For a good recent discussion of collection management, see Herbert D. Safford and Katherine F. Martin, "Collection Management: The Collection Development Alternative," in *Collection Development in College Libraries,* ed. Joanne Schneider Hill, William E. Hannaford and Ronald H. Epp (Chicago and London: American Library Association, 1991), 97–103.

12. In reality, of course, most selectors probably do not consciously arrange every citation encountered in a particular selection session in priority order, but that prioritizing is nevertheless the core of the work done, and every selector could with some difficulty produce such a prioritized arrangement of citations at the conclusion of the session.

13. Even in the case of a special library or an undergraduate library, the anti-collection will consist of all relevant items (e.g., all materials appropriate for undergraduates) not in the collection.

14. For a good summary of current progress in full-text electronic sources, see Reva Basch, "Books Online: Visions, Plans, and Perspectives for Electronic Text," *Online* 15 (July 1991): 13–23. See also Moid A. Siddiqui, "Full-text Databases," *Online Review* 15 (Dec. 1991): 367–72.

15. See Berndt Dugall, "Herausforderung an die Bibliotheken durch moderne Informationsmedien," *Zeitschrift fur Bibliothekswesen and Bibliographie* 39 (Jan./Feb. 1992): 34; "Die simultane Beherrschung traditioneller und neuer Medien ist die eigentliche Herausforderung. Es wird auf absehbare Zeit kein 'entweder-oder,' sondern ein 'sowohlals auch' die Maxime des Handelns sein mussen." ("The real challenge is the simultaneous control of both traditional and new [i.e., online] media. Not 'either-or' but rather 'not only-but also' must be the guiding principle for the foreseeable future.") [R.A. translation]

16. See Anne Woodsworth et al., "The Model Research Library: Planning for the Future," *Journal of Academic Librarianship* 15 (July 1989): 133; "Generally, staff who are involved in handling information in various formats & in designing access systems will be centralized, while those involved in delivering & evaluating programs & services will be dispersed, functioning in service clusters close to their main user groups."

17. Elaine F. Sloan, "The Organization of Collection Development in Large University Research Libraries" (Ph.D. diss., Univ. of Maryland, 1973): 38–50.

10 THE ACADEMIC LIBRARY COLLECTION IN AN ONLINE ENVIRONMENT

Selection is the very keel on which our mental ship is built. And in this case of memory its utility is obvious. If we remembered everything, we should on most occasions be as ill off as if we remembered nothing.—William James, *The Principles of Psychology* (1890)

What to keep and what to discard will remain very much an issue in the era of the virtual library.

Academic libraries exist for only one purpose: to provide local users—scholars and students—with access to the information they need for their education and research. The library achieves that purpose by ensuring that needed sources of information remain accessible and reliable (that is, authentic, unaltered) over time, and by establishing conventionalized relationships among published sources so that users can make decisions about which sources to consult and interpret in which order. Collection building is one of the primary means used by the library to ensure access and establish source relationships. Based on assessments and assumptions of the current and future information needs of local users, the library selects, assembles, and maintains certain publications, and in so doing relates those publications to each other, guarantees their continued existence, boosts their access for local purposes (effectively inserting them into local research and instruction), and privileges them with respect to the much larger universe of publication that exists beyond the collection.

We stand now at the edge of an information revolution sparked by advances in computer technology and telecommunications that will change fundamentally both the concept of the collection in the academic library and the role of the library in the academic institution. Many analyses have been made of the probable future of academic information services in this rapidly approaching, primarily online environment. (Several excellent overviews of the thinking on the future of information services have appeared recently.[1]) One expectation is that scholars—initially mainly in the sciences but eventually in other disciplines as well—will begin to exchange information with each other more routinely during the course of their work rather than mainly through formal publication. The result will be what has been labeled a "collaboratory."[2] Indeed, in some disciplines, this is already taking place. In a sense, therefore, the history of scholarly communication has come full circle: while the scholarly journal originated in the seventeenth century as a means to replace or broaden correspondence, today a form of correspondence on the network is beginning to supplant some functions of publication.[3] As this kind of scholarly communication increases, there are vital "knowledge management" roles that the academic library must be prepared to assume.[4] At the same time, however, we must not imagine, as some have, that formal publication based on peer review will become obsolete once all scholars are connected online.

This article first appeared in *New Directions for Higher Education* no. 90 (summer 1993): 43–62.

For a number of reasons, some of which will be discussed in this chapter, formal publication will remain an essential element of scholarly communication. But what happens, then, to the library collection as increasing quantities of information, both informal collaborative correspondence and formal publication, become available online? How should formally published information be assembled, maintained, and controlled? Can we even speak of a "collection" under such circumstances? And what will become of the paper materials wedged onto the shelves of today's libraries? This chapter will consider these questions. In so doing, I hope to assist academic administrators to identify and prepare for the kinds of decisions that will need to be made to accommodate and take advantage of the new information environment.

THREE STIPULATIONS

As we begin our discussion, we need to keep three issues in mind: the economics of attention, the educational dilemma, and the reification trap.

The Economics of Attention

Richard Lanham, in his recent book *The Electronic Word,* has presented a number of original and relevant observations about the future of information and literacy in an increasingly online environment.[5] Of the many ideas Lanham puts forward, we note especially his highly germane opinion that the scarcest resource in the information age will be the reader's attention. Because economics is the management of scarce resources, a primary challenge to educators in future will be to devise an economics of attention.[6] The modern library in its current mostly paper condition has, of course, always faced that challenge. The purpose of the collection is precisely to permit the user to focus attention on what is relevant amidst the din of the other sources that distract the user's attention, to increase the signal-to-noise ratio. But Lanham is doubtless correct in asserting that the need for such an economics of attention will increase as we move further into an online environment.

The Educational Dilemma

Thus the library aims to keep the user focused on a particular path, to arrange and relate sources so that time is not wasted and irrelevant "noise" does not distract. At the same time, however, the current culture and philosophy of information services demand that the library leave to the user as much discretion as possible in determining what information to use and in selecting the path most fruitful to his or her research. Thus the library's perpetual and existential dilemma is to control but not to regulate information, to guide but not to lead the library user. This dilemma is faced no doubt in many forms by all educators but it is especially acute for the library. The library's expertise is not in the information it provides but rather in the provision of information; in order to make specific information accessible, however, the library is obliged to make some value judgments about it.

The Reification Trap

The third point that we need to bear in mind is that reality is fundamentally and unavoidably social. In contrast, publications are things. Although the function of the library is to relate these things to each other and to put people in a position to locate and understand these things, the more elemental forces that drive the library and its use are the relationships among the people using the sources rather than the relationships among the sources themselves. To imagine otherwise is to fall victim to reification. In our zeal to analyze and postulate how the library provides and manages information, therefore, we need always to bear in mind that most of what we do has its primary motivation and purpose in human relationships.

THE TRADITIONAL ACADEMIC LIBRARY COLLECTION

To consider where we are going we must first understand where we are. Let us examine some of the concepts that underlie academic library collection building in today's paper environment.

Three Screens

Library collections are created primarily for economic reasons, for to provide the user with relatively immediate access to all information is neither possible nor desirable. The point of building a collection is to differentiate works added from works excluded. Even the largest research libraries acquire only a small percentage of what is actually published. Collection development is, therefore, a screening operation. Collection development functions as the central or secondary screening process in a trio of screening processes, the succession of which determines or at least significantly affects what users have access to and thus what they know from published scholarly information over time. The primary screening process today is publishing; the tertiary one is collection retention. Each of the three successive processes is intended to reduce for economic reasons (both financial and attentive) the number of publications available to the user. More is written than can or should be published, more is published than can or should be collected by libraries, more is collected than can or should be retained by libraries over time.

Source Types and Attributes

Although library collections are used differently by students and scholars working in different disciplines, academic library use can be divided into two broad fundamental categories, each with a corresponding source type. These are data and notification. (Certainly more source types and functions can be defined than these two. For a fuller discussion, see Atkinson.[7])

Data sources provide or record information that is used for research purposes. They can be historical, statistical, or bibliographical. Some data sources are used to aid research (for example, reference sources) whereas others are the object of research (such as literary or historical documents). The former are used in all subjects whereas the latter, which constitute a large portion of the holdings of research libraries, are used primarily by the humanities.

Notification sources are publications produced by contemporary scholars for purposes of communicating with one another: these are the scholarly books and articles that often make up the bulk of our acquisitions and absorb most of our acquisitions budgets. Notification sources are the material stuff of scholarship. The faculty users of academic libraries are at once the primary consumers and producers of notification sources.

Publications are selected for most academic library collections by the library staff (usually called bibliographers or selectors). Generally speaking, the selector makes decisions based on particular attributes of available sources that, in his or her judgment, will meet the defined or assumed needs of the current, local constituency. Although the selector can identify materials that will be useful to local students or scholars and can often determine that one source will be more useful than another, there is normally no way for the selector to determine whether a work will be totally useless. In a research library almost any source can have some use; this is the universal utility syndrome.

Source attributes can be divided into two fundamental categories. Let us call them extrinsic and intrinsic. Extrinsic source attributes can be easily, or at least relatively objectively, determined. They include such features as subject, publisher, format, language, and possibly such qualities as the reputation of the author and the level of difficulty or sophistication of the work. These attributes are used not only for selection but also for cataloging and reference purposes. But the library does not and cannot fulfill its responsibilities by restricting its attention to extrinsic attributes. To fulfill its educational mission, the library must also—again, for economic reasons—try to identify intrinsic attributes, that is, the potential value or significance of the work for local users. This is a far more difficult and subjective operation, but collection building (not to mention reference services) always requires some knowledge and application of intrinsic attributes by library staff.

In the course of identifying or defining intrinsic source attributes, the library most clearly faces its educational dilemma: it must contrive to focus user attention and lead users in particular directions while at the same time allowing as much flexibility as possible to decide what to read in what order. Faculty can, of course, contribute to the identification of intrinsic attributes and their participation in the building of college library collections, which are frequently based heavily upon the current curriculum, is particularly prevalent for this reason.

Why, then, do faculty not play a larger role in the selection of materials for research libraries today? To differing degrees, the faculty are regularly consulted on research library selection decisions and policy, but there are several reasons why they cannot build research library collections. First, there is the mundane problem of time. So much is being published that selection has become a full-time profession. Second, there is the problem of collection bias. Heavy faculty selection results in unbalanced collections because certain faculty members will inevitably build more actively than others. Third, such participation is not politically or economically feasible because no institution has adequate resources for all faculty to acquire all the sources they want. Therefore, to the dismay of some faculty, there must always be an objective arbiter or agent—the library selector—who decides on the basis of systematic criteria those materials that should be acquired in the best interests of the institution as a whole.

Publishing and Collection Development

Collection development can only be understood in relation to the screening operation that precedes it, publication. Publishing and the library effectively divide between themselves the main responsibility in the paper environment for mediating between the writer and the reader in all aspects of formal scholarly communication. Many of the budget issues that affect collection development and indeed the operation of the library in general derive from decisions made and actions taken by the publishing industry.

In most cases of scholarly publication, especially the publication of notification sources, the author does not own what he or she produces, but rather deeds ownership through copyright to the publisher in return for publication. The modern publisher as copyright holder does not, therefore, sell information but rather sells the material sources from which information may be extracted or created and the limited right to extract that information from those sources. Even after the reader extracts or learns that information, the reader does not "own" it, that knowledge is still legally owned by the publisher. (For an especially informative review of these issues, see Okerson.[8]) The convention of transferring the ownership of scholarly information to publishers has in some cases proven highly prejudicial to scholarly communication. So many publications have come into existence and their prices are often so high that institutions cannot afford to acquire what users legitimately need. This situation is not, I hasten to add, the fault of the publishers. The problem derives at least partially from the demands of scholars for effective publishing outlets. It should also be remembered that the primary goal of the publisher is not to exchange information (that is merely a means) but rather to increase revenue and a few publishers specializing in scholarly publication have achieved that goal spectacularly. The exchange of information is the goal of the library and the academy and entrusting that responsibility—contracting out knowledge dissemination—to publishers (especially commercial ones) has been in some instances a serious error because it increases the economic barriers to scholarly communication.

What most vexes many librarians is that the scholars who produce much of the work that librarians acquire are often at the same institutions as the librarians. In effect, scholars are giving their work to publishers who then package it and sell it back to the librarians, sometimes at extremely high prices. (Probably the most balanced and authoritative discussion of these concerns is found in Cummings and others.[9]) However, some of this anger and anxiety probably has its source in reification. The assumption is that the purpose of publication is information exchange. But what publishers appear to know somewhat better than librarians is that scholarly publication actually has many competing purposes, one of which is communication about the author. Notification sources tell the reader not simply what the writer knows but that the writer knows it—that the writer knows something that an editorial board of experts agrees is worth communicating to other experts, that the writer belongs to that community of experts and through such publication is playing a leadership role. Thus, publication is certification. As such it is inextricably bound into the highly stylized social and cultural fabric of the academy.

We must also recognize that scholarly journals "have a natural tendency to be hierarchical, with scholars generally in agreement on the relative rankings of the journals that publish material in their fields."[10] Most scholars strive, therefore, to publish in high-ranking core journals (that is, journals that are frequently cited) that have established records of articles that have contributed significantly to what is known on a subject. It has become easier for publishers to create core journals because disciplines have become so extremely specialized. Because "faculty prefer to avoid a lengthy hierarchy of journals in a discipline, in some sense all new journals are 'essential' in that they constitute a natural home for articles of value. In a sense, all journals become at least second best in the hierarchy for a small number of scholars. Hence, libraries face not only increasing average prices owing to declining average circulation, but also intense demand to subscribe to all journals because every one is in some sense important."[11]

Thus what the publisher aims to provide is not simply a medium through which information can be exchanged but also a mechanism that adds status to any item it accepts for publication. That is in fact the value added by the publisher. In the closed and competitive culture of the academy, the value of such a mechanism is difficult to measure in mere dollars.

Interinstitutional Cooperation

As the costs of library materials have consistently outpaced the ability of libraries to purchase them, libraries have resorted increasingly to interlibrary lending. (According to Stubs, interlibrary borrowing per student increased by 60 percent in academic research libraries between 1986 and 1993.[12] During the same period subscriptions per student decreased by 14 percent and monographs purchased per student decreased by 30 percent.) This has led to efforts at interinstitutional cooperative collection development, that is, formal agreements among institutions so that different institutions take responsibility for collecting different materials. Materials can then be shared and (so goes the concept) the collections of all institutions treated as if they were our own. Without such cooperative agreements, institutions risk canceling the same journals or avoiding the purchase of the same monographs so that eventually some materials would become inaccessible. The idea therefore has been to aim for the creation of a single, national collection owned by and located at different institutions but accessible to all scholars at all institutions.

University administrations have urged this eminently logical goal on the library community for decades but, with a few exceptions, libraries have failed to achieve it. The few real successes in cooperative collection development have been regional; probably the best known of these is the arrangement between Duke, North Carolina State, and the University of North Carolina.[13] The reasons for the low success rate are varied but clear. To begin with, we cannot share core journals or monographs. All institutions with active faculty must hold these materials if the faculty are to do their research and students are to receive instruction. Some publishers know which journals are core and charge much more for them. Most efforts at cooperative collection development, therefore, have concentrated on peripheral materials. Because the costs of these materials are often much lower this has seldom resulted in any significant dollar savings. Moreover, as the costs of core journals have increased, our ability to purchase peripheral materials has declined, which is particularly unfortunate because just such items make for rich research collections.

What makes interinstitutional cooperative collection development from the outset most difficult, however, is the *local imperative,* that is, the unremitting political pressure to spend local funds to meet local needs. The library exists to provide access to those materials its users require. A truly cooperative program would compel the use of local funds to meet national rather than local needs. For cooperation to work effectively, in other words, a library would be obliged not only to spend its budget on some materials its local users do not need but also to do so at the expense of some materials they do need. This is not something that any academic library has the political strength to achieve, nor is it something the library really wants to do even though it may claim it does. Libraries are local service bureaus. They measure their success and derive most of their rewards from responding directly to the needs of their local clientele. Library selectors are trained to empathize and identify with faculty users in order to make decisions in the best interest of those users. Thus the selector always gives precedence to the local over the national (and to the present over the future). As a result, libraries are regularly willing to duplicate material held elsewhere, even if that means that some items will not be collected anywhere and may for that reason eventually become inaccessible.

In the past year, the Association of American Universities (AAU), in collaboration with the Association of Research Libraries, has embarked upon yet another program to coordinate the acquisition of foreign materials; the initial pilot projects will concentrate on materials from Latin America, Japan, and Germany.[14] This new initiative is based upon the same synergistic method of dividing responsibilities among institutions that has always been used for cooperative collection development and it therefore will face the same obstacles, especially the local imperative. What differentiates this effort from previous ones, however, is its strong endorsement by the presidents of the AAU institutions. Although I am not certain if all of the political implications have been understood by all of the institutions involved and although I believe that most faculty will probably view such a program initially as a significant diminution of services, the new initiative is a very promising step indeed. Only the AAU presidents acting in concert could bring about such a revolutionary alteration in the academic culture.

But even with such hopes on the horizon we must not delude ourselves. Even if institutions were to succeed in binding together in this way, such a cooperative initiative would by itself be doomed to failure because libraries do not control publication prices and we are operating in a publishing environment that is a near monopoly. If institutions use cooperative collection development and interlibrary loan to subscribe to fewer journals, publishers will simply increase prices to cover revenue loss. In the long run, therefore, interinstitutional cooperation is not the answer to the crisis in the cost of library materials.

The Weight of History

The tertiary selection screen in the paper environment consists of retention decisions as the library decides which materials it wishes to preserve and which to withdraw. Research libraries, however, rarely practice this operation. Regular withdrawal is something done primarily by smaller libraries, public and academic, that have limited space, clearly defined user needs, and few historical obligations. Research libraries generally prefer to add more shelves (even at the expense of user space), build extensions to library buildings, and construct large off-site storage facilities when space is no longer available on central campus. The main reason for the resistance to withdrawal is the universal utility syndrome described earlier. Because any publication has potential use for research, the retention of any publication is not only justified but expected. In a way, therefore, the very act of bringing a publication into a research library collection enhances its value to such a point that we are often unable to dispense with it.

However, withdrawal is an area in which some interinstitutional cooperation should be possible. Because candidates for withdrawal are of low use, institutions should be able to coordinate withdrawals to ensure that one or two copies of individual items are retained somewhere in the country. Once again, however, libraries have, with a few regional exceptions, never managed to achieve this. One possible reason is that it could be cheaper, or at least faster (which is another form of cheaper), to store an item in a warehouse and retrieve it as needed than to find it at another institution and borrow it through interlibrary loan. Another reason is certainly that the cost of coordination would be quite high: assigning responsibility to particular institutions for specific titles and ensuring that the institutions give exceptional treatment to those titles would be an expensive undertaking. There can be no doubt, therefore, that duplicate copies of very low-use materials are being retained by research libraries throughout the country.

ACADEMIC LIBRARY COLLECTION ONLINE

Let us now turn our attention to the library in a primarily online environment.

Vision

When compared with our present circumstances, scholarly communication in an online environment would at first glance appear to be something approaching an information utopia. Because everyone in the country or in the world would in theory have access to a single "copy" of a publication in a single server, the long-pursued national collection could, at least technically, finally become a reality. Many of the political impediments to interinstitutional cooperation, and most importantly many manifestations of the local imperative, would be eliminated because the amount of time required by a local user to gain access to an item of information would be the same whether the item is at the user's institution or an institution on the other side of the country. In a totally online client-server environment, therefore, all institutions could divide collection responsibilities, possibly in some cases in cooperation with scholarly associations. Each institution could concentrate all of its resources on building comprehensive online collections in narrowly defined subject areas to which all users everywhere would have access.[15]

There would be costs, of course, in the form of equipment, programming, and telecommunications, but as the cost of some technology (especially storage) continues to decline, total costs could conceivably not exceed what all institutions now spend on the creation of separate discrete collections. A scholar specializing in a particular discipline, moreover, would no longer require that the library at his or her institution support that expertise with research-level collections built by subject experts. Those bibliographical experts, the online librarians who understand how to develop and service an online collection in that particular discipline, could be concentrated at whatever institution assumed responsibility for the subject area. The scholar could work with that remote collection as easily as if it were stored on campus and communicate online with the bibliographers building the collection.

In an oversimplified nutshell, the foregoing is one vision of the online collection of the twenty-first century. It is a somewhat naive vision, perhaps, for there are certainly significant impediments to its realization, some of which we will examine in this chapter. It is, however, a vision toward which scholars, university administrators, and academic librarians should nevertheless strive, for such a system would inestimably enhance scholarship and higher education. Its realization is technically, and probably financially, feasible. The technology needed is already emerging and academic institutions could, as a group, by collaborating closely and pooling their funds, create this kind of distributed scholarly information network.

Dual-Collection Adjustment

Many academic libraries now speak in terms of a "format-free" collection policy, by which it is meant that the objective of the library is to collect all relevant information within the confines of available funding without regard to format. Whether the item needed is in paper, in microform, or online, therefore, is irrelevant and should not influence the selection decision.

Such a "format-free" policy serves not only informational but also political purposes. It is useful in allaying concerns that the library may be purchasing less useful online sources at the expense of more useful (but less glitzy) traditional paper sources. It is safe and fashionable, therefore, for libraries to claim utility as the paramount criterion for all selection. But things are, of course, not nearly so straightforward. To begin with, any publication's format must always be factored into the selection decision if for no other reason than that different formats require different kinds of support. A bibliography on magnetic tape may provide much better access than a paper version but there is little point in acquiring it if the equipment and programming skills necessary to make it accessible do not exist in the local institution. Even more fundamentally, we must avoid what we might call the format fallacy, that is, the misdirected assumption that utility is somehow incidental to the format. That is never the case. Utility is always at least partially a product of format. If utility is the avowed fundamental criterion for the building of library collections then the format must (and does) play a major role in the selection decision. Online sources do not, therefore, constitute simply "another" format to be equated with the traditional formats of paper and microform. There are fundamental differences between analog and digital information that libraries must understand and exploit. If the current fashion is to downplay those differences, this is done for political purposes or in order more easily to insert—from a process perspective—digital information services into a library infrastructure designed to provide access to analog information.

For some time into the future, therefore, we must be prepared to live not so much with a two-format collection as with two separate collections, one digital and one analog, that have very different qualities, provide very different services, and require very different relationships between users and information. If everything continues to proceed as expected, most scholarly use will gradually shift from the analog to the digital but the transition will doubtless take many years and be very uneven.

In order to hasten and promote the digital library, we will probably need to do exactly what the traditionalists fear: acquire (in the sense of provide access to, pay for) what are some initially less useful materials in digital form at the expense of more useful materials in traditional form. We will need to build a critical mass of digital materials with which users can work, a collection that can begin to compete with the analog collection for the user's attention. Eventually, the very fact that a source is online will begin to render it more useful than sources in traditional formats.

Building the Digital Library Collection

The digital library collection will be created from two sources. The first will be those materials that are directly available to the library in digital form, either because they were originally produced in that form or because, although initially in analog form, they were converted to digital form. The second will be materials that the library owns in some analog form and then decides to convert to digital form. (For a summary of projects currently underway to convert analog information to digital form, see Drabenstott.[16])

Although the first category will be subject to special selection problems already described (notably the need for adequate support and infrastructure), many of the criteria now used for the selection of analog materials can be used to make decisions on publications already in online form. We must assume that digital versions of both data sources and notification sources will be published initially by a variety of for-profit and not-for-profit publishers as well as by some individuals who take advantage of the network to become their own publishers. Libraries may add selected sources to their collections either by loading the publications on tape, disk, or another medium into local servers, or by linking to the publications on remote servers. If managed correctly, the local user should notice no difference between the two.

Far more problematical will be the full-text retrospective conversion to digital form of a carefully selected subset of materials that the library already owns in analog form. This will require entirely new selection criteria for which we have few models in the traditional library. Another difficulty in this process will be a political manifestation of the format fallacy: if we are suffering from such severe budget pressures, some will ask, why devote our scarce and shrinking resources to making another copy of something we already own? To ask such a question is to assume that the business of the library is to acquire symbols on surfaces and that once those symbols have been received, cataloged, and stored, the library's job is done. However, the business of the library is not to acquire but rather to provide access to symbols on surfaces, to relate those sources to each other, and to relate users to those sources. Mere ownership never accomplishes that (even in the analog environment). If by converting publications to digital form we substantially enhance their accessibility and utility, then such conversion is fully justified, even if it must be done at the expense of providing access to other unowned information.

Thus conversion is an entirely new form of selection. We must also bear in mind that the use of information in analog form will necessarily decline over time. Analog information that is not converted will become increasingly obscure. It must be the library's responsibility, therefore, in building the (national) digital collection to decide which materials in analog form are to be injected into the digital collection, to compete there for the user's attention.

How exactly do we decide what to move from the analog to the digital collection? This is a difficult question that will cause considerable controversy for many years to come. Initially we will probably want to undertake some large-scale conversion projects in which certain kinds of materials for use in particular disciplines or research projects will be converted en masse. But I would also strongly urge a parallel approach. What is converted should be at least partially driven by what is being published, in the sense of what sources are cited in current online publications. It should become one of the routines of online publishing that as many of the paper publications as possible cited in an online notification source be converted to online form so that a hypertext link between the citation and the item can be established. Admittedly, this will lead in the beginning to an odd collection of digitized materials. Some obscure items that happen to have been cited will be in digital form while some fundamentally important core materials remain in paper. Quickly, however, many of the core materials should become digitized in this way and the content of the digital library will grow based on what active scholars are actually using. Scholars will themselves define the significant publications in their fields by citing those in the notification sources they produce. (In a sense, this continues the tradition of preservation through copying that has been in effect since antiquity: the publications preserved are those that scholars and librarians at the time deem important enough to justify copying.)

The Primary Impediment

What stands in the way of achieving these goals? Neither technology nor lack of funding (for we do have the funding, if we are prepared to use it for these purposes) nor lack of vision nor even political opposition. All of these can be overcome through some combination of planning and will power. What truly stands in our way is ownership: even though we have paid publishers large sums of money for paper publications we do not own the information content. Even though our faculty have produced large portions of that information neither they nor their institutions own it. We cannot therefore decide to convert our analog holdings to digital form because some owners—some publishers—will not permit it or at least not without what will no doubt be prohibitive prices. (The position of the Association of American Publishers was presented in a press release [August 5, 1994]: "Reproduction is an exclusive right of the copyright holder; therefore, scanning, a form of reproduction, generally requires the permission of the copyright holder. Since the copyright law already addresses reproduction, *no new right is necessary* to deal with scanning."[17]) We are rapidly approaching a point, therefore, at which we may finally have the technology to provide equal access for all scholars everywhere to much of what is published but will be unable to provide that access partially because we have had the poor judgment to transfer away the legal control over the information itself.

Publishing Future Notification Sources

Clifford Lynch has warned us not to become preoccupied with publishing, "which is on . . . [our] minds because of the pricing crisis. But publishing is only a part of (and, in some sense, a byproduct of) the overall system of scholarly communication, which is much larger and more complex."[18] This is certainly true. As noted earlier, libraries do have a major reference services role to play in assisting informal communication, which is becoming increasingly central to scholarship in some disciplines. But formal publication will remain essential to scholarly communication. Indeed, it may become even more vital in the online environment where so much information will be immediately accessible and reader attention will be in increasingly short supply. It will be through the formal publication process (that is, involving peer review) in online form that primary screening must continue to occur. The alternative would be informational chaos. Through peer review, the scholarly community will separate out core information, so that the scholar or the novice will know to concentrate his or her attention upon that information first.

If we assume that the current client-server model continues to evolve and eventually most notification sources are created and disseminated online as electronic publications that replace paper books and journals, how will publication of notification sources be accomplished? Let us posit two general scenarios.

The first scenario, which we will call the *commercial model,* is a replication in the online environment of the publisher-author-library relationship that now exists. Each publishing house will own by virtue of copyright its particular publications. Scholars will continue to sign over the ownership rights of their writings in return for publication. The publisher will mount those publications in one or more privately owned servers. Local users—scholars and students—will then access the remote server of the publisher. The institution—probably but not necessarily the library—will be billed in some way either for each publication in the server accessed by a local user (the "by-the-drink" option) or more likely (and preferably) through some kind of site license allowing any user at the institution access to any of a set of articles in a server (the "all-you-can-eat" option). In the by-the-drink option, the user will probably be prohibited by law from transmitting a copy of the publication over the network; in the all-you-can-eat version, the user will probably be prohibited from sending the publication over the network to anyone outside the institution. This scenario will be indeed "a great irony" because "while these networks promise to largely eliminate the accidents of geography as an organizing principle for interinstitutional cooperation and to usher in a new era of cooperation among geographically dispersed organizations, the shift to licensing essentially means that each library contracting with a publisher or other information provider becomes . . . [an] isolated, insular organization that cannot share its resources with any other organization on the network."[19] Commercial publishers will use every means at their disposal to make this scenario a reality because their survival will depend upon it.

The second scenario, which we will call the *institutional model,* represents a radical departure from the situation that now exists. The servers and their contents will be owned not by the publishers but by the institutions, possibly in collaboration with scholarly associations. Each institution will be responsible for maintaining a set of servers that hold publications based perhaps on some division of subjects among institutions; all electronic publications, or at least all formally published notification sources, of each discipline, in other words, may be held in particular servers at designated institutions. All servers will be network-accessible. Each discipline will establish editorial boards. When the boards accept an item for publication, it will be added to the appropriate server, which will then be maintained indefinitely by the institution responsible for it. The copyright will be owned by the institution responsible for the server and any item in any server should be freely accessible to anyone, provided it is not for commercial purposes. Instead of spending money to buy notification sources, institutions will spend money to make collections of notification sources available. Some of the funding currently used for the purchase of books and subscriptions in the print environment would be spent instead on client-server infrastructure and telecommunications. (For two often-cited calls for variations of the institutional model, see Rogers and Hurt, and Dougherty.[20])

It is likely that we will see some manifestations or combinations of both scenarios for some time into the future. One scenario, however, will eventually dominate the other. Because publishers already own large quantities of scholarly information in analog formats and because some of the more adventurous publishers will likely soon begin to publish in electronic form, some version of the commercial model is at least initially inevitable. However, it does not need to become the dominant model. If institutions move decisively, they can begin gradually to shift the "action" from commercial servers to institutional servers so that eventually most of the use falls on the latter.

It is important to recognize that online publication does not in and of itself improve access to information. Rather it improves the control of information and such control can be used not only to enhance access but also to constrict it. If institutions do not fight to put such an open network of scholarly communication in place we will see no improvement and possibly even a degradation in access as more scholarly information becomes available online. Some publishers will still own the information needed by scholars and students at institutions of higher education and that information will be kept as scarce as possible in order to maintain market value.

Three Probable Objections (of Many) to the Institutional Model

Needless to say, the institutional model just described would be an enormous undertaking requiring the mobilization and merging of information services on each campus, in the form of the library, the computer center, the press, and possibly the bookstore, not to mention much more extensive, formal coordination among institutions than is now practiced. The extent to which the institutional model is possible will depend partially upon costs but if it is found to be within the financial reach of the academy and if we are interested in moving toward it, we need to be prepared for many concerns and objections. Three of these seem especially important.

The complication of interinstitutional competition. In today's environment, institutions are in constant competition with each other for the best faculty, the best students, the greatest endowment, the most grant funding. The relative availability of scholarly information at different institutions—the quality of their libraries—plays a highly visible role in this competition. Exceptional libraries attract exceptional scholars who attract, in turn, exceptional students and funding. Rich, prestigious institutions become in this way richer and more prestigious, giving poorer institutions something to which they can aspire—the American Way. So what happens to this long-established prestige relationship if all scholars, regardless of their institution, have access to the available information, or at least to most of the key, current notification sources? Bigger institutions having more funding available would presumably play a larger role in the national scholarly information effort than smaller, poorer institutions; however, the latter would have a part as well. But what advantages does the institutional model offer the larger institutions? The essential point about Harvard's library, after all, is that every institution really wants it but only Harvard has it. Harvard's library is a scarce resource. Its value depends on that very scarcity. If some of that scarcity is removed (which is what the institutional model is partially intended to accomplish over time), then some of that value is lost. Will we see a collusion, therefore, between the large commercial publishers and the great academic libraries to move toward the commercial model so that both can retain their superior positions? Probably not.

Even the great academic libraries are under severe budgetary pressures today. Even they must depend on other libraries (primarily, other research libraries) because they can no longer acquire all that they need. There is some hope, therefore, that perhaps the largest academic libraries in the country (for example, the Association of Research Libraries) could jointly identify the funds among themselves in a relatively equitable fashion to undertake something approaching the institutional model. For some time into the future, moreover, the advantages of the very wealthy academic library will remain in its analog holdings, items that will become increasingly rare because they have not been converted to digital form. It is likely, therefore, that those disciplines that rely heavily on historical materials will become more centralized at the larger institutions, which can continue to maintain large paper libraries, while those disciplines (mostly in the sciences and the professions) that depend on current notification sources will remain dispersed at institutions of all sizes.

Loss of hierarchy. A second problem that could block a move toward the institutional model involves the cultural function of scholarly publication discussed earlier. Some journals or publishers are seen to be more standard or "core" than others and an article or a book published through them bespeaks a greater expertise on the part of the author. If the institutional model were to be put fully into effect, many individual journals and publishers would presumably disappear.[21] All scholarly publications presumably would be published in a single set of servers so that there would be little hierarchical differentiation of the kind now provided. Don Schauder uncovers a basic ideological conflict in our move toward the digital collection between the "tradition of the free sharing of academic knowledge" represented by libraries and the "tradition of the prestige journal" represented by publishers.[22] Schauder's research showed that scholars want both of these fundamentally conflicting traditions retained.

The reputation of the journal or publisher is indeed a key extrinsic attribute, one of the only such attributes, in fact, providing an indication of a publication's value (that is, its intrinsic attributes). That reputation is an important means for scholars and students to determine what to read and in what order. Online publication in a distributed client-server environment, however, offers us an extrinsic attribute that will serve the same purpose. Indeed, the attribute will be so reliable and direct that it is likely to make us uncomfortable. As in the case of retrospective digital conversion, we should aim to let the scholarly community decide as much as possible for itself what is important. Each item, once in the server, should therefore have attached to it some kind of counter indicating how often the item has been used or accessed (possibly by different groups). Probably most useful to scholars in a particular field would be knowledge of which publications have been accessed not only generally but also by those scholars they consider to belong to their peer group. Special care would need to be taken in devising such a system in order to protect the privacy of the individual. Hyperlinks should also be provided to other sources in which the publication has been cited so that the extent to which the item is cited will be easily apparent. Thus, rather than the potential significance of an item being defined indirectly by its publisher, the item can be determined to be a core publication directly based on the level and type of use it is receiving. The impact of the publication on current scholarship will be in this way at least partially quantified and immediately demonstrable. What a practicing scholar will want to read first is what everyone else in the field is reading, and that will change the sequence in which the scholar and student approach information. This will have implications for their assessment of the literature and their approach to the discipline.

The specter of bureaucracy. A recent argument against the institutional model is that "the bureaucratic ineptitude of many large institutions would threaten to become a major barrier to the dissemination of new knowledge—a situation meriting concern."[23] As a bureaucrat myself, I must admit to a similar apprehension. Of all the objections to the institutional model, this is the one I find most difficult to counter. Private businesses are often able to do things much more efficiently than public organizations such as government agencies or academic institutions. It makes little sense for institutions to assume responsibility for publishing if what is gained by such a radical step is immediately lost to political conflict and poor management. Somehow the work of using (institutional) money to exchange information must be made as efficient as the work (now done by publishers) of using information exchange to make money If we cannot manage this, then the institutional model admittedly makes little sense and we will need to accept the fact that it is the institution itself that is the real impediment to the creation of an effective scholarly communication system.

Rescreening

If the commercial model eventually comes to dominate, the three selection screens will presumably remain in effect although in somewhat different form from what we experience in today's environment. Publishers will continue to undertake the primary screening operation, deciding through their editorial boards which materials to publish. Individual institutions will still provide a secondary screening step because they will not be able to afford to provide their users with access to all of the online publications needed. The "collection" will in many ways be shifted in the commercial model from institutions to publishers and we must expect some of the main service responsibilities of libraries to shift to publishers as well. The tertiary screening step (retention decisions) for online sources will also shift mainly to publishers and will become therefore all the more problematical because some publishers will presumably only retain the information they own for as long as it is profitable to do so. The fundamental archival role of libraries may therefore be seriously jeopardized. Some agreement would be needed so that publishers either going out of business or seeking to jettison information that is no longer profitable would be prepared or obligated to pass (preferably for free but at least at a fair price) the older information (back) to the academic community for storage. It is at this point that the institutions can exercise their tertiary screening role and decide which older materials they will retain online.

If the institutional model is accepted, only two screening operations will exist and they will be entirely different from those of the commercial model. At least in the case of most notification sources, publishing and collection building will merge into a single operation. (I am assuming that many data sources will continue to be published by for-profit publishers. In the institutional model, academic institutions would assume responsibility, from my perspective, primarily for current notification sources.) To add an item to an official institutional server would be simultaneously to publish it and add it to the national collection. This would be the new primary screen. It would be the scholarly community in each discipline that would then decide what is in such a collection. Of course, large quantities of network-accessible information would not be officially published in this way and certainly some groups of scholars would become disgruntled and establish their own servers. The status of such "renegade" servers would need to be determined. Another variation on this theme would be played by scholars who cannot get their material through the primary screen, that is, published in the official disciplinary servers, but who feel their material contributes significantly to the field and therefore decide on self-publication, that is, putting their material on their own servers. This would be more difficult for users to find and such material would normally always be read after that in the official servers but it could still have considerable influence. We must also expect some traffic in preprints, depending on how long editorial boards take to make their decisions, although the heavy use of online preprints now in effect in some disciplines should be significantly reduced when all publications are immediately published online upon acceptance. The AAU Task Force on *A National Strategy for Managing Scientific and Technical Information* envisions a national online repository. that consists of two parts, a current collection and one or more permanent collections. The permanent collections would consist of materials that have been subject to peer review; the current collection would be the equivalent of preprints. Any item in the current collection not transferred to the permanent collections in two years would be deleted.[24]

Remembering to Forget

Information stored online will be subject to some physical degradation over time and its accessibility will be in constant jeopardy from hardware and software changes. As a result, a process of what is now called "refreshing" will need to be put into effect: stored information will need to be routinely and periodically recopied if it is to remain accessible.[25] Preservation in the online environment, therefore, is likely to become a fairly automatic process. This will have important financial implications for preservation. It may become more cost-effective in at least the early days of a primarily online environment to keep something rather than withdraw it. Withdrawal requires human intervention and decision making; it may be more cost-effective simply to recopy along with the rest of the collection. Eventually, however, the cost of not withdrawing anything will become burdensome. Servers will become overloaded, congested, "noisy," regardless of how sophisticated the technology is, and the user will become increasingly more occupied with finding information than with interpreting and applying it. We will need therefore to learn how to "forget" certain documents, to omit them from the current discussion.

Thus it is likely that libraries will need to develop an entirely new screening method for online publications. The question is, do we simply move such publications somehow to one side, in the way we do now through off-site storage, or do we consign such withdrawals to oblivion? (Since there may be only one "copy" of a publication in the national collection, a decision to discard or delete in the online environment will often prove irreversible.) The universal utility syndrome will force us in many cases to select the former, that is, to develop a procedure that would still leave the scholar the opportunity to find, albeit with more difficulty, some of the screened-out information. The "difficulty" part is important: while this new tertiary screen need not result in a permanent loss, the recapture of such information should be difficult enough so that only those who truly want it will have the impetus to gain access.

What exactly should we do with such material to downgrade its accessibility? We have already noted that some materials considered less important will probably remain in their original analog form. By the same token, some items that are no longer useful might be converted back into the analog library, that is, transferred to microfilm (still probably the most secure and lowest maintenance medium) or even printed on acid-free paper and stored in a warehouse. They would still be retrievable but in a digital environment such manual access will probably appear so time consuming that the material would appear to most users as virtually lost. Only the largest, most prestigious institutions are likely to maintain such archives and they will be considered well endowed (both financially and informationally) for that reason.

The information congestion that will lead to such tertiary screening may arrive more quickly than we think. We must bear in mind that hypertext as it is now developing has the very real potential to atomize publication. (For a useful, recent introduction to hypertext, see Borman and von Solms.[26]) Although knowledge and understanding are based on intertextual connections, we are now preparing to establish mechanical systems that create so many connections at such a speed that the result may be not new knowledge but total chaos. The fact that all language and all knowledge are connected becomes a reality through hypertext, which can move the reader from one text to another to another. In some kinds of research, such textual "channel flipping" may be desirable but much other research will require a concentration of attention on a continuous text. The library may need to develop the capacity selectively to disable or restrain those intertextual connections that we have sought for so long to establish. The library should be able to segregate information from the current discussion, to cause the user to forget about it long enough to concentrate on the text at hand. In addition to the process for moving information from digital to analog storage, therefore, some new form of temporary withdrawal may also be needed.

CONCLUSION

Rapid advances in information technology present us with an unprecedented opportunity to reenvision and redesign all aspects of scholarly information exchange, including collection building and the scholarly publication process. We must grasp that opportunity, not only to take advantage of the improvements that the new environment will provide but also to apply in that new environment what we have learned—and to correct some of the mistakes we have made—in the old one.

REFERENCE NOTES

1. K. M. Drabenstott, *Analytical Review of the Library of the Future* (Washington, D.C.: Council on Library Resources, 1994); C. A. Lynch, "Accessibility and Integrity of Networked Information Collections," contractor report prepared for the Office of Technology Assessment, 1993 (NTIS PB93-218923); J. S. Rutstein, A. L. DeMiller, and E. A. Fuseler, "Ownership Versus Access: Shifting Perspectives for Libraries," *Advances in Librarianship* 17 (1993): 33–60.

2. R. Clarke, "Electronic Support for the Practice of Research," *Information Society* (Jan.–Mar. 1994): 10, 25–42; National Research Council, *National Collaboratories: Applying Information Technology for Scientific Research* (Washington, D.C.: National Academy Pr., 1993).

3. B. Houghton, *Scientific Periodicals: Their Historical Development, Characteristics and Control* (London: Clive Bingley, 1975).

4. R. E. Lucier, "Knowledge Management: Refining Roles in Scientific Communication." *EDUCOM Review* 25 (fall 1990): 21–27; R. E. Lucier, "Toward a Knowledge Management Environment: A Strategic Framework," *EDUCOM Review* 27 (Nov./Dec. 1992): 24–31.

5. R. A. Lanham, T*he Electronic Word: Democracy, Technology, and the Arts* (Chicago: Univ. of Chicago Pr., 1993).

6. Ibid.

7. R. Atkinson, "Old Forms, New Forms: The Challenge of Collection Development," *College and Research Libraries* 50 (Sept. 1989): 507–20.

8. A. Okerson, "With Feathers: Effects of Copyright and Ownership on Scholarly Publishing." *College and Research Libraries* 52 (Sept. 1991): 425–38.

9. A. M. Cummings et al., *University Libraries and Scholarly Communication: A Study Prepared for the Andrew W. Mellon Foundation* (Washington, D.C.: Association of Research Libraries, 1992).

10. R. Noll, and W. E. Steinmueller, "An Economic Analysis of Scientific Journal Prices: Preliminary Results," *Serials Review* 18 (spring/summer 1992): 32–37.

11. Ibid., 35.

12. K. Stubs, "Introduction," *ARL Statistics 1992–93* (Washington, D.C.: Association of Research Libraries, 1994).

13. P. B. Dominguez, and L. Swindler, "Cooperative Collection Development at the Research Triangle University Libraries: A Model for the Nation," *College and Research Libraries* 54 (Nov. 1993): 470–96.

14. Association of American Universities Research Libraries Project in Collaboration with the Association of Research Libraries, *Reports of the AAU Task Forces on Acquisition and Distribution of Foreign Language and Area Studies Materials, a National Strategy for Managing Scientific and Technological Information, Intellectual Property Rights in an Electronic Environment* (Washington, D.C.: Association of Research Libraries, 1994).

15. American Physics Society, "Report of the APS Task Force on Electronic Information Systems," *Bulletin of the American Physical Society* 36 (1991): 1119–51. The society has predicted the evolution of a single physics database.

16. K. M. Drabenstott, *Analytical Review of the Library of the Future* (Washington, D.C.: Council on Library Resources, 1994).

17. Association of American Publishers, "An AAP Position Paper on Scanning," press release, Aug. 5, 1994.

18. C. A. Lynch, "Reaction, Response, and Realization: From the Crisis in Scholarly Communication to the Age of Networked Information," *Serials Review* (spring/summer 1992): 111.

19. Lynch, "Accessibility and Integrity of Networked Information Collections," 22.

20. R. M. Dougherty, "A 'Factory' for Scholarly Journals," *Chronicle of Higher Education* (June 17, 1992): B1, B3; S. J. Rogers and C. S. Hurt, "How Scholarly Communication Should Work in the 21st Century," *Chronicle of Higher Education* (Oct. 18, 1989): A56 (reprinted in *College and Research Libraries* 51 [Jan. 1991]: 5–8).

21. American Physics Society, "Report of the APS Task Force on Electronic Information Systems."

22. D. Schauder, "Electronic Publishing of Professional Articles: Attitudes of Academics and Implications for the Scholarly Communication Industry," *Journal of the American Association for Information Science* (Mar. 1994): 93–95.

23. C. A. Lynch, "The Transformation of Scholarly Communication and the Role of the Library in the Age of Networked Information," *Serials Librarian* (1993): 15.

24. Association of American Universities Research Libraries Project, *Reports of the AAU Task Forces on Acquisition and Distribution of Foreign Language and Area Studies Materials.*

25. A. R. Kenney and L. K. Personius, "The Future of Digital Preservation," *Advances in Preservation and Access* 1 (1992): 195–212.

26. H. Borman and S. H. von Solms, "Hypermedia, Multimedia, and Hypertext: Definitions and Overview," *Electronic Library* 11 (Aug.–Oct. 1993): 259–68.

11 CRISIS AND OPPORTUNITY

REEVALUATING ACQUISITIONS BUDGETING IN AN AGE OF TRANSITION

The academic library has but one purpose, and that is to support the educational and scholarly objectives of the institution it serves. The new information era we are now gradually entering, however, calls into question the ability of the library's traditional operations to support those institutional objectives. The continued participation of the library in the academic enterprise will therefore depend increasingly on the facility with which the library is able systematically to replace those current operations—on the basis of which it has defined its existence for so many decades—with new ones that will be able to respond more effectively to the new information needs and expectations of higher education. The many challenges the academic library presently faces in the current environment, including especially the endemic erosion of library resources, must be confronted and can be overcome, therefore, only within this context of transition.

Certainly one of the most visible and highly publicized economic challenges facing the academic library at this time is the decline in the purchasing power of the acquisitions budget. Large-scale serial cancellation projects have become a way of life for all academic libraries. The prices of many library materials are growing much more rapidly than library acquisition budgets, which has led to an increasingly evident degradation in the quality and depth of library collections in all types and sizes of academic institutions.[1]

Major efforts by libraries to combat this decline have been directed primarily outward in the form of public denunciations of publisher prices and of overtures to other libraries to establish cooperative or coordinated acquisition agreements. Neither of these tactics has proven very successful—partially, in my opinion, because of the competitiveness and internal fragmentation of the academic community and the academic library. This is not to claim, of course, that adjustments to relationships within and among academic institutions and their libraries will lead miraculously to a decline in externally imposed costs of library materials, but rather only that such adjustments must form an essential first step toward the creation of a practicable strategy to manage the costs of scholarly communication during this period of transition. The purpose of this paper, therefore, will be to consider why and how the acquisitions budget should for that purpose be integrated into the broader library and institutional budgetary and planning process.

THE COLLECTION DEVELOPMENT ETHOS

Research library collection development in its modem form evolved in the 1960s as a kind of organizational and political mitosis. Inside the library, collection development

This article first appeared in *Journal of Library Administration* 19, no. 2 (1993): 33–55. Copublished simultaneously in *Declining Acquisitions Budgets: Allocation, Collection Development and Impact Communication,* ed. Sul H. Lee (Binghamton, N.Y.: Haworth Pr., 1993), 33–55.

disengaged itself from the processing side of library operations—principally the acquisitions function—basing this separation on the distinction between selection and acquisition. This led to the division of the academic library into its current tripartite structure of public services, technical services, and collection development. At the same time, academic library collection development defined itself outside of the library by assuming responsibilities previously in the hands of some faculty users.[2] This process was undertaken deliberately but gradually—aided by such innovations as the modern collection policy, which in its early form doubtless functioned as a kind of guarantee or assurance to faculty that their bibliographic needs would be effectively met even after they themselves were no longer initiating selection decisions. This assumption of responsibility was possible and necessary at least partially because of the fundamental fragmentation of the faculty. One purpose of collection development, therefore, has always been in effect to provide a form of adjudication in order to ensure that the bibliographic resources needed by different faculty users and programs would be equitably distributed. Fulfilling this responsibility—and indeed retaining the authority for fulfilling it—will admittedly become increasingly difficult in an age in which users interact directly with information online.

The essential instrument that drives and sustains collection development has always been the acquisitions budget. Outside the library, the budget permits collection development to respond to faculty needs and to function as an equitable distributor of bibliographic resources. Inside the library, it is at least partially by means of the acquisitions budget that collection development is able to guide and influence library policy. "The form the budget takes, and the process used to achieve it, . . . reflect the decision-making authority within the library."[3] In the same way that different faculty groups or members are in frequent competition for institutional resources, different segments of the library are also often unavoidably in some form of competition with each other. The budgetary authority of collection development, combined with its close linkage to faculty, has empowered it to play a role equal and complementary to the more established functions of public services and technical services.[4]

Competition among different library operations is understandably exacerbated by austerity. "What heightens competition most of all is the perception of a finite sum of money to allocate."[5] Because library resources are so clearly in a state of decline, they are as such inadequate to support properly all library operations. Each operation naturally assumes its contribution to information services is among the most critical and therefore deserves preferential treatment. What is different about collection development is that in its case this preferential treatment has often been forthcoming. In many institutions, the acquisitions budget is maintained separately from the rest of the library's budget, because of its perceived significance, and in order to counteract the traditionally higher level of inflation for library materials. This convention of a separate acquisitions budget has also contributed to collection developments autonomy. The university administration further strengthens this autonomy by stipulating often that funding allocated for materials is to be spent for no other purpose. The administration recognizes, moreover, that the acquisitions budget is—theoretically—a source of value to the entire institution, and therefore represents a safe and nonpartisan budget increase even (or especially) in times of austerity. Such preferential treatment of the acquisitions budget, it must be admitted, may result in part from a misunderstanding of the information services process by the institutional administration: the implication seems to be that the acquisitions budget must be protected—even, if necessary, at the expense of staff and library infrastructure, as if information sources could be made accessible merely by purchasing them. This is obviously absurd, yet to deny this assumption too vigorously might well result in the library receiving no preferential treatment from the institution at all. The end result has been in any event that collection development budgetary resources have increased much more rapidly than those of other library operations—possibly to the detriment of information services as a whole.

The Library as Agency

All well functioning service organizations, including especially information services, understand themselves to be representatives of their clientele. All academic librarians see themselves more or less as agents of their users. The library is therefore in many respects an agency, in the narrow sense of an organization created and sustained for the sole purpose of acting in the interest of some group other than itself. We do well to bear in mind, therefore, as G. Stevenson Smith points out, the existence of a substantial literature on agency theory, a basic premise of which is that agencies sometime unwittingly or even perhaps intentionally tend to act in their own self-interest, rather than in the interests of their principals or clients.[6] In order to avoid such situations, contracts are agreed upon between agents and their principals. In academic libraries, budgets and collection policies presumably serve those same contractual purposes.

Let me stress at once that I do not mean to imply that collection development has ever intentionally acted in its own self-interest or has ever intended to misrepresent anyone, including especially the institution or faculty it serves. We must admit at the same time, however, that the function of research library collection development has gained somewhat in significance as a direct result of the so-called serials crisis. Demonstrable scarcity increases budgets, and it increases the authority of budget managers. Nowhere in the library is scarcity as visible or as easily demonstrated as in collection building. Indeed, the costs of library materials (due in part to the price increases of European science publishers) are increasing so rapidly that no university could ever expand the library's acquisitions budget year after year at a rate which could even begin to keep pace with such price increases.

This condition of demonstrably declining purchasing power has been evident now in the acquisitions budget for the better part of two decades—in other words, for practically as long as collection development has been in existence. It is especially important therefore that we begin to recognize that collection development, both as a library function and as a political entity, is at least in part a product of this seemingly inexorable budgetary decline. Collection development is in its modern form inseparable from, and perhaps now even inconceivable without, the decline in library resources in general and the serials crisis in particular. Collection development has defined itself, established its goals, and measured its successes mainly in terms of that decline. Collection development has in fact become that library (or information service) function which seeks to build collections and to provide access to information in an environment of inadequate resources and negligible control over the means of publication production. Again, I certainly do not mean to imply that collection development either desired or conspired to create this condition. I am saying, however, that collection development would be a very different function in the absence of those extreme budgetary pressures typified by the serials crisis. It is important to understand therefore that the successful eradication of those factors that have created such budgetary pressures will fundamentally alter the profession of collection development administration.

The Pursuit of Cooperation

Of the several courses of action which collection development has considered to alleviate this condition, certainly the most visible and perhaps most innately logical has been cooperative collection development. Several versions and theories of cooperative collection development have evolved, but certainly the best known and most discussed has been the synergistic version, in which different libraries take responsibility for collecting different publications, according to some coordinated plan. The most successful instance of such synergism was surely the Farmington Plan, which was intended to divide responsibilities for the selection and acquisition of foreign publications.[7] The effort to apply that same process to the acquisition of higher use materials, such as science journals, was, as Richard Dougherty and others have since pointed out, somewhat flawed from the beginning—if for no other reason than that, if we succeeded in dividing such responsibility for expensive serials among institutions, this would reduce the total number of subscriptions, which would in turn almost certainly encourage the publishers of those serials to increase subscription rates, thus eliminating any savings for the libraries participating in such a strategy.[8] The cancellation of expensive, commercially produced serials, in other words, will not reduce costs, because it will generally result in the increase in the prices of those remaining commercially produced serials to which the library continues to subscribe. As long as the library does not control publication production, it will not control costs. The large science publishers, who account for an increasing proportion of that production, will demand increasing revenues, regardless of how academic libraries divide selection responsibilities among themselves. The copyright laws also conspire against cooperative collection development, because the publishers are of course intelligent enough to charge higher prices for their higher use materials—and if we were to cancel such high use items, we would doubtless end up borrowing them so frequently through interlibrary loan that we would be legally compelled to resubscribe.

But these are not the only reasons we have failed to put broad cooperative collection development programs into effect. Indeed, we have seldom brought our cooperative planning far enough even to test these assumptions, although we have discussed and analyzed cooperative collection development from every conceivable angle. Perhaps the most extended and certainly one of the most energetic and altruistic efforts to create a national cooperative collection development program was the Research Libraries Group (RLG) Collection Management and Development Committee (CMDC). This group, which included during its existence many of the best minds in research library collection development, met at first quarterly, and then biannually for over a decade. It was supported and encouraged financially and morally by many of the largest research institutions in the nation, and it examined cooperative collection development from many perspectives. It devised detailed plans, and it worked industriously to put those plans into effect. Some of those efforts notably the group's greatest monument, the Conspectus—but also some other programs, such as the Long-Term Serials Project—are still in operation and still have some influence. But it must be admitted that the calculable effect of this decade of effort on the acquisitions budgets of the participating institutions, when compared especially with the cost of the Committee's operation, were probably negligible. There are many reasons for this, including most notably the inability of any institution to participate successfully in any program that entails the purchase of materials needed by scholars at another institution at the expense of materials needed by its own users. One further reason for the inability of CMDC to develop more effective cooperative programs may have been that the RLG program committees were designed to mirror the academic libraries they were intended to support. Separate committees were formed, therefore, for collection development, technical services, public services, and preservation, thus perpetuating the divisions among those primary library functions and impairing further their coordination. While the CMDC, moreover, worked hard and long on a unified collection policy, the Conspectus, a unified budgeting process was seldom if ever considered. This inability or unwillingness to reconsider or revise local budgeting methods, which do indeed reflect "the values and priorities of the library, and of the broader institution itself," bears witness both to the inability of libraries to transcend their internal divisions and to their reluctance to look beyond their own walls for the potential provision of traditional library services to their local clientele.[9]

Using What We Have

In the absence of control over key sources of library expenses, including especially publication production, the library must at the very least ensure that it is making optimum use of what resources it does have at its disposal. This will require, first, some mechanism that allows, or indeed forces, the library routinely to consider cooperative programs of all types with other institutions. Some process for quantifying and assessing the cost benefits of cooperation, and of regularly comparing the benefits of cooperation with those of independence must be put in place. Second, the optimum use of library resources will require greater participation of clientele in decisions as to how resources are to be used. We must expert this expanded participation to develop in any event as users become increasingly able to obtain access to information electrically without using the library directly. If the library is to continue to fulfill its function as both intermediary and adjudicator, if it is to move successfully at all through the age of transition it is now entering, better opportunity for faculty participation in—or at least observation of—the resource allocation process must be provided. Third, and equally important, the optimum use of library resources requires within the library the creation of library-wide priorities, and the application of those priorities across library functions—or more exactly: it will require the ability (a) to determine which aspects of which library functions will contribute most effectively to the fulfillment of those priorities, and then (b) to support those functions accordingly. Such an expansion of the resource allocation process inside and outside the library threatens the autonomy and authority of collection development more than any other library function—and it is precisely for this reason that collection development must initiate this process.

REMODELING THE LIBRARY BUDGET

The primary instrument for this transformation must be the budget. We must adopt budgeting methods that will permit us to use the budget as a planning tool and as a communications device. Several methods have been devised to respond to such needs, but few have proven satisfactory.[10] Program Planning and Budgeting, while an arguably effective budgeting method for the Department of Defense thirty years ago, has been very difficult to apply in many other organizations, including libraries. Zero-base budgeting has been somewhat more effective, and remains potentially applicable to some library budgeting needs.[11] Whatever method is selected, however, it is essential that the budget project the true costs of academic information services, and that it clarify the priorities the library intends to adopt in order to meet those costs. In collection development, we have in the past relied primarily on written collection development policies to achieve some of these purposes. Collection policies are, however, often difficult for faculty (or indeed for anyone outside of collection development) to understand easily, and they remain in any event meaningless abstractions for staff and faculty alike when not directly connected to the budget. The other major drawback of collection policies is that they can also serve to isolate (or insulate) collection development from other equally essential library services which directly affect access. While a collection policy may therefore guide or reflect the library's selection of materials, it only partially regulates their accessibility to users, because the policy does not necessarily stipulate the priorities of other library functions.[12]

Both the collection policy and the materials budget in their current forms, therefore, can lead to a fragmentation of library operations: the policy and the budget give the impression—propound the illusion—that different library operations are undertaken for different purposes—rather than that all library operations are merely different methods, or links in a chain, to achieve the single purpose of local access. If the fragmentation of the academic research library into separate and competing jurisdictions is to be even somewhat alleviated, therefore, fundamental redistributions and redefinitions of operational authority and responsibility throughout the library system may need to be effected. Care must be taken in any event to avoid a condition in which different traditional library operations are perceived and run as relatively separate enterprises, each with its own self-defined objectives. We must consequently redesign and learn to use the library budget to serve not only as a communications vehicle with the institution but also as a process to bring about a more effective coordination and coalescence of traditional library operations.

Our immediate goals should be therefore (a) to foster a reintegration of the acquisitions budget with the full library budget, so that the true costs and cost benefits of library services and information access will be apparent, (b) to extend the collection policy into a full library operational policy, defining priorities in unified terms for all library "selection" activities, including especially cataloging, ILL location (off-site storage), and preservation as well as collection building, and (c) finally to amalgamate this expanded budget and this expanded policy into a single document that will engage the library, the user community, and the institutional administration in the planning and budgeting process, that will promote the assessment of potential cooperative programs with other institutions and that will support the gradual transformation of academic information services. This is admittedly a tall order—but one upon which the future effectiveness of academic information services directly depends. I will spend the remainder of this paper making a few suggestions as to how the first step in this process—budget integration—might be achieved.

Multidimensional Budgeting

Academic libraries need to look more to the commercial sector for organizational and budgetary models. In our exasperation over what we view as our exploitation by commercial publishers, we have failed to appreciate their success. Their purpose is to make money, and we must admit they have achieved that purpose spectacularly. We must not be repelled by the commercial sector, therefore, but should rather study and learn from it, even though the objectives of academic libraries often diverge significantly from those of commerce. One innovation recently proposed for larger businesses is what Jeffrey A. Schmidt calls multidimensional budgeting, the purpose of which is to convert "conventional budgets into formats that are more relevant to management."[13] Schmidt suggests four separate budgets, or budget dimensions: an activity budget, a product budget, a customer budget, and a strategy budget, each of which is connected or mapped onto the previous one.

> [M]anagement can assess resource allocations by working down from the strategic budget to the base conventional budget. At each level, management can test the correct alignment of resources against its priorities, and the budget can be adjusted, as necessary, until an optimal statement is achieved.[14]

Certainly multidimensional budgeting is intended to achieve some of the main goals as the planning-programming-budget system and zero-base budgeting, especially in its aim to use budgeting as a means to establish priorities—but multidimensional budgeting is not nearly as complex and exacting a process as PPBS or ZBB. It is rather, in my opinion, simply a call to look at the same funding from a variety of successive perspectives, in order to learn more about the rationale for past expenditures and to understand more clearly the implications of potential allocation decisions. Viewed from another perspective, multidimensional budgeting, which some companies, or even some libraries, may well be practicing in one form or another already, is merely a method to move systematically from an incremental budget to one which better reflects programs and policy.

How might multidimensional budgeting be applied in academic libraries? To be sure, with some difficulty. Not only is the redefinition of budget categories a problematic and potentially controversial undertaking, but such categories must also permit accounting procedures to be devised that will permit the capture of appropriate expenditure data. Such challenges must nevertheless be confronted, if the budget is to serve as a mechanism for communication and functional integration.

In designing a multidimensional budgetary model for libraries, we could try to adopt Schmidt's four budget dimensions to library purposes; it is probably preferable, however, to define our own dimensions. Most academic libraries will presumably want be to shown how library services support academic programs, and they will want the budget to provide insights and facilitate decisions on how the costs of those services should be distributed. We need therefore to move through a minimum of three dimensions: from (a) the traditional operating budget through (b) a service budget to (c) some kind of program or policy budget. The process of mapping one budget on to the next will necessarily strain some budget categories, and will require that some of these categories be modified. This categorical review and redefinition should be accepted, however, as an inevitable and ultimately beneficial consequence of any planning effort. We will therefore develop a budget with three budget dimensions, each of which should be used in order to allocate *the same* available funding. (The grand total of each budget dimension, in other words, should be the same.) The same categories should be used to record expenses, of course, both to track spending and to produce historical information that can be applied to future allocation decisions.

First Dimension: The Operational Budget

We will list the budget categories on the vertical axis, and the cost (or "responsibility") centers on the horizontal axis. See figure 1. Most academic libraries will use some version of this traditional line-item budget. Funding is allocated by category to the cost centers, each of which has a budget manager responsible for suballocation and expenditures. The cost centers in the standard library budget are often library units—individual libraries in the system or central departments. Each cost center then has its own subbudget within which it will define its own budget categories. When there is a separate collection development operation, of course, the materials budget is suballocated, usually by subject.[15] We will use the standard budget categories of personnel, materials and "other," in which the latter often refers increasingly to online services. As Werking has shown, the "other" category has been growing more rapidly in academic libraries than the categories of materials and personnel.[16]

This standard form of budgeting provides considerable flexibility—

	Main Library	Branch 1	Branch 2	Central Processing	TOTAL
Personnel					
Materials					
Other					
TOTAL					

FIGURE 1. Operations Budget

with the notable exception that many libraries are prohibited by their central administrations from shifting funds between materials and personnel. The independent authority given to individual fund managers, moreover, shields much of the use of the operational budget from external scrutiny, protecting it from many outside pressures, and ensuring that the administrative integrity of the library budget remains intact.[17] For these same reasons, however, the standard operational budget is not very helpful for purposes of planning or communication. The real application of the budget takes place relatively out of sight, so that the transformation of fiscal resources into information services is obscured. While this can be seen to safeguard the library's autonomy, it also makes it difficult to argue for increased funding—or even to explain how changes in allocation affect the availability and utility of information to meet the scholarly and instructional needs of the institution. While the standard operations budget remains essential as a first budgeting step and should be retained, the budgeting process should not be concluded with such a budget. A more effective budgeting mechanism is also required, therefore, by means of which the uses of the budget can be displayed more visibly. This should be the purpose of the service budget.

Second Dimension: The Service Budget

I would suggest that the service budget be mapped onto the operational budget by retaining the same budget categories, replacing the units with services as the cost centers, and then rebudgeting the amounts in the final column of the operational budget across the new service budget.[18] The process of designating services as cost centers is of critical importance, because these will be viewed by the institutional community as the primary justifications for the library's maintenance and support. The library will in effect define itself through these categories. Whatever services the library decides to select, they should be understandable or easily explainable to users, and they should be adaptable to transition, i.e., simultaneously applicable to both traditional and online services.

I am convinced that the major service division in the library must be between mediation (which encompasses the traditional functions of reference, collection development, and cataloging) and delivery (e.g., acquisitions, circulation, ILL, preservation, library systems).[19] I would therefore aim to divide all services into these general categories as soon as possible, although certainly more traditional categories may be initially preferable for most libraries.[20] Since we must account for the entire budget in each dimension, we are compelled to add a third cost center, which is not a service, but which nevertheless must be supported: administration. The administrative budget should be kept on principle to a minimum in order to ensure that most budgetary decisions and uses are effected at the service level, and to avoid using the administrative category as a catch-all to evade the chore of distinguishing between the operational service categories.

An important part of any budget as a planning or management tool must be the consideration of alternatives or options. These might be added to the service budget as subcategories. Such options should be included, it seems to me, in any planning budget, even if some of them are not used. In such cases, the amount allocated for unaccepted options is simply zero, but the option should remain in the budget as a record of the decision, and so that the possible use of that option in future can be revisited. Many different kinds of alternative options might be included. The development of alternatives should promote discussions not only of adjusted or improved services, but also of so-called "opportunity costs," i.e., those activities or opportunities that will be forfeited by selecting one option over another.[21] For the purposes of our example, let us consider the fundamental alternative between funding something internally and contracting it out to an external agency. We will therefore include the simple (and oversimplified) options of "internal" and "external" as subcategories in our services budget example. See figure 2.

Care must obviously be taken in defining "external services"—specifically, whether this refers to operations external to the library or external to the institution. In my opinion, which is admittedly based on experience in larger academic institutions, it is preferable to define "external services" as external to the library, thus encouraging comparisons between the costs of institutional services and those of agencies outside the institution. So long as the library's budget is separate from that of the rest of the institution, whether one transfers funds to another campus operation or to a distant commercial enterprise makes no difference to the budget (although it may to the institution).

	Mediation	Delivery	Administration	TOTAL
Personnel Internal				
External				
Materials Internal				
External				
Other Internal				
External				
TOTAL Internal				
External				

FIGURE 2. Service Budget

We now begin to perceive the first strains on our standard budget categories. Using external personnel for administrators, for example, while certainly a tantalizing idea, is probably not very practicable. On the other hand, such a budget format would encourage some estimation of the cost benefits of using external staff for some mediation services: cataloging or selection or even reference. The more we advance into the online era, the more feasible will become the use of external staff for such purposes. The same is true, of course, for the various services that come under the heading of delivery: while today most delivery staff will no doubt be in the library, the storage and delivery of online information will be increasingly contracted out or shared among institutions. This should be reflected and anticipated in the budget.

The most problematic category is no doubt materials, by which we mean publications regardless of format that are read or accessed primarily by library users—but arguably also by library staff. Materials that fall within the mediation category include those that identify or describe or refer to other materials, i.e., reference sources. These sources—e.g., bibliographies, indexes—should be understood as falling primarily in the external option category. This is important: we must recognize that we are in effect contracting out to publishers for the production of such sources. There is, on the other hand, one large and expensive reference publication that is now produced internally, which is the library catalog. We notice at once, however, that the cost of the catalog as a publication manifests itself primarily in the cost of the staff producing it. In other words, most internal costs for the production of materials would normally appear in the budget as personnel costs. Materials costs are therefore probably by definition external, and I would recommend that we include all nonreference library materials in the category of external delivery, because all publications are fundamentally delivery mechanisms that have been in a sense contracted out to external agencies (for the most part, to publishers).

It is in this category of external delivery, then, that the enormous costs of materials—the origin of the serials crisis, and of much of the decline in the fiscal resources of the library generally—are located in the budget. The structure of the budget should force the institution therefore to recognize publication—especially commercial publication—as essentially an external, contracted service; the budget should further require us to consider, as we did in the case of personnel, the potential cost implications of shifting those costs or allocations from, in this case, external to internal. By generating an initially somewhat contradictory category of "internal materials" (which would admittedly ultimately manifest itself as an internal personnel cost), the service budget compels us to consider this as an alternative delivery mechanism—not on the airy theoretical level, but on the highly practical level of budget allocation. Each time the budget process is enacted, therefore, the prospects of a shift from external to internal—from commercial to local, institutional publication—will or should be weighed. The further we move into the online age, the more opportunities to transfer delivery responsibilities from external publishers to the institution (or preferably the library) will become apparent.[22] And the more open the budgeting process, the more users who need publications to be delivered to them (and who want their own publications delivered to others) will be made aware of these opportunities.

Administrative materials, to complete our review of the service budget categories, might consist mainly of management information, some of it produced externally, and some internally.[23] Access to this information is increasingly important for research library management, but its costs are rarely articulated, and the resources needed to create it are seldom clearly allocated. Finally, the "other" category will consist of the same kinds of items as those in the operational budget—mainly supplies and equipment—except that one might prefer to budget bibliographic utility fees—e.g., for OCLC and RLIN—not in the "other" category in the services budget, but rather as an external mediation cost for materials.

Third Dimension: The Program Budget

In order to map the service budget to the program budget, I would suggest using the previously identified services as the new budget categories, then defining the programs as the new cost centers. This will involve the final row of costs (total) in the service budget and rebudgeting those costs across the new budget, so that the final column in the program budget will be identical to the final row in the service budget. The purpose of the program budget is to shift the perspective from the information service programs, as conveyed in the service budget, to the client or institutional programs.[24] How such programs are designated in the budget depends upon the values and priorities of the individual institution, and upon the message the library wants to convey to its clientele community. Obviously the users themselves need to identify with the programs listed—to understand the needs and capacities with which they are affiliated—so probably the most effective approach might be simply to use the administrative divisions within the institution, such as colleges or departments.[25]

For purposes of our example, let us simply use as our programmatic cost centers the standard subject categories of humanities, social sciences, sciences, and interdisciplinary. See figure 3. Ideally we might prefer in many instances to budget information service costs across other cost centers, for example: instruction, current research, long-term/potential research. Instruction and research are certainly the two most frequently cited divisions of institutional programmatic responsibilities, and if we could divide research into current (needed now for ongoing research) and long-term (needed potentially in future to maintain quality collections), this would provide a fine opportunity to establish funding priorities: we could demonstrate that, as purchasing power erodes, we must shift costs increasingly from long-term to current research, and then from current research to instructional support. We could use what we budget for long-term research as a basis for cooperative collection development programs. Such categories might also be useful for calculating indirect costs for federal grants, which often support materials acquired for research, but not for instruction. While this may appear to be a reasonable budgetary structure in theory, however, anyone who has tried it must readily admit that it is highly problematic in reality, because we cannot in most cases determine whether materials acquired and cataloged will be used for

instruction or research. Materials acquired for graduate instruction, for example, are often the same as those used for faculty research—and whether an item will be used for current research or only in the longer-term future is impossible to predict.[26]

	Humanities	Social Science	Sciences	Inter-Disciplinary	TOTAL
Mediation Internal					
External					
Delivery Internal					
External					
Admin Internal					
External					
TOTAL Internal					
External					

FIGURE 3. Program Budget

In reality, further subject breakdowns than humanities, social sciences, sciences and interdisciplinary would likely be needed at least for larger institutions. The other and more problematic requirement for program designation is, of course, that the program costs be realistically and readily quantifiable. Establishing program costs in this fashion is especially difficult for most libraries—except perhaps for the collection development operation, which traditionally divides its materials budget by subject or program. The costs of supporting some of the most important program categories may not be easily identifiable. On the other hand, not only do different subjects or other programmatic categories have different needs and values, they also have different developing research infrastructures, with online uses and capacities evolving at very different rates. These different needs and different access opportunities can at least be reflected in the program budget. We cannot avoid the interdisciplinary category, since the parameters of subjects are notoriously permeable—although like the use of the "administration" category, we must take care not to use the interdisciplinary category as an excuse to avoid difficult categorical budgetary decisions. Tracking and budgeting mediation costs, while difficult, should be within our means. Mediation personnel (presently in reference, collection development and cataloging), for example, frequently have subject specialties. Many paraprofessional staff, on the other hand, such as searchers, reference assistants or copy catalogers, will still need to be included in the interdisciplinary categories.

As in the service budget, it is especially important to include in the program budget "internal" and "external" alternative options. In both the mediation and delivery categories, most of the personnel costs will remain internal and most of the materials costs external using the definitions established in the service budget. An important part of the program budget process must be to consider how costs can be reduced and/or services enhanced by examining alternatives, as they apply specifically to different institutional programs.

Finally, we will no doubt find in the program budget that administrative costs are even more difficult to integrate than in the service budget but again, we must not lose sight of the fact that administrative costs are real, and must be accounted for. Including administrative costs provides a clear indication of their effect on program support, requires that they be regularly and, routinely justified, and ensures that they will be systematically factored into any budget planning rather than hidden and protected. Such administrative costs might either simply be included in the interdisciplinary column, or some effort might be made to distribute them across institutional programs.

The difficulties and values of such a method as multidimensional budgeting should now be apparent. Like other budgeting methods—although perhaps in a rather simpler fashion—library-wide, multidimensional budgeting would in a sense purchase planning and coordination capabilities somewhat at the expense of clear and easily managed accounting procedures. But such benefits may be worth the costs. A primary drawback of such budgeting methods is the significant expenditure of staff time and energy necessary to quantify and track the expenditures in some of the more important categories. The value added to the budgeting process, however, should be substantial. In the case of multidimensional budgeting, the budget format will force the creation of priorities and encourage the consideration of the full effect of allocation. In the example presented above, in which the same funding is viewed from three different but connected dimensions or perspectives, not only must the first draft of such a budget present all three dimensions, but each change to the initial draft in the review process leading to the final budget also requires adjustments to all three dimensions, providing much more detailed insight into the implications of such adjustments for library services and academic program support. This should enhance significantly the communication and planning value of the deliberation and negotiation process that leads to the final budget draft.

CONCLUSIONS

If the library must indeed position itself for the gradual but inexorable transition into an age in which information exchange is characterized by the prevalence of online sources, then a major aspect of this work must inevitably be to shift more of the responsibility for scholarly communication to the academy itself. The adverse effect of the practices of commercial science publishers on scholarly information exchange presents only one argument—although certainly a very compelling one—for such action. If the academic library is to participate in—and facilitate—this transformation in scholarly communication, as indeed it should, a more detailed budgeting process, possibly of the multidimensional type suggested above, must be devised and implemented. This redesign will not be without political risk for the library, for to make budgeting a more public process is to invite some controversy. It is, however, only by opening up the budgeting process that the library can successfully inform the community of the true costs of information services, and begin to urge the community to adopt more economically reasonable methods of information transfer. Only through such a public and expanded budgeting process, moreover, can the library demonstrably ensure that it is functioning consciously as the agent of its users—and not in its own interests. And only through such an expanded budgeting process, finally, can the competing traditional jurisdictions within the academic library be somewhat alleviated, and the opportunities for interinstitutional cooperation assessed.

The fundamental rationale for the academic library will remain the same in the online era as it has always been: to provide current and future local users with access to that information they need to do their work in the shortest possible time. In order to continue to achieve that objective in our radically changing technical and economic environment, the library and its institution must consider how to change more of its mediation costs from internal to external, and how to shift more of its delivery costs from external to internal. We need, in other words, for our local users to begin to rely more on mediation services provided (online) by other institutions—in effect, dividing responsibility for specialized subject expertise among institutions. At the same time, more of our delivery costs need to be at least partially internalized by contriving for individual institutions to assume the role of publisher—either of the scholarship of its local faculty or on the basis of some division of subject publication responsibilities across institutions. If this transition is managed gradually and deliberately, moreover, the effect on the availability of library jobs may be minimal: such jobs that are lost by contracting out for mediation might be replaced by the assumption of increased internal responsibilities for delivery.

All such work presupposes, of course, a much closer coordination of responsibilities among institutions than has been practicable in the past. The reasons we have failed to achieve such cooperation are not so much bibliographical or even economic, as they are cultural and political. This failure has been to our disadvantage, and the chronic inability of libraries—and institutions—to form effective alliances will become an increasingly serious impediment to scholarly communication. While economic pressures may force increased coordination among—and within—institutions, and while technical advances may provide improved means for such coordination, each institution must still develop internal techniques that will permit it to overcome those political and cultural obstacles. Since the budgeting activity is by far the most politically driven and culturally revealing process in any institution, it is only reasonable that our work begin there.

REFERENCE NOTES

1. This is the conclusion of the forthcoming Andrew W. Mellon Foundation report on *University Libraries and Scholarly Communication.* For a preview of that report, see *ARL: A Bimonthly Newsletter of Research Library Issues and Actions* 165 (Nov. 23, 1992): 1–2.

2. See Richard Flume Werking, "Allocating the Academic Library's Book Budget: Historical Perspectives and Current Reflections," *The Journal of Academic Librarianship* 14 (July 1988): 140–41.

3. Eugene L. Wiemers Jr., "Budget," in *Collection Management: A New Treatise,* ed. Charles B. Osburn and Ross Atkinson (Greenwich, Conn.: JAI Pr., 1991), Part A: 71.

4. See the remarks by Nancy A. Brown and Jerry Malone on resource control as one base of power in their "The Bases and Uses of Power in a University Library," *Library Administration & Management* 2 (June 1988): 142.

5. Jasper G. Schad, "Fairness in Book Fund Allocation," *College & Research Libraries* 48 (Nov. 1987): 486.

6. G. Stevenson Smith, *Managerial Accounting for Libraries and Other Not-for-Profit Organizations* (Chicago: ALA, 1991), 6–7. For a good summary of research on agency theory, see Kathleen M. Eisenhardt, "Agency Theory: An Assessment and Review," *Academy of Management Review* 14 (Jan. 1989): 57–74.

7. See Edwin E. Williams, "Farmington Plan" in *The Encyclopedia of Library and Information Science,* vol. 8 (New York: Dekker, 1972), 361–68.

8. Richard M. Dougherty, "Turning the Serials Crisis to Our Advantage: An Opportunity for Leadership," *Library Administration & Management* 3 (spring 1989): 60–61.

9. Wiemers, "Budget," 73.

10. For a good review of library budgeting, see Michael E. D. Koenig and Deidre C. Stam, "Budgeting and Financial Planning for Libraries," *Advances in Library Administration and Organization* 4 (1985): 77–110.

11. On zero-base budgeting, see Ching-chih Chen, *Zero-Base Budgeting in Library Management: A Manual for Librarians* (Phoenix: Oryx Pr., 1980); and more recently, Carol Hodlofski, "Zero-Base Budgeting: A Tool for Cutting Back," *The Bottom Line* 5 (summer 1991): 13–19. For one of the original accounts of the planning-programming-budget system, from which the goals but also the difficulties of the system are readily apparent, see "Program Planning and Budgeting Theory: Improved Library Effectiveness by Use of the Planning-Programming-Budgeting-System," *Special Libraries* 60 (Sept. 1969): 423–33. See also Michael E. D. Koenig and Victor Alperin, "ZBBB and PPBS: What's Left Now That the Trendiness Has Gone?" *Drexel Library Quarterly* 21 (summer 1985): 19–38.

12. Collection policies may, of course, as noted in Bonita Bryant, ed., *Guide for Written Collection Policy Statements,* Collection Management and Development guides, no. 3 (Chicago: ALA, 1989), 3, establish "useful priorities to guide cataloging, retrospective conversion, and preservation decisions," but if the policy does not expressly designate priorities for decision-making outside of collection development, they may well have only a minimal effect on broader library operations.

13. Jeffrey A. Schmidt, "Is It Time to Replace Traditional Budgeting? A Method to Make a Budget More Useful to Management is Proposed," *Journal of Accountancy* 174 (Oct. 1992), 104.

14. Ibid., 104.

15. For current guidelines, see Edward Shreeves, ed., *Guide to Budget Allocation for Information Resources,* Collection Management and Development Guides, no. 4 (Chicago: ALA, 1991), especially section 4.3 on "Structuring the budget."

16. Richard Hume Werking, "Collection Growth and Expenditures in Academic Libraries: A Preliminary Inquiry," *College & Research Libraries* 52 (Jan. 1991): 11–12.

17. This is perhaps one manifestation of "administrative secrecy" as described in Max Weber's classic account of bureaucracy in Part 2, Chapter XI, of his *Economy and Society.*

18. Schmidt does not suggest using the same categories for successive budget dimensions, but this seems to me desirable from a practical perspective in order to map one dimension on to another

19. See my "The Acquisitions Librarian as Change Agent in the Transition to the Electronic Library," *Library Resources & Technical Sciences* 36 (Jan. 1992): 7–20.

20. It would also be possible, of course, to further subdivide mediation into such activities as identification and description, and to add a separate subcategory of storage to the category of delivery.

21. On opportunity costs, see Michael Koenig, "Budgets and Budgeting, Part 1," *Special Libraries* 68 (July/Aug. 1977): 230–31. More recently, see Dennis P. Carrigan, "Improving Return on Investment: A Proposal for Allocating the Book Budget," *The Journal of Academic Librarianship* 18 (Nov. 1992): 294.

22. Dougherty, "Turning the Serials Crisis," 62–63.

23. If we define "materials" as only those items used by clientele, then we would, of course, need to budget management information as "other."

24. This is admittedly a change to the usual use of the term "program budget," in which budgeting is normally based on agency programs rather than clientele programs. In my example, agency programs are instead the focus of the service budget.

25. For the drawbacks of allocating by academic department, see Jasper G. Schad, "Allocating Materials Budgets in Institutions of Higher Education," *The Journal of Academic Librarianship* 3 (Jan. 1978): 328.

26. In a totally online environment, of course, in which every use is the equivalent of a kind of online circulation transaction, it may be possible at least to track use, and extrapolate expenses on that basis—but whether even the availability of such data would permit the use of such budgeting categories remains doubtful.

12 THE COMING CONTEST

If, as now seems likely, many of the services provided by publishers and libraries in the current print environment will be done increasingly by writers and readers for themselves once the most heavily used information becomes available online, opportunities for both libraries and publishers to provide their services to academic users well may diminish. While the new online medium will doubtless spawn new service possibilities, the plain fact is that there may not be enough room in a primarily online environment for both academic libraries and commercial publishers of specialized scholarly information to grow and to remain key players in the academic information services arena. It is possible that libraries, if they are to continue to fulfill effectively their functions as primary service agents, will decide either to take on additional responsibilities for specialized scholarly publishing—or that publishers, in order to survive and expand, will need (and will have the technical capacity) to assume many of the mediation and distribution functions previously performed by libraries.

If this is true, and either academic libraries or scholarly publishers—but not both—will eventually prevail in a primarily online environment, then which should it be? Of course, academic libraries will agree easily that ultimately libraries should succeed, because they are more directly concerned and better able to deal with the information needs of academic users. Publishers, or at least the commercial ones, are indeed business enterprises, and customer service is not the fundamental purpose of business despite the proclamations of the current "quality" movement. The fundamental purpose of business is to stay in business: to grow and to increase return on investment. Customer service is merely a means to that end. If growth and revenue could be better achieved by ignoring or maltreating customers, then customers would be ignored or maltreated. Therefore, service quality is relatively simple for a business to define: high-quality services are those that generate increasing revenue, and low-quality services are those that do not.

In contrast, libraries have at their disposal no such straightforward method to measure quality of service, and are also obliged by their professional culture and their institutional commitments to view service not as a means but rather as an end—so that all actions taken and all resources expended are justified exclusively by that purpose. That being the case, what would happen, one wonders, if at a certain point academic libraries began to suspect that commercial vendors were developing a capacity to provide better service at a distance than libraries were able to provide on site? If service is the exclusive purpose of libraries, rather than a means to "stay in business," then would libraries, seeing that publishers could do a better job, simply convert themselves into warehouses, and advise their institutions to use the funding previously spent on libraries to provide instead access to the services of publishers (which would by that time have expanded themselves into full-service scholarly information brokerages)?

Of course not. But the reason this will not happen is neither because libraries are imbued with some supercompetitive spirit, nor because libraries are necessarily equipped to provide better services, but rather because libraries know so little about the quality of the services they do provide, that they would probably never notice that an outside agency was capable of doing a better job. Because service is so difficult (in the absence of a convenient gauge like revenue) to monitor and assess, and because the real needs of academic users are so diverse and complex, and because the library has always had (by virtue of its proximity to its users) what amounts to a monopoly on campus for print information services, and

This article first appeared as a "Guest Editorial" in *College & Research Libraries* (Nov. 1993): 458–60.

finally because service is the library's only purpose for existence, the library has preferred and has been permitted to define service quality on the basis of whatever service levels it—the library—provides. Since high-quality service is the only purpose for the existence of libraries, and since libraries exist, what they are providing must be high-quality service. Libraries consequently will never be able to recognize, let alone admit, that another agency is providing academic information services superior to those provided by libraries, because that is by definition impossible. Only after users have in effect rendered libraries totally superfluous by abandoning them for commercial vendors will libraries in their current condition be able to recognize that their services were inferior.

What is to be done? To begin with, academic libraries need to acknowledge and to prepare for a situation in the not-too-distant future in which they will enter into a very real and strenuous competition with commercial scholarly publishers and other vendors to become the dominant information service providers for students and faculty users. The more online publication becomes the accepted mode, the more opportunities, temptations, and incentives libraries and publishers are going to find to bypass each other. While one result of this might be that libraries and publishers will become so preoccupied with each other's traditional activities that they will end up simply exchanging responsibilities over time, a much more likely scenario is that one or the other will become the prevalent academic information provider. Academic libraries (and publishers) would be very foolish not to begin preparations now for that coming competition.

Second, as part of this preparation academic libraries must dispense with the mistaken notion that publishers and libraries are in entirely different businesses. Both libraries and publishers are fundamentally information intermediaries between academic writers and readers. It makes no difference whatsoever whether those services are understood as ends or as means. In a primarily online environment, moreover, it will be users (i.e., writers and readers) rather than libraries who define quality service.

Third, libraries need to begin learning as much as possible about specialized scholarly publishing. To this end closer links should be established with computer centers and university presses. The aim should be a condition in which a faculty member, having completed something for publication, will bring that material to the library. The library will then ensure that the material is referred to a nationally qualified editorial board; if the board accepts the item for publication, then it will be the library (after having done the necessary cataloging or indexing) that ensures through its links with other libraries around the nation and around the world that the item is published; that is, that it is made known and available to students and scholars who are interested in the subject.

Fourth, and perhaps most important, academic libraries now need to begin to concentrate on personalizing and humanizing relationships with their users, because it is only through continuous personal contact and interaction that libraries effectively can begin to assess and refine service quality. We have become so absorbed and preoccupied with the ability of computer-mediated communication and publication to eclipse location as a factor in scholarly collaboration and information services that we have ignored—or at least resigned ourselves to the unfashionability of discussing—the very real isolation and dehumanization that increasing reliance on online sources will necessarily entail. While proximity to users may no longer allow academic libraries to assume a service monopoly, it does continue to provide libraries with their greatest opportunity to tailor services (including publishing) to meet local user needs—services that are demonstrably superior to those available exclusively at a distance. It will be risky and difficult, but there is no alternative: the more rapid the advances of information technology, the more willing academic libraries must be to invest in enhancing their human resources. This is the real challenge, and if we are able to meet it, then we will succeed finally in supplying a truly superior information service as defined not by ourselves but by the preferences of our users.

13 NETWORKS, HYPERTEXT, AND ACADEMIC INFORMATION SERVICES

SOME LONGER-RANGE IMPLICATIONS

Because computer network use is increasing so rapidly, we must begin to consider some of the longer-term issues that relate to scholarly information exchange in a networked environment, and the possible future roles of academic information services in that exchange. The growing capacity of the network, combined with the eventual ability to link any textual units with any others, may well have profound effects on scholarly communication and higher education, especially the relationship between readers and writers. Three examples of key responsibilities that may be assumed by academic information services in the online environment are (a) assistance with institutionally based publication, (b) work with authors on the indexing of their publications, and (c) the design of new, network-based document structures.

The application of computer-mediated communication and resource sharing to the creation and exchange of scholarly information has been anticipated for decades, but only recently have librarians begun to witness the kind of rapid increase in the use and utility of networked information that we have for so long been expecting. The use of the network is now expanding so rapidly that the statistics recording that increase are difficult even to comprehend.[1] In response to the rapidly rising demand for computer networking—not only for scholarly purposes but also in support of government and commercial transactions—Congress has passed the High-Performance Computing Act of 1991, which is intended to "support the establishment of the National Research and Education Network (NREN), portions of which shall, to the extent technically feasible, be capable of transmitting data at one gigabit per second or greater by 1996.[2] Newly introduced legislation, "The Information Infrastructure and Technology Act," would authorize an additional $1.15 billion over five years to provide for the effective use of such a vastly expanded national network.[3] Perhaps the most pressing challenge to those of us responsible for academic information services, therefore, will be to remain somehow conceptually ahead of such developments in order to guide them whenever possible in directions that will ensure the greatest benefits for scholarship and higher education.

We appear to be succeeding in our effort to meet this challenge in the short term—at least to the extent that issues which must be settled before fully effective use of the network for research and instruction can be achieved are becoming increasingly well defined. Such shorter-term issues include controversial policy questions, most of which reduce to concerns about who owns or will own which parts of the network, and the extent to which

This article first appeared in *College & Research Libraries* (May 1993): 199–215.

the network should be publicly supported and controlled.[4] Many of these policy questions derive from the fact that a variety of constituencies will rely increasingly on the network for very different purposes.[5] Also of immediate concern are legal issues that must be clarified and negotiated, before published information can become broadly available in electronic form. The most important of these for scholarly communication have to do with copyright, and considerable effort is now being devoted to their definition and resolution.[6] There are also other legal issues relating to privacy and security, although many of these will be of much greater concern to commercial users of the network than to scholarly or academic users.[7] Vaguer and more vexing are the short-term social and cultural considerations that must be confronted. The most problematic of these from the standpoint of scholarly communication have to do with the willingness of scholars to accept electronic formats as a vehicle of formal publication.[8] Finally, a variety of shorter-term technical issues that will need to be resolved relate to such issues as network capacity, standards, and protocols.[9] It is perhaps indicative of the times in which we live that these technical impediments will doubtless be by far the easiest ones to overcome.

Because events and innovations are now finally accelerating so rapidly, however, concentration on the definition and solution of such shorter term issues is not enough. Taking "a 'wait and see' attitude on many key issues," as Richard Katz has recently noted, "is not a viable strategy."[10] If academic information services are to exercise some influence over the future direction of scholarly information exchange and higher education, then some thought must also be invested in what appear at the moment to be longer-term issues. (We must designate these as "longer-term" rather than "long-term," not only because such notions are always relative but also because these issues, too, will certainly be upon us much sooner than we expect.) We need to begin to prepare for these developments now; we need to begin to define concepts, to agree upon values, to take positions, if we are to lay the groundwork for decisive action in the future. This preparation will entail, unavoidably, some prediction and speculation about the qualities and uses of the network in its fully developed form. We must be willing, in other words, to undertake a certain amount of conjecture in public about what a network is and what *the* network will become, if we are to have any chance of influencing its evolution. The consideration of a few of these longer-term implications will be the purpose of this article.

INITIAL DEFINITIONS

Information Services

There are clearly many kinds of information, but let us restrict our definition to those groups of (often natural language) signs created by people for purposes of communicating their ideas.[11] The user—scholars, students—locates such sets of signs or information units, therefore, and produces information from them. The primary purpose of information services has always been and will always be to reduce to a minimum the amount of time required by local users to obtain access to that information they need to do their work.[12] All information service activities are intended ultimately to achieve that single objective. As we move increasingly into an online environment, those service activities will change, but that primary objective will remain the same. Results, in terms of access time reduction, should presumably improve substantially in an online environment. However, information overload—a primary retardant to academic information access since at least the advent of the machine press—will probably also become even more pronounced as more information becomes available online. Efforts to control such overload will no doubt drive the renovation of many information service operations.

An essential responsibility of information services must be to assist users in determining *what* information they need to do their work. Without this assistance, the amount of time the user will require to locate such information can be greatly extended. Information service operations provide this assistance by acting upon information—by selecting, distinguishing, referring to, and otherwise privileging individual information units, in order to enhance the user's ability (a) to locate those units and (b) to decide which of those units is worth the time to retrieve and absorb. In the paper environment, this service is provided most clearly through traditional library operations such as collection development, cataloging, and reference. All such services, moreover, regardless of the dominant information format, are necessarily intended to add value to individual information units by differentiating those units from each other in such a way that clientele will be able to make decisions as to the *sequence* in which they access information. All information exchange is necessarily sequential. Meaning is, in fact, at least partially a product of sequence; to change the sequence, therefore, is always to change the meaning. This is true not only at the sentence (syntactical) level but also at the document level, in the sense that the understanding of an information source is necessarily conditioned at least in part by the reader's (or hearer's) previous knowledge or experience of other sources. A primary purpose of academic information services, therefore, is to assist the student or scholar not only in locating needed information but also in determining which items of information to read (or hear) in which order.

The Network

John S. Quarterman defines a computer network as "a set of *computers* communicating by common conventions called *protocols* over *communication media.*"[13] A useful and concise definition—albeit one that also displays a problem that we encounter frequently in the literature on networks and computers—i.e., reification the confusion of human and material relationships. We must assume that it is information which is being communicated, and we have already defined information as consisting of signs. Computers, however, do not exchange signs. They exchange signals, i.e., "units of transmission which can be computed quantitatively irrespective of their possible meaning."[14] It is these signals that are then later converted into signs, so that users can extract or create information from them. Since communication entails the exchange of signs, it should not be supposed, as Quarterman apparently does, that a computer network consists of "a set of computers communicating." Networks are material transportation devices. At its most basic level, a network is a machine designed to move very small physical objects *(packets* in the current technology) from one place (or *node*) to another. It is important, therefore, that we continue to bear the materiality of the network in mind—that we recognize it for the mechanical apparatus it is.

Although there are many computer networks now in existence, these different networks are in some cases very difficult to differentiate.[15] It is, moreover, the nature and the purpose of networks to be indistinguishable—what we now call "transparent." For our purposes, therefore, it is most convenient to refer, as we have done so far, simply to *the network* in the generic sense of all of the networks now accessible. We must also note, however, the term *computer network* is often used to refer to several different concepts. One is clearly the *network proper,* i.e., the links or *highways* down which the signals are sent—the transportation system described above. By extension (metonymy), however, the term *network* is also often used to refer to the content of the databases accessible through the network—so the *extended network* also includes the information available through (i.e., derivable from) the network proper. Finally, there is what we might call the *functional network,* that includes the rules or *grammar*—not only technical (e.g., protocols), but also administrative and legal—which regulate the network's operation.[16] While information services have in the past been concerned primarily with the extended network, it will become increasingly important for academic information services to participate more actively in the direction and operation of the functional network as well.

Hypertext

The network proper is, in any event, a formal telecommunications instrument designed to connect computers. In considering the future of scholarly information exchange, we must therefore take into account not only the facility of the network but also the effects of computers on scholarly reading and writing. Certainly one of the best approaches to such an assessment is to focus on the phenomenon of hypertext because it is through the concept (if not yet the reality) of hypertext that we begin to sense the most fundamental and far-reaching effects of the computer on communication in general and scholarly information exchange in particular. Hypertext may be viewed both as a symbol and as the most visible manifestation of the radically new capabilities made available by computers. Hypertext also deserves the special attention of librarians because one of its most obvious and frequently described applications will be for bibliographical citation.[17]

A useful current definition of hypertext is provided in a 1988 article describing a hypertext system at Brown University:

> In essence, a hypertext system allows authors or groups of authors to link information together, create paths through a body of related material, annotate existing texts, and create notes that direct readers to either bibliographic data or the body of the referenced text. Using a computer-based hypertext system, students and researchers can quickly follow trails of footnotes and related materials without losing their original context; thus, they [students and researchers] are not obliged to search through library stacks to look up referenced books and articles. Explicit connections—links—allow readers to travel from one document to another, effectively automating the process of following references in an encyclopedia. In addition, hypertext systems that support multiple users allow researchers, professors, and students to communicate and collaborate with one another within the context of a body of scholarly material.
>
> *Hypermedia* is simply an extension of hypertext that incorporates other media in addition to text. With a hypermedia system, authors can create a linked body of material that includes text, static graphics, animated graphics, video, and sound.[18]

The term *hypertext* was originally coined by Theodor Nelson in 1965.[19] He then developed the concept further in other publications, most fully in his now classic *Literary Machines.* It was in that work especially that Nelson introduced the definition of hypertext as *nonsequential writing.*[20] That concept is frequently echoed in other current definitions.[21] As we noted above, however, sequence is a fundamental component of language, and there can obviously be no such thing as writing or reading "without sequence." What Nelson and others mean, of course, is that hypertext allows the reader to move parts of a document out of their "original" sequence, i.e., to embed them in, or to connect them to, contexts other than those in which the author originally placed them.

To change the sequence is, again, to change the meaning—so that hypertext provides the reader with the power and authority to affect the meaning of the text. We must also recognize, however, that the reader has always had that power anyway. The text consists of signs, and the reader has always brought the meaning to the text by relating the text to previous texts he or she has experienced. Indeed, the potential interrelationship or interconnectedness of all texts has become one of the dominant preoccupations of late twentieth-century philosophy and especially literary theory. In 1966, Julia Kristeva first coined the term *inter-*

textuality: "[A]ny text is constructed as a mosaic of quotations; any text is the absorption and transformation of another. The notion of *intertextuality* replaces that of intersubjectivity, and poetic language is read as at least *double*."[22] This concept, as developed especially by Roland Barthes, has become highly influential, and has been applied to a variety of critical purposes.[23] Care must be taken, as Kristeva noted later, however, not to imagine intertextuality as a linear concept, i.e., "in the banal sense of 'study of sources.'"[24] In 1976, Lauren Jenny pointed out that the fundamental metaphors of literary criticism were in fact noticeably shifting from aquatic linear images (e.g., "influences," "sources") to metaphors of webs, fabrics, or networks.[25] Roland Barthes, in a classic essay on the nature of the text, even noted that the word *text* itself derives from the Latin *texere,* which means to weave (cf. "textile").[26] The concept of linearity, therefore, has gradually been replaced in the late twentieth century by the realization that understanding is achieved only through a constant rearrangement of a network or matrix of texts.[27]

Hypertext does not engender intertextuality, therefore, but rather merely heightens its utility and effect. More precisely, hypertext permits the easy creation of new syntagmatic contexts, in the sense that it permits any text or group of texts to be reduced to its constituent elements, so that these elements can be rearranged or reconstituted in new sequences. While such a function has many uses, the one that is most frequently noted, as in Nicole Yankelovich's definition above, is fore purposes of increasing the application and extent of bibliographic citations (i.e., surrogate references to other texts). The reader in the fully formed hypertext network should be able to choose to read in two temporal directions—synchronically through the text as provided by the author but also diachronically back through the citations to which scholarly texts refer, and of which any text is necessarily composed—a kind of bibliographical reading. Each of the texts cited by the author can be read in a hypertext environment, including any parts of those cited texts not specifically quoted by the author—so that the reader can enter the cited text, and read on both sides, so to speak, of the quotation. Any citations in the cited text can in turn be followed backward to their original sources, and so forth.[28] And these are only the *explicit* citations. The reader will in all likelihood also have the ability to use implicit citations, i.e., to create new networks of references by looking for similar texts that use the same signifiers (words, sounds) in similar sequences or proximities in other files accessible throughout the network.[29] The reader can indeed approach the entire content of the extended network as a single unit (rather like approaching the entire library as a single, multivolume set). Research on the network thus comes to consist fundamentally of defining and redefining parameters, so that the reader does indeed become a writer, creating new texts through new contexts.

Hypertext's main strength, however, is also its greatest potential drawback: its infinite flexibility could create an environment in which the original expression of the author could become obscured or lost altogether:

> Hypertext fragments, disperses, or atomizes text in two related ways. First, by removing the linearity of print, it frees the individual passages from one ordering principle—sequence—and threatens to transform the text into chaos. Second, hypertext destroys the notion of a fixed unitary text. Considering the "entire" text in relation to its component parts produces the first form of fragmentation; considering it in relation to its variant readings and versions produces the second.[30]

This propensity for mutability has already been recognized as a potentially serious impediment to scholarly communication, and one which information services will certainly need to confront.[31] Nelson himself stipulated that a document in its original form—i.e., defined as finished by the author—should be subject to no further alterations, which are not made or condoned by the author.[32] But at the level of reading, of course, the reader can do whatever he or she wants to the original context—that is the nature of hypertext. At the level of reading, there can be no question that the writer will lose substantial authority and autonomy. Hypertext "infringes upon the power of the writer, removing some of it and granting it to the reader."[33] The unity and closure of the text as understood by the writer are no longer inviolable. To be sure, the writer, regardless of format, always merely recommends to the reader that the text be considered in a certain form, that it be read in a certain sequence, that it be related to certain parts of certain other texts. The reader is obviously always in the primary control of the reading—but the availability of hypertext and the network, it must be admitted, increases that control dramatically.

FREEDOM AND AUTHORITY

This diminution of authorial control is only one manifestation of a far more fundamental quality of hypertext and networking—and more generally of information exchange in the online era: the potential *forfeiture of origin.* We encounter this quality now probably most clearly in the reduction of the significance of location: where a particular segment of information is located is a far less important attribute of that information in a networked environment—not because location no longer exists (the signals that "carry" information are always material and must therefore always reside some*place),* but rather because those material signals can now be transported at such speeds that the effect of that transportation on access time becomes imperceptible to the user. All locations become relatively equivalent on the network: they lose their difference, and therefore their significance.

We have noted above that it is people (not computers) who communicate by means of networks; although this, too, is an oversimplification—in the sense that no one ever communicates directly *with* another person, but rather always with a text of some kind produced *by* another person. While print certainly tends to level or standardize such communication, the elimination of the perceived differences between one text and another, and thus the obfuscation of origins, becomes even more prevalent in a networked environment. All texts are manifested in the same form on the individual's computer screen. The text with which the reader interacts is something always already written (or copied) by someone on the network. Regardless of whether that someone wrote that text a few minutes or a few seconds before in response to a query by the reader on e-mail, or whether the original writer produced that text years or centuries or millennia ago under totally unknown circumstances—the reader is still engaged in a dialogue not with that person, but rather with the graphic, material signs. The network by virtue of its endemic neutrality encourages the reader to view all texts as current and all authors as contemporaries.

Jay David Bolter has examined these issues in some detail in his recent book *Writing Space.* He concludes that hierarchy in writing is a convention of the print culture, and that the advent of the fully developed hypertext network will free the reader from that hierarchy.[34] The hypertext network will also liberate the reader from the tyranny of the author, bringing about a welcome "end of authority."[35] This will lead to a "new dialogue" between reader and writer, "which replaces the monologue [of the author] that is the conventional printed essay or monograph."[36] This tyranny of the author has throughout the print era been most evident, according to Bolter, in the literary canon, which will be replaced in the online age by the "rich texture of allusions and references" of the network.[37] Sequence becomes the responsibility of the reader: since works in hypertext "do not have a single linear order, corresponding to the pages of a book or the columns of the papyrus roll, . . . there is no order to violate."[38]

Bolter clearly misinterprets some of the fundamental textual and epistemological requirements of communication and scholarship. Some structure, some hierarchy, must be preestablished, some works (canon) and terminology (indexes) must be privileged if communication is to take place. The alternative is babel. It is not that the user should be denied flexibility—quite the contrary; but such flexibility must be voluntary. Indeed, flexibility is only possible if there is a structure against which some variation is possible and permitted. The "new dialogue" for which Bolter hankers would itself result in a tyranny—one exercised entirely by the reader. But that is certainly no dialogue. A dialogue rather entails some balanced authority for both parties; the author's recommendations on sequence and structure must be provided and consciously observed (or rejected), therefore, if true dialogue is to take place.

We glimpse perhaps the root of Bolter's misconceptions in his challenge to the infinity of reference:

> Semiotics regards representation as a process without end. . . . The interpretant, the definition of the sign, may in turn be treated as a sign requiring definition. The process continues in theory as long as we like, because each new interpretant allows for a further interpretation. In fact any practical system is limited. In the dictionary each word is defined in terms of other words that are themselves entries to be consulted, but no dictionary is infinite. If we had the patience, we could examine all the words in the network of definitions contained in the dictionary. By starting often enough at different entries, we could ultimately exhaust the dictionary's writing space.[39]

What Bolter fails to recognize or accept is that all of the terms in the dictionary refer to *each other*—and to nothing else. Language is a network of self-references. Because each term is only understandable through its relationship to other terms, the signs of which the language is composed are in a state of continuous and ultimately circular reference. That is why referentiality is theoretically infinite. That is why one can never "exhaust" the dictionary's "writing space." That is why it is possible to claim that there is no beginning and no end to the referentiality of language, and that nothing exists outside of the text. And that is, above all, why some structure needs to be imposed upon the text by some acknowledged authority. Some words, some sentences, some documents need to be specially privileged, to influence the order in which texts are encountered and experienced. This need not mean, of course, that there is some kind of natural or endemic value to one text rather than another—as the concept of the canon might indeed imply. The order imposed on the literature is always artificial, in the sense that it reflects relative decisions made by individuals in authority. It is precisely because there are theoretically no natural origins, no beginning and end to language, that we must impose that kind of order—origins, sequence—for purposes of understanding.

We must assume, therefore, that selection in some form will continue to be a primary activity either undertaken or facilitated by information services. Selection in the online era will presumably consist of someone attaching (i.e., linking) something to the text which the reader can use to decide not only whether to retrieve and read that text but also when to retrieve it (i.e., in the reading sequence). Online selection as an information service is, in other words, an act of appending to the text some evaluation of it, and this literally "added value" is the indispensable service that will make possible networked scholarly communication.

At the same time, however, we must admit that Bolter and others are fully correct in their realization that networking and such computer applications as hypertext "democratize" information, and permit unprecedented flexibility in text production and manipulation. The "history of information technology from writing to hypertext reveals an increasing democratization or dissemination of power."[40] That may be *in nuce* the conundrum, the core challenge, of information services in the early online era. Control, to be sure, must be provided, selection must take place, order of some kind must be imposed, if access time is to be reduced and overload circumvented for the purposes of scholarship and education—but paradoxically a primary responsibility of academic information services must be to leave the reader at the same time the freedom to ignore such control, and indeed perhaps under some circumstances even to encourage him or her to do so.

FORMAL CONSIDERATIONS

The Literature

Will formal publication survive the online age? It need not necessarily. All scholarly communication could conceivably take place through the kind of informal interchanges we now see on the network discussion lists. The homogeneity or neutrality of the network described above reduces also the difference between formal publication and informal communication—but, in the interests of control and sequence, some kind of distinction does need to be made in the online environment between writings that the author alone decides should be made public, and writings that experts in the field (editors) endorse and recommend to other experts to read. Special databases or segments of general databases will therefore need to contain subject or topical files that include publications, i.e., writings that authors declare finished, and that duly authorized peer review boards declare significant. Anyone working in the field will then normally consult these publications *first,* before beginning to search the network for other information of relevance.[41] In this way, the core of the subject can be defined, and progress in the discipline can proceed.

The clear risk of such a procedure, of course, is that it could lead to an extreme centralization of control over formal publication. If the only categories we have available are (informal) discussion and (formal) publication, and if there are only subject files and no individual journals, and if there are only a few "core" subject files for each discipline, then the editors responsible for deciding what deserves the status of a publication in such subject files could exercise virtually dictatorial control over the development of their respective disciplines. This problem is circumvented somewhat in the print environment through the availability of noncore journals. If there is no equivalent of such a multiplicity of journals in the networked environment, then there may be no opportunity to publish new or unpopular ideas (i.e., outside of "normal science"). It is for this reason that some other categories of scholarly communication will need to be established beyond publication and discussion. Some form of quasi- or individual publication needs to evolve, in which the author alone could vouch for the completeness, quality, and consistency of the publication, and which the reader could then consult on that basis after (presumably) first consulting core or refereed publications.[42] There is nothing at all wrong with vanity publishing either in paper or online—provided that it is clearly identified as such. Hypertext will in any case ensure that any "peripheral" publications of this type that are of real significance will be linked to future core publications through references.

If the online discussion (as opposed to formal publication—or quasi-publication) is a legitimate part of the network (as it already is), information service operations will need to decide soon whether such discussions should be archived in the same way that we will need to archive and safeguard publications. The archiving of online discussions is a temptation at the present time in the partially developed network, and it is one we need, in my opinion, generally to resist. To feel obliged to retain every human utterance in graphic form makes little sense in the print environment, and none at all in fully networked circumstances. In all probability, we will need to look at the question of storing network discussions in a manner similar to the way we now approach the retention of manuscripts in the paper environment. It is ultimately a preservation question best left in the hands not of librarians but of archivists. Only a small subset of the manuscripts produced are now retained, and similar decisions based on similar criteria will need to be made for networked discussions. As is the case now of manuscripts in the paper environment, most discussions will presumably be preserved by individuals rather than institutions.

The Document

Monographs and Periodicals. The most basic formal distinction in printed scholarly communication, at least from the standpoint of libraries, is that between monographs (i.e., single books on specific subjects) and periodical articles. The scholarly monograph permits a fully developed statement on a well focused subject, approached usually from a multiplicity of perspectives or examined in a broad context. The monograph is, as its name implies, unitary and separate. The advantage of such closure is that the monograph can define its own terms and create its own internal, self-referring context—a kind of network in print.[43] The reader must invest some time in the monograph, and while its boundaries are predetermined by the author, the reader always has the option of varying the sequence in which he or she reads the composite parts of the monograph, or of reading it only selectively; most scholarly treatises are doubtless seldom read cover to cover by scholars, but are rather read *in*. There are also well-known drawbacks to the monograph, however—one being that, aside from some knowledge of the publisher, the reader seldom has adequate advance information about either the quality of the monograph's scholarship or the precise nature of its content. The scholar must first locate—find out about the existence of—the monograph, a task which enumerative bibliography, cataloging, and book reviewing have been able to assist only to a limited extent; and he or she must then invest time reading "into" the monograph to gauge its quality and utility. Information services, with their primary objective being the reduction of access time, have likewise in the paper environment seldom succeeded effectively in reducing the time needed by readers to digest, assess, and make use of monographic information.

Periodical articles, on the other hand, overcome to a certain extent some of the monograph's drawbacks. The value of periodicals for scholarly communication lies not so much in their periodicity, as in the concentration of their content and the predictability of their subject matter. Periodicals reduce the difficulty of location by establishing narrow boundaries for their subjects, so that much of the key knowledge of some disciplines is in effect defined by its inclusion in a relatively manageable set of core periodicals.[44] The articles published in these core periodicals, in other words, define or represent the current substance of the discipline; developments or ideas not expressed or referred to in the core journals are de facto of less importance—in the sense that the scholar will normally approach information published elsewhere only after he or she first absorbs the information in the core journals.[45] A subject that relies primarily on journal literature is not only more current, therefore, but also arguably under better control than a subject dependent mainly upon monographs, in the sense that the periodical-based literature has a more self-defined hierarchy of publication.[46] The periodical article also has the significant but seldom stated advantage that its absorption by the reader involves a considerably smaller investment of time. While the monograph tries to provide a (partially) closed intertextual network, the periodical leaves the reader more of the responsibility and authority for placing the information in a wider context.

Concentric Stratification. In a fully networked environment, formal scholarly publication can no longer be characterized by the dichotomy of monographs and periodical articles. That distinction makes no sense, if for no other reason than that the economics of online publication no longer requires periodicity: any article or monograph can be published as soon as it has been accepted and edited. Nevertheless, a fundamental objective of information services must be to ensure that the special advantages or capacities of both the monograph and the periodical article in the paper environment are somehow built into the online scholarly communication process. We need, therefore, a formal method of writing that is appropriate to the network—one that will exploit the special capacities of online publication, but that will at the same time retain the values (and avoid the drawbacks) of periodical articles and monographs. Any such method adopted must promote the reduction of access time and contribute to the counteraction of overload—and it should above all enhance communication, in the sense that it should improve participation by both the writer and the reader.

One such method may be for scholarly publications to be presented not in the traditional linear sequence, but rather as a set of linked or self-citing levels or strata. Let us give such a format the contradictory label of *concentric stratification* in order to emphasize simultaneously the concepts of separation and coincidence. Such a document structure might consist of a top level that would contain some kind of extended abstract; this level or stratum would then be connected to the next level, and so on. Each succeeding level would include the information contained in the previous level, but would provide in addition greater degrees of substance and detail. Scholarly communications that require an extended context, and would therefore deserve a monograph in the paper environment, would in the online environment merely include more levels than would a communication that would in a print environment have been published as a journal article. The top level should contain for indexing and access purposes all terms in the work considered by the author to be critical. There should be some standardization of levels, such that the reader would be able to decide which level to access first, depending on his or her previous knowledge of the subject and on the extent of the information required. Such a document structure would also restore to the author some of the authority and control that will necessarily be forfeited in a hypertext and networked environment, since it would permit the author through such a hierarchical structure to privilege—to assign different values or significance to—different parts of the text.

Three-Dimensional Textuality. If formal scholarly publication on the network does indeed shift from a linear form to some kind of hierarchical structure, then reading on the network will be something that is done, so to speak, in three dimensions: first, one can read horizontally or linearly within any level of a given publication; second, one can read vertically or hierarchically through the levels of any particular publication; and, third, one can read referentially back through the constituent citations (be these explicit or implicit) into other texts on the network.[47]

This has, needless to say, some important implications not only for scholarly communication but also for instruction. Students could be given one group of texts or a single text that could conceivably consist of a single key paragraph; from that one text, the student could then construct (reconstruct?) the entire subject by moving linearly, hierarchically, and referentially—rather like growing a complete organism from a single cell. Needless to say, no two students would end up with the same "subject," or rather the same composite text; the responsibility of the instructor would then become to guide the students through the intertextual connections, making certain that the standard or canonical connections are not overlooked but also providing each student with the capacity to build his or her own connections beyond the canonical.

If the reader is going to read in three directions, then the writer is, of course, going to have to learn to write in three directions—a very different notion of writing from that done in the linear print environment. At the very least, the writer will need to create the work hierarchically in linked levels. One assumes that in a paper environment, for example, most authors start with an outline, and then write each section more or less linearly, i.e., seriatim. Writing by using some system like concentric stratification would presumably also begin with some kind of outline, but then the outline of the whole work might be expanded in stages—with each stage functioning eventually as a separate text-stratum.[48]

Writing will also need to include connections to explicit citations. The author should be prepared, moreover, not simply to cite another publication but possibly also to do something to it (i.e., to some copy of it)—to tag it or annotate it in such a way that the reader is able to infer the author's evaluation or application of the cited work. In this way, the author can guide the reader through the cited work, but the reader will still be able to make alternative sequencing decisions. If the author is referring to statistical data rather than to a narrative text, the software needed for that data and the tagging of particular data elements would also be expected. In any case, interaction with the textual history of the subject should become a much more integral aspect of both writing and reading in a fully networked environment.

INFORMATION SERVICES

Certainly one of the most basic changes for which libraries as information service operations will need to prepare will be the blurring of the distinction between the reader and the writer. Libraries, at least in North America, have developed an aggressive (and admittedly somewhat self-righteous) philosophy based primarily on assistance to—and protection of the rights of—the reader. Libraries have seldom catered to the full needs of the writer (even though most of the readers in academic libraries are usually gathering information in order to write something). In a networked hypertext environment, the writer must be accepted as a client deserving of a level of service at least equal to that of the reader—if for no other reason than that it will become increasingly difficult to separate the activity of reading from that of writing, since both will consist mainly of some manipulation of text on the network. "In a full-fledged hypertext the distinction [between writing and reading] can disappear altogether."[49] We must in any event expect the information environment in the online era to be such that, while the library will obviously continue to assist the user in locating information, the main information retrieval service provided by the library may well be indirect—through assistance to those who input or publish information. A central function of information services in the online era, in other words, will be to ensure that information is made available by its originators in such a form and according to such standards that it will be most rapidly accessible and useful to those who need it.

Publishing

It is very unlikely—and it would certainly be very undesirable—for the commercial publishing industry to continue to play the same dominant role in scholarly publication in the online environment that it has in the paper environment: that would be economically unacceptable and technically unnecessary. There will certainly be important and profitable opportunities for commercial publishers in the online environment, but the routine publication of scholarly notification sources should not be one of these.[50] Since the majority of the authors, readers, and editors of scholarly publications are members of academic faculties, it will make very little sense to continue to "contract out" to commercial publishers the responsibility for distributing the written scholarly products of the faculty. The academy, as Richard Dougherty, Ann Okerson, and others have strongly advocated, must assume that responsibility.[51]

It should be the function of academic information services to ensure that national—or preferably international—peer review structures are in place. These editorial boards will then continue to do what they do in the paper environment: they will add value to individual articles by endorsing them for publication. The network of "core" servers for each subject area mentioned above needs to be established as soon as possible, so that such publications can then be easily available to all students and scholars. Access to the network for academic users should be free, in the same way that access to the library is free; the cost of its maintenance, in other words, should continue to be borne—as it is today—by the institutions. An infrastructure for individual or vanity publications must also be in place. Each institution will need to establish policies on archiving—especially for such individual publishing and for network discussion list input. It is also highly advisable that institutions retain copyright control for all or most publications by their faculty. In the interest of scholarly information exchange—and because scholarly authors traditionally and correctly receive rewards for publication indirectly in the form of peer recognition and promotion rather than direct remuneration—all scholarly information published by institutions should be free for any person or institution to copy for any noncommercial purpose.[52]

Indexing

Providing effective access in a networked environment must become increasingly *the responsibility of the writer,* with the assistance of local information services. The indexing of the text—or whatever we call the additions to the text that will allow the user to locate, understand, and evaluate it—must become in a networked environment an integral part of the writing of the text. Assisting the author with the indexing of his or her writing, so that such indexing (and this may well include specialized software) becomes part of the publication, should become a responsibility that information services undertake at the time the publication is being produced, rather than something libraries or commercial indexers do, as is now the case, subsequent to publication. This professional activity of assisting the writer to produce his or her indexing within the network context, so that readers needing it can find it, will presumably be fundamentally the same activity or service, approached from the opposite direction, requiring the same bibliographical knowledge and skills, as assisting the reader to locate information on the network.

Document Structure

The replacement of linear reading and writing by a hierarchical structure of some kind (e.g., *concentric stratification)* will be justified only if that new structure is standardized so that information access is improved. The practicability of the whole enterprise will certainly depend upon prearranged, universally accepted conventions. In the kind of hierarchical structure suggested above, for example, there would need to be some set of abstract guidelines applicable to writing on any topic that would define the characteristics of information to be written or located at each level—or more exactly, that would standardize the relationship of the strata or levels to each other. Only in this way would the user be able to exploit the conventions of the structure, in order to arrive at the information needed in the shortest possible time. Defining that structure for all formal scholarly writing, obtaining international agreement on its implementation, assisting authors in their writing so that they make effective use of the structure, and assisting readers in locating the information they need in the shortest time by exploiting that structure—all of these functions should become routine responsibilities of information services in an online environment.

CONCLUSIONS

Librarians are admittedly control freaks. We yearn to regulate all information exchange, and we have a morbid fear of losing anything. We traditionally interpose ourselves between the user and the information. And now, just when it appears that technology will finally liberate the user from the tyranny of mediation, the library, in its new guise as information service provider, appears poised to insert itself once again between the information seeker and the information sought. There will be some objection to this role, and some rejection of this service—but if information professionals recognize that the imposition of some order and structure on networked information is an essential prerequisite for effective scholarly communication and higher education in an online environment, then plans should be made, regardless of the opposition, to provide that service and to demonstrate how it adds significant value to the functional network. This effort should be made, moreover, even if—or especially if—it is not in the best administrative interest of libraries to do so. If the kinds of information services discussed above are successfully implemented, then not only will the traditional operational divisions within the library (e.g., selection, cataloging, reference) dissolve and be reconstituted in other forms but also the currently clear administrative divisions between the library, computer center, university press, and campus bookstore will become increasingly obscure—so that the need to effect some kind of amalgamation of all campus information services may eventually become irresistible.

Neither networks nor hypertext will separately bring about a true revolution—but in combination they are indeed very likely to engender a radical transformation in scholarly information exchange. Together they provide not simply a new and improved version of what has been done before in paper form, but rather represent fundamental revisions in the very modality of communication; they may even affect and alter some of our basic assumptions about the nature of information itself. The ability especially to augment a text's content through implicit and explicit citation has the most far-reaching implications, which users of networks and hypertext must learn to appreciate. If there is one lesson we have learned, one conclusion we must draw, from the experience of such critical methods as deconstruction, it is surely this: if we push intertextuality far enough, if we take it upon ourselves to explore a large enough range of the previous uses of the signs of which a text is composed, if we broaden the context enough, then the reference of those signs and the meaning of that text will diminish and dissolve. Meaning is fragile, and the capacity of the network for a theoretically infinite combining and recombining of texts can jeopardize meaning in a fundamental sense. The hypertext-enhanced network is indeed a machine of enormous power and promise, but like all powerful machines, it will need to be skillfully designed and responsibly operated by those who understand and respect its potential.

REFERENCE NOTES

1. According to testimony of Douglas E. Van Houweling in the House Committee on Science, Space, and Technology, Subcommittee on Science, *Management of NSFNet,* 102d Cong., 2d sess., Mar. 12, 1992, 38 (also currently available by FTP from nis.nsf.net/internet/legislative. actions/hearing, Mar. 12 1992), between July 1988 and March 1992, "traffic on the [NSF] backbone has grown almost 7,000 percent, an average of 11 percent compounded every month, and new applications and uses are constantly emerging."

2. *Congressional Record* 137:174 (Nov. 22, 1992), S17730. The NSF Backbone is just completing its transition from T1 (1.5 megabits per second) to T3 (45 megabits per second). See the *Link Letter* 5, no. 1 (Mar./Apr. 1992), 1, 8–9 (also currently available by FTP from nic.merit.edu/ newsletters/linkletter). A megabit is one million bits; a gigabit is one billion bits. By contrast, the original ARPANET put into operation in 1969 was run over wideband telephone lines that permitted transmissions of 50 kilobits (i.e., 50,000 bits) per second (Dennis G. Perry, Steven H. Blumenthal, and Robert M. Hinden, "The ARPANET and the DARPA Internet," *Library HiTech* 6, no. 2 [1988]: 51).

3. This bill, sponsored by Senator Albert Gore, is currently (summer 1992) pending in the Senate as S-2937. For the text of the bill, see *Congressional Record* 138, no. 97 (July 1, 1992): S9539-

41. A copy of the press release describing the bill is currently available by FTP from nis.nsf. net/internet/legislativeactions/iita.1992/gorebill.1992.txt.

4. For good summaries of these issues, especially as they relate to the development of the NREN, see Clifford A. Lynch, "The Development of Electronic Publishing and Digital Library Collections on the NREN," *Electronic Networking* 1, no. 2 (winter 1991): 6–22; Edwin Brownrigg, "Developing the Information Superhighway: Issues for Libraries" in Carol A. Parkhurst, ed., *Library Perspectives on NREN: The National Research and Education Network* (Chicago: Library and Information Technology Assn., 1990), 55–63; and Charles R. McClure et al., *The National Research and Education Network (NREN): Research and Policy Perspectives* (Norwood, N.J.: Ablex, 1991), especially chapters 3 and 9.

5. We must be especially careful in the academic environment to avoid assuming that most uses of the Internet are for scholarly purposes. See the testimony of Mitchell Kapor in House Committee on Science . . . , *Management of NSFNet,* 78: [nearly] "60 percent of all registered computing sites in the Internet are commercial organizations. Within two years the number is expected to grow to nearly 90 percent."

6. Two good summaries of the copyright issues are Paul Hilts, "Through the Electronic Copyright Maze," *Publishers Weekly* 239, no. 26 (June 8, 1992): 35–37; and Robert L. Oakley, "Copyright Issues for the Creators and Users of Information in the Electronic Environment," *Electronic Networking* 1, no. 1 (fall 1991): 23–30.

7. See Gordon Cook, "A National Network That Isn't," *Computerworld* 26, no. 10 (Mar. 9, 1992): 91–95.

8. The interviews undertaken by the McClure team showed a clear aversion by scientists to publishing in online journals: this is because "the reward structure of science is based on formal publication history and . . . electronic publication does not enhance one's status or image; in fact, it may very well harm them." (McClure, *The National Research and Education Network,* 103.)

9. One major technical issue still to be resolved, for example, is protocol interoperability. On this see Lorcan Dempsey, *Libraries, Networks and OSI: A Review, with a Report on North American Developments* (Bath: U.K. Office for Library Networking, 1991), especially chapter 2; see also the review of this report by Clifford Lynch in *The Public-Access Computer Systems Review 2,* no. 1 (1991): 171–76.

10. Richard N. Katz, "Academic Information Management at the Crossroads: Time Again to Review the Economics," *Serials Review* 18, nos. 1/2 (1992): 43.

11. A sign, according to Umberto Eco in his *A Theory of Semiotics* (Bloomington, Ind.: Indiana Univ. Pr., 1976), 16, is *"everything* that, on the grounds of a previously established social convention, can be taken as *standing for something else."*

12. See my "The Conditions of Collection Development" in Charles B. Osburn and Ross Atkinson, eds., *Collection Management: A New Treatise* (Greenwich, Conn.: JAI Pr., 1991), 37–42.

13. John S. Quarterman, *The Matrix: Computer Networks and Conferencing Systems Worldwide* (Bedford, Mass.: Digital, 1990), 6.

14. Eco, *Theory of Semiotics,* 20.

15. A good example is the relationship of the NREN to the Internet and NSFNet. Will the Internet "Evolve into NREN," (Vinton G. Cerf, "Introducing the Internet" in Parkhurst, *Library Perspectives on NREN,* 20, figure 6); or will "the current NSFNET . . . become the Interim NREN" (Michael M. Roberts, "Positioning the National Research and Education Network," *EDUCOM Review* 25 [fall 1990]: 12); or is the NREN already well in place, with NSFNET "currently" serving "as the primary cross-continental backbone for the NREN, which now links over one thousand university and college campuses . . ." (Stephen Gould, "Building the National Research and Education Network," *CRS Issue Brief* [IB90126] [Washington, D.C.: Library of Congress, updated Dec. 18, 1991], 1)? It is perhaps not so much the network itself as the literature describing it that is becoming too complicated to understand.

16. These three views of the network are perhaps roughly equivalent to Robert Kahn's three infrastructure components: the network, the databases, and the infrastructure intelligence— except that he quite rightly includes protocols as part of the network rather than as part of the infrastructure intelligence—in his "National Information Infrastructure Components," *Serials Review* 18, nos. 1/2 (1992): 85–87.

17. For a readable introduction to hypertext, see Carl Franklin, "Hypertext Defined and Applied," *Online* 13, no. 3 (May 1989): 37–49. See also Michael Knee and Steven D. Atkinson, *Hypertext/ Hypermedia: An Annotated Bibliography* (Westport, Conn.: Greenwood, 1990).

18. Nicole Yankelovich et al., "Intermedia: The Concept and the Construction of a Seamless Information Environment," *Computer* 21, no. 1 (Jan. 1988): 81. Jay David Bolter, in his *Writing Space: The Computer, Hypertext, and the History of Writing* (Hillsdale, N.J.: Erlbaum, 1991), 27, notes that "the principle of hypertext has been implicit in computer programming" for some time. "Hypertext is the interactive interconnection of a set of symbolic elements, and many kinds of computer programs (databases, simulation programs, even programs for artificial intelligence) are special cases of that principle."

19. T. H. Nelson, "A File Structure for the Complex, the Changing and the Indeterminate," *Association for Computing Machinery: Proceedings of the 20th National Conference* (New York: Assn. for Computing Machinery, 1965), 96, 98.

20. Ted Nelson, *Literary Machines: The Report on, and of, Project Xanadu concerning Word Processing, Electronic Publishing, Hypertext, Thinkertoys, Tomorrow's Intellectual Revolution, and Certain Other Topics including Knowledge, Education and Freedom,* 3d ed. (Swarthmore, Pa.: the author, 1981), 1 /22 and 2/21. This is a difficult work to cite, in that it has been updated and reissued several times. The copy I used is owned by the Harvard University Law Library.

21. For example, Philip Seyer, in his *Understanding Hypertext: Concepts and Applications* (Blue Ridge Summit, Pa.: Windcrest, 1991), 1, describes hypertext as "nonlinear, or nonsequential, text. That is, the text is organized so you can easily jump around from topic to topic. You do not need to read the text in fixed sequence."

22. Julia Kristeva, "Word, Dialogue and Novel," trans. Alice Jardine, Thomas Gora, and Leon S. Roudiez, in *The Kristeva Reader,* ed. Toril Moi (New York: Columbia Univ. Pr., 1986), 37.

23. Several good surveys of intertextuality are available. See, for example, Marc Angenot, "L' Intertextualité: enquête sur l'emergence et la diffusion d'un champ notionnel," *Revue des sciences humaines* 60, no. 189 (Jan/Mar 1983): 121–35; Ottmar Ette, "Intertextualität: Ein Forschungsbericht mit literatursoziologischen Anmerkungen," *Romanistische Zeitschrift für Literaturgeschichte* 9, nos. 3/4 (1985): 497–522; Thais E. Morgan, "Is There an Intertext in This Text?: Literary and Interdisciplinary Approaches to Intertextuality," *American Journal of Semiotics* 3, no. 4 (1985): 1–40.

24. Julia Kristeva, "Revolution in Poetic Language," trans. Margaret Waller, in *The Kristeva Reader,* 111.

25. Laurent Jenny, "La Stratégie de la forme," *Poétique* 27 (1976): 261.

26. Roland Barthes, "Theory of the Text," trans. Ian McLeod, in *Untying the Text: A Post-Structuralist Reader,* ed. Robert Young (Boston: Routledge & Paul, 1981), 32.

27. Probably the most effective analysis of the relationship between hypertext and post-structuralist literary theory will be found in George P. Landow, *Hypertext: The Convergence of Contemporary Critical Theory and Technology* (Baltimore: Johns Hopkins Univ. Pr., 1992).

28. Bolter, *Writing Space,* 15.

29. This would presumably be one use of the so-called knowbot. See Robert E. Kahn and Vinton G. Cerf, *The Digital Library Project: An Open Architecture for a Digital Library System and a Plan for its Development,* vol. 1: *The World of Knowbots* (draft), (n.p.: Corporation for National Research Initiatives, 1988). See also Bennett Daviss, "Computer Watch," *Discover* 12, no. 4 (Apr. 1991): 21–22.

30. Landow, *Hypertext,* 54.

31. See Gordon B. Neavill, "Electronic Publishing, Libraries, and the Survival of Information," *Library Resources & Technical Services* 28, no. 1 (Jan./Mar. 1984): 76–89; and Peter S. Graham, "Electronic Information and Research Library Technical Services," *College & Research Libraries* 51, no. 3 (May 1990): 241–50.

32. "Ordinarily a document consits [sic] of its *contents* (including history and alternatives) and its *out-links.* These out-links are under control of its owner, whereas its in-links are not." (Nelson, *Literary Machines,* 2/27.) An "out-link" is presumably a link from the original, owned document to another document, while "in-links" are presumably the links from other

(not owned) documents to the owned document. See also the chapter in *Literary Machines* on electronic publishing (2/34–2/45).

33. Landow, *Hypertext*, 71.

34. Bolter, *Writing Space*, 22–25 and 112–14.

35. Ibid., 153.

36. Ibid., 117.

37. Ibid., 153.

38. Ibid., 119.

39. Ibid., 203.

40. Landow, *Hypertext*, 174.

41. This is a combination of the Acquisition-on-Demand Model and the Discipline-Specific Literature Base Model as defined in Czeslaw Jan Grycz, "Economic Models for Networked Information," *Serials Review* 18, nos. 1/2 (1992): 12–13. See also in the same issue of *Serials Review*, 78–81, the article by Charles W. Bailey Jr. on "The Coalition for Networked Information's Acquisition-on-Demand Model: An Exploration and Critique."

42. See Stevan Hamad's very reasonable idea of a hierarchy of discussion groups, out of which would emerge a hierarchy of online publications, in his "Scholarly Skywriting and the Prepublication Continuum of Scientific Inquiry," *Psychological Science* 1, no. 6 (Nov 1990): 343–44.

43. I hasten to note that no publication is, of course, ever fully self-contained, since it is connected with other publications specifically through references and quotations, and more broadly by virtue of intertextuality.

44. See Charles B. Osburn, "The Place of the Journal in the Scholarly Communications System," *Library Resources & Technical Services* 28, no. 4 (Oct./Dec. 1984): 322.

45. It is not, again, that information A in a core journal is somehow endemically superior to information B in a noncore journal, but rather only that information A in the core journal will normally be read first, and will therefore normally condition the understanding of information B.

46. It is in fact this hierarchical quality or position which is actually being marketed by commercial science publishers: that is what the highly reputable or core journal provides to the material it publishes. Whether that value added is worth the price some commercial publishers now charge is, of course, another question.

47. Reading would probably also take place at the same level across different but related publications; although this might also be viewed as a further form of referential reading, since it might be based on "implicit" references or links.

48. It would probably be possible for some kind of "outliner" software to be produced that would assist with this work, although care would obviously need to be taken to leave the evaluative decisions entailed in such outlining fully in the hands of the author. For a discussion of the concept of the outline as it relates to word processing, see Michael Heim, *Electric Language: A Philosophical Study of Word Processing* (New Haven: Yale Univ. Pr., 1987), 139–45; see also his discussion (243–46) of Gabriele Lusser Rico's concept of "clustering."

49. Bolter, *Writing Space*, 216.

50. By "notification sources" I mean those publications that scholars write in order to keep each other informed of the results of their research and scholarship. Most scholarly publications today—both monographs and journal articles—are notification sources. See my "Old Forms, New Forms: The Challenge of Collection Development," *College & Research Libraries* 50, no. 5 (Sept. 1989): 514–15.

51. See, for example, Richard M. Dougherty, "A 'Factory' for Scholarly Journals," *Chronicle of Higher Education* 38, no. 41 (June 17, 1992): B1 and B3; and Ann Okerson, "Back to Academia? The Case for American Universities to Publish Their Own Research," *Logos* 2, no. 2 (1991): 106–12.

52. This is roughly the copyright policy of *The Public-Access Computer Systems Review*. Robert L. Oakley ("Copyright Issues," 25) has noted, however, that this could create some legal difficulties "because of the potential for disagreements over the line between commercial and noncommercial use."

14 MASS DEACIDIFICATION IN THE CONTEXT OF ACCESS TIME REDUCTION

My assignment is to discuss mass deacidification as one function of preservation within the broader context of library operations. I will try to fulfill this charge by describing a general model of information services, and then by locating preservation and mass deacidification within it. Some time will therefore need to be devoted at the outset to the definition of this model. Two caveats are in order before we begin. The first is that I will be saying very little that is new; the purpose of using such models must be rather to "make strange" those routine issues and operations that have become so familiar to us that we have become insensitive to them. If we can approach such routine concepts as strangers, we can perhaps see them anew. The second caveat is that the model will be described in a language appropriate to an age that accords science and technology the highest status. I will try unavoidably to add credibility and legitimacy to the model by describing it as if it were a physical object or law that we have built or discovered, and that we are in the process of measuring or testing. Please bear in mind, therefore, that the model is, of course, nothing of the kind; it is simply a linguistic construct intended to help us discuss how we do our work, and, as such, is subject to neither observation nor calibration.

THE MODEL

Change is the only absolute. The only thing that does not change is the fact that everything changes. This includes not only information but also the processes by which information is transferred. Let us therefore concentrate on change as the basis for our description of information transfer and information services. Let us begin by reducing information transfer to three continually changing concepts or "transitional components."

The Aggregate Source Collection

The first of these is the total collection of sources of (let us limit it to graphic) information at any point in time, i.e., those material objects, like books, from which people produce information. This total aggregate of information sources is obviously transitional: it changes from one moment to the next—first, because new sources of information are being continuously created, but also, second, because all information sources (including electronic sources) are necessarily material objects and are as such subject to decay.

The primary responsibility for information sources rests with their creators, the authors—aided, to be sure, by certain specialists in the information services community such as publishers, printers, and programmers. Anyone working to improve or to influence the condition

This article first appeared as a presentation at the New York State Seminar on Mass Deacidification, 84–98.

or effectiveness of an information source is acting as an agent or representative of the author (even though that author may be unknown, or may have died centuries or millennia before).

The origin of the information conveyed by the source is usually the graphic text—which librarians customarily refer to as intellectual content. Because information can be produced—inferred—from any physical object, however, the physical source can itself convey information apart from the text, so that we may also speak of a physical content. Information produced from this physical content can in turn be used for a variety of purposes, such as tracking the physical history of the production of sources, or of the production of the source in hand, or to complement or extend the reader's understanding of the intellectual content (so-called analytical bibliography).

Information Needs

The second transitional component is very different from the first, and is much more difficult to define, because it has, unlike the source collection, no immediately evident physical basis. Quite the contrary: it is the continuously evolving information need of each individual client. While information sources are public and subject to physical inspection and management (although admittedly not in the aggregate), information needs are private and personal, and can be understood only by an individual in consultation with himself or herself. Responsibility for the definition, management, and satisfaction of such subjective requirements necessarily rests therefore primarily with the individual—i.e., the user or reader. Anyone who tries to assist in this activity is a representative of the reader. The aggregate of these subjective requirements for each individual changes continuously over time in response to external conditions (such as classroom assignments), but also as a result of psychological and other entirely private factors.

Access Facilitation

Between the physical, public sources and the private, subjective needs resides the component of greatest interest to us, and the one to which we will devote most of our attention, access facilitation. The term access, for all its use and overuse, is vague and problematic—occasionally almost ethereal—and not at all conducive by itself to modelling or planning it is much preferable therefore to concentrate not on the process of access, but rather on the efficiency of its facilitation, which must always be measured in terms of time.

This means, to begin with, that information services should be designed and understood in a primarily temporal context—that is, as a system of operations intended to promote access time reduction. It has always been and will always be, the purpose of information services to reduce the time required or spent by clients (normally those individuals who have contracted directly or indirectly for the service) to obtain access to that information they need to do their work. This holds true regardless of whether we are talking about the New York State Library, or the library at Alexandria, or some mega-computer of the future. All information services, including all library operations, are devoted to that single process and are intended for that single purpose. While it may appear that some library operations are designed to achieve related but different objectives, those objectives will be found upon closer inspection to be manifestations of this more fundamental purpose. If there were no reference departments, for example, our users could eventually define, identify and locate the information they need, but it would require an enormous investment of time—an investment most users would be unwilling to make. If we eliminated our catalogs and bibliographical tools, users could with enough industry eventually locate the information they need by browsing through the stacks. If we stopped building collections altogether, users could still presumably gather needed information by travelling to distant cultural centers as was done in antiquity and the Middle Ages. Life is, however, simply not long enough to locate all of the information needed; my point is rather that if it were long enough, if there were enough time, such information could be identified, located and exploited by the individual in need of it without the assistance of information services. But there is in fact not enough time (nor has there probably ever been) to achieve that end—which means that efficient information services in some form are an essential prerequisite for education and all intellectual progress.

The primary responsibility for access facilitation, measured in access time, belongs to information services. Information services as a function, however, has control over neither the aggregate source collection, which is the primary responsibility of the authors, nor over the subjective information needs, which are known exactly and in detail only to the users, readers, receivers. The purpose of information services is rather always to reduce the time needed by those users to satisfy those personal requirements by using those in public sources. (It is worth noting that, as we move further into the online age, the user will probably become increasingly independent or solitary. Information services will then begin, in my opinion, increasingly to shift their primary focus from the receiver to the sender. Information services will fulfill their responsibility for access time reduction increasingly by influencing what is available, and how it is available, on the network; this will involve much closer work with writers than with readers, even though the end purpose of services will continue to be intended ultimately for the reader. The quality of the output needed by the user, in other words, will be maintained and improved by the increased participation of information services at the point of input. The role of preservation in this process is, of course, yet to be determined, although it is certainly worthwhile noting that, of all the information functions now performed by the library, it is preservation which, because of its focus on the material source collection, is perhaps that information service operation which most serves needs of and as representative of the author at this time.)

We can best describe or understand the third transitional component in our model of information transfer by positing that for any person, at any point in time, all information sources in existence—the aggregate source collection—can be distributed along a single theoretical access time continuum that ranges from a positive end ("immediately accessible") to a negative end ("never accessible"). This continuum (or more precisely the relationship of the sources on the continuum to each other) is also in a continuous state of flux: the time required by the user to obtain access to each source on the continuum relative to all of the other sources is constantly changing. The user's objective is always to aim for a condition in which those sources are as much as possible arranged in such an order that best serves to respond to that user's individual information requirements at the moment—so that those sources which best meet the most immediate information needs of the individual reader are most immediately accessible—i.e. accessible in the shortest possible time, as close as possible to the positive or "immediate" end of the continuum.

The distribution of the sources on the continuum—the speed with which the user can gain access to each of the sources relative to each other—changes constantly in response, again, to subjective and objective factors. The subjective factors derive from the knowledge and activity of the individual. Which sources of information the individual encounters, and how the individual understands and exploits those sources has the most obvious and profound effect on the order of the sources along the continuum (as always: what you understand depends on what you already know)—and in a sense this subjective ordering is one of the main goals of education and research.[1] It is the objective factors, on the other hand, affecting the order of sources along the access time continuum that are of most interest to us, because those represent most specifically the true work of information services, and it is for those services and for that rearrangement of sources that the user becomes a client and contracts either directly or indirectly with an information services operation. Taking the paper-based library as an example: let us say that a particular information source exists at this time that can respond to the need of a particular Cornell student. I can reduce the amount of time that student needs to gain access to that source by making an arrangement with, say, SUNY Binghamton according to which Binghamton will buy and maintain that source so that my local user can borrow it through ILL from Binghamton, if and when my user decides he or she needs it (in return presumably for my buying something a user at SUNY Binghamton might need). I can reduce that access time still further by purchasing a copy of the source for my institution and housing it in the collection in closer proximity to the student. I can reduce that time still further by having the author and title of that item included in the library catalog; and access time can probably be reduced further still by including a full subject description of the item in the catalog. Access time can be reduced even further by employing a reference staff that will personally assist the user in deciding that he or she needs access to that particular item and in physically locating it.

Each of these information service functions has not only a value for the user, but also a cost for the information service operation—in terms of time or money (which are really the same thing, money being stored labor time). The information service operation has resources at its disposal, all of which (in the case of the non-profit operation, at least) are, directly or indirectly, devoted to access time reduction for current (and future) clientele. These resources are, however, seldom` adequate to meet all information needs of all clientele. In general, the greater the access time reduction—i.e. the shorter the access time for any single source—the higher the cost. The function or responsibility of information services management (in our case, library administration) is to distribute the use of its resources in such a way that the greatest access time reduction is achieved in the case of those resources most needed by local clientele. This is often impossible to provide for each user individually (except perhaps in the case of some special libraries), so that the information service operation must normally assume an idealized user or group of users, and an idealized access time continuum. Even so, the information service process is extremely complicated, precisely because of the continuous evolution of the three transitional components of the model, and because of the subjective nature of information needs and of the continuum itself at any point in time.

THE THREE OBJECTS OF INFORMATION SERVICES

If we view information services from such a perspective, we find three objects or central issues of information services upon which we must concentrate our analysis.

The first of these is the act of positioning sources or source groups on the individual or (more often) idealized continuum. This is what most of the operations of information services are intended to accomplish. The purpose of positioning, as we have seen, is normally to reduce access time. Most information services—practically all—are intended to move specific sources forward on the continuum. In other words, by acting on the source in some way (publishing it, selecting it, cataloging it, putting it in a server, reading it to somebody over the telephone), information services seeks to reduce the time needed for access to it. There are, to be sure, some information service actions that have—not so much the intent as—the result of increasing access time for certain information, and such services are among the most difficult to perform for that very reason. The most obvious examples are various forms of deselection, such as journal cancellation and weeding. In many of these instances, scarcity of resources, such as budget or space, force a rearrangement of items on the continuum.

The second object of information services is an extension or refinement of the first; it is migration control. As a result of the many subjective and objective factors and forces acting on the continuum, most sources would appear to move on the continuum in the negative or entropic direction. Bear in mind that this is a true continuum, with each point representing a source. Because there is necessarily only a limited amount of space toward the front of the continuum, the positioning or repositioning of the sources toward the front causes others to move in the negative direction. I call this phenomenon the "displacement imperative."[2] Making the necessary adjustments to impair (or occasionally to accelerate) the migration of certain sources on the continuum is therefore also a key responsibility of information services, although one that in a sense counterbalances the operation of positioning. This is a further reflection of the very complicated dynamics of information services. Positioning is only possible if displacement, and therefore migration, take place, but information services also seeks in specific cases to impair that migration. Different information service operations therefore sometimes act in opposition or contradiction to each other, which can cause political as well as bibliographical ambiguities. Migration control may often concentrate in the center or more on the negative side of the continuum; unlike positioning, which normally pushes sources forward, migration control tries to impair their slippage further back—to provide some stabilization.

It is also important to understand that absolute stabilization on the continuum—by which we would mean the freezing of certain sources in a position relative not to other sources on the continuum but rather relative to the front of the continuum—is probably not an option. The continuum—or rather the movement of sources on the continuum—is too volatile. All sources now must move, mainly toward the negative end, regardless of what is done. The most that can be done is that, through the intervention of some very specialized information service operations, the migration of particular sources down the continuum is somehow impeded.

The third object of information services is, inevitably, resource utilization. It is the responsibility of the information services operation to convert its resources (which, as noted above, can also be understood and expressed in terms of time—mostly staff time) in the most efficient way possible into access time reduction in response to the collective information needs of local clientele.

All information services must be assessed in terms of these three objects.

PRESERVATION IN CONTEXT

The information service activities that we normally group under preservation are concerned primarily with migration control. They are intended to deter or retard the migration of specifically targeted sources toward the negative end of the continuum in those instances when that migration is a consequence of physical deterioration. What differentiates preservation from most other information services (i.e., most other library operations) is its focus not on current access time but on projected access time over the longer term. The purpose of most information services is positioning, i.e., to reduce access time to (in each case) a particular source in relation to other sources at that time. The purpose of preservation (and of other historically oriented information services), on the other hand, is to reduce access time to a particular source in relation to its potential position (potential access time) on the continuum at a later time as a consequence of its migration. And it is in relation to that potential position that preservation must measure the success of its operations. In other words, the success of the activity (at T2) is not measured against the position of the source on the continuum (at T1) before the activity took place. (which is how positioning works), but rather against the potential location of the source on the continuum at some future period (at Tn) after the source has been subject to migration.

The preservation effort to halt migration on the continuum as a result of physical deterioration is perhaps the most ancient of information services, and has been accomplished since the very beginning of graphic communication by two means: (a) maintenance, which is the effort to retain the physical source in—or to restore it as much as possible to—the condition in which it was originally created or received, and (b) substitution, which entails copying the content either manually or mechanically onto a newer or more durable medium.

Substitution has always been the preferable option in most instance, for the very good reason that it provides—within the context of the above model—the more effective method of longer-term migration control. By transferring the content of the source to a new medium, the migration of the source as a result of physical deterioration is obviously slowed significantly; the only reason we have inherited those works that we have from antiquity is that our predecessors resorted to substitution. But substitution, in comparison to maintenance, is also potentially problematic because of its radical effect in some cases on the positioning of the source on the continuum in the short term (T1 to T2). We can cite at least three instance of this radical effect. First, if the copy is not a completely accurate duplication of the content (and let us not get stuck in defining what that might be), then substitution can be only partially achieved, and access time for parts of the text may move more rapidly to the far negative end of the scale, because what was miscopied may never be accessible again. This has been the persistent drawback throughout history in the case both of handwritten copies and of new editions printed from reset type. It has only been since the application of photography to graphic communication that this particular liability has been eliminated.

Second, substitution achieves some stability of intellectual content only by separating the intellectual from the physical content, and then usually moving the physical content to the negative end of the continuum. In a few cases, to be sure, the physical content of a source is of equal or greater value than its intellectual content; those sources clearly warrant maintenance rather than substitution. In all other cases, and that means most cases (and I strongly believe this), retention of the physical content is not alone adequate justification for the selection of maintenance over substitution.

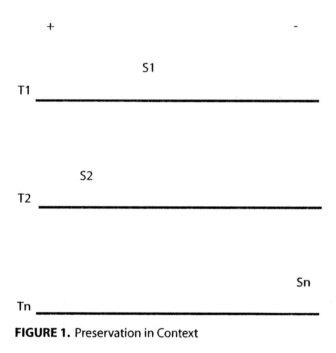

FIGURE 1. Preservation in Context

The third and most problematic instances of these radical changes in positioning on the continuum that result from substitution have evolved only in the modern era when we have begun to alternate media—to undertake what we now commonly refer to as reformatting. Such a change of format can have a most significant effect on the position of the source on the continuum. The most obvious and no doubt the most controversial method of substitution recently has been microformatting. This is because the replacement of a paper copy with a microfilm will move the source radically toward the negative end of the continuum. Once again, this is because preservation, unlike most other information services, is primarily prospective, i.e., it is concerned about the location of the source on the continuum in the future. Microfilming does reduce access time—moves the source toward the positive end of the continuum—but only when compared with the source's potential condition at some future date. The controversy arises primarily because users and other information service operations are focused on the present, and preservation must frequently accelerate migration—increase potential access time, i.e., act contrary to the routine goals of information services—in order to carry out reformatting. Once again, we see that preservation's primary aim is to retard migration mainly through stabilizing it on the continuum, even if that stabilization is purchased paradoxically at the expense of access time reduction in the short term. The user—and the user's representative (often in the form of the bibliographer)—compares the access time of the original with the access time of the reformatted copy, while the preservationist compares the access time of the reformatted copy to the access time of the original if left untreated.

Maintenance, as opposed to substitution, often provides a much lower level of any real migration control. Adjustments to the physical condition of a source will, to be sure, slow its deterioration, but that source will nevertheless continue to move down the continuum as a result of the natural and inevitable decay of all physical objects. It is, in a sense, a far less satisfactory form of preservation, if we assume that the goal of preservation is primarily migration control. A major—probably the major—value of maintenance over substitution, on the other, hand, is that it is singularly undisruptive for the continuum of any particular individual. Maintenance has, in other words, normally only very minor effects on short-term positioning. Conservation and repair, for example, as perhaps the most common forms of maintenance, move the sources slightly forward on the continuum: they reduce access time modestly by ensuring that the sources remain for the time being in an improved physical condition, but they do not radically change the position of those sources in relation to their previous position (in T1).

Deacidification is probably a form of maintenance—and if the technology of mass deacidification continues to improve, it may become an increasingly acceptable method of maintenance. Compared to other methods of preservation, and even other methods of maintenance, the most striking feature of successful deacidification from the standpoint of the access time continuum is its lack of striking features. Deacidification is in a way the most conservative of the major conservation processes, which accounts, in my opinion, for much of its popularity. While other maintenance processes have at least some modest effect on positioning, deacidification is even more subtle, and, if successful, would seem to create not the slightest perceptible change in the source's position on the continuum (i.e., in relation to other sources) for any individual over the short term.

This conservative quality of deacidifcation has several clear advantages. From the bibliographical perspective, deacidification allows the sources treated to migrate (obviously much more slowly than in their untreated form) down the continuum as part of the broader collection. Deacidification serves to promote, therefore, the concept of the local collection as a consciously constructed assemblage, and contributes to keeping that assemblage intact—or to say the same thing in a very different way, it leaves positioning on the continuum to those other information service operations that are responsible for it. As we have noted, maintenance provides some minor stabilization on the continuum, but nothing approaching the level of stabilization achieved by some forms of substitution. In a sense, therefore, deacidification produces a kind of short-term stabilization (between T1 and T2—a stabilization of the collection in place), which in many cases does indeed facilitate the individual retrieval process—research and education—although admittedly only at the expense of longer-term stabilization.

In addition to this bibliographical rationale for deacidification, therefore, the most pragmatic argument for deacidification is clearly a political one. In the extremely conservative atmosphere of the academy (or of the large public library), this most conservative of all treatments is probably in many cases the most welcome. It may indeed even be used for political purposes to offset or counterbalance the political liabilities of other preservation treatments or other library operations.[3] The retention of the physical content is also advantageous politically. Even though the physical content normally provides (or permits the creation of) information of much less value than the intellectual content, there is often a reluctance on the part of many scholars—especially historians, for obvious reasons—to relinquish access (i.e., to permit an increase in access time) to any information, because the true value of any information always changes over time, and may therefore be found to be much valuable later than it was thought to be originally.

Given these advantages, is mass deacidification—as perhaps the most efficient and politically correct form of maintenance—generally preferable to substitution? All other things being equal: probably not. All other things being equal, mass deacidification is in most cases a less preferable alternative to substitution at this particular time. The reason is that technology now provides us with the ability to reduce at least some of the effects of radical positioning that are so often the result of substitution. Possibly photocopying (on high quality, acidfree paper), and certainly digitization (once we learn a bit more about managing it) can provide some short-term stabilization, while at the same time also presenting opportunities to achieve a much more acceptable level of long-term stabilization than is possible through deacidification. (With digitization, for example, very high levels of long-term stabilization are possible, because one can simply produce replica paper copies indefinitely.) All other things being equal, therefore, we should simply photocopy or (preferably) digitize all materials printed on acidic paper, or poor paper of any kind—as soon as those materials enter the library or as soon as they are discovered in it. The reason we do not do this now is to be found, of course, in our third object of information services: resource utilization. All other things are not equal. The costs are not equal. We can achieve superior preservation (if we define preservation as I have above), and we can provide superior levels of service (in terms of access time reduction) through photographic or digital substitution than we can through mass deacidification, but the costs of photographic or digital substitution remain presently somewhat prohibitive. Certainly the costs of all of these technologies can be expected to decline—especially digitization—but the costs of mass deacidification (if it is truly a mass process) will remain in all likelihood less than any form of substitution.[4] That may motivate us to opt for mass deacidifcation on a broad scale—but if we do so, it will be because we cannot afford to provide the level of information services that modern forms of substitution will allow. Mass deacidification will always be a compromise: it provides a less than optimum level of service—although one that will admittedly reduce access time (over time) to an extent that would clearly not be possible without its intervention. Mass deacidification in the preservation sector of information services is, in a way, somewhat similar to minimal level cataloging in the area of technical services: both result in some access time reduction, although we could and would prefer to reduce access time still further, if adequate resources were available to do so.

We must not make the mistake, however, of assuming that decisions relating to preservation procedures will be made within the narrow context of preservation alone. That has never been the case. Preservation options will be evaluated within the broader context of all information service operations—and from that macroperspective, the access time reduction attainable through mass deacidification may well be found wanting when compared with the access time reduction that can be realized through other information service operations outside of preservation. This is presumably what Dick DeGennaro meant by declaring at the Andover Conference that we "cannot afford to foreclose the library's future by giving excessive priority to preserving our deteriorating print-on-paper collections at the expense of positioning our libraries to cope with the opportunities and demands of the new information technology."[5] It could well be, therefore, that a process such as digitization, even though it may cost more than mass deacidification, may have such controllable, positive effects on both short term and longer term access time reduction (positioning and migration control in the above model), that it will be found preferable to less expensive forms of preservation, such as mass deacidification. Even if digitization, in other words, were to remain substantially more expensive than mass deacidification, its value in terms of access time reduction may be such that it is more competitive than other preservation options (including mass deacidification) with other information service operations beyond preservation, and might therefore be supported in our institutions, while those other procedures might not be. I rather expect this will be generally the case.

But if, finally, that is not the case, and if institutions around the country, or in New York State, were to make mass deacidification a routine and regular operation, to what extent is cooperation among institutions possible and desirable? There are, of course, many forms of cooperation. The joint funding of a central facility—if it ever came to that—would certainly be a reasonable prospect, if financially justified, and the preservation community certainly has the experience and the reputation to achieve the objective. (MAPS is an obvious precedent.) Cooperation in support of infrastructure—e.g., transportation—might also be practicable. Cooperation at the selection level among institutions, however, is probably not a realistic goal, and I would like to argue strongly here and now against such an option, lest we end up expending large quantities of time in a vain effort to establish such a coordinated selection program among ourselves.

We must learn from our experiences—especially those to try to create broad and intricate cooperative structures and programs for purposes of coordinated collection development. Again: the purpose of information services is to move the most needed material forward on the continuum, and to impede the migration of some sources further down the continuum—within the confines of available institutional resources. Cooperative agreements, from the standpoint of the local institution, are normally intended to affect access time as it relates to material for which there are far lower needs—materials which are expected to be located more toward the negative end of the continuum. Since cooperative collection building cannot move sources very far forward on any individual continuum, the focus of such cooperation has necessarily been on those sources for which extended access time is acceptable. Cooperative collection development has been relatively unsuccessful, precisely because libraries have been understandably unwilling to alter their patterns of collection building, and to devote their scarce resources to the reduction of access time for materials acceptably located toward the negative end. Trying to reposition sources at the negative end, at the expense of trying to reposition sources at the positive end, is always counterproductive and will never justify the expenditure of resources necessary to create and administer a complex cooperative program.

We will encounter the same failure for the same reasons, if we attempt to coordinate selection for mass deacidification. Instead, we should accept the so-called "complementary" approach to cooperation: each library should deacidify those materials, the migration of which on the continuum it wishes to impede from the standpoint of its local priorities. This will result in some duplication, but some duplication is always justified, if warranted by local needs. If the complementary approach were used nationally, it would, to be sure, result in the migration of some materials to the far negative end of the continuum: as those publications work their way down the continuum, however, there will be opportunities to preserve some of them using other preservation procedures perhaps more conducive to cooperation. Works that arrive at the far negative end of the collective or idealized continuum, having never received any such form of preservation attention along the way, will be in jeopardy, and may well be lost. There will, therefore, be some losses of information. The new age we are now entering, with its new view of information as overabundant and partially expendable, will not only condone such losses—it will insist on them. And, in my opinion, rightly so.

REFERENCE NOTES

1. The distinction between instruction and research is one to which our faculty users are understandably sensitive. From an information services perspective, however, that distinction is much less pronounced, because what is called research is to a great extent self-education; the job

of information services is to provide information assistance. Whether it is for the user to teach a student or for the user to teach himself or herself is less of a concern.

2. This is most obvious in the source that occupies the front place in any continuum, which is the source the user is reading at that particular point. As smart as the user may be, as technically advanced as information services may become, the user can read only one source at a time. As the user stops reading one source and starts reading another, the source that was being read is displaced by the source now being read. This same kind of displacement probably takes place constantly among all of the sources located toward the front of the continuum as other sources are moved forward by (among other factors) information services. We have not yet fully grasped this reality—nor have, I think, our colleagues in computer technology. We cannot make everything immediately accessible: while that may be a logical technological goal, it is epistemologically impossible. This "displacement imperative" is, of course, simply the manifestation in this model of what will be the central issue of information services as we enter the online age, namely information overload.

3. If a library were devoting a large quantity of its materials budget to the acquisition of electronic sources, and if this activity were making some of the more conservative segments of the library's constituency uneasy, the library might want for this purpose alone to select mass deacidification as one of its main preservation methods rather than some form of substitution.

4. See Anne R. Kenney and Lynne K. Personius, *Joint Study in Digital Preservation Phase 1* (Washington, D.C.: Commission on Preservation and Access, 1992), 25–32.

5. Richard DeGennaro, "The Institutional Context for Mass Deacidification," in *A Roundtable on Mass Deacidification,* ed. Peter G. Sparks (Washington, D.C.: Association of Research Libraries, 1992), 14.

15 IN DEFENSE
OF RELATIVISM

Theory is never an end in itself—especially when presented within the context of a profession's literature. Rather, its purpose is always to enhance or illuminate practice. David Henige has received no response to his criticism of the Conspectus *not* because of some defect in the way librarians assess and exchange professional information, but rather because his criticism, while certainly vigorous and provocative, has probably had no more than a negligible effect on the practice of collection development and administration. This lack of impact derives primarily from Henige's failure to recognize the multiplicity of motivations for the Conspectus, but also, I think, because of some misconceptions on his part about the realities of librarianship and collection development. At this point, I'd like to examine some of the main uses served by the Conspectus.

THE CONSPECTUS AS DECLARATION OF COOPERATIVE INTENT

In an era of continuously declining resources, interlibrary cooperation has become not only respectable but expected. To put a broadly based cooperative collection development program in place, some method must be devised to summarize not only the collection content but also the collection priorities of the participating institutions in such a way that those summaries can be easily communicated and compared. (The raw data of the National Shelflist Count provide no such basis for communication.) To complete the Conspectus is already to begin to engage in a form of cooperation, therefore, to the extent that it represents an effort to convey to other institutions—in admittedly a highly stylized, summary form—past and present collection priorities. Work on the Conspectus further serves to notify university administrations, funding agencies, library users, and other institutions that the library undertaking that work is convinced of the possibility and desirability of comparing and coordinating collections.

THE CONSPECTUS AS FOCUS FOR COLLECTION THEORY

One of the most beneficial products of the Conspectus—both inside of RLG and in the collection development community at large—has been the level and intensity of the discussion it has generated. The availability and demands of the Conspectus have compelled some of our best minds to confront some of our most fundamental questions. What is a collection? How can we refer to its qualities? What is the relationship between collection strength and utility? We would never have found the time or the energy to consider such issues had it not been for the presence and pressure of the Conspectus. In fact, nothing testifies more profoundly to the usefulness of the Conspectus in this very specific sense than the frequency with which it has, over the years, been declared to be useless.

This article first appeared in *The Journal of Academic Librarianship* (Jan. 1992): 353–54.

THE CONSPECTUS AS EXERCISE IN LOCAL POLICY ARTICULATION

To complete the Conspectus, the bibliographer must externalize and compare the work he or she is investing in the development of different subject areas of the collection. This is important, because all knowledge and insight derive ultimately from conclusions drawn about relationships. Although the Conspectus was certainly designed to compare rankings of the same subject at different institutions, there can be no doubt that a major benefit of the Conspectus (and its success as a basis for internal collection policies) has been to force a comparison of the quality of different subjects at the same institution. To be sure, as Henige implies, some bibliographers may (consciously or unconsciously) lie about their collections when completing the Conspectus, but even committing such an unproductive and unmannerly act should at least improve the bibliographer's perception of his or her collection effort and priorities.

THE CONSPECTUS AS INTER-INSTITUTIONAL COMMUNICATIONS VEHICLE

We arrive finally at some of Henige's criticisms, which are specifically leveled at the capacity of the Conspectus to communicate useful information among institutions about collection strength and intensity. But just what useful information is the Conspectus intended to communicate? Henige considers the Conspectus "a largely undifferentiated, highly subjective, and abstract aggregation of selectors' opinions concerning the strengths of their libraries' holdings."[1] Fair enough. He then concludes that the "Conspectus is little more than an extravagantly designed and assiduously propagated bushelful of best guesses," and urges that the national utilities (OCLC and RLIN) and, above all, the National Shelflist Count be used as our principal cooperative tools, because they provide much more objective and reliable data.[2] But Henige then ends his article with the assertion that, while many disciplines want to be "scientific," collection development (which Henige apparently believes—quite mistakenly, in my opinion—to be a discipline) does not qualify as scientific. It is, in fact, "difficult to imagine how collection development can transform itself from an 'art' into a 'science.'"[3]

So why does Henige feel compelled to criticize at such length the inherent subjectivity of the Conspectus? The whole point of the Conspectus is, after all, to convey a series (or, if you prefer, a bushelful) of opinions—subjective assertions about the value and utility of subject collections presented by those who are responsible for developing them. The question is not how to compare the assertion to the reality: the assertion is the reality in this subjective "discipline" which is necessarily more "art" than "science." As a communications vehicle, as a means for bibliographers to declare their individual opinions about their collections, the Conspectus remains, for all of its flaws, the best instrument available.

THE CONSPECTUS AS CATALYST FOR COOPERATIVE COLLECTION DEVELOPMENT

We must admit in the final analysis, however, that Henige and his fellow Conspectus detractors are correct in their charge that we have failed to follow up on the assertions made in the Conspectus; we have failed to refine those assertions through dialogue among institutions; we have failed, in short, to put in place the kind of systematic cooperative collection program envisioned by RLG and the ARL NCIP initiative.[4] But we must also bear in mind that such failure is hardly attributable to the abstract, "unscientific" nature of the Conspectus. The Conspectus remains a highly necessary but far from sufficient prerequisite for cooperative collection development. The reason we have been unable to achieve a broadly based cooperative program is quite simply that collection administration continues to be fundamentally influenced by that most subjective for all forces: politics. We have so far failed to counter those powerful internal pressures at all of our own institutions which demand that we devote all of our collection resources to the satisfaction of short-term, local needs.

Most of us envy the status of the natural sciences. Most of us hanker for scientific objectivity, for the clean, reassuring procedures of the scientific method. But librarianship, and especially collection development, has very little to do with science or objectivity. Bibliography always has been a mutable, obscure, ambiguous, messy pursuit, and those of us who practice it must accept that the instruments we create to help us manage our work will necessarily reflect those qualities.

REFERENCE NOTES

1. David Henige, "Epistemological Dead End and Ergonomic Disaster? The North American Collections Inventory Project," *Journal of Academic Librarianship* 13 (Sept. 1987): 213.

2. Ibid., 212.

3. Ibid., 213.

4. The availability of the National Shelflist Count, which is a uniquely useful tool in many ways, has certainly *also* failed to lead to a national cooperative collection development program. The now classic description of the background and purpose of the RLG Conspectus can be found in Nancy E. Gwinn and Paul H. Mosher, "Coordinating Collection Development: The RLG Conspectus," *College & Research Libraries* 44 (Mar. 1983): 128–40. The standard statement on the National Collections Inventory Project can be found in David Farrell, "The NCIP Option for Coordinated Collection Management," *Library Resources & Technical Services* 30 (Jan.–Mar. 1986): 47–56.

16 THE ACQUISITIONS LIBRARIAN AS CHANGE AGENT IN THE TRANSITION TO THE ELECTRONIC LIBRARY

All information services, regardless of the format used to convey the information, can be divided into the two fundamental categories of delivery and mediation. Delivery is the less visible but no less critical service responsible for shifting the physical information package among different locations. Delivery will become an increasingly significant—but no less invisible—function after the arrival of routine electronic publishing. Acquisitions administrators—who, along with circulation, interlibrary loan, and preservation officers, have primary responsibility for delivery in the paper-based academic library of today—need to begin planning now to expand their knowledge and responsibilities to respond to the new requirements for information delivery in the rapidly approaching age of networked information. If they can achieve such objectives, acquisitions staff will play a key role in improving the future contributions of the library to the academy.

If there is any period one would desire to be born in, is it not the age of Revolution; when the old and the new stand side by side and admit of being compared; when the energies of all men are searched by fear and by hope; and when the historic glories of the old can be compensated by the rich possibilities of the new era? This time, like all times, is a very good one, if we but know what to do with it.—Emerson, *The American Scholar*

Anyone seeking a quick, concentrated glimpse into the current state of the academic library, its self-esteem and its self-depreciation, its hubris and its paranoia, need look no further than the library's acquisitions operation.[1] The place and image of the library in the institution is mirrored in the position and perception of the acquisitions operation in the academic library. In both cases, as Joe Hewitt has implied, we find complex responsibilities seldom understood by those in authority and perceived by most clientele (if indeed they are noticed at all) as being primarily clerical and flagrantly bureaucratic.[2] We find, above all, in both the acquisitions operation and the library as a whole, a vague apprehension of a creeping superfluity, a sense of pending obsolesence engendered primarily by advances in information technology so rapid in their development and so complex in their potential as to be barely intelligible to many line librarians. Discussions of this situation are often

This article first appeared in *Library Resources & Technical Services* 36, no. 1 (Jan. 1992): 7–20. A version of the article was presented at the Acquisitions Administrators Discussion Group on July 2, 1991, at the ALA Annual Conference in Atlanta, Ga.

complicated by a tendency to confuse functions with administrative units. The function of acquisitions is for the time being not at all in jeopardy, but the acquisitions department might be, and we have indeed seen transformations in such departments in several institutions; in some cases we have even seen parts of the traditional acquisitions responsibility shifted into other functional areas, such as collection development. In the same way, the information services function in the academy now performed by the library can never be eliminated if the institution is to pursue its educational and research mission, but there are prospects that at some institutions the library as an administrative unit will merge with or be relegated to other information service units on campus, such as academic computing.

Regardless of whether such administrative reorganizations enhance or impair the performance of library functions, the fact that such restructuring is even considered presents a clear signal that acquisitions may have failed to convince the library—and that the library may have failed to convince the institution—of its ability effectively to meet the needs of its clientele as we gradually but inexorably enter the new era of online information. The question that immediately presents itself, therefore, is whether adjustments might be introduced into the acquisitions function that would not only lead to an improvement in its role in the library but at the same time improve the effectiveness of the library's contribution to the institution. The purpose of this paper is to present some general ideas and tentative suggestions that, I hope, will serve as a basis for further discussion on this issue.

FUTURE PROSPECTS

We have in recent years witnessed a small but growing number of standard information sources published in electronic form. This shift from paper to electronic publishing has so far had its primary impact in public services, especially reference and collection development. This is because many such electronic sources either are directly accessible to users or public services staff over networks or are shipped to libraries as computer files in such forms as CD-ROMs or tapes, so that they can be managed by acquisitions operations in somewhat the same way that traditional paper sources are treated. No one will doubt, however, that the point is rapidly approaching at which an increasing amount of full-text information will be made routinely available to libraries and their users by transmission over networks, and it is that inevitable innovation—its approach now already heralded for decades—which upon finally arriving will have the most profound effect on all aspects of library operations, including especially the acquisitions function.[3]

The question acquisitions administrators need to consider is whether they plan to continue simply to maintain their current focus, retain their present methods, and restrict their responsibilities to those paper (or paper-like) publications that will no doubt continue to be published for some time (this is fully possible, since one could presumably bypass acquisitions in ordering access over networks to online sources) or whether the acquisitions function should be prepared to undergo some radical, fundamental alteration, so that it would gradually begin to play, with respect to networked information, a role analogous to what it now plays in the provision of information transferred via paper. There is still time for acquisitions to begin to plan for such a transformation. The development of electronic publishing has for several reasons not evolved nearly as quickly as was once predicted.[4] But electronic publishing is nevertheless making noticeable progress, and it is likely to move forward very rapidly and very suddenly once it gains momentum and critical mass of user acceptance. While opportunities remain, therefore, to adjust to, and to take advantage of, these rapidly evolving developments in the techniques of information exchange, we are probably approaching the eleventh hour.

We now have available to us a variety of well-conceived predictions about the future of the library as publications become increasingly available online.[5] These discussions are very useful in preparing ourselves for the changes we must shortly confront; however, it is important to bear two further points in mind. First, more precise projections of the conditions of libraries in the coming decades can be little more than exercises in pure speculation, which are, for the most part, not helpful in planning, especially given the restricted time we have available to spend on such work. Second, well-managed planning, if successful, is not simply an effort to prepare for future events; it should also be an attempt to shape them: by considering and readying ourselves for the future, we can and probably will change it. It is essential, therefore, that any planning we do leaves us with broad flexibility to absorb and to take advantage of unforeseen future developments while at the same time provides us with some kind of clear framework within which, or target toward which, we can orient ourselves in the course of the transition. One way to begin this process is to agree upon a general description or model of the whole operation—in this case information services—that is applicable to both the present and the probable future condition. Such an abstract model can be used as a context within which to make adjustments to the concrete conditions or activities now in place, in order to move the operation through the transition toward the preferred future. Creating such a description applicable to both the present and the probable future is in a sense simply a way of looking at the present and future simultaneously as we begin to make our adjustments: if one changes or upgrades activities or concepts, and these continue to fit into the model, then one is probably moving in the right direction. Let us therefore attempt this—but first we need to insert two presuppositions.

TWO PRESUPPOSITIONS

The Potential Primacy of Notification Sources

Graphic information is communicated in many formats for a wide variety of purposes. Many categories of information sources—belles lettres, for example—will almost certainly continue to be published in paper form well into the future, and the relationship between those materials and the library's acquisition function will presumably remain unaltered for some time. We have recently become aware, on the other hand, that certain types of information sources are particularly amenable to electronic publication—for example, bibliographic files and numeric data. The next major advance will presumably be the routine publication online of narrative full text. Of the various sources for which the academic library is responsible, it will most probably be the large category of library materials that I have elsewhere called *notification sources,* which will be published increasingly in full-text electronic form in the near future and which will be likely to have the most significant impact on library operations.[6] Notification sources are those materials written by scholars to describe the results of their research and thought for the information and assessment of other scholars working in the same or related fields. Most scholarly journal articles and monographs fit into this category, and there have recently been repeated calls from scholars, librarians, and network administrators to publish more information of this kind in electronic form.[7] It is in notification sources that the greatest opportunities for online scholarly communication should be available.[8] The delay in routinely publishing most notification sources online surely derives less from any limitations of technology than from cultural habits and the economics of publishing. Once these two (admittedly substantial) impediments are bypassed or moved aside, as they must eventually be, the floodgates will open, and we will experience a deluge of online scholarly publications, which some institutional agency—one hopes it will be the library—will need to ensure are available to scholars. Most of these publications, at least in the beginning, will probably be electronic journals, many of them no doubt in the sciences.[9] But the other scholarly disciplines will not be far behind, because all subjects will benefit so demonstrably from remote access at personal workstations to the latest published information.

For reasons of convention, aesthetics, and ease of access, we may expect that monographic publications will continue to be published in paper form for a somewhat longer period than their journal counterparts, but we must anticipate that the scholarly monograph as well will succumb to online publication in the relatively near future.[10] It may be that the scholarly monograph will be replaced by some form of online monograph, or that lengthier materials will be published in digital form with the expectation that they will be printed by or for the library user on site and on demand, or even that the monograph as a method of scholarly communication will be replaced by shorter essays more conducive to publication as electronic journal articles. In any event, the driving force behind the replacement of the paper monograph by some online form of publication will undoubtedly be primarily economic. The publication of lengthier studies on highly specialized subjects, especially in those disciplines without industrial or commercial applications, is already becoming so expensive as to be prohibitive. I suspect in fact that there has seldom been enough of a true demand for such specialized monographic notification sources to justify their publication economically. We have perhaps succeeded so far in circumventing this problem primarily though the agency of the academic library, which creates a kind of artificial demand for specialized scholarly publications. Under the current system of collection development, the library imputes a use-value to materials for which no actual use-value has been demonstrated. The library purchases the publication on the basis of that potential use-value (or on the assumption that the publication by virtue of its availability on the shelf will acquire use-value). As a result, enough of a reliable demand of this kind presumably exists to permit publishers to bring out short runs of highly specialized monographic publications. The pressures on library budgets in recent years (caused in part by rapidly inflated journal prices), however, have now become so paralytic in their effect that some libraries can no longer afford to acquire materials based on potential—as opposed to demonstrated or expressed—use-value. Since a reduction in publication costs appears unlikely, it may well be that only through some form of restructuring of the scholarly publication process will it remain possible economically to communicate such specialized information for very much longer in lengthier publication formats.

In light of these considerations, therefore, let us restrict our inquiry, at least initially, to services promoting the exchange and use of notification sources published electronically.

The Inclusion of Input

The purpose of notification sources is, obviously, scholarly communication. Communication entails the transmission and the reception of information—input and output. Modern libraries have restricted their responsibilities to reception—or, more precisely, to the facilitation of receptions—of information, leaving responsibilities for transmission for the most part to other agencies, mainly publishers. This has always been a potentially problematic approach to the promotion of scholarly communication, because transmission and reception are so fundamentally interdependent. If the library intends to continue to play a key role in scholarly communication in the online age, therefore, it must be prepared to assume some responsibility itself for ensuring that the entire scholarly communication system operates effectively—and that must necessarily include input.

The need and the potential for the academic library to play a much greater role in publishing as we move further in to the online era is by now a relatively common idea.[11] Little has been done so far, however, to chart the processes by which such responsibilities might be assumed. At this point, we need only stress two implications of such an expansion of the library's traditional activities. First, if such new responsibilities are to be accepted by the library, a key role in that undertaking will need to be played by those library staff with the most advanced understanding of the processes and economics of publication—and those staff will for the most part be located in our acquisitions (and also collection development) departments.

The second implication is mainly economic. If the library does assume greater responsibility for assisting and promoting the entire process of scholarly communication, much of which is achieved primarily through notification sources, then the present methods of funding that communication must soon be recognized as ineffective. We must bear in mind that scholarly communication is an admittedly slow but nevertheless progressive dialogue. Scholars read publications primarily to write more of them—to continue the conversation. (Much more "interactive" publication will no doubt become possible online.) Both sides benefit from the dialogue: not only the reader, but also the author and his or her institution. (The institution's primary "product" or "commodity," which is sold to prospective students and to funding agencies is, after all, the reputation of its faculty—and that reputation is established mainly through publications.) Most of the readers and writers of notification sources are, moreover, the clientele of academic libraries. Under such circumstances, we must conclude that our current funding methods for notification sources are largely counterproductive. We will be wasting our money—and in a very real sense we are already doing so—buying information (packaged as notification sources) from each other. Instead, we should be using that funding to send such information to each other. Libraries must maneuver themselves into a position from which they will be accepted as credible and legitimate conduits for the transmission of notification sources.[12] Needless to say, such a shift in the method of scholarly communication raises many questions, but there is no doubt that academic libraries are fully capable of putting such a system into effect and that such an arrangement managed by the library would promote the interests of scholarly communication substantially. It would also, if properly managed, bring about a much more egalitarian distribution of scholarly information.

Having posited our two presuppositions, we may now turn to our primary task of presenting a general description of information services.

THE DIALECTIC OF INFORMATION SERVICES

Information services are those facilities designed to improve the ability of (in the sense of reducing the time required by) the individual client to identify, organize, transmit, receive, exploit, and develop and maintain standards for communications, usually in the form of sets of graphic signs, for predefined purposes. In the academic library, those purposes are for the most part education and research.

The basis of our description will be a division of information services into two fundamental functional categories. The first of these two functions, which we will call *delivery*, is charged with the transportation or conduction of the material information package or carrier; the other function, which we will call *mediation*, is designed to assist the sender and the receiver of the package in the transmission, receipt, and the application of the so-called information content of the package.[13] Together these functions form a kind of dialectic of information services, so that one cannot in reality be disconnected from the other. At the more elementary level, it is obvious that mediation, in order to achieve its function, must play a role in the delivery process—it must, for example, take economic issues into account in document assessment and consider location as part of the process of identification. By the same token, delivery can seldom be effectively achieved without some understanding of or reference to the content, and the needs of the communicants—i.e., the senders and receivers of the information—must be understood by those responsible for delivery if, for example, effective priorities for delivery are to be established.

On a more fundamental level, the dialectic reduces perhaps most clearly to the realization that all communication could and might be understood as a form or process of delivery. The package and the content are both primarily means of delivery. The medium is selected by the communicants through a kind of mutual agreement that such a medium provides the best prospects for delivery, and that decision will be driven or conditioned by the relative delivery potential of different media. Even the capacity, which most electronic media now provide the user, to manipulate the data received—that, too, can and must be understood in a sense as a delivery function, for the data needed by the receiver are in effect made deliverable and are delivered by means of that manipulation. The user in effect through manipulation creates and delivers the data for his or her own use. Mediation itself can in fact be understood—and must sometimes be viewed—as that segment of information services responsible for ensuring and enhancing delivery.

We could, of course, expand on these connections indefinitely. The only important point is that, in the heat of our efforts to divide information services into these two types of activities, we not lose sight of the fact that such categorical distinctions as delivery and mediation are always artificial abstractions. We can no more separate delivery from mediation than we can divide transmission from reception: each is understandable and practicable only as an extension of the other. At the operational level, however, it does appear very likely that some staff in the electronic library will specialize in delivery and others in mediation.

Both delivery and mediation are, of course, services in themselves, designed to serve the needs of the communicants. Both delivery and mediation are also concerned with the material containers of information—albeit in very different ways. This is, again, as true in the electronic environment as it is in the paper environment. It is admittedly sometimes tempting to view information exchange in electronic form as something done "without having to rely on tangible physical objects as the medium of communication."[14] This is, of course, incorrect. All communication is achieved through some kind of material media. In the case of online communication, those media are difficult to observe and they can be moved about very quickly, but they remain nevertheless material objects, and their transmission and reception remain material manipulations.

We must be careful to distinguish, therefore, between: (a) the carrier or what we are calling the information package (e.g., a book or a database); (b) the content of the package, which most often consists of linguistic or pictorial symbols (e.g., the print on the page or on the screen), which is, of course, also material; and (c) the information symbolized by the content, which is encrypted (encoded, turned into symbols) for purposes of communication by the writer and decrypted by the reader. Bearing in mind that these three entities are, of course, also inseparably interdependent, we might say that, in the grossest possible terms, the responsibility for managing the carrier or package belongs in large part to the delivery operation; the content forms in many ways the central focus of mediation; which the information itself must always be the primary concern and responsibility of the communicants.

We can best begin to distinguish delivery services from mediation services by differentiating their respective relationships to the information package and to the user. Delivery is primarily a logistical operation aimed at the transportation of the package or the carrier from one location to another. The material nature of the package, its physical composition, is of critical importance to the delivery operation, because it has the most fundamental effect on the package's portability. It is in general much easier (or, at least, much faster) to move information packages from one location to another in electronic form than in paper form. Regardless of the package's physical composition, however, delivery requires a thorough knowledge of the technology of transmission as well as an experienced understanding of many of the peripheral factors—administrative, economic, legal—upon which the successful movement of the information package depends.

Mediation, on the other hand, is primarily a linguistic or hermeneutic operation, designed to optimize or amplify the exchange of information among the communicants; this service reduces in most instances to assisting the writers and readers in making different kinds of selection decisions: what and how to transmit, what to receive and what to filter out, how to search, what uses to make of the information once it is obtained. While delivery is concerned more with the transportation of the information package (which may admittedly sometimes involve some transcription of the content), mediation must concentrate more upon assisting in the translation of meaning into material symbols, and of the material symbols into applicable meaning. This requires knowledge of the needs and interests of the communicants, as well as the methods of identifying and interpreting information packages. Delivery services work primarily with matter "out there" in the material world (including, increasingly, segments of electronic databases); their activities, operations, and success are for the most part objective, public, and measurable. Mediation services, on the other hand, while also working admittedly with material content, are nevertheless designed to facilitate private, subjective activities—writing, reading, evaluating, interpreting, applying—which are neither observable nor precisely measurable.

In spite of their relatively observable activities, however, delivery services are normally separate from, and seldom observed by, the communicating clientele. That aspect of information services that is de facto public, in other words, and that could be objectively evaluated is paradoxically seldom even perceived, let alone evaluated by the public. Mediation, on the other hand, is subject to constant scrutiny and aggressive public assessment. Even though delivery operations in the traditional paper environment are already barely visible to most library users, such services in the online environment have the potential to become even more obscure. How often have we heard it said that in the online environment, it makes no difference where the information is located: the user can gain access to it over the network regardless of its location? This is indeed true, provided that those invisible technicians and information service specialists responsible for delivery have done and continue to do their work. The extensive technical and administrative effort invested to provide such immediate access to large volumes of information in different locations remains relatively unnoticed by most users—unless, of course, the system malfunctions.

This also means among other things that delivery services always function as a kind of direct representative of the user. Delivery services act for the communicants in their absence, and carry out their presumed bidding, in effect making decisions for them. One of the major liabilities of delivery services, therefore, to which we have already made reference, is that delivery staff can for this reason alone easily become detached from the clientele in whose interest they are charged to operate. Mediation services, on the other hand, can seldom if ever act entirely for the communicants but rather must work frequently in their presence as (often very much less than equal) partners. Precisely because mediation services depend for their success on a close coordination with the user, they are highly visible and are subject to all of the benefits and liabilities of that exposure. It is mediation services, moreover, that always have functioned as the library's link to the user and will no doubt continue to do so.

We must also distinguish between our two basic services at the economic level. Mediation services, with various degrees of input from the communicants, try often to assess the value of information from the perspective of utility or use-value. The willingness to pay the cost of the transmission and receipt of the document depends upon how much (i.e., how fast) that access is needed by the receiver. Delivery services, on the other hand, tend to view the value of the document more in terms of its exchange-value or market value—i.e., in financial terms. The value of the document or package is assessed or inferred mainly by comparing it as a material object to other packages of like quality, origin, and design. Thus, while mediation services are more inclined to view scholarship as a form of specialized communication and documents as products of research to be communicated, delivery services tend perhaps to view the document more as a commodity and scholarly information exchange more as a specialized form of commerce. This tendency is perhaps one further manifestation of the fact that delivery services are accustomed to objectivity and relatively exact measurement, while mediation services understand their operation as promoting primarily subjective and relatively private action.

We should note, finally, that the citation of an information package—its bibliographic surrogate—may refer to different concepts in delivery than in mediation. While the citation for mediation purposes is used mainly to characterize or identify the content as it relates to the content of other documents, the citation for purposes of delivery is used mainly as a means to determine where the document is or could be physically located and perhaps where it should be sent—in other words, a kind of address. What the document is about—in the sense of what its content refers to—is for the most part irrelevant to delivery services, except to the extent that it can serve as an indication of its origin and destination.

In order to examine these concepts further, let us resort to a diagram that summarizes the distinctions we have been discussing but that also retains at the same time the terms we use now in the primarily paper environment. See figure 1.

The broken vertical line between input and output today separates also the library's responsibilities on the output side from those of the publisher, who is now primarily responsible for input. As noted earlier, at least as far as notification sources are concerned, which are both written and read primarily by the clientele of academic libraries, there is no reason, especially in the online environment, not to expand the library's role in information services to include input—to fuse more effectively the inputting and outputting operations. Even in the primarily paper environment, as already noted, we pay dearly for this unnecessary and highly contradictory division of responsibilities. Our goal, therefore, must be not simply to add input responsibilities to those we already have for output, but also in so doing to bring about a closer coordination or consolidation between the two.

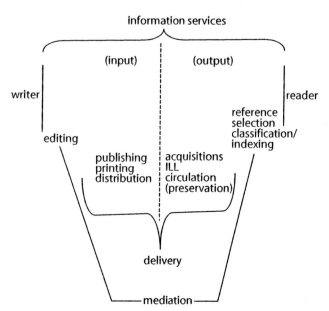

FIGURE 1. Structure

This is admittedly perhaps most demonstrably practicable in the diverse realm of mediation. Certainly the library has the potential, and should assume much more responsibility for, assisting and organizing the editing or input-filtering function. Much more is being published today than needs to be for purposes of scholarship, because, among other things, there is an inadequate system of quality control.[15] Working with scholars to establish standards and procedures for editing notification sources should be a fundamental library service, which should aim to bring about a much more effective and dependable quality control over scholarly communication. But we must also strive to combine what are now conceived primarily as outputting responsibilities with inputting activities. This is especially needed in selection and in cataloging and indexing. An integral aspect of the selection responsibilities for notification sources should be the influencing and assisting of what gets published; part of selection activity, in other words, as mediation service, should be to work closely with scholars to select those writings that should be made public through standard channels and to determine the levels of access that should be provided for different publications. The classification and indexing of notification sources should also properly be done by the library—again, as mediation service, that is, in partnership with the author at the inputting stage. When the library transmits (i.e., publishes) a notification source, the cataloging or indexing should be part of, or one further form of, that publication. As mentioned earlier, collection development funding budgeted for notification sources should be used at least partially for inputting, i.e., for transmitting those sources to other libraries for the use of scholars elsewhere.

Such an amalgamation between input and output should also occur in the area of delivery services. Those staff responsible for receiving transmissions—or for ensuring that such transmissions are available to local scholars—should be the same staff responsible for the transmission of the work of local scholars to other institutions—or at least for ensuring that other institutions can effectively request and receive such transmissions on demand. In this way, we can guarantee critically important uniform standards and procedures in the online exchange of notification sources, much as we have succeeded to a limited extent in achieving such standardization today in interlibrary loan.

We must bear in mind, finally, that delivery not only is concerned with the movement of information in to and out of the institution for research purposes, but is also responsible for the transportation of information within the institution for instructional purposes. Information, for example, "scattered throughout the library can be brought together or interconnected to form a useful collection for teaching and learning purposes. These facilities can be supported by not only the library but also the computer center and offices of instructional development on campus."[16]

BEYOND NOTIFICATION

Although we have restricted our discussion to notification sources, we must also pay at least some passing attention to the fact that other sources will also become increasingly available online in full text, although not as quickly, I suspect, as current notification sources. One very large body of potential online information, which may well become prevalent shortly after the initial emergence of notification sources, consists of materials previously published in paper form but later digitized. The purpose of such digitization may be preservation, storage, or simply improvement of access. Whatever the purpose, we must expect large numbers of digitized documents eventually to replace their paper originals at most of our institutions. These digitized items will be transportable over networks to readers throughout the country and the world. The direct intervention of libraries in this transfer of information might possibly be less necessary, although the screening or selection skills of mediation will very probably remain essential services. In any event, such transfer will be impossible without not only technical innovations but also complex economic and political negotiations. Creating and maintaining an infrastructure that can promote and link such innovation and negotiation must be the responsibility of delivery services. Once again we find the special skills of delivery staff in clear demand: technical and administrative knowledge and skills, not to mention an understanding of the economic base upon which the whole structure must be erected. In addition, the legal work to be done on such digitized reprints, and which should also be accepted as part of the responsibility of delivery services, will be considerable, because most of the materials to be transferred to online form will be protected by copyright. Some agency within the academy familiar with the economics of information and publication will need to negotiate with publishers on the provision of access in this form.

There is also no reason not to assume that all scholarly publications—not only notification sources—might eventually be published online, in the sense that they would be sent to institutions over a network, and then either printed and put on the shelf or maintained and read in digital form and, if necessary, printed on demand. We are now, I believe, technically able to accomplish this. Once again, however, it will not be the technology that deters this innovation, but rather the fact that a critical portion of the current input side of delivery services—i.e., publishing—remains primarily in the hands of commercial publishers whose goals are not communication but rather revenue and who therefore must control and restrict the distribution of their publications. Online publication, with its potential for immediate proliferation, would jeopardize that restriction. This is one more reason that it is essential for the academic library to assume increasing responsibility as soon as possible for the input side of delivery services, for only in that way will scholarly communication realize the full benefits of online publication.

CONCLUSIONS

While libraries have recognized for some time that substantial changes in what we have been calling mediation will issue from advances in electronic publishing, libraries have reflected much less upon the changes that are bound to occur in delivery—changes that will be at least as significant as those we anticipate in mediation and, given the increased independence of the user from direct mediation in the online age, possibly even more significant.[17] Delivery, redefined or specified in some manner as we have tried to do above, will remain a highly critical function, therefore, in the electronic library.

It is clear that, if we adopt perspectives similar to those presented above, a variety of relatively disparate operations in the current environment—acquisitions, interlibrary loan, publishing, network design, telecommunications—are in fact all oriented toward very similar objectives and are perhaps most productively understood as variations of a single service concept. There is, moreover, at least some potential, as we move increasingly into the era of online information exchange, for these now separate functions and responsibilities to be synthesized into a unified system of scholarly information delivery.

There can be no doubt that the current delivery operations in the library have the leverage and the potential, the position and the connections, to play a much expanded coordinating role in future information services. The ability of the library to manage and adapt to rapid changes in information technology will depend, moreover, precisely upon such a conscious "interaction with the environment."[18] This does not mean, I hasten to add, that our current library delivery services will necessarily assume such a role. Certainly such opportunities will not materialize *ex nihilo*—nor is it likely that such responsibilities will simply devolve to any operation anywhere in the information services system without some action being taken by that operation to attract those responsibilities. It will be, as always, those segments of the system that best discern how to take advantage of the present to create their own future that are most likely to play an enhanced role in that future (albeit not always in the way they had originally planned). Whether acquisitions staff in academic libraries today will have the motivation and the foresight to create for themselves a more influential and critical position in the kind of information services structure we have been describing is a question to which I have no answer. What I do know is that the necessary (if not alone sufficient) condition for the assumption of a major leadership role by acquisitions will be at the very least a breadth of knowledge and perspective not today traditionally associated with the acquisitions function. Gaining that knowledge, forming that breadth of perspective, would no doubt be the most effective first step by acquisitions administration toward that preferred future. What kind of knowledge are we talking about?

To begin with, the knowledge acquisitions already possesses in the economics of publishing will need to be broadened. Above all, the same level of expertise acquisitions is reputed to possess in the area of traditional publishing must be extended to electronic publishing. The library, and indeed the institution, should be able to look to acquisitions as the authority on advances in electronic publishing for purposes of scholarly communication. This knowledge must encompass not simply the techniques but also the economics of scholarly publication, precisely because, again, the major impediments to the evolution of electronic publishing are not electronic. They are economic. If the library is truly to serve the interests of scholarly communication, it must appropriate increased economic responsibility for scholarly publishing. The economics of scholarly communication cannot be left solely in the hands of either the information technicians or the commercial publishers, although both of those groups—one in the interest of expediency, the other for purposes of profit—have been and will continue to be quite prepared to assume that control. Rather, it is the library that is in the bets position to assume responsibility, as it has always sought to do, for ensuring that scholarly information is available to all who need it for educational and research purposes.

Second, and closely related to the need for acquisitions to broaden its knowledge of the techniques and economics of publishing, is the need for acquisitions to work to gain a more in-depth understanding of information technology and telecommunications. This is necessary in order both to promote electronic publishing and to begin to guide and influence technical innovations in the information industry more effectively. A durable and open link has yet to be forged between the library and information engineering; if this is not put in place relatively soon, two distinct and competing cultures are certain to emerge. This is not to deny, of course, that the development of information technology should be left in the hands of the technicians. It certainly should be, but those technicians should and will need much more precise guidance in the potential applications of that technology, and it is through the library's delivery services—those staff most knowledgeable in the material aspects of information management—that such guidance should be supplied.[19]

Finally, were acquisitions to assume such an expanded role in the electronic library, it would need to begin now to strengthen its understanding of mediation services as these will evolve in the online era. This is necessary not only to gather the information needed to advise information engineers on future technical development requirements, but also more fundamentally to ensure that all delivery operations are meeting the needs of scholarly information exchange. Mediation services will, as already noted, very probably remain the primary link between delivery services and the clientele—the communicants. The potential for delivery services to become isolated, to act as independent representatives of the communicants with only a vague or indirect understanding of their needs, can be avoided only by delivery services establishing and maintaining routine and functional connections with mediation services.

This is admittedly an almost absurdly ambitious agenda for acquisitions—but we face unprecedented changes and opportunities, and these call for radical action. If such goals as those just described could be achieved in the near future by the acquisitions operation, delivery services would be able to assume the kind of pivotal coordinating or linking function necessary ultimately to attain the level of efficiency and productivity that users of information services in an online environment will demand and deserve. This linking function is schematized in figure 2.

The ideal function of delivery within such a structure is not only to manage the logistics of the transmission and reception of graphic information for the institution, but also in doing to represent the needs of scholarly communication to the technical arm of information services and to convey the technical capacities and options, including their administrative and economic advantages and perquisites, through the agency of mediation services, to the scholarly

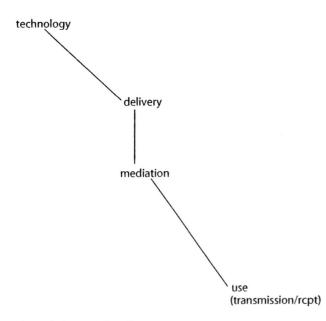

FIGURE 2. Coordination

user community. Delivery services would function in such a capacity as a kind of regulatory mechanism within the national system of scholarly information exchange, which would define what material forms of exchange are technically available and economically feasible. This service, if well managed, would have the most beneficial effects for the communication of scholarly information in the online era, for the service contribution of the library to the institution, and, needless to say, for the position of delivery services within the library.

Despite the forward-looking philosophies adopted by a small number of acquisitions departments, few operations in the academic library today appear as ill-prepared as acquisitions for the advent of online information exchange. Certainly no operation will be more profoundly affected by that development than acquisitions. No operation has so much to lose by deferring such preparation or so much to gain by beginning now to plan and to implement whatever functional changes are needed to accommodate and to exploit these opportunities. If acquisitions does not assume these responsibilities, they will certainly be absorbed by other agencies in the information services community, probably ultimately to the detriment of scholarly communication.

REFERENCE NOTES

1. I use the term *acquisitions* to refer to those library functions responsible for the ordering and receipt of library materials in all formats including serials.

2. Joe A. Hewitt, "On the Nature of Acquisitions," *Library Resources & Technical Services* 33 (1989): 107.

3. See *Managing a New Library Resource: Results of the RLG Machine-Readable Data File Project in Six Member Libraries* (Mountain View, Calif.: The Research Libraries Group, 1989). For a recent, very adaptable effort to integrate electronic publications into the current academic library, see Paul Metz and others, *Report of the Task Force on the Electronic Journal* (Blacksburg, Va.: Univ. Libraries, Virginia Polytechnic Institute and State Univ., 1991).

4. Participants in a 1980 Delphi study, for example, predicted that "25 percent of existing reference books will be available only in electronic form." Reported in F. W. Lancaster, *Libraries and Librarians in an Age of Electronics* (Arlington, Va.: Information Resources Pr., 1982), 61.

5. The classic work remains F. W. Lancaster, *Libraries and Librarians in an Age of Electronics.* For a more recent discussion by Lancaster see his "Electronic Publishing" in *Library Trends* 37 (1989): 316–25. For a recent critique of Lancaster's position, see Svend Larsen, "The Idea of an Electronic Library: A Critical Essay," *Libri* 38 (1988): 159–77. For a summary of different perspectives in the published literature, see Meredith Butler, "Electronic Publishing and Its Impact on Libraries: A Literature Review," *Library Resources & Technical Services* 28 (1984): 41–58. For a selected bibliography on electronic publishing, see Barbara M. Robinson, "Managing Change and Sending Signals in the Marketplace," *Library Acquisitions: Practice & Theory* 13 (1989): 223–25. The best recent overview is certainly David W. Lewis, "Inventing the Electronic Library," *College & Research Libraries* 49 (1988): 291–304.

6. Ross Atkinson, "Old Forms, New Forms: The Challenge of Collection Development," *College & Research Libraries* 50 (1989): 514–15.

7. For a very recent example of such a call to publish more online, see N. David Mermin, "Publishing in Computopia," *Physics Today* 44 (May 1991): 9–11.

8. See Brian J. Perry, "The Impact of Electronic Publishing on Library Collection and Services," *IFLA Journal* 14 (1988): 129.

9. See Lewis, "Inventing the Electronic Library," 296: "Disciplines where the results of research can be separated from the reporting of results will find the transition easier than disciplines where a large part of the scholarly task is the expression of understanding. A biochemist receives a Nobel Prize for work done in the lab, but a historian will receive a Bancroft, not for work in an archive, but only for a book." See also Eric Wainwright, "The University, Its Library, and the Information Age," *Australian Academic & Research Libraries* 16 (1985): 75.

10. Michael Gorman would disagree. See his view on the future of the monograph in his "The Academic Library in the Year 2001: Dream or Nightmare or Something in Between?" *Journal of Academic Librarianship* 17 (1991): 7.

11. See, for example, Edwin Brownrigg, Clifford Lynch, and Mary Engle, "Technical Services in the Age of Electronic Publishing," *Library Resources & Technical Services* 28 (1984): 67. More recently, see Peter S. Graham, "Electronic Information and Research Library Technical Services," *College & Research Libraries* 51 (1990): 249. The Coalition for Networked Information has established a Working Group on Non-Commercial Publishing, which is considering among other things how institutions can be assisted in undertaking more electronic publishing.

12. See Patricia Ohl Rice, "From Acquisitions to Access," *Library Acquisitions: Practice & Theory* 14 (1990): 18–19. See also Eldred Smith's idea of a centralized "electronic collection" for the use of all research libraries in his "Resolving the Acquisitions Dilemma: Into the Electronic Information Environment," *College & Research Libraries* 52 (1991): 236.

13. See Clyde Hendrick, "The University Library in the Twenty-first Century," (*College & Research Libraries* 47 [1986]: 128), who divides the user's task in the coming online age into two parts: (a) mastery of the physical means of getting at the information and (b) mastery of the conceptual systems for the organization of the library's store of knowledge. See also Gorman, "The Academic Library in the Year 2001," 6:

    > The purpose of libraries is, and always has been, twofold: (1) to acquire, store, disseminate, and allow access to carriers of knowledge and information in all forms, and (2) to provide services based on those carriers of knowledge and information. The fact that there are now new carriers and new technologies ('twas ever thus) has not changed that enduring purpose one whit.

14. Gordon B. Neavill, "Electronic Publishing, Libraries, and the Survival of Information, " *Library Resources & Technical Services* 28 (1984): 76.

51. See Carolyn J. Mooney, "Efforts to Cut Amount of 'Trivial' Scholarship Win New Backing from Many Academics," *Chronicle of Higher Education* (May 22, 1991): A1, A13, and her "In 2 Years, a Million Refereed Articles, 300,000 Books, Chapters, Monographs" (on A14 in the same issue).

16. Deanna L. Roberts, "Needs-Led Service Not Acquisitions-Led Service in the Research Library," *Collection Building* 11, no.1 (1991): 24–25.

17. See, for example, Forest Woody Horton, Jr.'s idea of "The Emerging Information Counselor," *Bulletin of the American Society for Information Science* 8, no. 5 (June 1982): 16–19.

18. "Interaction with the environment" is one of the seven major issues relating to the successful adaptation to change identified by G. Edward Evans in his "Research Libraries in 2010," in *Research Libraries, The Past 25 Years, The Next 25 Years: Papers for a Festschrift Honoring Le Moyne W. Anderson,* ed. Taylor E. Hubbard (Boulder, Colo.: Colorado Associated Univ. Pr., 1986), 77–94.

19. See Martin Faigel, "The Library as Marketplace in a Collection Management Environment," *Library Acquisitions: Practice & Theory* 12 (1988): 194. Academic libraries have so far often been less than successful in influencing decision-making on technology at the institutional level. See, for example, Kenneth E. Flower, "Academic Libraries on the Periphery: How Telecommunications Policy is Determined in Universities," *Journal of Library Administration* 8, no. 2 (summer 1987): 93–114.

17 THE CONDITIONS OF COLLECTION DEVELOPMENT

The technical revolution we are now experiencing in information processing and telecommunications has so far had mainly an indirect effect on collection development. Automation has, to be sure, radically transformed the identification and ordering of library materials, but the object of collection development—the information sources themselves—and the uses to which those sources are put, remain relatively unchanged. It has not been so much the practice of collection development which information technology has influenced, therefore, as the theory of bibliography and collection services. The major impact of technology has been perhaps—to borrow a term from Russian Formalism—to "defamiliarize" collection development: although the operations and objects of collection development have remained relatively unaltered, our anticipation of the Great Leap into the electronic age has made these operations and objects appear unusual and unfamiliar, as if we were obliged to view them through some kind of distorting lens.[1] What follows is an attempt to describe the current process of collection development—to answer the question, "what is it that collection development librarians do?"—by identifying and defining four fundamental concepts which together inform and underlie that process: (a) combination, (b) locality, (c) temporality, and (d) focus. These are, of course, not the only concepts that condition our current perception of collection development, but they are in their aggregate adequate for a general theoretical mapping of the field. Such an approach is both a response to and a product of the defamiliarization of collection development brought on by our present, restless preoccupation with transition and technology. The intent is to describe and interpret collection development in a manner that is applicable to both the traditional and the online environments—for it is evidently our lot for the time being to remain balanced on the cusp between these two potentially very different eras.

TERMINOLOGY

The decade of the 1980s has witnessed an avalanche of publications on collection development. Between 1980 and 1989, no fewer than nine new (or newly edited) book-length studies—textbooks, manuals, overviews—on the nature and method of collection development were published in the United States.[2] Each of these books approaches the subject from a slightly different perspective, although most provide information on the standard canon of topics: selection and deselection, policy, budgeting, collection evaluation, and—in some cases—acquisitions, cooperation, preservation, and historical bibliography. In the past fifteen years, moreover, three specialty journals relating to collection development have been founded (*Collection Building, Collection Management,* and *Library Acquisitions: Practice and Theory*), and the articles on collection development in the general library literature are becoming so numerous as to be difficult to track.[3] If there is one conceptual thread that connects most North American publications on collection development theory in the

This article first appeared in *Collection Management: A New Treatise,* ed. Charles B. Osburn and Ross Atkinson (Greenwich, Conn.: JAI Pr., 1991).

1980s, it is probably the insistence that collection development should be distinguished from acquisitions on the one hand, and from selection on the other. The most immediate root of these distinctions is what we might call the "Edelman Triad." At the 1977 RTSD preconference on collection development in Detroit, Hendrik Edelman posited his highly influential terminological hierarchy:

> The first level is collection development, which, although it can be interpreted as a passive term when it describes collection growth, should in fact be seen in the active sense. . . . Collection development is a planning function. . . . From the collection development plan flows the budget allocation in broad terms.
>
> The second level is selection, which is a direct function of collection development. It is the decision-making process concerned with implementing the goals stated earlier.
>
> The third level of this hierarchy is acquisition. The acquisition process implements in turn the selection decisions. It is the process that actually gets the material into the library.[4]

The uncoupling of acquisitions from collection development culminated on the theoretical level in the early 1980s with the realization that collection development must be "service-oriented rather than collection-oriented," and thus at least as focused upon the information needs of the public as upon the technique of importing materials.[5] This distinction is reflected in the organizational structure of most North American research libraries today, in which collection development is a separate and relatively autonomous operation, while acquisitions continues to function primarily within the technical services structure.[6] The other branch of the Edelman Triad, which distinguishes between collection development as the planning or policy-making function, and selection as the activity deriving from collection policy, now pervades the literature, although the understanding and definition of that distinction does vary.[7]

Even though the term *collection development* was initially intended to stress the broader policy and budgeting functions, yet further collection-related activities such as deselection, cooperation, and especially the rapidly growing field of preservation occasioned the creation of the term *collection management,* which came rapidly into vogue in the early 1980s.[8] This new term was apparently expected to subsume collection development, in the same way that collection development subsumed selection and acquisitions in the Edelman Triad. The problem is that the term collection development was not very well defined to begin with—and the efforts to create yet another term have consequently caused considerable confusion. The term collection management, while gaining wide popularity in the early 1980s, appears nevertheless not to have displaced the term collection development. The two terms often now receive equal or at least parallel billing. Two of the most influential national committees on collection development today, for example, are both called the "collection management and development committee"—one in the Association for Library Collections and Technical Services (ALCTS) of the American Library Association (ALA), and the other in the Research Libraries Group (RLG). At the present time (1990), the two terms are becoming increasingly synonymous, with *collection development* often being used to refer to all of those expanded responsibilities which the term *collection management* was created to encompass. Buckland is typical in his willingness to accept either term, provided it is understood to "denote the whole process of forming and managing collections of library materials."[9]

The distinction between selection and collection development, now so common in the literature as to qualify practically as a cliché, deserves some reconsideration, for the distinction is not nearly as clear as is frequently assumed. All aspects of collection development reduce in a sense to selection. Collection building, weeding, preservation and main-tenance—all of these are finally a matter of choosing individual sources or source groups over others for some purpose. From this perspective, budgeting and policy are tools of selection—manifestations or generalizations drawn from past experiences of selection. This is obviously not to claim that collection development does not exist: it does exist, of course, but primarily as the administrative extension of selection.[10] The term collection development is especially useful and significant to the extent that it connotes plurality: the "preference today for collection development instead of book selection reinforces an emphasis on the quantity of works comprising the collection rather than on individual books."[11] This is important. The term collection development (or management) does not merely indicate that the assembly of textual units into a group in one place at one time requires administration—for example, policy, coordination and budgeting. It also implies that the systematic assembly of textual units necessarily entails actively relating those individual units to each other. The development of library collections depends ultimately upon "the capacity to make the parts fit the needed whole."[12] We must, therefore, begin our examination of collection development with a discussion of this concept.

COMBINATION

All perception, all understanding, appears to be grounded at least partially in comparison, in difference, in opposition, in dialectic—in the invention or discovery of relationships. This would seem to be true even at the most elemental level of sensory perception. In a recent treatise on information science, for example, Howard L. Resnikoff discusses color perception:

> . . . there does not exist a color which can be absolutely discriminated by the human visual system: all colors are equivalent; and only certain relationships which depend on *pairs* of colors presented to the retinal light receptors within sufficiently brief intervals of time can have any perceptual significance.[13]

A color can only be perceived, therefore, by contrasting it with another color. Contrastive relationships have also long been identified as the fundamental force behind natural language:

> . . . in language there are only differences. Whether we take the signified or the signifier, language has neither ideas nor sounds that existed before the linguistic system, but only conceptual and phonic differences that have issued from the system.[14]

The understanding and evaluation of graphic communication, while depending to be sure upon the individual reader's linguistic competence and experience, is also clearly a product of the connections that the reader notes or establishes between the item in hand and other recalled documentation. There are no self contained documents which have meaning without reference to any others. The content of any document depends rather upon its association with other documents, that is, the active placement of the item by the reader/ user within some kind of context, some accumulation of texts, some collection. Every reader is, therefore, always a kind of selector, in the sense that every reader is always in the process of building a personal, private collection. Each document used is selected and judged in relation to some part of the user's private collection already in place, is added to that collection, and by that addition changes the collection, that is, affects the relationship of the items in that collection to each other. The reader's private collection is necessarily changing all the time, but at any particular point in time, it is always a single, self-defining text. Such downloading to a private collection can take many forms; materials can be downloaded electronically, photocopies can be made, notes taken, or the material can simply be read, remembered, and related by the user mentally to previous readings.[15]

What are then the sources and criteria used by individuals to build such private collections? These will obviously vary broadly depending upon the verbal and bibliographic skills of the user, and the uses to which the personal collection is to be put. In general, however, such personal collections are being built by selecting—downloading—from larger public collections at hand. There are a variety of public collection types—for example, most visibly bookstores, databases, and libraries, each of which serves to provide what we can term an *intermediate sort*. The purpose of such an intermediate sort is precisely to combine textual units into a single macrotext, which will serve as a source from which the user may in turn select or download, and thus create a personal collection in response to individual information needs. Such public collections are "intermediate," in the sense that they are, at least in theory, subsets or sorts of some total "universe of publication."

There is at any time, however, a network of interacting collections, which serve as different intermediate sorts. These are often in competition for the reader's attention, and vary in their purpose, comprehensiveness, and accessibility. Depending upon the information needs of the user, some sorts are more useful or effective than others. While combination, moreover, is the critical factor within any collection, including an intermediate sort, it also plays a key role *among* intermediate sorts. A secondary purpose of intermediate sorting, therefore, is to create in the aggregate what passes for the universe of publication. There is from the practical standpoint of information production and consumption no such perceivable, comprehensive universe; there are only information galaxies, so to speak, which consist of combinations of intermediate sorts. The universe of publication exists only as an abstraction, which has little meaning or application outside of bibliographical theory. In any case, the principle of textual combination—of the interaction and influence of individual texts upon each other to form a single collection—lies at the basis of all types of collection building, be it the creation of a public collection by a professional bibliographer, or the creation of a personal collection by the user, who uses the public collection as an intermediate sort. In all cases, the document is changed through its addition to the collection, and by such addition (or deletion), the collection itself is altered. While the linking of texts into a single whole to establish meaning may not necessarily be a conscious act on the part of the reader, the bibliographer's creation of the public collection should entail such a conscious act of fusion. The builder of public collections "reads" large segments of the collection in an abbreviated fashion, usually by means of citations, and gauges the relationship of the textual units to each other; the potential effectiveness and utility of the entire collection is estimated on the basis of that abbreviated information.

If the understanding of graphic texts depends fundamentally upon combination, then we must assume that the accumulation, use, and evaluation of graphic information is done over time, in a sequential or linear fashion.[16] As the reader proceeds through the text, the meaning and significance of the sentence is gradually established; different parts of the text begin to shed light on other parts; understanding of the beginning of the text is conditioned by expectations of the content of the remainder, while the experience of the remainder causes the reader to revise in his or her memory the meaning and significance originally attributed to the beginning.

Because textual understanding is cumulative, the *sequence* in which a reader encounters different textual units is significant. The value or content of the information is continually altered or adjusted sequentially. The information is not simply changed (i.e., understood differently) by sequence, but rather the sequence is itself a kind of information. While it is true, therefore, that collection development "has to do with the location of copies of materials" in a single place, as we will discuss further below, and that books do indeed "have existence whether or not they are added to any given library collection," we must at the same time be very careful not to confuse information sources—books, serials, computer files—with the information itself.[17] Users derive or produce information through the use of sources; the availability of some sources rather than others, and the effect of that availability on the sequence in which these sources are encountered, must, therefore, affect the information derived or produced from such a combination of sources, even though it will obviously have no effect on the physical existence of those books at any point in time. It is, therefore, problematic to view library materials as "sources . . . whose substance is unaffected by being collected," if we consider the "substance" of a source to be the information derived or produced by the user.[18] The library or information center directs the user in some respect to one item rather than another; the resulting sequential experience will thus influence the meaning and use of the information for each user. This is the crucial function and purpose of the intermediate sort. Regardless of the nature of the channel—paper or electronic—it has always been and will remain a primary purpose and responsibility of collection development to create that sort, and in that way to influence the sequence in which the reader encounters, decrypts, and thus understands and evaluates information. Combining graphic texts into a collection is therefore not simply a function of discrimination, that is, defining the collection's focus—or of location, that is, downloading to one place in response to local needs. The role of sequence ensures that collection development is also a function of time. Any theory or definition of collection development must pay close attention to the temporality of information use.

The most effective structure for the processing of information is hierarchical.[19] The intermediate sort is one means by which such an information hierarchy is created. A subset of documentation is selected and acquired—downloaded—into a local, public collection. This downloading is a relatively continuous operation, and is driven by such factors as the rate of publication, the library's processing or system capacity, and, as we will discuss below, local political-economic conditions and stipulations. The hierarchy derives from the fact that the materials downloaded in the intermediate sort are given increased significance over items not selected because those items downloaded will normally be encountered by users earlier in their searching sequence. The final stage of the hierarchy is completed when the individual further downloads particular items from the intermediate sort into his or her own private collection.

It is likely, therefore, that the future of collection development will turn at least partially upon the effectiveness or utility of the intermediate sort as created by libraries and as perceived by local users. If bibliographical "surrogates" (e.g., citations and abstracts) are found to provide an adequate link to the amorphous, undefined universe of publication, then public collections, such as those created in and maintained by libraries will become increasingly unnecessary as we move further into the online age. If, on the other hand, some weighted sampling or representation, some narrowing of choice to effect a sequencing of materials is accepted by local readers as an essential intermediate step to information gathering, then collection development—or whatever the activity will eventually be called—will remain an indispensable mainstay of education, learning and research for the indefinite future. Because of the mere quantity of publication, some kind of intermediate sort would certainly appear to be desirable. If a hierarchical structure is indeed an essential prerequisite for the systematic selection and transfer of information, then public collections of some kind, which can perform the functions of intermediate sorts, must invariably be built. The individual's private collection and the information universe, staring starkly at each other across the void, do not constitute much of a hierarchy. The sequencing which would result from the downloading of sources from such a vast mass of publication would doubtless be unacceptably random without the sifting definition of "significant" publications—publications to be read first—through the intermediate sort. The final decision on whether local public collections of some kind are justified, however, must be made finally by the local user community. Let us now turn our attention, therefore, to the role of that community in collection development.

LOCALITY

All libraries are local libraries, in the sense that all libraries are built and sustained in response to the needs of a defined user group, normally affiliated with a particular institution or residing in a particular geographical region. This is true regardless of the size or specialization of the library. It is true for public libraries, as well as for academic and special libraries. (It is even true for national libraries: the geographical region served is merely larger.) In all cases, the user community subsidizes—directly or indirectly—the services provided by the library, and the library creates and adjusts its services to meet the information needs of its local clientele. Regardless of advances in information technology, regardless of whether local collections continue to exist or whether they are eventually replaced by terminals affording access to data located elsewhere, local information needs will persist, as will the demand for local information services designed to respond to those needs.

While the individual library can make the microdecisions concerning the particular items to which access should be provided, the broader policy decisions that define the parameters within which the library's collection building effort must operate, are largely based upon stipulations made in advance by the supported (and supporting) user community. Local clientele always define the political-economic boundaries within which every library must operate and every collection must be developed. It is the community which perceives the need, and it is the community which pays the cost of fulfilling that need. The development of each collection will necessarily reflect the resources, values and biases of the society it serves. Many user communities, for example, demand and deserve some form of censorship, although the term "censorship" is not normally used to describe the political selectivity which influences the building of all collections. The values driving such selectivity vary widely from one locale or user community to another. A school library may reasonably decide to exclude materials that communicate viewpoints contrary to the general values of the local community, such as works suggesting racism or sexism. Many research libraries, on the other hand, will expend enormous energy trying to identify and acquire just such racist or sexist publications for use by scholars as primary social or historical data. It is, without doubt, public libraries which face the most difficult challenges in responding to the political values of their clientele, because those values are often so disparate, and because the library must protect the rights and respond to the legitimate needs of users with minority interests.

The political and intellectual values of the local community are manifested and sustained by the community's economic support of the library. The library must be responsible for indicating to the community the levels of support required to provide access to certain types of information needed. The local community—be it a town or city, a school, a university, or a specialized agency—then decides what proportion of its total budget it is willing to devote to information services. It is, therefore, an essential administrative responsibility of the library not simply to identify and assess the information needs of the supporting community, and to recommend the best (i.e., most cost effective, most productive) methods to meet those needs, but also to evaluate and understand the underlying political and intellectual values which motivate those needs.

Because each community defines its own needs, and often controls much of its own economic resources, there is, in reality, no such thing (in North America at least) as a national collection, that is, a collection systematically created to serve the needs of users throughout the nation. There is merely an accumulation of collections or databases—intermediate sorts—built or designed in response to local specifications. The political economics of library collections ensures that no collection effort will ever be undertaken which serves national needs at the expense of local needs. A library will support the maintenance of databases held elsewhere—either centrally for national use or connected with another local institution—only to the degree that such remote databases or collections respond directly and demonstrably to the information needs of the local user group. That is now and will remain indefinitely the challenge facing cooperative collection development.

The information policies of most societies in the late twentieth century—at least when compared to those of previous ages—are relatively open. Some serious transgressions persist, of course, in the form of excessive government censorship, and further limitations are imposed upon access by the economics and technology of information. For the most part, however, most people in North America today can gain access to just about any of the information they need—if they are willing to invest the time locating it. Let us now consider the concept of time in collection development.

TEMPORALITY

How long it takes to do things is one measure of their value. One measure of the value of information is the amount of time needed to gain access to it. Access time, therefore, plays a key role in many library decisions, including especially those relating to collection development. If we are to arrive at a fuller understanding of what collection development is, and is becoming, we need to devote much more attention to the role of time. There are, needless to say, many different aspects of time which affect information access and use. In order to establish some structure upon which to mount this discussion, let us posit three closely linked, general categories: (a) access time, or how long it takes the user to locate needed information; (b) service time, or how long it takes to create a local collection or to establish systems which ensure access to information; and (c) source longevity, or the amount of time sources of information remain useful, both intellectually and materially.

Access Time

As noted previously, most individuals could gain access to most of the information they need—if they were willing to spend the time locating it. In this sense, therefore, the primary function of the library is not so much to provide access to information, as it is rather to reduce the amount of time needed by local clientele to gain such access. This has always been and will remain an essential purpose of libraries, regardless of changes in information technology and telecommunications. Every library operation including especially collection development, every library decision, every task undertaken by every library staff member, is aimed ultimately at achieving that single objective. Particular information sources are acquired by particular libraries because ownership is the most secure and consequently the most timely mode of access. The effect of sequence on use, noted above in our discussion of combination, is at least partially a function of time. From a temporal perspective, every local collection serves as a kind of core collection, in the sense that it is a set of sources which is used first, and upon which subsequent use (understanding, application) of other sources or collections is, therefore, necessarily based. An item of information which is more rapidly available is more useful and more likely to be used. Potential relative utility is, therefore, a very unsatisfactory criterion for selection, because it is at least partially a *product* of the act of selection: utility is not something entirely endemic to the document before the selection decision is made, but is rather at least partially a quality *added to the document by virtue of its selection.* The fundamental question of collection development, therefore, is not how useful the document is, but rather how useful it should be made, or more precisely: how rapidly it should be accessible to current and future local users.

Service Time

Time expended by staff in any service organization, including a library, can only be viewed as a supplement to the time of the organization's clientele. All of the staff time expended on selecting, acquiring, or providing access to sources is always a kind of advance temporal investment intended to reduce the expenditure of user time in the future. The success of the library's enterprise can only be gauged by the extent to which the expenditure of service time has reduced the access time for local users. There are, of course, different users, and how the relative time of each is valued by the library must be factored into any such evaluation. Public libraries will presumably try to view each user (i.e., each legitimate user as defined by the rules of locality), and, therefore, the time of each user, as being of equal value; libraries which support institutions or agencies, on the other hand, such as academic or special libraries, are more likely to distinguish categories of users, and may devote more service time to the reduction of the access time of some users rather than others. Such decisions will always be conditioned by the values and political forces of the locality: many college libraries may invest more service time in reducing the access time of undergraduates; some university libraries, on the other hand, may feel compelled to devote more effort to reducing the access time of faculty. Because all service time is rationed and expended with the sole aim of reducing access time, service time is best defined in terms of access. We can distinguish several subcategories of service time as relating to collections, for example: (a) time needed to define and assemble collections (the intermediate sort), which is the time spent in a traditional environment on collection development; (b) the time needed to analyze that collection (currently cataloging, but also reference); (c) the time needed to assist users in the location of information beyond the collection (now primarily reference, but also collection development). The further we move into an online environment, the more these traditional functions are likely to coalesce; they are in fact even now becoming so closely interconnected as to be sometimes indistinguishable.

While different amounts of time can be spent by staff providing different types of services, decisions as to how much time should be devoted to any operation must finally be driven by the primary criterion, namely how long it should take for local users to gain access to the information affected by that operation. We must be careful, however, not to approach this fundamental principle too simplistically, lest we make the mistake of imagining that collection quality or utility might somehow be calculated arithmetically. Such quantification would remain very difficult for several reasons. The selection decision will always be a private, subjective act of the selector, regardless of whether that selection involves the intermediate sorting by a professional bibliographer, or whether the selection is a matter of downloading to a private collection by a user. Quantification of selection quality is also practically impossible, because time must be invested in negative decisions, that is, in deciding not to select or download certain sources of information; this activity is virtually impossible to track or measure. In an undergraduate library, for example, considerable service time may be very wisely spent in deciding not to order title A, if the presence of that title in the collection might function as noise which would obscure the availability or utility (i.e., might reduce the access time to) the potentially more significant title B. This negative decision making lies not only at the basis of weeding, but also more generally of selection: most selection time is doubtless spent in such proactive deselection.

Source Longevity

If access time is the amount of time spent locating needed information, and service time is the amount of time needed to create a system which facilitates that access, source longevity, our third temporal category, refers to the amount of time access remains needed and possible for individual information sources. We can again distinguish several subcategories.

There is, to begin with, what we might call channel longevity, that is, the amount of time the physical medium is capable of carrying its message. Maintaining or extending channel longevity is the primary purpose of preservation. Currently, preservation is concerned mainly with the deterioration of paper materials, but the increasing availability of electronic information will require quite different preservation efforts, including perhaps equipment repair and the development of methods to combat hardware obsolescence. Preservation (or whatever name we eventually end up calling it) will remain that segment of library operations responsible for the struggle against all forms of material entropy and for defining the options for safeguarding material or mechanical access.

Another subcategory may be code longevity, that is, the length of time the code in which the information is embedded continues to lend itself to decryption by library users. The most frequently used code is natural language. Depending upon local interests and abilities, some lesser used natural languages may over time become less accessible to local clientele. This issue also blends into channel longevity, however, in the area of digital codes. The machine languages used for software may become obsolete over time, in which case access to the affected information will become difficult or impossible.

The most subjective level of source longevity is message longevity, the length of time the message or "content" of the source remains useful from the perspective of the user. Because message longevity is so intimately dependent upon constantly changing user competence and interest, measurement of message longevity is virtually impossible. Use and user studies, as imprecise as they may be, remain the only means to assess message longevity systematically. There would appear to be several weaknesses of use studies as a measure of message longevity—especially for research materials. The first is that use studies can consider only past use, and must draw conclusions from that review about future use; actual use is thus being applied to project potential use. The only problem is that utility is driven by external factors which also change over time. New fashions in research, new theories or discoveries can easily change the utility of any publication, that is, can extend the length of time it remains useful. There is, in addition, the eternal difficulty posed by historical research, which in a sense runs consistently counter to the normal use of publications by practitioners, and thus can extend source longevity indefinitely. We will define this phenomenon more precisely in our examination of the concept of focus.

Excursus: The Garbage Can Model

Before we leave the subject of time, it behooves us to make a brief excursion into the subject of the so-called garbage can model of decision making. Charles A. Schwartz has recently suggested that this model be applied to the study of collection development.[20] The garbage can model was originally developed to explain how decisions are made in "organized anarchies," such as educational institutions, which are characterized by "problematic preferences, unclear technology, and fluid participation."[21] What is of special interest to us is that garbage can models:

are attempts to understand those phenomena within a temporal context. Rather than relying on a consequential order to form linkages within decision making, garbage can models of decision making assume a temporal order. That is, problems, solutions, and participants are assumed to be connected by virtue of their simultaneity.[22]

According to the model, decisions are a result of the confluence of four "streams" within the organization—I imagine them as four chutes leading into a container, the garbage can: down these chutes flow (a) problems, (b) solutions, (c) decision makers, and (d) opportunities.[23] Which of these join together depends primarily upon time, that is, when they come together in the garbage can. Schwartz does not explain the model in much detail, nor does he indicate very exactly how the model actually applies to collection development; this vagueness is, however, part of his intent, since he is basically taking a position against theorization—or at least against the creation of models which try to explain very much.[24]

If the garbage can model can be applied to collection development more rigorously (which is admittedly precisely what Schwartz is trying to caution us against), it might be as follows. Selectors are basically decision makers; perceived user needs are problems; publications are solutions; funding (probably the most tenuous link) equates to opportunity. Applying the garbage can model: the selector does not look at the needs of the users, review the universe of publication, and then acquire or make accessible through the application of available funding those publications which best meet those needs. Quite the contrary: the decisions depend much more upon temporal circumstances, that is, upon particular selectors with particular levels of funding at their disposal, encountering or recalling particular user needs and particular publications which might meet those needs within roughly the same time intervals. That confluence or simultaneity of circumstances would determine in effect which publications are selected for which collections.

It might be objected, of course, that the whole point of collection evaluation is to avoid just such randomness in the collection building process: the quality of the subject collection is supposed to be measured against a stable representation of literature on the subject, user needs are supposed to be identified through surveys or liaison, and then the most important publications (i.e., those most suitable for the user community) are selected or otherwise made accessible from among those available. Selection based primarily upon such systematic collection evaluation and use studies, therefore, would seem to contradict or at least subvert an application of the garbage can model, because selectors are under such circumstances actually choosing from among all alternatives on the basis of preestablished norms. But are we not rather merely increasing the capacity of the can by using such evaluations, or at least the volume of the flow down the chutes for problems and solutions? Even when we apply systematic evaluation, collection building may still be primarily a matter of which needs are linked to which publications by which selector with access to which resources at which time.

The real value of the garbage can model, and the real contribution Schwartz has made by drawing attention to it, is that it may seriously challenge some of the most fundamental concepts of collection development theory—especially the view that selection can be and is influenced primarily by a systematically and evenly applied collection policy. The model does not, as far as I can tell, prohibit the identification of priorities, but it does accentuate the instability and relativity—the highly temporal and temporary nature—of collection policy and standards.[25]

FOCUS

Collections are built (theoretically, metaphorically) from the center. The central, or so-called *core* materials, as defined by the library's collection policy, are those given priority, that is, theoretically acquired first; effort can then be turned to providing access to increasingly "peripheral" information until acquisitions funding is depleted. Admittedly, no such sequencing of selection normally occurs in reality: core materials and peripheral publications are acquired—or access to them is provided—more or less simultaneously. There is rather a continuum of candidates for selection running from those viewed as highly relevant to those perceived as mainly peripheral; the line on that continuum between what can and cannot be selected shifts in response to budgetary pressures. Nevertheless, the term *core* remains a vivid and useful metaphor for those particular sources upon which the collection should concentrate or focus—and to which access should be provided sooner than access to other sources. The real challenge to both the collection development administrator and the library selector is, therefore, clearly to identify or define those sources which the user should spend the shortest time locating.

The main problem in establishing collection priorities and core sources is that every topical collection necessarily contains within itself a multiplicity of cores. This becomes clear, if we define core publications as those sources relating to any subject which are essential for a user to understand that subject. Because the levels of competence and expectations of users vary so widely, we must expect any single subject area to contain several overlapping cores. Core sources on, say, the Japanese economy, will be different for an interested citizen using a public library, than for an undergraduate taking a course on the subject; the core materials needed by those two will be different still from the core sources required by an economics professor, and different yet again from those sought by a business executive considering a move into the Japanese market. It is a serious mistake, therefore, to imagine that each subject contains a single core of materials, defined without respect to locally driven needs and values.

The variant nature of information sources themselves further complicates the focus of collections. In the cases of the humanities and the social sciences, the initial problem of assigning priorities would be considerably simplified, if we would begin with the assumption that every topic contains within itself at least two centers, one of primary materials, and one of secondary materials. The criteria and the selection tools used for defining and building or providing access to these two cores are very different. Primary materials represent a kind of canon—in the humanities it is the works of the established authors, while in the social sciences it consists of the standard data sources. Secondary materials, on the other hand, are the means by which the subject is summarized for the layman, or by which specialists communicate with each other about their work.[26]

In a library that serves clientele with significantly different knowledge levels and expectations, therefore, there necessarily are a variety of cores, or what I would now prefer to label *focal points*: these are in a state of perpetual competition with each other for attention and funding. On the basis of the foregoing discussion, we could perhaps define, for example, at least four such focal points for each humanities and social science subject: basic-primary and advanced-primary materials, basic-secondary and advanced-secondary materials. The basic materials would be used as introductions to, or summaries of the field, while the advanced materials would be needed by specialists. Depending on the range of experience of the local clientele, of course, more levels would probably need to be defined than simply basic and advanced.

Responding more or less simultaneously to the pressures related to each of these focal points is how a library selector spends much of his or her time. The pressures of each focal point will vary, and each certainly can be ranked in relation to the others for different subjects. In college libraries, for instance, undergraduate secondary material may well exert the greatest pressure in the social sciences, while undergraduate primary material may cause more pressure in the humanities. It is, however, never a matter of totally relieving the pressure relating to any one focal point, but rather of balancing those pressures as well as possible in response to local demands and requirements. As soon as some of the pressure relating to one focal point is relieved, the pressure associated with another builds until it begins to assert its control over the selector's attention and budget.

We must, finally, add a fifth focal point to our original four: the historical focus. As a result of the factors influencing source longevity discussed above, most sources added to a collection or otherwise made accessible necessarily migrate over time from the center of focus to the periphery. As time passes, in other words, the utility of such sources diminishes from the standpoint of the subject's practitioners or educators. From an historical perspective, on the other hand, the utility of those sources persists and even increases over time; in fact, in a certain (no doubt oversimplified) sense, as the actual utility of an item decreases for the practitioner or educator, the potential utility of the same item as a primary historical source increases for the historian of the subject or of that subject's instruction. See figure 1.

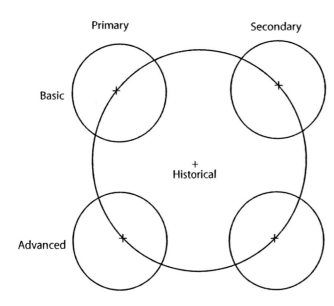

FIGURE 1. Focal Points

New sources, or new access to sources, are acquired in response to the four current focal points. While sources can also be acquired for historical purposes, such sources are often already held; the historical focal point exercises its main pressure, therefore, on deselection and preservation decisions. The main reason research libraries weed so seldom is precisely because the migration away from the current focal points often seems to represent a movement toward the historical focal point.

CONCLUSIONS

Each of the four concepts we have examined—combination, locality, temporality, and focus—is an aspect of a single process, and is, therefore, intimately related to the other three. Each can, in fact, be approached as a function or product of the others. At the same time, every specialist in collection development, depending upon his or her individual understanding of the purpose of libraries and collections, probably assigns priority (consciously, or as an implication of decisions made) to one of these fundamental aspects over the others. The collection developer who views the response to user demand as the ultimate rationale of libraries may view locality as the most important. Those who see subject areas and the external world of publication as the guiding principle against which libraries must measure their quality will probably perceive focus as being the most significant. Those who approach collections primarily from the perspective of structure or system may well prefer to give precedence in their thought and planning to the role of combination.

For my own part, the aspect of collection development I consider most critical to the future of the field is temporality. We understand so little about the function of time in information services, and yet it is just that function which may well contain the key to the successful transportation of collection development into the online environment. It is the concept of time that connects service costs to the fulfillment of user needs. It is time that provides the most practicable framework for creating and connecting library operations. It is time also that, on a more specific level, supplies us with the clearest link between collection development and preservation: we need to define preservation theoretically and administratively—as an essential component of collection development because it is through preservation (among other collection services) that the library exercises control over the length of time sources of information remain accessible. Above all, the concept of time must play a critical part in our understanding and measurement of information utility, and should, therefore, be factored into all collection decision making. Selection, budgeting, policy, evaluation, cooperation—all of these can, should, and must eventually be understood in temporal terms. Regardless of the form in which information is published—paper, electronic, or something else—the fundamental questions which drive a collection's creation must remain the same: (a) how long will it take a member of the local community to gain access to a particular unit of published information? (b) based on the projected or specified information needs of the locality, how long *should* it take to gain access to that information? (c) how can access to that information be adjusted so that no more time than should be expended will be expended by local users to gain access?

What do we need in order to accomplish this? To begin with, we probably need to develop a scale of temporal access levels (perhaps related to our abstract Conspectus levels) which any library selector can apply to any publication. We need shared databases, which contain the records for as many potentially useful publications as possible, to create a network of intermediate sorts. In response to local policies, selectors in each library must contrive to assign those temporal access levels to the records of all appropriate publications. On the basis of those assignments (or—in a totally online environment—perhaps automatically as a result of such assignments), the publications to which those records refer need to be shifted around, downloaded, transferred somehow within the network of intermediate sorts, in order to influence and adjust the amount of time needed by local users to gain access to individual publications. The most important publications, that is, those needed in the shortest time, should be owned and maintained in a local collection or database. Publications to which less immediate access is needed may be maintained in other locations—in the case of paper materials, these items may be held in libraries nearby to which users may travel; electronic publications falling into that category might be held in remote databases easily accessible. Other publications, to which access is needed less immediately, could be held in more distant libraries, or in databases more difficult or problematic to access. In this fashion, a constantly shifting network of access could eventually be established which would reflect and respond to changing local user needs. Only through this (or some similar) technique will libraries be able finally to increase and refine their systematic control over service and access time.

REFERENCE NOTES

1. For a discussion of defamiliarization in Russian Formalism, see Fredric Jameson, *The Prison-House of Language: A Critical Account of Structuralism and Russian Formalism* (Princeton, N.J.: Princeton Univ. Pr., 1972), 50–54.

2. *Collection Development in Libraries: A Treatise,* Robert D. Stueart and George B. Miller, eds., (Greenwich, Conn.: JAI Pr., 1980), 2 vols.; William A. Katz, *Collection Development: The Selection of Materials for Libraries* (New York: Holt, Reinhart and Winston, 1980); Robert N. Broadus, *Selecting Materials for Libraries,* 2d ed. rev. (New York: Wilson, 1981); Richard K. Gardner, *Library Collections: Their Origin, Selection, and Development* (New York: McGraw-Hill, 1981); Arthur Curley and Dorothy Broderick, *Building Library Collections,* 6th ed. rev. (Metuchen, N.J.: Scarecrow, 1985); G. Edward Evans, *Developing Library and Information Center Collections,* 2d ed. rev. (Littleton, Colo.: Libraries Unlimited, 1987); David Spiller, *Book Selection,* 5th ed.

(Chicago: ALA, 1988); Rose Mary Magrill and John Corbin, *Acquisitions Management and Collection Development in Libraries,* 2d ed. rev. (Chicago: ALA, 1989); William A. Wortman, *Collection Management: Background and Principles* (Chicago: ALA, 1989).

3. This becomes clear from a perusal of the (usually) annual reviews of the work in collection development (previously "resources," originally "acquisitions") published since 1958 in *Library Resources & Technical Services.*

4. Hendrik Edelman, "Selection Methodology in Academic Libraries," *Library Resources & Technical Services* 23 (winter 1979): 34.

5. Charles B. Osburn, "New Directions in Collection Development," *Technicalities* 2 (Feb. 1982), 3.

6. See Joe A. Hewitt, "On the Nature of Acquisitions," *Library Resources & Technical Services* 33 (Apr. 1989): 106–07.

7. Curley and Broderick, in *Building Library Collections,* 27, for example, apparently view collection development as a more resourceful or active kind of selection: "In the narrowest sense, . . . the term selection suggests known entities among which choices are made, entailing most often the limitations of reliance on reviews in a few popular publications, acquiring only what one's regular jobber can supply, or subscribing to only 'indexed' periodicals." Collection development, on the other hand, includes such things as "a wide and diverse range of review sources, active acquisition of small and alternative press publications, collection analysis and evaluation, regular retrospective purchases . . . and collection goals which acknowledge intangible (not just utilitarian) aspects of the library's mission."

8. See, for example, Frederick C. Lynden, "Collection Management," *The ALA Yearbook* 5 (1980): 117; also Paul H. Mosher, "Collection Development to Collection Management: Toward Stewardship of Library Resources," *Collection Management* 4 (winter 1982): 41–48.

9. Michael K. Buckland, "The Roles of Collections and the Scope of Collection Development," *Journal of Documentation* 45 (Sept. 1989): 215.

10. Administration is infrequently considered in discussions of collection development. A refreshing exception is Wortman's *Collection Management,* 11–13, 217–23.

11. Marcia Pankake, "From Book Selection to Collection Management: Continuity and Advance in an Unending Work," *Advances in Librarianship* 3 (1984): 201.

12. Mosher, "Collection Development to Collection Management," 42.

13. Howard L. Resnikoff, *The Illusion of Reality* (New York: Springer, 1989), 194.

14. Ferdinand de Saussure, *Course in General Linguistics,* ed. Charles Bally and Albert Sechehaye, trans. Wade Baskin (New York: McGraw-Hill, 1966), 120.

15. For a further discussion of some of these issues, see my "The Role of Abstraction in Bibliography and Collection Development," *Libri* 39 (Sept.1989), 201–16.

16. Saussure, *Course in General Linguistics, 70.*

17. Buckland, "The Roles of Collections," 215–16.

18. Buckland, "The Roles of Collections," 217. It should be noted that Buckland equates "substance" with material—so that he is obviously correct in claiming that the addition of such substance to a collection does not alter that substance.

19. Resnikoff, *The Illusion of Reality,* 98–117.

20. Charles A. Schwartz, "Book Selection, Collection Development, and Bounded Rationality," *College & Research Libraries* 50 (May 1989): 328–343.

21. Michael D. Cohen, James G. March, and Johan P. Olsen, "A Garbage Can Model of Organizational Choice," *Administrative Quarterly* 17 (Mar. 1972): 1–25.

22. James G. March and Johan P. Olsen, "Garbage Can Models of Decision Making in Organizations," in *Ambiguity and Command: Organizational Perspectives on Military Decision Making,* ed. James G. March and Roger Weissinger-Baylon (Boston: Pitman, 1986), 11.

23. Cohen et al., "A Garbage Can Model," 3. See also Michael D. Cohen and James G. March, *Leadership and Ambiguity: The American College President* (New York: McGraw-Hill, 1974), 82.

24. Schwartz, "Book Selection," 339.

25. In the course of his presentation, Schwartz explains that the weakness of some "interpretive models" of collection development is that they "represent after-the-fact generalizations" (331). In other words, first we do things, such as build collections, then we rationalize those activities using values or concepts which may in fact have played no role whatsoever in the original activity. Post hoc, ergo propter hoc. This would be a valid objection, if the development of collections were an action which occurred only once, and if those individuals responsible for devising the theories were different from those engaged in the action. Since collection development is an ongoing activity, however, and since those of us doing the selection are often the ones who are also creating the theories, it is not unlikely that there is a kind of circular influence: our theories may indeed not describe or explain how we have actually selected in the past, but they may well condition how we understand selection, and, therefore, how we select in the future. Life imitates art.

26. In the case of the sciences, there are no primary materials—aside from the "Book of Nature." Scientists, therefore, call their journal literature, for example, "primary materials." The competition for the funding of science materials would seem often to derive more from outside the library, especially from the equipment needs of the laboratory. In the humanities and social sciences, on the other hand, for which the research library is the rough equivalent of the laboratory, no such dichotomy exists: the competition for funding remains primarily for access to publications.

18 TEXT MUTABILITY AND COLLECTION ADMINISTRATION

I have been asked to make some brief, speculative comments about the possible long-range effects of the increasing availability of electronic information on collection building and administration. I will therefore limit my remarks to some thoughts on the place of collection development in a predominantly online information environment. I want to note at the outset that I agree fully with Peter Graham's views expressed earlier at this conference on the role of technical services in what he calls "intellectual preservation," and that my ideas will be quite consistent with his—although presented, of course, from the collection development side of the house.[1]

Let us take as our point of departure that quality of online information which separates it most demonstrably from information available in more traditional forms: text mutability. Clearly the most revolutionary quality of the online format is that it empowers the user to enter easily and quickly into the text in order to add, delete, substitute, supplement, amalgamate, purge, manipulate—in short, to produce a personal text which uniquely suits the needs or inclinations of the individual user.[2] This capacity for unlimited adjustment is available regardless of whether the text is numerical or narrative (and indeed the narrative text is doubtless already coming increasingly to be perceived as a series of manipulable data elements). The broad implications of such text mutability have yet to be fully grasped either by bibliographical theorists or by library administrators.

If we understand the term *text* in the broadest sense to indicate not only the physical signs—the print on the page or on the screen—but also the ideas to which such signs refer, then mutability is, of course, a quality of any text. The interpretation of the meaning of the text, the decryption of the signs, is after all a relatively subjective operation, depending as it does upon each individual's continuously evolving textual experience. It is on the basis of that personal textual experience that each person assigns his or her meaning to the text; in this sense, therefore, the meaning of any text is constantly shifting. What makes communication possible at all under such circumstances (both communication between people, and "communication" with oneself—i.e., individual study and learning over time) is the relative stability of the material, graphic signs of which the physical text is composed. Communication depends upon a stable, objective text, to which different people can refer, and against which they can compare their subjective interpretations. It is precisely that stability which may well become increasingly jeopardized in a predominantly online environment.

It is becoming clear, therefore, that it is not only the quantity and flow of information, but also its fragility, its perishability, which will characterize the online era. It is becoming clear that we can purchase the ability to manipulate information only at the expense of its stability—at the expense, in a manner of speaking, of the information's own history. Online technology provides us with unprecedented individual control over information, but it is precisely that control, that ability to make unlimited and continuous changes to the graphic text, which threatens the historical basis upon which communication and understanding

This article first appeared in *Library Acquisitions: Practice & Theory* 14 (1990): 355–58.

finally depend. The online ethos harbors within itself unexamined antihistorical forces, for we must bear in mind that history is ultimately textual. There is in fact no history: there are only historical texts. History is, in this sense at least, material—which means that it can be lost, if there is no agency vested with the responsibility and the authority to preserve it.

This is, of course, one reason that our history departments are so often in the forefront of support for academic libraries: the library physically contains—defines the limits of—history. And yet we are not talking only about history in the narrower sense of that discipline practiced and pursued by our history departments. We are talking here rather about history in the sense of the record *per se,* about that which has already been written in *all* disciplines. It is, once again, that stable body of graphic information, upon which each discipline bases its discussions, and against which each discipline measures its progress. Without such a history, without such a fixed, discrete, objective textual canon against which to compare its new thoughts and utterances, no discipline can communicate or evolve.

The definition of the record—the designation of those publications which should constitute the record—has always been one of the library's primary social and epistemological functions. That is finally the underlying rationale for and responsibility of collection management. Of all of the "graphic utterances"—publications—that exist, the library selects and maintains only a limited number, and in so doing defines or creates the record through which communication takes place across space and time, and according to which new ideas are compared and assessed.

The question is: do those traditional library functions and responsibilities change in a predominantly online environment? What role does the research library play, if most research consists primarily in the searching and downloading of information from a distant database by a scholar at a personal workstation? Where is the collection to be managed and developed? Many of the answers we have devised so far merely beg the question. Of course, there is a technical role for the library as mediator between the user and the information. Of course, the library can and should continue to assume an economic responsibility, since there will always be more information needed than any institution can afford, and some agency—the library—will need to decide how the institution's information dollars will be most effectively spent. What we have perhaps failed to recognize, however, is that the library must also continue to maintain its responsibility for record definition—for collecting, i.e., for moving a carefully selected assembly of graphic utterances from the environment into a library database, and thereby stabilizing that information for future reference. The most serious error the library could make at this time would be to assume that its role in a predominantly online environment will be mainly that of a switching point. That role as switching point belongs not to the library side, but rather to the computer center side of information service. The library's function has always been—and will remain regardless of changes in technology—to select, stabilize, protect, and provide access to significant or representative graphic texts. In a primarily online environment, in which textual stability—and therefore communication—is perennially at risk, those responsibilities become more essential than ever before.

How, finally, will the continued assumption of these traditional library responsibilities affect library organization and administration in a predominantly online environment? In the long term, I expect—or hope—libraries will structure their operations around three basic functions. The first function is the obvious one of *mediation.* The library will clearly need to maintain and enhance its ability to identify needed information in appropriate databases, and to assist users in the downloading of such information. This will entail an amalgamation of what have become the reference and cataloging functions in the traditional library. And about time, too: perhaps the greatest error made in modern library administration has been to allow cataloging and reference (which are, after all, merely two ends of the same stick—putting information in, and getting it out) to develop along such divided paths that they have become two separate cultures which can now barely communicate with each other. The advent of the online era should at least provide us with the opportunity to reconnect these two essential and adjacent components of library service.

The second function of the library in a primarily online era will be, I would hope, *primary record definition*. This is the equivalent of traditional collection development, as I have briefly (and no doubt simplistically) been trying to describe it. The purpose of this function will be to create a stable database by downloading discrete, carefully selected online publications. Fulfilling that function will require, as it does now, considerable subject knowledge, i.e., an understanding of the content and significance of the constantly evolving network of public data from which the selected publications are to be downloaded.

Mediation and primary record definition are essentially downloading functions, and both have their equivalents (reference, cataloging, collection development) in the traditional library. The final function I envision in the electronic library has no real equivalent today. I will call it, for want of a better designation, *secondary record definition*. This will be the library's uploading function. When a scholar at an institution has written something which is deemed by a select group of peers to be worth communicating broadly to other scholars, that communication should take place by the library's uploading that publication into the library database, thus disseminating it to other libraries, and thereby to other scholars, throughout the nation and the world. The ultimate purpose of the academic library is to provide bibliographic support for education and to serve as a basis for communication among scholars—in short, to disseminate significant information. In the predominantly paper era, we rely heavily upon commercial publishing for that purpose, but such commercial publishing is merely a means to achieving that ultimate end—and already that particular means is becoming economically prohibitive and technically unnecessary.[3] The library—in conjunction with the computer center and the academic press—must assume direct responsibility for disseminating information among scholars. Providing scholars with the channels through which to communicate, working with scholars to establish the technical and bibliographical standards and procedures for online publication in this fashion—these are responsibilities which should therefore also be assumed by the library in the online era.

The role of the library in general—and of collection management in particular—in a predominantly online environment can and should be more central and more vital to research and communication than in the era of traditional formats. Whether we achieve such success and relevance in the fast-approaching age of electronic information tomorrow depends entirely upon our willingness to create, evaluate and adopt radically different concepts of information service today.

REFERENCE NOTES

1. See Peter S. Graham, "Electronic Information and Research Library Technical Services," *College & Research Libraries* 51 (May 1990): 244–47.

2. This potential is perhaps most clearly visible in the form of what is being called hypertext. For a review of current developments in hypertext, see the May 1989 issue of the *Journal of the American Society for Information Science.*

3. Sharon J. Rogers and Charlene S. Hurt, "How Scholarly Communication Should Work in the 21st Century," *College & Research Libraries* 51 (Jan. 1990): 5–8.

19 PRESERVATION AND COLLECTION DEVELOPMENT

TOWARD A POLITICAL SYNTHESIS

Preservation and collection development can be effectively coordinated only when the underlying political forces that drive these two operations are defined and compared. Toward this end, this article explores some of the functions and values of preservation and collection development from a primarily political point of view in three contexts: the institutional, the interinstitutional, and the commercial.

All information is transferred by material means. Strictly speaking, libraries do not, cannot, provide information, but are rather responsible for assembling and protecting the material objects—documents, film, data tapes—from which users can derive or produce information. The essential purpose of building a library collection is to locate such material objects in an environment in which their use can be mediated, monitored, adjusted, protected. From this perspective, preservation and collection development may be understood as two aspects or phases of a single, primary function: the provision of access to material information tools. For administrative and bibliographic reasons, therefore, we must make certain that preservation and collection development are driven by identical—or at least closely compatible—values.

POLITICAL IMPLICATIONS

We can approach this objective from several directions. Economic, organizational, and bibliographic issues obviously need to be addressed and resolved locally if a closer synchronization of preservation and collection development is to be achieved. But before planning toward any such synthesis, the political implications of a closer connection between collection development and preservation will need to be defined and understood. The purpose of this paper is to take an initial, tentative step in that direction—to explain and compare some of the functions and values of preservation and collection development from a primarily political point of view. This is an especially necessary exercise in the case of preservation, because that activity presents some unique political challenges and opportunities. Preservation can and should be understood in many instances as a political act of appropriation—i.e., an assumption of responsibilities previously held by (or previously the property of) other agencies or authorities. The political issues underlying preservation and collection development will be examined in three contexts: the institutional, the interinstitutional or cooperative, and the commercial.

The Commission on Preservation and Access claims that, of the 305 million volumes housed in ARL libraries, approximately 75 million are currently at risk, and a very large amount of preservation reformatting will have to be completed by the nation's libraries in

This article first appeared in *The Journal of Academic Librarianship* 16, no. 2 (May 1990): 98–103.
An earlier version was presented at the ACRL New England Chapter Spring Conference, May 5, 1988, University of Lowell, Mass.

the relatively near future if significant portions of the national collection are to survive.[1] The assumption made in this article is that the Commission is correct.

THE INSTITUTIONAL CONTEXT

From a purely political perspective, the selection of library materials may be regarded as a rhetorical skill. Selection criteria are, in effect, arguments used initially by the selector to persuade himself or herself—or to persuade other selectors—to acquire or reject available titles; related arguments are devised to convince library and institutional administrators of the need for funding, and to assure library users of the wisdom of collection policies and decisions. The use of selection criteria as argumentation is especially relevant to the politics of collection development, for although the responsibility for academic library collection building has now passed almost entirely to the library, that responsibility is probably in many cases still considered to have been delegated rather than transferred. That is, many bibliographers may, with justification, perceive that their function is to act primarily as agents of current faculty clientele.

Utility and Use

It is for this reason especially that potential utility is the central topos in the warehouse of arguments used to support selection decisions. Selection can be justified if demonstrable use by current clientele can be projected. Definitions and measurements of use will vary widely, of course, from one library (or even from one bibliographer) to another. Smaller academic libraries may be compelled to define potential utility as the high probability that a number of students will read the document as part of a classroom assignment. Large academic libraries, on the other hand, may view potential utility as the possibility that the document may be perused by a single scholar; even if the scholar concludes that the document is insignificant or deficient, moreover, such a conclusion would not have been possible without access to the document, and its acquisition on the basis of potential utility would probably remain justified.

Needless to say, if a library had the resources to acquire all relevant publications, if it could achieve the representational ideal of every research library—i.e., to represent in its collection virtually what is known (in the sense of what has been published) on all relevant subjects— then the library would by definition contain all present and future high-use material, and the topos of potential utility would be superfluous. Very few (if any) libraries are able, however, to strive for such a representational ideal beyond very narrow subject areas. While representation remains an ultimate objective of collection development, efforts to achieve that objective are now made primarily through library consortia. In broad subject areas, most individual academic libraries are clearly obliged to limit their collection-building objectives—and therefore their rhetoric—to the supply of information tools perceived (by users) or inferred (by collection officers) to be needed for current instruction and research at the institution.

Because collection development—when viewed from this political perspective—is so heavily rhetorical, and because potential utility is such a *locus argumentarum*, it is very difficult for collection development administrators to assume a contrary position and to argue that resources should be expended on materials falling below the standard for potential utility. These lower use materials must be viewed as a sort of surplus, which it is permissible to acquire only if there are assurances that projected high-utility items have been and will continue to be routinely received.

Contemporary versus Historical Materials

Potentially high-use materials are defined and understood by contrasting their qualities to those of documents that are seen to receive—or can arguably be expected to receive—low use. Older items held by the library that receive demonstrably infrequent or negligible use form one of the classic examples of low-use materials. That resources should *not* be spent on such materials is, therefore, an obvious implication of any collection arguments based on potential utility. It is just these older materials, however, that are now the targets of many of our large-scale, national cooperative preservation programs.

While collection development and preservation have a common objective—to provide and protect access to the material means of producing information—considerable disagreement may arise over which material means should be made available. Collection development values have in many cases been designed to emphasize the perceived needs of *current* users, and only a small minority of our current users are fundamentally concerned about historical materials—the vast majority are interested almost exclusively in immediate access to contemporary materials. Given a steady-state budget—or a budget with declining purchasing power—a library that makes a materials budget allocation to preservation of any amount even approaching the 10 percent recommended by ARL will, in effect, be purchasing guaranteed access to lower use material at the expense of immediate access to higher use material.[2] This will probably be true even for libraries that use circulation (or some other measure of use) as the basis for preservation selection.[3] Most older materials that circulate are probably still receiving relatively infrequent use; if they were candidates for acquisition, they could seldom compete successfully with newer materials.

Considerable political liabilities are therefore inherent in the decision to establish a preservation program, for that decision could be interpreted as not serving the best interests of current users. It is for this reason that the resources for a preservation program must always be approved and endorsed at the highest level of the institutional administration; the decision to support such a program must represent an ideological commitment by the institution. For similar reasons, funding allocated for preservation by the library must always remain separate from subject lines in the collection budget: the values underlying preservation will frequently collide with the rhetorical-political preconditions for much selection work. Bibliographers should, of course, be able to recommend materials in their subject areas for preservation, but if they are forced by the funding structure to make decisions between preserving older materials and acquiring new ones, then they will be compelled as agents of their current clientele to favor newer materials at the expense of those items that reside by definition beyond the perimeter of potential utility.

In West Germany, major political obstructions to cooperative collection development have been overcome by relying on an agency external to the universities—the Deutsche Forschungsgemeinschaft—to acquire lower use foreign scholarly materials and to distribute those materials among university libraries. In this way those libraries are able to use their local funding primarily to respond to the immediate needs of current users.[4] In a similar manner, supplementary external funding has provided the only fully practicable solution for our large-scale preservation projects in which considerable quantities of low-use materials are preserved. The assistance received from the National Endowment for the Humanities (NEH), the Council on Library Resources, Mellon, and other enlightened foundations is, for the political reasons described above, an essential precondition for large cooperative projects.

Risk and Responsibility

Even with the assistance of external funding, however, a library must still allocate a portion of its budget to any preservation project, and this allocation carries with it some risk. It is a risk many larger libraries have recently become increasingly willing to take, and one that some smaller academic libraries are now also probably poised to assume. It is a risk that all academic libraries are morally obliged to accept, for to initiate such a program is to take an important step closer to the representational ideal. It is to confirm that the library has an educational and scholarly function that extends beyond the support of the information needs of its current clientele; it is to stipulate that the library also has a responsibility to history—and to posterity—a responsibility that, if not accepted by the library, will not likely be assumed by any other agency. We find in the institutional context, therefore, our first clear instance of preservation as appropriation, for it is through the decision to channel some modicum of funding—with or without external support—into the preservation of lower use materials that the library is in effect appropriating responsibility for defining its own functions and values.

THE INTERINSTITUTIONAL CONTEXT

Let us distinguish between two general methods of cooperative collection development. The first, which I designate the synergistic method, entails the division of responsibilities among libraries for selecting certain categories of materials that have, for the most part, not yet been published.

A Synergistic Approach to Collection Development

The Farmington Plan is the classic instance of this type of cooperation. It is probably most effective when responsibilities are divided among institutions by very clearly or narrowly defined subjects, such as the Research Libraries Group's "primary collecting responsibilities," or by very specific and distinguishable characteristics of publications, such as country of imprint.[5] Some of the cooperative agreements of the Triangle Research Libraries Network in North Carolina provide a successful present-day example of regional synergism.[6] In the case of broad, standard subject areas, a frequently conceived synergistic approach is to divide responsibilities among institutions by levels of documentation. Thus a library within a partnership can assume responsibility for research (as opposed to instructional) materials, or for advanced (as opposed to basic) publications, or, of course, for potentially low-use (as opposed to potentially high-use) documents.[7]

The problem is that such categories are highly abstract, and such distinctions vary widely from one institution to another. Institutions agreeing to assume responsibility for research-level collecting also risk forfeiting considerable autonomy and may be obliged by such agreements to acquire materials in the interest of the consortium at the expense of those materials perceived to be needed by current clientele. The attraction and value of the synergistic approach, on the other hand, is that it provides an opportunity for planned, systematic coordination among institutions. The synergistic method is the consortial answer to the representational ideal: if all subjects are represented at all levels somewhere in the consortium, then the composite collection of the consortium will represent what is presently known (i.e., has been published) on all relevant subjects.

A Complementary Approach to Collection Development

The other general method of cooperative collection development can be called the complementary method. In this case, each selector at each institution proceeds to acquire those materials perceived at the time to fall within the currently defined perimeter of utility. Any funding still available for materials outside that perimeter is then used to acquire items considered to be closest to the perimeter and which have not already been acquired by other institutions in the consortium. This method allows each selector at each institution (1) to define the perimeter appropriate both to current user needs and to currently available resources at the institution, and (2) to avoid duplicating items held elsewhere that are defined locally as falling outside the perimeter. The complementary method is therefore a form of collection interdependence that affords a high degree of autonomy for participating institutions, and allows each institution maximum latitude to build its collection in direct response to current user needs. At the same time, however, it allows for no systematic coordination, because participants are not assigned responsibility for covering specified subject areas. Gaps can easily develop throughout the consortium. The representational ideal cannot be pursued, therefore, by means of a purely complementary system.

Disparities

Regardless of which of these two general methods are used in a cooperative collection development program—and there are, needless to say, many potential variations and hybrid forms of these methods—one of the most serious obstructions to cooperation remains the economic and bibliographic disparity among libraries seeking to cooperate. The selection parameters of larger libraries will normally extend far beyond and encompass those of smaller libraries, so that in a complementary program, the smaller or medium-sized libraries will often have little to offer to large library holdings.[8] Except for a few special collections, a very small proportion of the uniquely available items in any consortium will be held by the smaller members. Smaller libraries tend, therefore, to become heavily dependent members with little influence over the direction of cooperative programs or over the criteria for any division of responsibilities within the consortium. Larger libraries, for their part, may sense increasingly that they are being exploited by smaller members having little to offer in return.

Condition and Use in Preservation

When we turn our attention to cooperative preservation programs, we find that, once technical and processing standards have been agreed upon, and procedures have been established for exchanging information on titles already preserved or in the queue to be preserved, a complementary system of cooperative preservation can be put in place which affords each participant the broadest autonomy. Barclay Ogden's "condition and use" method of preservation selection is perhaps the ideal complementary system.[9] This method proposes that any item in need of preservation that is used locally should be preserved, unless that item has been preserved at another institution; if the item has been preserved elsewhere, the library obtains a copy from the other institution in lieu of duplicating that preservation. Because Ogden believes that brittle materials, if left untouched on the library shelf, will not reach a true level of disintegration for a very long time, the complementary method would appear to provide an excellent means to navigate between the Scylla of local user demands and the Charybdis of the long-range brittle book crisis. If every library can preserve all items at risk that are being used—except for those already preserved elsewhere—then eventually a large portion of the brittle documents throughout the nation may receive treatment.

The full implications of the condition and use method of preservation selection, argued so skillfully by Ogden, deserve much further consideration, however it is possible that the application of such a method could diminish significantly the research quality of the national collection over time. Because only a portion—probably a relatively small portion—of our brittle books are used or will be used in the near future, many of them could well be lost eventually, if current use is our sole criterion for preservation selection.

This is a situation which has, of course, been the norm throughout history: what has been copied and thus preserved over the past 4,000 years has been what was thought at the time of copying to be of utmost importance. What is different about today for us—the new generation of copyists who rely upon photography (and increasingly, one hopes, upon optical disk technology) rather than upon stylus and parchment—is that we are now technically capable of preserving a significant segment of what was thought by the writer, rather than by readers, to be worth retention. In preservation, we have, in other words, the opportunity to achieve a limited, retrospective version of collection development's most cherished goal, the representational ideal. Although collection development has been unable to achieve that ideal on any scale in individual institutions, it certainly remains a primary goal of consortia, and it should remain a fundamental purpose of consortial preservation efforts.

The underlying concept of the representational ideal is that the user—not the library—should be responsible for deciding what information is important and relevant. In order for the user to have that opportunity, he or she must have access to the broadest possible representation of what is known (in the sense of what has been expressed or written) on the subject. In the same way that the research library should ideally not make evaluative decisions about the quality or relevance of information, but should rather leave those decisions as much as possible to the users, the library should also not allow current users to make such evaluative decisions for future users, but should rather leave that opportunity to those future users.

It must be the library's responsibility, therefore, to relay to the future a broad representation of what has been *said* (i.e., written)—not a representation of what was *heard* to be important at this particular time. We must strive to provide to future generations the same opportunities of access that we aspire to provide to our current clientele, namely the opportunity to provide texts with meanings and to interpret for themselves the broader significance of those meanings. To achieve even a limited version of that objective, the condition and use method could well prove inadequate.

Complementary methods such as condition and use, when applied to preservation, exhibit the same benefits we observed in cooperative collection development—but also the same liabilities. They provide each institution with the flexibility to base all of its selection decisions upon local priorities, but this flexibility can mean that the net result is an uncoordinated and randomly developed national collection. If unused brittle materials are indeed imperiled, then the application of a purely complementary method will result in the survival of a very fragmented collection indeed.

Cooperation in Preservation

Much preferable is the application of a synergistic method that divides responsibility within (and among) consortia by subject. As stated, one main disadvantage of the synergistic approach when applied to cooperative collection development is that it must be based upon abstract categories or levels of materials that are sometimes difficult to apply to actual publications. In the case of cooperative preservation, on the other hand, all methods—complementary, synergistic, or hybrid—are necessarily specific because the target collections already exist. Synergistic divisions of responsibility are not based upon abstract subject categories that must be interpreted by each participating institution, but rather upon actual subject collections already in place and classified.

Equally important is that cooperative reformatting projects are designed to permit the acquisition of a reformatted item by other institutions at a very low cost. Unlike cooperative collection development—and this will become especially significant when we turn to the commercial context—one result of cooperative reformatting is a considerable reduction in the cost of duplicating holdings once the initial reformatting has been achieved. Thus while both cooperative collection development and cooperative preservation have the same final objective—namely, to secure access—their effects on individual collections and the distribution of holdings are very different. While cooperative collection development is intended to reduce duplication among institutions for certain categories of materials, cooperative preservation reformatting has the effect—within the confines of copyright restrictions—of enhancing opportunities for duplication.

Cooperative preservation programs also offer more potential for parity among different sized institutions in the same consortium than is possible in cooperative collection development programs. Equity among different sized institutions is, of course, never possible, but a closer interdependence among cooperative partners can be achieved in programs designed to coordinate preservation. Presumably because the large collections contain far more deteriorating items than one could ever hope to salvage, given current funding and technology, the nation's largest and most prestigious research libraries have been fully ready to omit the preservation of materials already preserved elsewhere (providing that such preservation has been done according to adequate standards), and to depend upon those other institutions for access to those materials. Thus a document held by larger institutions that has been preserved elsewhere will eventually disintegrate and be discarded. The reformatted (or otherwise preserved) item held by the other library—which may be a much smaller library—will then eventually become a relatively rare item, potentially unique in the consortium or even in the nation. The balance of unique holdings within the partnership and within the national collection will therefore be at least somewhat realigned through cooperative preservation programs. Because such a system makes all institutions increasingly interdependent, smaller institutions have a much greater opportunity to become more equal partners in the cooperative enterprise.

The interinstitutional context, therefore, yields a second instance of preservation as appropriation: by taking responsibility for preserving a low-use item (which all other institutions agree is a low-use item), an institution is in effect appropriating that item from other institutions at which the item is currently held. The positive result of this type of appropriation is a more equitable and practicable division of responsibilities among cooperating institutions.

THE COMMERCIAL CONTEXT

Why Replacement?

When the decision is made that the renovation of a document—through conservation, mending, deacidification—is not possible, two options usually remain available: replacement or reformatting. Depending upon projections of use, replacement, when possible, will probably often be preferred to reformatting. There are several reasons for this. One is clearly legal: a document protected by copyright cannot normally be reformatted if a new replacement copy can be acquired. Because the physical document is a product of the commercial sector, its replication and therefore its use is restricted like any other patented product.[10]

In addition to the legal motives for choosing replacement over reformatting, there is also the functional issue of ease of use. If the document may receive considerable use, microfilm is not a suitable option; one must either acquire a replacement or, if none is available, reformat into a more convenient form (e.g., a photocopy).

A third motive may also influence the preference for replacement over reformatting, and that is a commercial bias. There exists a tacit, unexamined presupposition that the library's responsibilities are restricted to that of a secondary distributor—which means that the library is not responsible for the generation of the material means of producing information, but only for its collection and maintenance. It is therefore with a very clear sense of a last resort that the library finally takes matters into its own hands, assumes independent responsibility for the material document, and copies the document's graphic content onto an arguably more durable medium.

Certainly one of the most significant consequences of a library's decision to reformat is that this action—of all of the methods of preservation available—seems most to extract the document from the marketplace, and thus, if the document is no longer subject to copyright restrictions, to transfer responsibility for primary distribution to the library. Therefore, preservation becomes a political act of appropriation in the commercial context: by reformatting according to agreed upon standards, a library appropriates the authority for primary distribution, i.e., republication. Through such appropriation, the document is relieved of its status as a commodity and is transformed from something produced for profit to something produced for use.

This action provides the document with its ultimate safeguard. As an information tool in the custody of a library, its availability is no longer jeopardized by the values and forces of the marketplace: its accessibility is guaranteed, because it has become the sole responsibility of an institution—the library—which measures its success not by a profit margin but rather entirely by the extent to which it can supply access. In this sense, it is difficult to imagine another library function so successful in achieving that objective as preservation reformatting.

CONSIDERING PRESERVATION IN A BROADER CONTEXT

The only remaining question is: Why are we content to restrict our preservation efforts to older brittle materials? Certainly we are experiencing a crisis of brittle books, but just as surely one reason we are having such difficulty confronting that crisis is that we are compelled to devote such a large portion of our resources to securing access to current, higher use materials. If we are professionally and morally committed to preservation, then we should not limit that commitment to older materials—materials already in place in the library. The focus and definition of preservation should be broadened. In the same way that it is self-defeating and contradictory in the institutional context for a library to ignore its responsibility to preserve older materials in order to maintain immediate access to current materials, it is equally short-sighted in the broader political-economic context to restrict the concept of preservation to older, already published documents. It is time to consider applying the same energy, skill and sense of mission to the protection of materials not yet published as have been applied to retrospective preservation.

This involves more than simply lobbying publishers to use acid-free paper. That some scholarly publications are still being printed on acidic paper is simply one surface manifestation of a far more fundamental and threatening corrosion at work within the relationships of the production of scholarly information: the increasing commercialization of scholarship and the exploitation of academic libraries by some scholarly publishers. It is the duty and the destiny of the academic and research library community to assume full responsibility for protecting scholarly publication from those commercial and economic malignities that threaten its longevity and availability, just as surely as does acidic paper. At least some of the responsibility for the primary distribution of scholarship must be taken out of the hands of some commercial publishers. Scholarly publications cannot be properly protected so long as they remain initially defined as commodities. One of the most important accomplishments of the national preservation effort is that it has finally moved libraries into the business of independent scholarly publishing: we simply call such work preservation reformatting. In cooperation with university presses and computing centers, the technical and economic skills that we are now rapidly developing in our preservation programs should be applied to the publication and distribution of future scholarship—in the interest of its preservation. This should be adopted as a logical, expanded goal of the preservation movement and as an essential step in the direction of the eventual political synthesis of preservation and collection development.

CONCLUSION

All innovation entails political risk. Academic and research libraries will need to take substantial risks in the coming decade to ensure that the nation's collections—past and future—receive the protection minimally necessary for their survival. Such action is very risky because it requires the alteration of deep-seated political values underlying the library's relationships with users, other libraries, and scholarly publishers. Acceptance of such political risks brings with it, however, the prospect of significant political gains for the library through the appropriation of new responsibilities. The academic library is, of course, never an end in itself, but is rather always a means to achieve the long-term goals of education and scholarship. It is in the best interest of those long-term goals that academic libraries accept the risks and exploit the benefits of a vastly expanded, nationally coordinated preservation program as a basic component of the national collection effort.

REFERENCE NOTES

1. *Brittle Books: Reports of the Committee on Preservation and Access* (Washington, D.C.: Council on Library Resources, 1986), 22.

2. *Guidelines for Minimum Preservation Efforts in ARL Libraries* (SPEC Kit #137) (Washington, D.C.: Office of Management Studies, Association of Research Libraries, 1987), 3. See also Susan E. Bello, *Cooperative Preservation Efforts of Academic Libraries* (Urbana, Ill.: Univ. of Illinois GSLIS, 1986), 28.

3. See Barclay W. Ogden's definition of the "condition and use" method in "Preservation Selection and Treatment Options," in *Minutes of the 111th ARL Membership Meeting* (Washington, D.C.: Association of Research Libraries, 1988), 38–42. See also the definition of the "condition-driven approach" by Roger S. Bagnall and Carolyn L. Harris in "Involving Scholars in Preservation Decisions: The Case of the Classicists," *Journal of Academic Librarianship* 13 (July 1987): 141.

4. Paul Kaegbein, "National Collection Building in the Federal Republic of Germany," *Journal of Academic Librarianship* 13 (May 1987): 82–83.

5. Nancy E. Gwinn and Paul H. Mosher, "Coordinating Collection Development: The RLG Conspectus," *College & Research Libraries* 44 (Mar. 1983): 134–35.

6. Joe A. Hewitt, "Cooperative Collection Development Programs of the Triangle Research Libraries Network," in *Coordinating Cooperative Collection Development: A National Perspective*, ed. Wilson Luquire (New York: Haworth, 1986), 143–44.

7. This is a division of levels used by RLG. See the *RLG Collection Development Manual,* 2d ed. (Stanford: Research Libraries Group, 1981), 1.

8. Joe A. Hewitt has written on the Triangle Research Libraries in "Cooperative Collection Development," 148: We have found that there must be a certain degree of parity if cooperative collection development is to work as a mutually beneficial enterprise. Our [University of North Carolina, Chapel Hill] success with Duke is closely related to our relatively similar size and mission. Collectively, small and medium sized academic libraries contribute enormously to the materials available for resource sharing, but this collective strength is not by design. I can think of only a few cases in North Carolina where a smaller library can collect systematically at a level that would be useful to the research libraries, without seriously overbalancing the collections of the smaller library.

9. Ogden, "Preservation Selection and Treatment Options," 40–41.

10. One question that should be asked, however, is whether the person whose intellectual labor created the document in the first place, the author, is fully served by such restrictions, or whether those restrictions have the effect of protecting primarily the owner of the distribution system, the publisher. It seems to me that there is a clear need to distinguish between scholarly documentation, which is intended mainly for education and research, and publications aimed at the broader public, such as novels, which are often intended from the outset as commodities. Different copyright restrictions should apply to these different types of publication.

20 THE ROLE OF ABSTRACTION IN BIBLIOGRAPHY AND COLLECTION DEVELOPMENT

Wer denkt abstrakt? Der ungebildete Mensch, nicht der gebildete.
—*Hegel*

Although bibliography is one of the most ancient branches of scholarship, it remains today one of the least studied. Some of its subdisciplines—notably descriptive and analytical bibliography—have, to be sure, received some scholarly attention and regulation, but the characteristics and functions of the generic discipline of bibliography continue to be for the most part only vaguely defined.[1] Even more problematic is the relationship of collection development to bibliography—a particularly vexatious state of affairs, given that many librarians responsible for collection development in North American research libraries hold the job title of "bibliographer."

Let us define bibliography quite simply as that discipline which takes as its object the record *as such*. Although all disciplines are involved with or depend upon records, bibliography is unique in its definition of the record as its object of inquiry rather than as a means to attain its object. It is further possible to posit a distinction between a theoretical-historical form and an applied form of bibliography. The theoretical—historical form focuses upon how information is conveyed and diffused; this branch of the discipline is manifested in many specialized concerns, ranging from the study of the history of graphic communication to the highly technical investigation of information transfer. The main problem in trying to define the theoretical historical aspect of bibliography is that such an area of study is virtually impossible to disentangle from many other subjects, such as philology, communication studies and information science.

The applied form of bibliography is what I have elsewhere defined as "representational bibliography" i.e., the repetition or representation of the author is some text already expressed or presented, in order to relay or otherwise refer to that original text.[2] It is this applied type of bibliography that will occupy us in the following inquiry; we will use the term "bibliography," therefore, to refer exclusively to the applied ("representational")— rather than the theoretical-historical—form of the discipline.

It will be the purpose of this article to consider some of the manifestations, uses and consequences of one of the most elemental and problematic characteristics of bibliography and collection development, the quality of abstraction. We will begin by isolating certain aspects of bibliographical abstraction; these features will then be used as a basis for distinguishing different types of bibliographical activity. In so doing, an attempt will be made to define the location of collection development within the discipline of bibliography. The latter part of the essay will concentrate on aspects of abstraction which are associated with collection development—especially as it is practiced in the academic research library. Two general types of abstraction will be distinguished, what I will label "referential abstraction" and the "abstraction of reception." The former is intrinsic to all forms of bibliography and

This article first appeared in *Libri* 39, no. 3 (1989): 201–16.

derives mainly from the relationship of the bibliographic product to the material it represents. The latter type of abstraction is primarily a function of the relationship between the selection of library materials and their use.

The initial part of this article on abstraction tends to be somewhat abstract itself. Although the final intent of the article is to describe and evaluate some fundamental and, in my opinion, highly relevant features of bibliography and collection development, it will be necessary to indulge at the outset in a certain amount of definition and speculation to achieve that purpose.

THE MEANING OF ABSTRACTION

As one of the most fundamental and pervasive concepts in western thought, abstraction has had a long and somewhat complicated history.[3] In spite of these complexities, however, certain basic characteristics persist in the majority of the term's applications. The English term derives from the Latin verb *abstrahere* which means, among other things, to "separate, split (into parts)."[4] It was introduced into the technical vocabulary of philosophy, probably by Boethius, as a translation of two different (but conceptually related) terms by Aristotle. One of these, *αψαιρεσις,* means something equivalent to "removal," and was used by Aristotle with reference to the conceptual separation of qualities (such as numbers or colors) from material objects exhibiting them; the other term used by Aristotle, *χωριστος,* means *"separable,* logically or physically," and was applied by Aristotle to Platonic ideas.[5] Integral to the original meaning of the term, therefore, are connotations of separation, division, isolation, selection, partiality.

Such connotations remain visible in the philosophy of Locke, who understood an abstract idea as one which entails the removal of particular qualities of different individuals to reach a general concept.[6] Hegel (and Marx) viewed abstraction in a highly negative sense as a part which has been isolated and understood separately from its larger context.[7] Husserl, who devoted considerable attention to abstraction in his *Logical Investigations,* stressed the essential ingredient of dependence *(Unselbständigkeit):* abstraction is not simply any part of some larger unit, but is rather a concept that depends for its meaning and significance on its relationship to that larger unit.[8]

An abstraction can, therefore, be properly understood only with reference to the whole, of which it is an inseparable and dependent part. Such dependence is not, however, always immediately obvious. It is, in fact, a persistent feature of many instances of abstraction to appear as just the opposite, i.e., to present an illusion of independence. Thus Bartell Ollman defines an abstraction as "a part of the whole whose ties with the rest are not apparent; it is a part which *appears* to be a whole in itself."[9]

If we understand abstraction, then, as a dependent part that frequently gives the immediate impression of being an independent whole, than the application of the term to many of the activities and products of bibliography is especially appropriate. The most obvious form of abstraction in bibliography, what we can call referential abstraction, is a direct result of bibliography's unique relationship to the record as such.

REFERENTIAL ABSTRACTION

All (representational) bibliography consists of some form of conscious and selective repetition of previous texts—in a word: *quotation.* It is always the purpose of bibliography to represent in some respect what has already been presented at some other time and in some other form. The single essential prerequisite for bibliography is, therefore, the previous (or "primary") text, which it is the purpose of bibliography to relay or refer to. The exceptional relationship between the original text and its quotation is the source of referential abstraction.

In recent decades, quotation has generated considerable interest among philosophers of language because of its peculiar qualities of reference. Willard Van Orman Quine has singled out quotation as an especially clear example of what he has labeled "referential opacity." According to Quine, the "point about quotation is not that it must destroy referential occurence, but that it can (and ordinarily does) destroy referential occurence."[10] For example, the statement *"Three Men in a Boat* is in the stacks" would prove very confusing to someone unfamiliar with the conventions of citation (which is, of course, a form of quotation). Aside from the general perceptual problem of the statement (i.e., what are three men doing with a boat in the stacks?), such a person would doubtless be puzzled by what appears to be a sentence with a plural subject and a singular verb. The point is, of course, that *"Three Men in a Boat"* does not refer to the same thing that "three men in a boat" refers to—which is what Quine means by referential opacity. The use of the quotation (here symbolized by italics) subverts or deflects the reference, so that the same words refer to something quite different than they do in normal discourse.

It is helpful in trying to understand this odd feature of quotation to recall the traditional distinction between "use" and "mention": "the mention of a term" is an "occurrence of a linguistic expression in quotation marks for the purpose of talking about that linguistic expression. For example, in "'Cicero' has six letters" it is not the orator himself but the word referring to him that is being discussed. This is to be contrasted with *use of a term,* the occurrence of a linguistic expression for the purpose of talking about something other than the expression."[11]

The characteristics of bibliographical quotation noted above led information scientists some time ago to conclude that "documentary activities mention documents as such. They are not concerned with the use of what a document mentions. . . ."[12]

But documents are, of course, made to be used. The language of which they are composed (including their titles) is meant to refer in the normal way. Because bibliography involves quotation, however, such ordinary use and reference are altered. This is one reason that bibliography results in abstraction; normal language is being employed in bibliography, but the normal reference of that language—without which language is inconceivable—is at least partially lacking. Such reference need not, however, be lacking entirely. Although mention, as opposed to use, is clearly an essential feature of bibliographical quotation, it is also evident that vestiges, so to speak, of use—of normal meaning—often remain visible and relevant in a quotation. As Lawrence Lombard notes in his 1974 dissertation on quotation: "Just as quoting a name does not obscure for us whose name it is, reporting what someone has said, by quoting his words, does not obscure for us what he said. Quotation involves both a 'use' and a 'mention' of the quoted material."[13]

Even though it is clear in our example, therefore, that *Three Men in a Boat* is naming a document rather than referring to a trio of male human beings situated in a small seaworthy vessel, there can be no denying that the notion of the three men in the boat still remains very much imbedded in and understandable from the cited title. Such abstraction, therefore, can be mitigated.

In order to consider further this characteristic of bibliographical quotation and referential abstraction, we will need to distinguish between what we can label *primary and secondary reference.* The secondary reference is true bibliographical reference, i.e., the reference to the record. The primary reference, on the other hand, is the reference of normal discourse, i.e., to the object of the record, to *what* the record is referring to. Thus the secondary reference of *Three Men in a Boat* is, by virtue of the quotation, a novel by Jerome K. Jerome, while the primary reference is to a trio of male human beings occupying a small seaworthy vessel. The primary reference, in other words, is the usual reference of the language in the quotation when that language is used in normal discourse outside of the quotation.

Although primary reference is clearly possible within a bibliographical quotation—assuming the quotation is composed of natural language—secondary reference can take place even when the user of the quotation is unaware of the primary reference. It is fully possible for me to quote something (say, in a foreign language that I do not understand) perfectly correctly, without knowing what the quotation "means," in the sense of what the language in the quotation normally refers to. In such a case, the quotation would be devoid of meaning (primary reference), and therefore entirely abstract from the standpoint of the bibliographer—a signifier lacking a signified. It is this emphasis upon secondary reference to the diminution or exclusion of primary reference that results in the form of abstraction in bibliography that we are calling referential abstraction.

TYPES OF BIBLIOGRAPHICAL ACTIVITY

There are a variety of activities that traditionally fall under the rubric of "bibliography."[14] While all such forms of bibliography exhibit the potential for the referential duality described above, the relationship between primary and secondary reference varies in different types of bibliographical activity. It should be possible to distinguish varieties of bibliographical activity, therefore, by the relative degree to which the bibliographer pursuing each activity is compelled to take into account or to become engaged with primary reference. Because bibliography's focus on secondary reference is the essential source of referential abstraction, moreover, it should also be possible to rank—in a crude fashion—the relative role of abstraction in different bibliographical activities by ascertaining for each activity the extent to which secondary reference takes precedence over primary reference. Using this relationship as a basis, we can distinguish four fundamental bibliographical activities:

1. *The Synoptic Activity.* The purpose of synopsis is to paraphrase one or more earlier texts. (As is the case in all types of bibliographical activity, the form of such earlier texts is normally, but not necessarily, graphic.) When the synopsis is of a single text, the result is frequently and appropriately labeled an "abstract;" when a number of texts are distilled into a single synopsis, the product may be a research report *(Forschungsbericht),* or the kind of overview presented in many encyclopedia articles.

Like all bibliographical activities, the synoptic type is not intended to present new or original information; its sole purpose is, on the contrary, to say again what has all ready been said. The synoptic activity is unique among bibliographical activities, however, in that its product is composed of *indirect* quotation. While the synopsis may contain some direct quotations from the primary material (i.e., the original sources being summarized), it consists for the most part of language which the bibliographer (rather than the primary author) has selected. This special quality of synopsis places it on the periphery of bibliographical discourse, so to speak, as that form of bibliographical activity which is most analogous to normal discourse. Although secondary reference remains the central purpose of the synoptic activity, as it does in all forms of bibliography, the primary reference also clearly occupies the foreground of any synopsis. The objective of synopsis, in other words, is to document *that* something has previously been expressed; *what* was previously expressed can, however, effectively obscure that central purpose. In some cases, the synoptic bibliographer can even be misunderstood as speaking for or in the place of the original authors. The role of the bibliographer as a secondary author is most apparent, therefore, in the synoptic activity.

Needless to say, synopsis requires that the bibliographer interpret fully the meaning of the primary texts, and that he or she select appropriate segments of those primary texts to summarize. The result remains clearly an abstraction, as any summary must be, but the synoptic bibliographer must nevertheless become intimately involved with the primary reference of the original texts in order to create such a summary.

2. *The Critical Activity* The objective of the critical activity is to produce authorized texts, i.e., to create editions, the constituent signs of which correspond as closely as possible to the signs the author intended to appear in the original document.[15] The critical activity is traditionally viewed as the separate discipline of textual criticism. It is a discipline requiring considerable scholarly training and experience. Rudolf Pfeiffer, in his *History of Classical Scholarship,* defines aspects of this form of bibliography as the original activity of scholarship.[16]

Like all forms of bibliography, the critical activity is intermediary: the textual critic "is the agent of the writer to whom it matters what the reader reads. He is agent of the reader to whom it matters what the writer wrote.[17] The aim of the critical activity is, therefore, to quote the primary text correctly and completely; a principal responsibility of the critical bibliographer (i.e., the textual critic) is to design or to adopt the scale by which such validity can be measured. The main selective action of the critical bibliographer involves the application of that scale to the choice among (real or potential) variants that have occurred throughout the history of the text's transmission.[18] Unlike the synoptic bibliographer, the critical bibliographer must work within the confines of a given text, rather than creating a new text himself. The critical bibliographer's product consists, at least theoretically, entirely of direct quotation. Even so, the critical bibliographer does still retain considerable freedom and responsibility to interpret the primary text, and to make changes (emendations) on the basis of such interpretation.

As in the case of synoptic activity, the primary reference remains very much in the foreground of all critical products. Although the central function of the critical activity necessarily remains secondary reference—the edited text is always the critical bibliographer's best estimate of how the primary text probably appeared, or should have appeared, and is, strictly speaking, a reference to that primary text—the reader is frequently apt to overlook the secondary reference and to note only the primary one. Depending upon such factors as the history of the primary text's transmission, the editorial principles adopted, and the critical bibliographer's perception of his or her role as secondary author, the critical activity does not necessarily demand as high a degree of engagement with primary reference as the synoptic activity. This is true, if for no other reason than that the critical bibliographer is (theoretically) obliged to quote directly. Although hardly in keeping with the standards usually invoked for textual criticism, it is conceivably possible—in instances of ritual, for example—for the bibliographer to reproduce the primary text without attempting to understand what that primary text actually meant. We must conclude, therefore, that there is at least the potential for a higher level of abstraction in the critical than in the synoptic activity.

3. *The Enumerative Activity.* Enumeration consists of the identification of one or more texts by quoting directly some part of those texts; this part then serves as a sign which stands for the text as a whole.[19] We call these quotations, of course, "citations" or "references." When such quotations are collected into a single work according to some systematic principle, the result is a bibliography or catalog.[20]

It is in the enumerative activity that primary reference begins to recede behind secondary reference, and the exceptionally abstract character of bibliography becomes increasingly conspicuous. In enumeration the precedence of mention over use (as in our *Three Men in a Boat* example above) is especially apparent. The enumerative bibliographer also has considerably less latitude for creativity than his colleagues engaged in the synoptic or critical activities, for the selective decisions made by the enumerative bibliographer are limited to (a) which texts to cite, and (b) which parts of the text to repeat directly in order to effect such citation.

Unlike the critical or synoptic bibliographer, the role of the enumerative bibliographer as a secondary author is therefore greatly restricted. The enumerative bibliographer, moreover, need not necessarily have much (or, for that matter, any) knowledge of the text for which the citation stands, nor is he or she even obliged to understand the meaning (i.e., primary reference) of the components of the citation, providing that those components in the primary text can be mechanically identified. Indeed, the most significant bibliographical advance in the last quarter century has certainly been the proliferation of machines capable of drawing bibliographical citations from databases. This mechanization of the enumerative activity has provided a most dramatic demonstration of the abstract nature of bibliography.

It is clear, therefore, that a substantial part of the enumerative activity consists—or at least can conceivably consist—of extracting and representing a predetermined set of material signs, with no concomitant understanding by the agent (person or machine) responsible for such work as to what those signs refer to when they are used in normal discourse. The level of abstraction in the enumerative activity is, therefore, markedly higher than in either the critical or synoptic activities.

4. *The Aggregative Activity.* The most abstract of all bibliographic functions is what we will designate as the aggregative activity, i.e., the assembly of whole texts into a collection. If such aggregation is limited to a few shorter texts, the result may be an anthology. If it is extensive, the product is a collection of documents. We should, therefore, indeed accept collection development as a category of bibliography; like the other bibliographic activities, it is in fact a very specialized form of quotation, i.e., the representation of previous expression.

All of the abstraction and restriction inherent in the enumerative activity is also endemic to the aggregative activity. The aggregative bibliographer, moreover, has, strictly speaking, no opportunity whatsoever to play the role of secondary author, for the aggregative bibliographer's quotation is, in comparison with those produced by bibliographers practicing the other bibliographic activities, passive. The aggregative bibliographer disappears, so to speak, entirely behind the collective text it is his or her responsibility to assembly. Unlike the synoptic bibliographer who creates a new text, or the critical bibliographer who manipulates and adjusts a full text, or even the enumerative bibliographer who at least identifies the texts by actively quoting small but essential segments of those texts, the aggregative bibliographer normally has no right or responsibility to demonstrate his grasp of primary reference by actively quoting; expression is achieved solely through the selection and importation of already completed texts. Lack of familiarity with the full texts thus collected is not only possible, it is unavoidable and expected; the library selector, especially in a larger research library, may never personally encounter most of the materials he has selected. It is for this reason that the aggregative activity represents the most extreme form of bibliographical abstraction.

It is worth noting, in concluding this phase of our inquiry, that normal discourse admittedly also consists, in a sense, entirely of quotation. Because the vocabulary of any language is finite, normal discourse reduces ultimately to the combination of quotations. The real difference between bibliographical and normal discourse, then, is that bibliography entails selective quotation *without appropriation.* The bibliographer, as mentioner rather than user of language, never feigns creation of the segments of language he articulates, but is rather always compelled, to a greater or lesser extent, to attribute those segments of language to someone else. It is this "improper" use of language that renders all bibliographical activity abstract.

THE ABSTRACTION OF RECEPTION

Referential abstraction, which is a feature of all bibliography, derives primarily from bibliography's representation function. It is a consequence, in other words, of the relationship between the bibliographical product and the original document. Bibliography, however, always serves as an intermediary between the original text and the user. The other fundamental relationship in bibliography is, therefore, that of the reader of the text. Because of the service mission of libraries, moreover, and because of the importance of the use of library materials as a criterion for that form of aggregative bibliography which is collection development, the relationship of the user to the text is of exceptional importance to the library selector. This relationship is characterized, however, by another, equally problematic manifestation of abstraction, which we will designate as the abstraction of reception.

The meaning of any document is always variable, because such meaning depends, at least in part, on the personal knowledge and competence brought to the document by the user. The solid materiality of the document as a physical object, however, may deceive us on occasion into forgetting that the document's content possesses no such stability:

> "The objectivity of the text is an illusion and, moreover, a dangerous illusion, because it is so physically convincing. The illusion is one of self sufficiency and completeness. A line of print or a page is so obviously *there*—it can be handled, photographed, or put away—it seems to be the sole repository of whatever value and meaning we associate with it. . . . This is of course the unspoken assumption behind the word "content." The line or page or book *contains*—everything."[21]

The point is, of course, that the document "contains" nothing but paper and ink. Its "self-sufficiency and completeness" is an illusion, because most of the meaning "in" the document is in fact brought to it by the reader.

The same can be said about libraries as a whole: "A library may store books, microfiches, documents, films, slides, and catalogues, but it cannot store information. One can turn a library upside down: no information will come out."[22] Libraries contain material objects, from which information must be made. This creation of information is achieved by users placing texts they encounter into personal contexts. Information is, therefore, an "interactive product of text and context of various kinds, including linguistic, prior knowledge, situational, attitudinal, and task contexts among others.[23] The dynamic variability of such contexts among readers and over time means that the information, or utility, or value of any document will necessarily vary from one user to the next, and indeed from one reading to the next: no two users ever "read" (in the sense of understand or create meaning from) the same text, nor does any one reader ever "read" the same text twice.

While the library certainly does "produce" collections, the view of the library as a "production organization," or of library users as "in effect the consumers of what the library produces for use," is to note only one facet of the relationship of the user to library material.[24] Libraries only produce (in the sense of collect and organize) material documents. It falls to the user to produce information, for to use documentation is always to create information from it. The essential function of the library is not, therefore, to "produce" or to "provide" information, but rather to assemble the material *means of the production* of information, which are then employed by library users for such productive purposes.

The library selector, therefore, by virtue of his or her intermediate location and responsibility within the communication chain, is necessarily forced into a position of *abstract objectivism.* I borrow this designation from V. N. Vološinov, who applied it to that method of linguistics which erroneously presumes (in Vološinov's opinion) that "the system of language is an objective fact external to and independent of any individual consciousness."[25] According to Volosinov, language "exists for the speaker only in the context of specific utterances . . ."[26] Those linguists guilty of abstract objectivism have constructed their systems by extracting aspects of language from the situation in which such usage actually occurred. The resulting grammars and language theories are thus necessarily abstractions, because they are based on the removal of language from its natural context.

Although abstract objectivism is, at least in Vološinov's view, an unproductive and defective method for the study of language, it is precisely such an approach to human discourse (usually in graphic form) that necessarily serves as the very foundation of collection development. Because the full potential and significance of any product can only be ascertained by its use and because the use of the record, as we have already noted, is primarily a subjective operation that varies from one user to the next, collection development is nothing if not an exercise in abstraction.[27] The subjective contexts, which the reader combines with the material signs within the document to generate information, are unavailable to the bibliographer. Bibliography therefore focuses its attentions on what is available: the physical documents and their material "content." It is for this reason that collection development is necessarily objectivist, i.e., that it identifies, sometimes to the point of confusion, the physical objects in libraries with the information produced from them.

It is, of course, possible for the library selector to use the materials he or she has selected—to play the user—but such action can prove highly prejudicial to collection development, especially at the research library level. Because use is subjective and contextual, because it is dependent upon individual predilections and competencies, because much of the creativity of research derives indeed from just such individuality of use, it would clearly be detrimental to assign any special privilege or priority to any particular method or instance of use. It is for this reason that the library selector is to a great extent morally compelled to avoid extensive or in-depth use of the materials collected—regardless of the sacrifice such abstention entails—for to make use of documentation is necessarily to specify, to actualize, and thus ultimately to restrict meaning and significance. While the user can (and must) engage in such interpretation, the selector should routinely shun any such in-depth involvement, for the consequence of that involvement will necessarily be to affect future selection decisions. If the selector begins to privilege his or her own interpretations, as it is impossible to avoid doing whenever one becomes deeply engaged in a subject, then the selector will surely begin to usurp the user's opportunity to make evaluative decisions relating to library materials.

It is for this reason also that the building of research library collections cannot be left to individual users, such as university faculty. In fact, the more knowledgeable the user group, the greater the need for the collection to be built by an outsider who is willing to approach the documentation on the subject as an abstraction. In a free society, the library selector *must* adhere to abstract objectivism; his function is to relay to the user the material signs created by the author, and then get out of the user's way, so to speak, so that the user is free to decide for himself or herself just what those material signs stand for. It is essential, therefore, that the selector remain, to use Hegel's word, forever "ungebildet," i.e., "uneducated," "undeveloped," "naive."[28]

While such protection of the user is certainly the most significant application of abstraction in the field of collection development, it is important to bear in mind that this service to clientele is not and cannot be achieved, except at a high psychological cost to the individual selector. It has long been recognized that anyone obliged to create objects that belong to someone else will ultimately become alienated from those objects. The young Marx believed that private property "is (a) the product of alienated labour and (b) the means through which labour is alienated, the *realization of this alienation*."[29] Eventually such alienation must infect the worker's perception not only of his role in society but also of himself, because he has invested himself in the object from which he has become estranged."[30]

Selection officers, especially those working in academic libraries, are subject to very similar forces—with the same debilitating results. Some form of alienation is, of course, understandable and predictable for anyone employed in a service organization, especially when the administrators of that organization have traditionally been assigned a lower social status than their clientele. Anyone providing a service under such conditions will always be perceived as a servant. Regardless of such contrivances as "faculty status," therefore, the academic librarian cannot help but become somewhat estranged from the rest of the academic community as a result of the conservative social stratification of functions in the academy.

The problems deriving from the academic librarian's status, however, are only one source—and in many cases a relatively minor one—of the selection librarian's alienation. The more fundamental cause of that alienation is the inescapable abstraction inherent in the librarian's basic function, bibliography. While all bibliographers may experience some form of alienation, as a consequence of referential abstraction, it is the library selector who is most affected by the abstraction of reception, and who is therefore most subject to the malignities of alienation. Catalogers, who are primarily engaged in the enumerative activity, and reference librarians, who are involved in a form of work which is perhaps analogous to the synoptic activity, are far less vulnerable to such alienation, because the results of their work are somewhat more apparent.[31] The result, on the other hand, of the library selector's effort, the collection, must remain for the selector a relatively abstract and alien object. It is the user, not the selector, who "owns" the collections, i.e., the means for the production of information. The user appropriates that collection through use; because such use is a subjective and private activity, the collection becomes, in a sense, a kind of private property belonging exclusively to the user. While the objective of the collection's assembly is clearly its use, therefore, the restriction of that use to library patrons necessarily ensures that the builder of the collection will remain estranged from the object of his own creation. Thus the collection is indeed both the product and the means of the library selector's alienation.

SOME CONCLUSIONS

Many unusual and problematic features of bibliography (and especially collection development) are ultimately attributable to the pervasive effects of abstraction. It is also perhaps this property of abstraction which spawns the suspicion that bibliography, especially in its applied form, may not fully qualify as a legitimate academic discipline, that there may be something defective about it. It has been one of the purposes of this essay to explain that all bibliographical work is indeed characterized by a dependence upon a larger context, to which the bibliographer frequently does not have access. At least one such essential context, the use of library materials, can in fact never be available for observation. It is for this reason that professional practitioners of bibliography—and especially the aggregative activity manifested in collection development—are understandably susceptible to a sense of deficiency, fragmentation, illegitimacy, and estrangement.

The unavoidable complications of abstraction are also related to the failure of some common management methods—or at least the dissatisfaction with them—in collection development, and in libraries generally. Most management techniques have been developed initially by or for business or industry. We attempt to apply these techniques to libraries, even though business and industry operate according to an entirely different system of values. Libraries gauge their success almost exclusively on the basis of use-value. Because the true utility of anything, including especially library materials, is subjective and unobservable, use-value is necessarily an abstraction.[32] Business, on the other hand, evades the uncertainties of abstraction by measuring its success totally in terms of exchange-value. While commodities produced by industry and marketed by business do have use-value by definition (otherwise they would hardly be marketable commodities), the ultimate objective of business is not to create utility but rather to achieve a margin of profit, which is measured by how much (as symbolized by money) a commodity can be exchanged for. Exchange-value is quantifiable, therefore, while use-value, as an abstraction, is not. It is for this reason (among others) that many management techniques so successful in business and industry can be applied only partially and ineffectively to the administration of libraries.

Abstraction is so integral to the structure and epistemology of bibliography and much of library science that its excision from those fields is not an option. How, then, are we to deal with it? One answer would be to ignore bibliographical abstraction, to pretend as if there were nothing particularly unusual about bibliography, to act as if it were much like any other discipline, to delude ourselves into imagining that its failure to achieve that level of legitimacy and quality which attends other disciplines were due to extra disciplinary factors such as the low social status of librarians. The alternative to such pretense is to adopt a more candid and realistic attitude toward the inevitability of abstraction throughout the discipline—to accept and embrace it with all of the inherent complications and liabilities, to study its origins, to calculate its effects, and thus to lay the foundation for a more intricate and substantial discipline of bibliography. The time has come, in my opinion, for the library profession to embark upon the latter course, and to begin to devote increased energy to the enhancement and promotion of the discipline of bibliography. Such a program is needed not only to increase professional satisfaction, but also to improve library service, for the first step toward upgrading the practice of library operations must be to analyze and define the theory upon which such practice ultimately depends.

REFERENCE NOTES

1. The standard sources on analytical bibliography are Ronald B. McKerrow, *An Introduction to Bibliography for Literary Students* (Oxford: Clarendon, 1927), and Philip Gaskell, *A New Introduction to Bibliography* (New York: Oxford Univ. Pr., 1972). The major source on descriptive bibliography remains Fredson Bowers, *Principles of Bibliographical Description* (Princeton, N.J.: Princeton Univ. Press, 1949). The best survey of the divisions of bibliography is probably Roy Stokes, *The Function of Bibliography,* 2d ed. (Aldershot: Gower, 1982). For an excellent history of the use of the term "bibliography," see Rudolf Blum, *Bibliographia: An Inquiry into Its Definition and Designations,* trans. Mathilde V. Rovelstad (Chicago: ALA, 1980).

2. Ross Atkinson, "An Application of Semiotics to the Definition of Bibliography," *Studies in Bibliography* 33 (1980): 71.

3. Useful summaries will be found in the articles "Abstrakt/konkret" and "Abstraktion" in the *Historisches Wörterbuch der Philosphie, I* (Basel: Schwabe, 1971), cols. 33–65; and "Abstraction in the Formation of Concepts" in *Dictionary of the History of Ideas* (New York: Scribner's, 1973), 1: 1–9.

4. *Oxford Latin Dictionary* (Oxford: Clarendon, 1068-82), 13.

5. Henry George Lidell and Robert Scott, comps., *A Greek-English Lexicon,* rev. ed. (Oxford: Clarendon, 1968), 285, 2016. See also "Abstrakt/konkret," cols. 33–34; "Abstraktion," cols. 42–44; and "Abstraction in the formation of Concepts," 1–2.

6. John Locke, *An Essay Concerning Human Understanding,* ed. Peter H. Nidditch (Oxford: Clarendon, 1975), 410–11.

7. See Hegel's short essay "Wer denkt abstrakt?" in his *Samtliche Werke Jubildumsausgabe* (Stuttgart: Fromann, 1958), 20: 445–50. An English translation by Walter Kaufmann will be found in Kaufmann's *Hegel: Reinterpretation, Texts and Commentary* (New York: Doubleday, 1965), 460–65. See also Hathan Rothenstreich, *Basic Problems of Marx's Philosophy* (Indianapolis: Bobbs-Merrill, 1965), 72.

8. Edmund Husserl, *Logical Investigations,* trans. J. N. Findlay (New York: Humanities Pr., 1970), especially 1:428.

9. Bertell Ollman, *Alienation: Marx's Conception of Man in Capitalist Society,* 2d ed. (Cambridge: Cambridge Univ. Pr., 1976), 61.

10. Willlard van Orman Quine, *From a Logical Point of View: 9 Logico-Philosophical Essays,* 2d ed. (Cambridge, Mass.: Harvard Univ. Pr., 1961) 141.

11. *The Encyclopedia of Philosophy* (New York: Macmillan, 1967), 5: 68.

12. Robert A. Fairthorne, "'Use' and 'Mention' in the Information Sciences," *Proceedings of the Symposium on Education for Information Science,* Warrenton, Va., Sept. 7–10, 1965, ed. Laurence B. Heilprin et al. (Washington, D.C.: Sparton, 1965), 11. See also Yehoshua Bar-Hillel, *Language and Information: Selected Essays on their Theory and Application* (Reading, Mass.: Addison-Wesley, 1964), 324–25.

13. Lawrence Brian Lombard, "Quotation and Quotation Marks: Semantical Considerations," Ph.D. diss., Stanford Univ., 1974, 213.

14. See Stokes, *Function of Bibliography.* One of the best concise descriptions of the traditional divisions of bibliography remains Fredson Bowers' article on "Bibliography" in the *Encyclopedia Britannica,* 1970 ed., 3: 588–92.

15. See G. Thomas Tanselle, "The Editorial Problem of Final Authorial Intention," *Studies in Bibliography* 29 (1976): 167–211.

16. "Scholarship is the art of understanding, explaining, and restoring the literary tradition. It originated as a separate intellectual discipline in the third century before Christ through the efforts of poets to preserve and to use their literary heritage, the 'classics.' So scholarship actually arose as 'classical' scholarship." Rudolf Pfeiffer, *History of Classical Scholarship from the Beginning to the End of the Hellenistic Age* (Oxford: Clarendon, 1968), 3.

17. James Thorpe, *Principles of Textual Criticism* (San Marino, Calif.: The Huntington Library, 1972), 50.

18. The classic description of this process remains W. W. Greg, *The Calculus of Variants: An Essay on Textual Criticism* (Oxford: Clarendon, 1927).

19. I include under the enumerative activity not only enumerative or systematic bibliography but also descriptive bibliography: see my "Application of Semiotics," 67.

20. Most of the materials that inhabit the shelves of our reference rooms are the products of either the enumerative or the synoptic activity. Reference works are referential in the sense of secondary reference, i.e., they are intended to refer to other works. They are normally either synoptic (e.g., encyclopedias, handbooks) or enumerative (e.g. bibliographies, indexes, catalogs), or some combination (such as annotated bibliographies).

21. Stanley Fish, *Is There a Text in This Class? The Authority of Interpretive Communities* (Cambridge, Mass.: Harvard Univ. Pr., 1980), 43.

22. Heinz von Foerster, "Epistemology of Communication," in *The Myths of Information: Technology and Postindustrial Culture,* ed. Kathleen Woodward (Madison, Wisc.: Coda, 1980), 19.

23. Rand J. Spiro, "Constructive Processes in Prose Comprehension and Recall," in *Theoretical Issues in Reading Comprehension,* ed. Rand J. Spiro et al. (Hillsdale, N.J.: Erlbaum, 1980), 246.

24. David W. Lewis "An Organizational Paradigm for Effective Academic Libraries," *College & Research Libraries* 47 (July 1986): 337; George S. Bond, "Evaluation of the Collection," *Library Trends* 22 (Jan. 1974): 280.—See also Paul Bixler, "Development of the Book Collection in the College Library: A Symposium," *College & Research Libraries* 12 (Oct. 1951): 355. "There is a more or less steady flow into the book collection, and very often there is a more or less steady flow out. In other words, there are relationships to and from functions. One may immediately divide these functions into two types: first, production—or what leads into the book collection; second, consumption—or what leads away from the book collection into its use."

25. V. N. Vološinov, *Marxism and the Philosophy of Language,* trans. Ladislav Matejka and I. R. Titunik (Cambridge, Mass.: Harvard Univ. Pr., 1986), 65. The original Russian edition was published in 1929. There is some suspicion among scholars today that part or all of this book may have been written by Mikhail Bakhtin.

26. Ibid., 70

27. "The product only obtains its 'last finish' in consumption. A railway on which no trains run, hence which is not used up, not consumed, is a railway only δυναβει and not in reality." Karl Merx, *Grundrisse,* trans. Martin Nicolaus (New York: Vintage, 1973), 91.

28. Hegel, "Wer denkt abstrakt?" 447.—The job title "subject specialist" is, therefore, a misnomer, because the subject specialist is not, or at least should not be, a specialist in a subject, but rather an expert in the literature—the abstract material signs—of the subject. Crossley and Woodhead are two of the few who have recognized this: see John D. Haskell Jr., "Subject Bibliographers in Academic Libraries: An Historical and Descriptive Review," *Advances in Library Administration and Organization* 3 (1984): 79. See also Conrad Rawski's distinction between the "subject level" and the "metalevel," cited in Joseph C. Donohue, *Understanding Scientific Literature: A Bibliometric Approach* (Cambridge, Mass.: MIT Pr., 1973), 9–10.

29. Karl Marx, *Early Writings,* trans. Rodney Livingstone and Gregor Benton (New York: Vintage, 1975), 332. The *locus classicus* on alientation will be found in the final segments of the First Manuscript of Marx's *Economic and Philosophical Manuscripts.*

30. For an introductory overview of the different types of alienation, see Istvan Meszaros, *Marx's Theory of Alienation* (London: Merlin, 1970), 14–15.

31. Because of the restrictions inherent in the enumerative activity, the cataloger is also subject to alienation. There is little doubt to my mind (not being a cataloger) that the elaborate rules of cataloging in effect today are at least partially attributable to a need to counteract such alienation by providing the cataloger with more opportunities for decision-making and some semblance of secondary authorship.

32. Circulation statistics provide only limited insight into use, and even less into use-value. On the drawbacks of the increasing reliance on circulation statistics, see Scott Bennett, "Current Initiatives and Issues in Collection Management," *The Journal of Academic Librarianship* 10 (Nov. 1984): 259–60.

21 OLD FORMS, NEW FORMS

THE CHALLENGE OF COLLECTION DEVELOPMENT

Collection development is intended primarily to improve the academic library's ability to fulfill competing information responsibilities with chronically inadequate resources. In order to meet this challenge, collection development has sought to create a system out of the processes which are already endemic to selection. If this system is to progress, if it is to adapt to rapidly changing technical and economic conditions, it must have the capacity to exert greater control over scholarly and educational information. Steps toward this increased control should include the categorization of sources and access by function rather than merely by subject, the ongoing definition of a title-specific core, and the development of prescriptive access and collection policies.

It is testimony both to the perceived significance of collection development and to the status of the library in the academy that the primary responsibility for the selection of library materials has passed from faculty users to academic library staff. The transfer of that responsibility, which began in the 1960s, has still not run its course.[1] Most larger academic libraries have by now assumed full responsibility for selection, although even in some of these larger institutions the transfer of authority has occurred quite recently.[2] The development of collections has, to be sure, always been a basic concern of all types of libraries, but what we today understand as academic library collection development is to a great extent the ongoing systematization and professionalization of collection building and management which has evolved both as a product of and as a rationale for this transfer of the selection effort from faculty users to library staff. The reasons the academic library needed to assume responsibility for selection have been frequently discussed.[3] The most important of these were probably (a) a rapid increase in funding and research, supported mainly by federal subsidies, and (b) the increasing realization, which began at least as far back as the 1936 comparative study by Douglas Waples and Harold Lasswell, that superior research collections could be built by professional bibliographers.[4] From a more general perspective, the transfer of selection responsibilities was intended to create a mechanism to improve the academic library's ability to respond rapidly and rationally to the manifold information needs of its users. How collection development has sought to achieve that objective, and what further actions need to be taken in order to refine that ability, will be the subject of this paper.

THE RECONCILIATION OF LIBRARY FUNCTIONS

The academic library has neither a single mission nor a homogenous constituency, but rather is obliged to respond to a multiplicity of academic needs and interest groups.

This article first appeared in *College & Research Libraries* 50, no. 5 (Sept. 1989): 514–15.

Although there are many schemes which could be used to categorize these responsibilities, let us posit for the purposes of this discussion five essential functions which the academic library attempts and is expected to fulfill.

1. *The notification function.* The academic library continues to serve as the principal (although never exclusive) means by which scholars communicate the results of their research to each other across space and time.
2. *The documentation function.* The academic library maintains the essential raw data upon which many disciplines base their research.
3. *The historical function.* To all libraries, but to the academic library especially, falls the responsibility for maintaining the records of civilization, without which the future will be denied access to the past.
4. *The instructional function.* The students, whose education is after all the primary purpose of all academic institutions, depend upon the library as a means to supplement and enrich their learning.
5. *The bibliographical metafunction.* In order to achieve the preceding four functions, the library must promote and facilitate access to information sources.

We must note at once that these functions have very different characteristics. The first four functions are direct responses to user needs, while the bibliographic metafunction drives and regulates the other functions. The historical function exists to ensure that records which one day may be needed will still be available. It is closely connected to, but must be distinguished from the documentation function, which is not a long-range curatorial responsibility; the documentation function is rather intended to provide access to information presently needed, especially for the humanities and social sciences. To respond to the current needs of historians is to fulfill the documentary function. To maintain materials or access to databases for future generations, on the other hand, is to respond to the historical function. Thus while the historical function is intended to serve future scholars (or at least all future scholars concerned in any way with history), the documentation function responds directly to the needs and interests of contemporary clientele.

All academic libraries normally serve all five functions to varying degrees, depending upon available resources. Those resources—funding, staffing, space—are always and have always been limited. The five functions are therefore in a state of perpetual competition for inevitably inadequate resources. The fundamental responsibility of academic library collection development (although it may not always have been viewed in these terms in the course of its evolution) has been and remains the reconciliation of such competing library functions.

The balancing of competing responsibilities is, of course, necessary for all library operations, but collection development has been, as we shall see, especially well designed to achieve such a purpose. This capacity will doubtless become increasingly evident (and, one hopes, effective) as more sources of information become available in electronic format. Although electronic publication is not proceeding nearly as rapidly as was once expected, there can be little doubt that many paper publications will eventually be replaced by sources in electronic form. While this will alter the nature of collections significantly, it is unlikely that it will induce changes in the fundamental purposes of collection development, because the cost of meeting all information needs for instruction and research will very likely continue to exceed available resources. Mediating among those competing needs, reconciling divergent academic library functions with conspicuously inadequate resources, will remain the fundamental responsibility of collection development, regardless of the formats in which scholarly and instructional information is published.[5]

THE FOUR CONTACT GROUPS

In her frequently cited 1973 dissertation, Elaine Sloan characterized collection development as a boundary spanning activity:

> Collection development is viewed as an activity which is at the boundary of the organization and which also engages in extensive intraorganizational transactions. Those who are responsible for developing collections will be required to interact with users of the collections, who are outside of the boundaries of the university. Within the boundaries of the library, those responsible for collection development may interact with public service librarians who are in contact with users and with technical service librarians who are in contact with dealers and publishers. Those responsible for developing collections will therefore be required to coordinate their activities with many other organizational units.[6]

The competing functions which the academic library must fulfill are not only abstractions. Those functions are also powerfully represented by interest groups of varying authority with which collection development librarians maintain routine contact. We can distinguish these primary contact groups according to their relationships with the local institution and/or the library profession. See figure 1. Providing an acceptable but practicable response to the disparate needs, demands, aspirations, and biases of these four groups is the activity in which many collection development librarians are engaged much of the time.

Two initial assumptions relating to this scheme should be noted. First, the most immediately perceivable political influence clearly originates from above the horizontal line, i.e., from local institutional forces. When there is clear competition for resources between institutional and non-institutional contact groups, the former groups will usually prevail. Second, most of the economic power lies outside of the profession, to the right of the vertical line. One reason, for example, that the achievements of cooperative collection development have been relatively modest is that the main proponents or representatives of cooperative activities are often collection development staff at other institutions, and they have neither the political authority nor the economic influence to compete with the demands represented by other contact groups.

	Professional	Nonprofessional
Institutional	Local library staff outside of collection development	Users
Non-institutional	Collection development librarians elsewhere	Publishers

FIGURE 1. Collection Development Contact Groups

We should also note parenthetically that, while boundary spanning is indeed an accurate and insightful description, there are also aspects of collection development which have necessarily been at the same time boundary-defining. A linkage can only be achieved if the linking agent becomes a true third component, distinguished from those elements on either side of the boundary. Collection development, in order to establish its own identity, has been compelled to disengage itself from the two key contact groups at the institutional level, other library staff (usually in the acquisitions department) and faculty users. It is in fact very difficult to establish a collection development program without temporarily weakening the connection between the emerging program and those two institutional groups from which the program is assuming its responsibility and authority. Once the collection development program is in place, however, and its legitimacy is no longer suspect, a primary objective must be to reestablish and to reenforce those local contacts as rapidly as possible.

Let us now consider the relationship of collection development to each of its four main contact groups.

Library Staff Outside of Collection Development

Of all the diverse functions for which a library is responsible, it is the key bibliographical metafunction which remains the most obscure to users. This is especially the case with fundamental processing services. Because the main political and economic authority in the academy resides with the users, the bibliographical metafunction can become vulnerable. During periods of austerity, faculty users often lobby to protect acquisitions at the expense of other critical library operations. "Faculty members will accept many radical changes as long as funds are available with which to buy essential material. This is an area where mis-calculation can bring disaster; if allowed to grow haphazardly, this budget [i.e., for acquisi-tions] will devour other funds."[7] Because collection development has become the library's primary link with faculty, and because faculty generally recognize collection development librarians as the representatives of the collections, it becomes an essential responsibility of collection officers to educate faculty as to the dependence of the collection on quality processing and staff. Collection development is therefore in a special position to protect the bibliographical metafunction by translating the values and concerns of the library into those of the faculty users.

Library Users

Local library users are clearly the most prominent and influential contact group for any collection development operation. Much effort has been devoted to the design of surveys and other mechanisms to identify user needs and attitudes.[8] Recently the competing needs of current faculty users have become especially problematic as a result of the escalating prices of materials in the sciences.[9] We have now become very sensitive to the fact that such prices have driven the cost of fulfilling the notification function in the sciences many times higher than the cost of fulfilling that same function in the humanities and social sci-ences. Selection responsibility has been assumed by the library in order to ensure, among other things, that the basic information (notification, documentation) needs of all faculty users are being met as consistently as possible within the confines of available resources. In a very real sense, therefore, collection development has been created to deal with exactly the kind of crisis we currently face, so that a test of collection development is now under way: if methods can be devised and resources channeled to meet the competing informa-tion needs of different faculty user groups in the face of the rapidly declining purchasing power of library budgets, then collection development will have demonstrated its utility to its parent institutions.

Different constituencies among current faculty represent only one of the competing needs of library users. There are at least two other essential categories of competing user needs which collection development is expected to address. First, there is the competi-tion between undergraduate and faculty needs. Graduate students probably do not form an immediately apparent, separate constituency, because their needs are in many cases identical with those of the faculty, but undergraduates often require very different material from that pursued and used by faculty. For most subjects in most academic libraries, the instructional function will be the highest priority. The academic library must therefore acquire material specifically intended for and used by undergraduates in fulfillment of its instructional function. When the notification and the instructional functions begin to compete vigorously for strained resources, it becomes an urgent responsibility of collection development to ensure that the capacity of the collection to support education is not undermined by the library's obligation to foster communication among scholars.

In addition to the competing needs of current faculty, and the competition for resources between faculty and undergraduates, there is a third category of competing user needs, which is certainly the most difficult to mediate: it is the conflicting requirements of present and future users. To serve the needs of future scholars is the library's historical function. Materials no longer necessary for notification (or even documentation, such as superseded editions) must be maintained—not everywhere, but somewhere—for future historical research. This consumes space and staff resources which could be applied to the fulfillment of the other library functions. Responding to the historical function is difficult, because the constituency to be served has not yet arrived, while the other, competing functions (notification, documentation, instructional) all serve the needs of current users. The larger the research library, moreover, the more critical becomes the historical function, although academic libraries of all sizes can and must contribute to the effort. The realization of the historical function can in fact only be achieved effectively by the coordination of collection decisions among academic libraries.

The Collection Development Community

The successful development of academic library collections, especially during periods of budgetary distress, depends upon the exchange of information and the coordination of planning and operations among collection development officers at different institutions. One effort to improve coordination has taken the form of standards and guidelines to ensure adequate and equitable service to current and future clientele in all institutions.[10] Such published standards are essential, but also abstract, so that the value of their application is difficult to assess.

The other, more practical method to improve coordination has been cooperative collection development, which has been a goal of academic libraries for many years.[11] The first decade of *College & Research Libraries* contains several calls for improved cooperation in the development of library collections.[12] The arguments and the recommendations presented in those articles are not at all unlike positions still taken today, which is evidence of how modestly we have progressed in this area. There are a variety of cooperative programs now in operation, but few of these seem to be having demonstrable effects. The recent survey by Joe Hewitt and John Shipman on cooperation among ARL libraries revealed that cooperative programs "must, for the most part, still be described as somewhat poorly delineated or even embryonic. The most important finding of the study relates to the level of interest and activity directed toward establishing cooperative collection development *relationships*, rather than specific program activities."[13] While there is great enthusiasm for cooperation, there has been considerable difficulty actually implementing such programs. Why cooperative programs have not worked as well as expected, despite the significant quantities of time, money, and intelligence devoted to them, remains a source of continuous speculation and frustration for the collection development community. Joseph Branin has recently compiled a list of the standard reasons for program inadequacies, and he has also provided some sound suggestions for solutions.[14] The simple fact may be, however, that the historical function, which cooperative collection development is primarily intended to promote, is being given a lower priority in most academic libraries despite our efforts to support it.

The Publishing Community

The contact group that is least understood, most alien, and increasingly distrusted, is the publishing sector. The concerns and motives of publishers remain obscure to libraries, because publishers are normally not directly connected with either the institution or the profession. Publishers are critically important to the fulfillment of library functions, but unlike the other three contact groups, they are not proponents of any particular library function. The commercial publishers especially operate on the basis of a value system which is relatively foreign to those of both the academy and the library profession. It has become clear recently, that the values and aspirations of at least some members of this group are having the most significant impact on the library's ability to accomplish its multifold mission.[15]

THE DRIVE FOR SYSTEM

The professionalization of collection development derives in part from the realization that subject knowledge is a necessary but insufficient prerequisite for selection. Another special form of knowledge is needed to ensure the equitable use of resources and the creation of balanced collections which were sometimes jeopardized when selection was done exclusively by faculty. The primary motivation behind the burgeoning literature of collection development has been to create a system—a coherent, self-validating process—which can rationalize collection decision-making. The origination of such a system, we must also acknowledge, has some clear rhetorical benefits, in that it can be used to emphasize the care and professionalism with which the development of collections is now being conducted by library staff.

This systematization of collection development has been achieved, for the most part, by regulating or formalizing features which have always been central to the collection development process. Much of the literature on budget allocation, for example, has been concerned primarily with the use of formulas. But a budget formula is merely the automatic application of predetermined factors relating to such issues as needs and use, which are routinely taken into account in the course of allocation anyway. In a sense, therefore, budget allocation is always based on unwritten formulas, which are merely imperfectly applied. The formula simply ensures that those factors are articulated and invariably considered. The problem is that the demands on the acquisitions budget are so various, the competing needs so diverse, that no "magic formula" can possibly take all such factors into account.[16]

The major attraction of the budgeting formula is rhetorical: it serves "to convince faculty members and departments that their allocations are fair."[17] Most collection development budgeting remains in any case necessarily imprecise, because of the inability of the library to predict publication costs and patterns. (This is perhaps partially a result of the poor relationship and communication between libraries and the publishing community.) Most budget allocation is therefore based upon past spending rather than upon projections.[18]

The creation of a unified collection policy is also intended to articulate and render consistent criteria which are often already being applied by selectors. The purpose of the policy is to raise those criteria to consciousness, to compare and to coordinate them, occasionally as a prelude to adjusting them so that they meet the varied and competing needs of the institution as consistently as possible. But the collection policy, like the formula budget, while certainly a significant step in the direction of systematic decision making, remains defective as a coordinating tool. The reason is that most of our policy statements (including the Conspectus) are primarily descriptive: they merely articulate the current condition ("existing collection strength") and direction ("current collecting intensity") of the collections.

Some policies provide an indication of the direction in which the collection should be moving ("desired collecting intensity"), but even the inclusion of this feature cannot compensate for the policy's lack of prescriptive authority. Collection policies, in other words, fail to stipulate in detail how future collecting should be adjusted in response to changing economic and technical conditions. The collection policy also frequently fails to reflect clearly the broader goals of the library.

The pursuit of system has also been intense in the most fundamental area of collection development literature, selection theory. Publications on selection written in the 1940s and 1950s were for the most part elegantly phrased opinions of learned men who seldom doubted their capacity to distinguish between significant and inferior publications. Their major criticism of academic library collections was that the stacks were being clogged with materials of questionable quality.[19] Once the library assumed responsibility for collection development, however, it quickly found itself beset by precisely the same inability (previously presumed to be a faculty malady) to distinguish important from less essential publications. This prompted Margit Kraft to warn in 1967 that American libraries had "forsaken the responsibility for judging quality," and have thus become "enamored with quantity."[20] A decade later Daniel Gore was still making essentially the same charge.[21] Little progress has, in fact, been made refining and coordinating selection criteria. While academic libraries can no longer afford to collect as broadly as they did in the 1960s, the qualitative basis for their reductions have been poorly articulated and for the most part uncoordinated.

The desire to systematize selection may have reached a kind of apex in the recent work of Robert Losee, who has devised selection formulas, which he urges collection development officers to use in order to render selection "more scientific and thus more productive."[22] Like formula budgeting, such a quantitative approach to selection has great rhetorical value, but whether it is possible or desirable to apply such a system in the real world of competing information needs must remain open to question.

All selection methods, and especially those used for cooperative collection development, must be founded, to be sure, upon some kind of articulated gradation of source qualities. Of the many formulations of utility actually used in libraries and in consortial agreements, the most familiar and most frequently applied is probably the concept of the core. The word "core" certainly has its rhetorical value, too, because most people probably associate the word with the ultimate objective science, nuclear physics. Despite the frequent and confident use the term receives, however, it usually remains not much more than a metaphor for "important material." This is not to say that there is no core, or that there are no core publications. Such a statement would be cynical and counterproductive. Certainly there are core journals, core documents, core editions and texts which anyone familiar with the relevant field could identify. Such items are viewed by consensus as indispensable for research and education.

A real core must have a periphery—some boundary which separates it from the remainder of the universe of publication. Our effort to establish that boundary, to distinguish core from noncore materials, has been so far singularly unsuccessful, except through such retrospective methods as citation analysis or the use of circulation records.[23] For purposes of planning, budgeting, or coordination, the concept of the core, for all its use, is practically useless. Something between the algorithms urged upon us by our colleagues in information science and the currently vague metaphor of the core needs to be established, if our effort to develop a system for collection decision-making is to move forward.

It should be noted, finally, that the drive to create a systematic basis for collection development is also partially a response to and an application of the increasing serialization of scholarly information. Periodicals have long played an essential role in scholarly communication, but recently we have become especially conscious of the extent to which they have come to dominate our collections and our budgets. Between 1978 and 1987, the number of journals published in the sciences quadrupled.[24] This prevalence of serials will probably continue, so we had best learn as much as we can about their special bibliographic and epistemological qualities.

It is clear that the distinguishing characteristic of the serial, as opposed to the monograph, is its diachronic context: each article can be perceived as a dependent component of a single text which is the entire, ongoing journal. Thus the quality of any article published in a scholarly journal is at least partially anticipated and judged by the reader on the basis of his or her conclusions about articles read previously in the same journal.

Each article is a kind of chapter in an ever expanding treatise. Every selector is well acquainted with the problems this causes when there is a need to undertake cancellations: when a journal is cancelled, its users invariably interpret such action as an amputation. The backfile of the cancelled journal is then perceived as a defective part which is no longer useful, because it has been separated from its whole. To cancel a journal is to interrupt a conversation. This is traumatic not only for the user but also for the library, because it appears as a reduction or even a repudiation of that systematization which collection development strives with such zeal to create and maintain.

FUTURE DIRECTIONS

Much has been achieved in academic library collection development since the assumption of selection responsibilities by the library began almost thirty years ago. Collection development has created at least a rudimentary system for the balanced fulfillment of competing functions, and that system has been successfully applied. But it remains equally clear, that more must now be done, more responsibility assumed, more control sought, more boundaries spanned, if the success of collection development is to be sustained. The remainder of this paper will focus upon three specific recommendations to improve further the current effectiveness of collection development: categorization by function, core definition, and refinements in policy.

Categorization by Function

Collection policies, materials budgets, and the distribution of selection responsibilities among selectors tend to be divided along subject lines.[25] Collection development's heavy reliance upon subject divisions is at least partially a vestige of the time when selection was primarily a faculty responsibility. Many acquisitions budgets, for example, continue to be divided as if they were being allocated to academic departments.

One disadvantage of the subject division of materials budgets is that it throws into stark relief the competition among subjects for library resources. It is for this reason that the frequent reliance upon subject divisions has been a serious impediment to cooperative collection development. Such cooperative arrangements often entail the agreement by participating institutions that they will collect in certain subject areas to the exclusion or diminution of others. Faculty concerned with the subjects targeted for deemphasis understandably oppose the implementation of such cooperative plans.[26] We need, therefore, a more refined method of collection categorization—not to conceal the competition among subjects, which undeniably exists, but rather to clarify its complexities and to create a basis for more practical collection goals. Such categories should reflect the use of library materials, so that the effects of collection planning upon research and instruction will be more apparent to local clientele.

While it remains impractical to abandon subject categories entirely, we might improve selecting, budgeting and cooperation, by subdividing subjects according to function. For purposes of this discussion let us simply apply the five functions identified earlier as a basis for distinguishing sources (or, more precisely, source access regardless of format). For each subject we might identify the following:

1. Notification sources. These are mainly journal articles and monographs written by scholars for other scholars in the same or related fields of research.
2. Documentation sources. In this category are all primary materials. Examples of these include data sources for the social sciences, original publications such as diaries or newspapers used by historians, and the original works and authoritative editions of standard authors for the humanities.
3. Instructional sources. This includes summaries of knowledge, such as textbooks or manuals, intended to provide introductions to and exercises in standard subjects taught at the institution.
4. Historical sources. These are sources which are no longer in demand, but which may be needed one day for historical research.
5. Bibliographical sources. These are reference sources which organize and provide access to all other sources.

Notification and bibliographical sources are essential for all disciplines, and respond directly to the needs of scholars at the institution. The extent of the instructional sources required will depend primarily on the size and use of the institution's academic programs. The most divergent needs are met by the documentation sources. Some subjects, notably the sciences, have very little requirement for documentation sources (always depending upon how we define them), while subjects which view the library as their laboratory are heavily dependent upon documentation sources.

The division of sources by function would improve opportunities for establishing priorities among and between subjects. If we are to work with faculty to make the best use of increasingly shrinking resources, we must have the ability to divide sources in a manner clearly related to their actual use. We must be willing to decide when the fulfillment of one function can be reduced in order to maintain or enhance another, and that decision should be reflected in our collection building and management. At the same time, the library must also have the capacity to ascertain when weaker constituencies are not receiving adequate collection support, and to shield weaker constituencies from stronger ones. This can only be achieved systematically and openly by designating and monitoring source functions.

Cooperative collection development could also benefit from a method that bases cooperative agreements upon functional categories. Certain types of sources, such as most instructional sources and many notification sources, cannot be shared effectively among institutions, but must be owned. Faculty must receive assurances that cooperative agreements will not affect their access to such sources. Specific functional categories, with a direct relationship to use, therefore, should enhance communication among most of collection development's contact groups.

Core Definition

We can conceive of the functional categories as a kind of horizontal division of a subject. This is only a first step toward the kind of specification which will be needed if the library is to assume an even more responsible and active role in the reconciliation of competing demands on inadequate resources. No matter how carefully or creatively we categorize information sources, we are still obliged to devise some vertical or qualitative criteria within each functional category as a basis for selection. While such criteria will be necessarily different at each institution, they must also have some common characteristics among all institutions in order to maintain standards and to foster cooperation. A more exact and applicable definition of core materials is "essential to the rationality of collection development in the future."[27]

It is normally assumed that the core will vary from one institution to another depending upon local needs, but core holdings should overlap significantly. The core should ideally serve as a kind of common vocabulary for all those engaged in research on the subject—the accepted reference point, to which all work in the field orients itself. The only fair measure of progress in a field is by the relationship of current work to a consensually established core of information. Compatible research depends upon such common points of reference, as does the coordination of education at all levels, which presupposes a well-defined core of information to which all students are exposed.

If the core concept is to become truly useful we must be prepared to work toward the definition of a standard core, which would be consensually accepted as such by scholars and libraries. The most important attribute of such a core should be that it is endorsed in detail by the academic community at large. (From the standpoint of bibliographic administration, what constitutes that core is relatively unimportant; what is important is rather that everyone involved agrees on what constitutes that core.) This can only be achieved by defining specific titles as core items. Defining core titles, at least for notification sources, should be accepted, therefore, as a fundamental, ongoing responsibility of the academic library community.[28]

The consensual designation of core sources would have an immediately beneficial impact on acquisitions budgeting for academic libraries of all sizes. If it were possible to achieve some general agreement among all libraries as to which sources should be included initially in the core, each library could begin its budgeting process by projecting the funding necessary to acquire and maintain such materials. Our ability to compare the purchasing power of acquisitions budgets at different institutions would also be greatly improved by such a unified core definition; comparisons could be based upon what libraries have to spend once the core materials have been budgeted. Moreover, because the items defined as belonging to the core would be scrutinized by all participating libraries, the costs of these materials could be carefully tracked, routinely compared, and widely publicized. If certain items were found to be significantly overpriced, the suitability of those items for the core could be reconsidered.

Finally, a common definition of core materials would improve cooperative collection development. The first step in a cooperative program should not be to try to divide collection responsibilities for low use materials, because it is so difficult to agree on which materials fall into that category. The first objective of cooperation should be to decide upon which items should be duplicated among all participating libraries. Once that has been achieved, at least for notification sources, then potential areas for cooperative collection development can be much more easily negotiated. Our ability to rate aspects of our collections in relationship to each other would also be significantly enhanced, but only if we dare to define the dividing line between core and specialized materials.

How can a core definition be achieved? How are we to take charge of scholarly information in order to guarantee access to our users, if the utility of that information can only be gauged very imprecisely, and only after the item has already been acquired? One answer lies in the materiality of information. Libraries seldom control information directly. Rather they manipulate the containers the information is moved about in. To define a core is, therefore, to define the containers in which future core information will appear. One possibility is to exploit the contextuality afforded by the serialization of scholarly information. At least for notification sources, it should be possible for scholars and experienced subject or area bibliographers to arrive at a consensus as to which journals in each subject field should be categorized as core journals on the basis of the nature of the articles already published in them. The same could be done with databases, on the basis of the quality of information previously retrieved. It may also be possible to designate different types of core lists by level of academic program; a larger core might be defined for libraries with graduate programs in the subject than for libraries that support only undergraduate programs.

The Collection Management and Development Committee of the Research Libraries Group (RLG) has already taken a decisive step in this direction by working on lists of journals in selected subject areas necessary to build a very strong, research level (4+) collection. The purpose of the lists will not be to ensure duplication, but to make certain that at least one copy of each journal on the list will be available somewhere in the RLG consortium. These lists are not core lists because they are intended to represent works needed in the aggregate for exceptionally powerful research collections, but this potentially very effective project now being initiated by RLG has demonstrated that lists of essential periodicals can be assembled.

The RLG project has also shown that the construction of such lists requires a high degree of cooperative organization and collaboration. If core lists are to be devised at a national level, improved organization and communication among academic libraries will be required. The links between larger and smaller academic libraries will also need to be strengthened. It is essential that smaller libraries participate in the process, so that their users can be assured access to the same basic core materials in each subject as the users of larger libraries. This should improve the fulfillment of the notification function by smaller libraries. Care would need to be taken to ensure that the cost of the core does not exceed the budgets of smaller libraries. If such a core were defined, of course, all academic libraries, but especially smaller libraries, would be able to communicate their budget needs much more accurately and forcefully to their institutions. Accreditation might also eventually take core holdings into account.

The identification of core sources published in monographic formats is much more problematic. The retrospective circulation method could be used. An alternative for monographic notification sources might be to designate certain carefully selected monographic series in each subject as core series. This would doubtless be even more controversial than designating core periodicals, but it should not be impossible, especially if we are willing to work with editors and scholars in the field. There would also need to be mechanisms to review and update core lists periodically.

By designating core titles in this manner, the competition for publication in such sources should increase substantially, so that we could expect the quality of that material to remain consistently high. But would the definition of core materials constitute a form of censorship? Probably. Like all bibliographic decision making, core definition would necessarily involve the rejection of some materials or sources of information in favor of others. This is unavoidable, and it is a key aspect of the bibliographic function. As increasingly large volumes of data become available online, moreover, the art of bibliographic discrimination will become even more important to scholarly communication than it is now. No matter who makes the bibliographic selection, bibliographer or end user, it remains a collection development responsibility to ensure that the decisions are made consciously and according to consistently defined criteria.

Refinements in Policy

If functional categories could be established within subjects, and if title-specific cores could be defined, then the next step in improving control of and access to scholarly and instructional information would be to work on the design of prescriptive collection and access policies. Each institution must compare and prioritize the primary functions for the library as a whole, and for each subject area. Once access to the core materials in each functional category has been established, the remaining funds can be allocated on the basis of those priorities. The political difficulties should be allayed by the definition of core notification sources, because most faculty users at most institutions would thereby be able to depend upon the guaranteed availability of standard sources as nationally defined. Communication among scholars would be protected. The extent to which the library wants to develop its collections beyond those standard sources either individually or cooperatively would be based upon institutional directions and resources.

If each institution works toward a policy which is truly prescriptive, then the amalgamation of those policies should provide a clear indication not only of the current condition of the national collection, but also of the transformation the national collection would undergo in the event of substantial economic or technical changes. Only in this way can we have adequate control of access to scholarly information at the national level, and negotiate policy adjustments among libraries to ensure continued access.

Institutional policies afford opportunities for planning and decision making. If collecting were categorized by function, there can be little doubt that each institution would quickly confirm what we already know, namely that materials budgets are being spent increasingly upon notification sources, especially in the sciences. A prescriptive policy would determine the extent to which such notification sources should be permitted to consume the budget, or the degree to which the collection of other materials should be reduced in order to compensate for the increasing costs of scientific notification. Before this situation gets out of control, our policies must finally set functional limits to ensure that the needs of all constituencies are consistently met within the confines of current economic conditions.

The prescriptive collection policy must have the capacity to serve as a component of a general library policy regulating the use of all library resources. A clear and distinct link should be set between collection policy and all other library operations so that the effects of other operations on collections and access will be clarified for faculty clientele.

CONCLUSION

There are really only two ways to build a collection: on the basis of publication, or on the basis of use. Selection based on publication seeks to acquire a broad share of what has been published on the subject, while the use-based method imports only materials specifically applicable to current user needs. Most college libraries have always applied some form of the use-based method for most subjects, but larger university libraries have managed until recently to build many segments of their collections on the basis of publication. Today, however, even university library collections are becoming increasingly use-driven; they are being tailored to fit the special needs and interests of current users, because the publication-based approach is no longer economically feasible. Financial constraints are forcing a return to a kind of indirect selection by users. But things are now very different from the way they were thirty years ago.

The agency of collection development has begun to assume some control over the information needs of the academy. A system to regulate and focus selection and access, imperfect as it still may be, is now in place. The challenge facing collection development is to calibrate its operation more precisely, to define its rationale more persuasively, and to apply its methods more rigorously in preparation for the unprecedented economic and technical changes which we have only begun to experience.

REFERENCE NOTES

1. Mark Sandler maintains, in "Organizing Effective Faculty Participation in Collection Development," *Collection Management* 6, no. 64 (fall/winter 1984), that "the teaching faculty continue to serve as the primary agents of selection in the great majority of academic institutions."

2. The University of Florida Libraries, for example, continued to allocate its firm order budget to academic departments until 1987. Letter from Sam Gowan, 15 May 1989.

3. J. Periam Danton, *Book Selection and Collection: A Comparison of German and American University Libraries* (New York: Columbia Univ. Pr., 1963), 61–82. See also Jasper G. Schad and Ruth L. Adams, "Book Selection in Academic Libraries: A New Approach," *College & Research Libraries* 30 (Sept. 1969): 437–42; and John D. Haskell Jr., "Subject Bibliographers in Academic Libraries: An Historical and Descriptive Review," *Advances In Library Administration and Organization* 3 (1984): 73–84.

4. Charles B. Osburn, *Academic Research and Library Resources: Changing Patterns in America* (Westport, Conn.: Greenwood, 1979), 3–34; Douglas Waples and Harold D. Lasswell, *National Libraries and Foreign Scholarship* (Chicago: Univ. of Chicago Pr., 1936), 71, showed that the New York Public Library, which relied even then upon bibliographers, held collections of European social sciences materials which were superior to faculty-built collections in large academic libraries.

5. Allen B. Veaner, "1985 to 1995: The Next Decade in Academic Librarianship, Part I," *College & Research Libraries* 46 (May 1985): 219–25.

6. Elaine F. Sloan, "The Organization of Collection Development in Large University Research Libraries," Ph.D. diss., Univ. of Maryland, 1973, 47.

7. Gerard B. McCabe, "Austerity Budget Management," in *Austerity Management in Academic Libraries*, ed. John F. Harvey and Peter Spyers-Duran (Metuchen, N.J.: Scarecrow, 1984), 231.

8. See F. W. Lancaster, "Evaluating Collections by Their Use," *Collection Management* 4 (spring/summer 1982): 15–43.

9. Robert L. Houbeck Jr., "If Present Trends Continue: Responding to Journal Price Increases," *The Journal of Academic Librarianship* 13 (Sept. 1987): 214–20.

10. See *Guidelines for Collection Development*, ed. David L. Perkins (Chicago: ALA, 1979). Revisions of all of the guidelines included in this publication are now being undertaken by the Collection Management and Development Committee of the Resources Section, Resources and Technical Services Division, ALA.

11. David C. Weber, "A Century of Cooperative Programs among Academic Libraries," *College & Research Libraries* 37 (May 1976): 205–21.

12. See, for example, Louis R. Wilson, "The Challenge of the 1930's and the 1940's," *College & Research Libraries* 1 (Mar. 1940): 131; Verner W. Clapp, "Cooperative Acquisitions," *College & Research Libraries* 8 (Apr. 1947): 99–100; Ernest Cadman Colwell, "Cooperation or Suffocation," *College & Research Libraries* 10 (July 1949): 195–98, 207.

13. Joe A. Hewitt and John S. Shipman, "Cooperative Collection Development among Research Libraries in the Age of Networking: Report of a Survey of ARL Libraries," *Advances in Library Automation and Networking* 1 (1987): 225.

14. Joseph J. Branin, "Issues in Cooperative Collection Development: The Promise and Frustration of Resource Sharing," in *Issues in Cooperative Collection Development*, ed. June L. Engle and Sue O. Medina (Atlanta: Southeastern Library Network, 1986), 15–36.

15. See the Report of the ARL Serials Prices Project (Washington, D.C.: Association of Research Libraries, 1989).

16. Richard Hume Werking, "Allocating the Academic Library's Book Budget: Historical Perspectives and Current Reflections," *The Journal of Academic Librarianship* 14 (July 1988): 143.

17. Jasper G. Schad, "Fairness in Book Fund Allocation," *College & Research Libraries* 48 (Nov. 1987): 480.

18. See the reactions of Hugh F. Cline and Loraine T. Sinnott, *Building Library Collections: Policies and Practices in Academic Libraries* (Lexington, Mass.: Lexington, 1981), 79–81.

19. See, for example, Mortimer Taube, "Libraries and Research," *College & Research Libraries* 2

(Dec. 1940): 22–26, 32, and Garrett Hardin, "The Doctrine of Sufferance in the Library, *College & Research Libraries* 8 (Apr. 1947): 120–24.

20. Margit Kraft, "An Argument for Selectivity in the Acquisition of Materials for Research Libraries," *Library Quarterly* 37 (July 1967): 285.

21. Daniel Gore, "Farewell to Alexandria: The Theory of the No-Growth, High-Performance Library," in *Farewell to Alexandria: Solutions to Space, Growth, and Performance Problems of Libraries*, ed. Daniel Gore (Westport, Conn.: Greenwood, 1976), 164–80.

22. Robert M. Losee Jr., "Theoretical Adequacy and the Scientific Study of Materials Selection," *Collection Management* 10, no. 3 (1988): 25. See also his "A Decision Theoretic Model of Materials Selection for Acquisition," *Library Quarterly* 57 (July 1987): 269–83.

23. Richard W. Trueswell, "Growing Libraries: Who Needs Them? A Statistical Basis for the No Growth Collection," in *Farewell to Alexandria*, 72–104. In any case, to use circulation as a basis for core definition, one must first buy the document and see how it circulates, before one can determine whether it qualifies as part of the core. This is, of course, the weakness in the argument that a library should make the best use of its resources by acquiring only core materials.

24. *Ulrich's News* 1, no. 3 (Apr. 1988): 1.

25. The major exception to this rule is for area studies; area selectors are frequently responsible for many subjects from or relating to a single geographical area.

26. Fremont Rider recognized and criticized this same problem nearly fifty years ago in his *The Scholar and the Future of the Research Library* (New York: Hadam Pr., 1944), 68–85.

27. Charles B. Osburn, "Toward a Reconceptualization of Collection Development," *Advances in Library Administration and Organization* 2 (1983): 180.

28. The definition of the canon or the "classics" (i.e., materials belonging to the highest class), was a responsibility of the library at Alexandria. See Georg Luck, "Scriptor Classicus," *Comparative Literature* 10 (spring 1958): 152.

22 PREPARATION FOR PRIVATION

THE YEAR'S WORK IN COLLECTION MANAGEMENT, 1987

Collection management is in the broadest sense an economic responsibility, and its concerns and progress necessarily reflect prevailing economic conditions. If there is any link among the great variety of 1987 publications on collection management, it is an understandable preoccupation with a renewed onset of austerity. Pricing of library materials continues to occupy a prominent place in the literature, and cooperative collection development remains a favorite means to contend with eroding materials budgets—at least in print. However, most 1987 publications were written well before the uncertainties spawned by the stock market crash and subsequent accelerated decline in the exchange value of the dollar. Therefore, the 1987 preoccupation with budget inadequacies is only a prelude to what will doubtless evolve into the dominant theme of the 1988 literature.

What follows is a very selective overview of 1987 publications. A few items published too late to be incorporated into Wortman's very thorough 1986 review also have been included.[1] Excluded are reports on the content of individual collections, unless they are intended to be applied to collection management in general. Personal book collecting and bibliophily are also not covered. Most importantly, items relating specifically to the collection management of serials are excluded from this review by editorial policy: a discussion of those publications appears elsewhere in this issue.

GENERAL

Clearly, the most important general publication in 1987 is the new edition of Evans' *Developing Library and Information Center Collections*.[2] The book has been thoroughly updated and contains references to some materials published as late as 1987. New chapters have been added on fiscal management, preservation, and automation, making the book a more comprehensive introduction to the field than the original 1979 edition.

Successive editions of *Building Library Collections* are reviewed and compared by Gleaves in his discussion of recent, major publications in collection management.[3] Curt provides French readers with a long and detailed discussion of Magrill and Hickey, *Acquisitions Management and Collection Development in Libraries,* primarily to ensure that French librarians are acquainted with collection techniques and criteria used in U.S. libraries.[4] We in the U.S. could certainly profit from more in-depth reviews of foreign-language publications on collection management. Simonot describes French concerns about adapting U.S. methods of writing collection development policies to French library needs.[5]

This article first appeared in *Library Resources & Technical Services* 32, no. 3 (July 1988): 249–62.

In other articles on general subjects, Chamberlin examines the effects of institutional strategic planning, fundraising, and international programs on acquisitions in academic libraries, and Thomas considers the social and political relationships between bibliographers and faculty.[6] Thomas also draws attention to the contradiction between the 1970 Pittsburgh study, which indicated that significant portions of research collections are never used, and the 1985 survey by the American Council of Learned Societies, which revealed that many faculty members feel the holdings of research libraries to be inadequate.

ORGANIZATION

Cogswell defines eight standard functions of collection management; he then identifies six organizational models and estimates the effectiveness of each one in achieving each of the eight functions. He notes that none of the models is adequate to achieve fully the goals of either preservation or storage and weeding.[7] Bryant focuses upon critical points in the evolution of collection development organization and expands upon Sloan's classic tripartite definition of collection development structures.[8] She also provides a well-reasoned and long-needed summary of time-management difficulties that derive from the use of part-time selectors. Sohn reviews a survey of collection development organization in ARL libraries.[9] The survey revealed that such organizations vary widely and that most of the libraries surveyed have separate collection development units. Only three respondents relied entirely on full-time selectors: the standard collection development structure in larger research libraries still consists, therefore, of part time selectors who have other primary job duties and for whom the chief collection development officers normally do not have line responsibility. Cubberley finds similar problems of divided responsibilities facing collection development organization in medium-sized academic libraries and recommends that such libraries establish separate units of librarians who have collection development as their primary function.[10] Bobick's SPEC Kit on collection development organization in ARL libraries contains organization charts and descriptions, position announcements, orientation and training aids for bibliographers, and task force reports.[11]

COLLECTION BUILDING

In an important contribution to selection theory, Rutledge and Swindler define six basic selection criteria, and then place them on a matrix that theoretically permits each item being considered for selection to be rated on a scale of 1 to 100.[12] Losee, coming at the same problem from the more formal standpoint of economics and statistics, also devises a model for quantifying selection criteria and recommends, in addition, that his method be applied to a kind of retrospective analysis of selection decisions using MARC tapes.[13] Despite their emphasis on quantitative analysis, both Losee and Rutledge/Swindler acknowledge that subjectivity will and must continue to play a role in selection. Line, in a hardnosed review of two British studies on selection effectiveness, considers if selection should be improved, but decides that "a more realistic question is whether it matters much if it turns out that selection cannot be improved. What does 'improvement' mean anyway? . . . How good can selection actually get?"[14] Line provides no answers to these questions, but makes some suggestions about evaluating selection.

Heim describes the uses of statistical data in the social sciences and traces development of statistical data archives up to 1975.[15] On the basis of a study by Agrawal, it appears that information needs of social scientists in India are being relatively well met.[16] Broadus reports on a study of material uses by humanities scholars: the results show a somewhat higher percentage of periodicals and a somewhat lower use of foreign languages than expected.[17]

Both beginning and experienced bibliographers will profit from a careful reading of the wide range of essays on developing collections of English and American literature edited by McPheron.[18] Using business school materials as a basis, Vidor and Futas consider the special problems of building professional education collections.[19] In other publications on building subject collections, Palmer finds that Canadian fiction is generally held in U.S. libraries only when it has been reviewed in U.S. sources, and Makino decides that one of the main difficulties in building East Asian art collections is the coordination of selection decisions made by art librarians with those made by East Asian bibliographers.[20] Monnin warns against the skewing of public library collections of inspirational materials as a result of selectors' personal biases, and Iwaschkin charges that smaller public libraries (at least in Great Britain) tend to avoid selecting materials on such subjects as popular music, sex, or drug abuse, preferring instead to acquire less controversial material.[21] Gorman finds that publications espousing new right positions are being adequately collected in some Georgia libraries, and that public libraries tend to collect more of such material than academic libraries.[22] Sources and methods for building collections that respond to the needs of adult new readers are examined by Heiser.[23]

A survey by Mary and Victor Biggs on building academic library reference collections revealed that larger libraries often have written policies and select for reference on a title by title basis, while smaller libraries tend to place heavier emphasis on the selection of items traditionally categorized as reference materials.[24] They also note that, although libraries claim to weed their reference collections on the basis of low use, there seems to be little effort to gauge the use of reference collections with any accuracy. Johnson, Kelley, and Whitehead continue the discussion on the unique difficulties of building collections to serve students located far from the main campus.[25]

The lack of adequate criteria and methods for building special collections of twentieth-century nonliterary materials is lamented in an essay by Landon.[26] Streit reports on the results of a survey of Association of Research Library (ARL) libraries on rare book purchasing, and Weathers argues that public libraries need to put more effort into building special collections.[27]

The difficulties we experience building collections in U.S. libraries pale, needless to say, in comparison to the problems that must be confronted by libraries in developing countries. Olanlokun and Issah and Obiagwu describe current obstacles to building collections in Nigeria: they estimate that acquisitions at the University of Lagos in 1983 were only one-third of what they were in 1977.[28] Du Preez describes similar difficulties now experienced at the University of South Africa.[29]

On the subject of media collecting, Gatten and others provide an excellent introduction to collecting CD-ROM materials, describing the characteristics, advantages, and disadvantages of CD-ROMs, and reviewing particular CD-ROM products of interest to libraries.[30] Stewart relates the selection criteria for CD-ROMs used by Cornell University's Mann Library.[31] Webb describes how to build an adult nonfiction video collection in a public library.[32] The results of an extensive survey to determine the sources and criteria used by health educators and consultants (including librarians) to select audiovisual materials for health care teaching are delineated by Bratton and others.[33] Cornelius examines media collections in Australian academic libraries and finds them wanting, primarily because of inadequate funding, lack of trained specialists, and poor bibliographic control.[34]

On the subject of collecting for children, Elleman provides a current overview.[35] Beilke and Sciara emphasize a community-oriented approach to selecting materials that are culturally relevant to the needs of Hispanic and East Asian younger readers.[36] Berni, Forte, and Mussetto describe experiences building school collections in Italy.[37] A second edition appeared of Kemp's compilation of policies, procedures, and forms used for collection building by schools and media centers around the country.[38]

On the subject of gifts, Caswell explains in a useful, original essay that people donating or selling their private collections are often stricken with grief at the prospect of losing those collections; she urges that librarians dealing with such sellers or donors learn something about grief behavior.[39] Miller explains the purpose of the International Library Exchange Center, which was developed to link U.S. libraries with libraries abroad.[40] Poll describes exchange operations in Germany and argues that routine exchanges (as opposed to one-time exchanges for specified items) are no more labor-intensive than purchasing.[41] Leonhard presents a discussion of the exchange work of the German Research Society, which spends some DM 600,000 per year on materials for exchange with some 1,200 partners around the world; the society also maintains special offices in Washington and Tokyo to collect American and Japanese reports, government publications, and other materials difficult to order for research libraries.[42]

COLLECTION AND USE EVALUATION

The complexity—and perhaps even the impossibility—of precise collection evaluation is illustrated by an inventory of questions provided by Futas and Vidor.[43] Burrell suggests some refinements on statistical methods to predict future utility of materials, while Warwick rejects circulation as a basis for predicting use and offers instead a model for measuring "user utility" of titles recommended by faculty to students.[44] Uses of the Australian Bibliographic Network to reveal overlap, unique titles, and gaps in Australian library holdings are described by Rochester.[45]

Evaluation of the relationship between courses and collections remains a topic of perennial interest in academic libraries. Palais describes the use of course information, categorized by Library of Congress class number and sorted by computer, to produce a collection development policy at Arizona State.[46] Gabriel provides information on an experiment to match keywords in course descriptions at Mankato State with subject headings in the Minnesota State University system database to evaluate library support for the curriculum.[47]

In a study conducted at the East Carolina University School of Medicine, librarians asked medical school faculty to indicate subjects, based on National Library of Medicine classes, important for their teaching and research; the same faculty members were then asked to make selection decisions: the result showed little correlation between the subjects ranked as important and the items selected.[48]

COOPERATIVE COLLECTION DEVELOPMENT

Hewitt and Shipman provide extensive information on the variety of cooperative programs in place at large research libraries, the product of a survey they conducted among ninety-three ARL libraries.[49] In a paper read at a 1986 SOLINET conference, Branin presents a useful review of cooperative efforts, including delineation of the obstacles to successful cooperation. He focuses upon five strategies to overcome those obstacles and posits four models of cooperative collection development.[50] Medina describes the Network of Alabama Academic Libraries' work, which developed a collection assessment method to determine costs needed to support new academic programs throughout the partnership.[51] Using the Alabama Library Exchange as an example, Pike discusses the complexities of establishing a regional, multitype library cooperative program.[52]

Many cooperative programs are in place abroad. Korale describes the cooperative development of health science collections among seventeen Sri Lankan libraries. Amon and Lajeunesse recall the origins of cooperation among academic libraries in West Africa in the 1970s, while Lungu calls for an improved system of resource sharing in libraries of southern Africa.[54] In what is perhaps the most encouraging publication on cooperation in 1987, Kaegbein discusses the successful coordination of research library collection building in the Federal Republic of Germany.[55] One key to success is the responsibility assumed by the German Research Society to distribute funds to libraries for specialized foreign publications. This allows libraries to apply their local funds to the purchase of higher use materials. Further information on the West German program is provided by Kehr.[56] Tornier describes an East German cooperative collection development program in which 141 libraries have divided collection responsibilities for 296 subject areas.[57]

The need to improve collection of grey literature is becoming increasingly apparent.[58] Hasemann suggests enhanced methods of cooperation in collecting such material, which contains so much current information. Hasemann describes the new European Association for Grey Literature Exploitation (EAGLE), through which the collection of grey literature throughout Europe is being coordinated, and she calls for the eventual establishment of a central European grey literature library.[59]

The 1986 membership meeting of ARL was devoted to the North American Collections Inventory Project (NCIP).[60] Stam provided an informal, insider's history of the origin of the Conspectus; he also acknowledged that some resistance to the Conspectus by bibliographers derives from the fact that it is frequently imposed on collection development staff by library administration.[61] Miller stressed the value of the Conspectus for a rapidly developing library collection and noted that the Conspectus, to be successful, needs broader acceptance beyond the library community.[62] Scott, the National Librarian of Canada, discussed at the conference and elsewhere Canada's national inventory plan.[63] Ferguson described local uses of the Conspectus, most of which are similar to those benefits normally used to justify written collection development policies.[64] Abel skillfully manipulated the "Conspectus as map" metaphor and made the important point that the Conspectus does not contain data so much as opinions.[65] All of the speakers at the conference, especially Stam and Abel, emphasized the necessary limitations of the Conspectus and noted that some of its occasional unpopularity derives from the expectation that it alone can bring about cooperative collection development or can satisfy other cooperative needs for which it was never designed or intended.

Horrell calls for a national review of art holdings using the Conspectus as a basis.[66] Hanger traces the use of the Conspectus in the British Library as a tool to coordinate selection policy among different divisions within the BL, and he looks forward to the day when there will be a "pan-European Conspectus database."[67] Matheson describes uses of the Conspectus to communicate among research libraries in Scotland.[68] Finally, in an essay written in the "grand style," Henige undertakes a long-needed deconstruction of some of the rhetoric surrounding the Conspectus-rhetoric that has doubtless contributed to the kind of false expectations warned of by Stam and Abel.[69]

COSTS AND BUDGETING

The results of the 1986 market survey of libraries, publishers, and wholesalers are reported by Edelman and Muller and include a wealth of data on library budgets, responsibility for selection in different libraries, uses of reviews, criteria and sources of selection, and methods of processing.[70] Further analysis of these data is provided by Marsh.[71]

Clark summarizes methods used by collection managers to accommodate increased costs.[72] Montag provides a broad overview and seasoned advice on the selection and acquisition of international materials.[73] Martin describes the financial difficulties experienced in trying to build special collections during periods of austerity.[74]

Drawing upon research in social psychology, Schad considers the issue of equity in budget allocation in a highly original article; he discusses environmental factors affecting equitable allocation, principles that serve as a basis for equity in allocation, measures in applying those principles, and procedural rules of allocation.[75] Allen and Tat describe use of circulation statistics at the Western Australian Institute of Technology as a basis for budget allocation; Lane from the same library justifies such a method by confirming that circulation is a reliable indicator of in-house use and therefore presumably provides an accurate reflection of user needs.[76]

Hendrickson, in the lead paper at a 1986 conference on costs, delineates factors affecting the costs of library materials.[77] Schrift and Bauer reflect on how from their different perspectives publishers set prices, while Alessi provides a detailed and revealing discussion of factors affecting U.K. book prices.[78]

Current increases in the cost of library materials sustain interest in price indexes. Griebel provides a critical review and comparison of library materials price indexes available in Germany, the U.K., and the U.S.[79] Pallier also compares sources of pricing information in those three nations; Pallier then contrasts budgeting methods in those countries with budgeting in French libraries.[80] Fletcher discusses price indexes available to U.K. academic libraries and presents a composite index he developed that he believes tracks prices more accurately than any of the available indexes.[81]

Discriminatory pricing remains of interest, although much of the discussion relates to serials. A balanced view of discriminatory pricing is presented by Boissonnas, who reviews and adjusts previous studies on the subject, and also notes price markups by U.S. publishers selling to U.K. customers.[82] Dörpinghaus compares two issues of a Yale University Press price list, one distributed in the U.S. and the other intended for European customers: he finds that more than 80 percent of the monographic titles have higher prices in Europe.[83] Discriminatory pricing is not an injustice borne solely by North American libraries.

In an historical study, Danton traces acquisition budget increases for certain large German and U.S. libraries between 1860 and 1910. He concludes that increases in budgets over these periods probably did not keep pace with increases in demand for materials by library users.[84] So much for progress.

ACQUISITIONS

The results of a 1985 survey of acquisition departments in ARL libraries designed to compare organization and processes are discussed by Schmidt.[85] Most respondents showed an organizational division between monographs and serials; Schmidt finds that such segregated units seem to use their staff more efficiently. The most troubling conclusion drawn from the survey is that professional librarians in acquisition departments are responsible for work normally assigned to nonprofessional staff in other departments.

Several 1987 essays in *Library Acquisitions: Practice & Theory* focus on the subject of the business and ethical relationships between librarians and vendors.[86] Miller and Niemeier, acquisitions librarians at different universities, describe a test of vendor performance undertaken by ordering the same titles at the same time from the same vendors at their separate institutions; the results showed significant variations.[87] Mastejulia clearly defines what libraries need and expect from publishers, while Marsh advocates consumer action by libraries to protest or rectify questionable practices by publishers.[88]

Research on approval plans will now be much easier with the assistance of Rossi's annotated bibliography of seventy-seven publications on the subject.[89] Cargill confirms the cost-effectiveness of automatic ordering from a variety of perspectives, and Feller provides an overview of the rationale and procedures of approval plans as used by U.S. libraries.[90] Maddox discusses the uses of machine-readable data from an approval vendor and stresses the need to understand the reasoning behind vendor selections.[91] Smith and Gibbs explain the value of MARC records for automated acquisitions systems.[92] Nisonger provides an analysis of the costs of using Baker & Taylor's LIBRIS system, concluding that the system becomes more cost-effective as the level of ordering rises.[93] Advantages and weaknesses of the acquisitions subsystem of DOBIS are described by Khurshid.[94] Blauer, Bullard, and Miller discuss the essential role of standards developed by the Book Industry Systems Advisory Committee and the Serials Industry Systems Advisory Committee for automated acquisitions, and Somers describes the consequences of ignoring standards when creating an online acquisitions system, on the basis of firsthand experience.[95] Shuster writes about the use of a dBase III+ program for acquisitions, and Nuzzo presents dBase II and dBase III programs for creating online desiderata files.[96]

CONCLUSIONS

The collection management literature of 1987 contains a broad range of viewpoints and recommendations, all of which are ultimately intended to improve the methods libraries use to create and maintain collections. As always, the best publications ask the hardest questions, such as what constitutes fairness in budget allocation, or whether the Conspectus is indeed an "epistemological dead end." As we now hasten to ready ourselves for what will doubtless be a prolonged period of privation for all types of libraries, we must take special care not to become so distracted by the challenge of simply surviving the current budget year that we fail to continue to ask the kinds of difficult questions posed in the literature of 1987. That we can seldom express in fiscal terms the improvements we seek in collection services should in no way deter our pursuit of them.

REFERENCE NOTES

1. William A. Wortman, "Collection Management, 1986," *Library Resources & Technical Services* 31 (Oct.–Dec. 1987): 287–305.

2. G. Edward Evans, *Developing Library and Information Center Collections,* 2d ed. Library Science Text Series (Littleton, Colo.: Libraries Unlimited, 1987).

3. Edwin W. Gleaves, "Carter and Bonk Revisited: A Review of Recent Collection Development Literature," *Collection Management* 9 (spring 1987): 79–85.

4. Rose Mary Magrill and Doralyn J. Hickey, *Acquisitions Management and Collection Development in Libraries* (Chicago: ALA, 1984); Anne Curt, "A propos de PDC," *Bulletin des bibliothèques de France* 31, no. 2 (1986): 154–63.

5. Genevieve Simonot, "Paris-Texas: Analyse de la politique de développement des collections aux Etats-Unis et en France," *Bulletin des bibliothèques de France* 31, no. 2 (1986): 142–45.

6. Carole E. Chamberlin, "The Impact of Institutional Change: Opportunities for Acquisitions," *Library Acquisitions: Practice & Theory* 11, no. 2 (1987): 153–59; Lawrence Thomas, "Tradition and Expertise in Academic Library Collection Development," *College & Research Libraries* 48 (Nov. 1987): 487–93.

7. James A. Cogswell, "The Organization of Collection Management Functions in Academic Research Libraries," *Journal of Academic Librarianship* 13, no. 5 (1987): 268–76.

8. Bonita Bryant, "The Organizational Structure of Collection Development," *Library Resources & Technical Services* 31 (Apr.–June 1987): 111–22.

9. Jeanne Sohn, "Collection Development Organizational Patterns in ARL Libraries," *Library Resources & Technical Services* 31 (Apr.–June 1987): 123–34.

10. Carol W. Cubberley, "Organization for Collection Development in Medium Sized Academic Libraries," *Library Acquisitions: Practice & Theory* 11, no. 4 (1987): 297–323.

11. James E. Bobick, comp., *Collection Development Organization and Staffing in ARL Libraries*, SPEC Kit 131 (Washington, D.C.: Association of Research Libraries, 1987).

12. John Rutledge and Luke Swindler, "The Selection Decision: Defining Criteria and Establishing Priorities," *College & Research Libraries* 48 (Mar. 1987): 123–31.

13. Robert M. Losee, "A Decision Theoretic Model of Materials Selection for Acquisition," *Library Quarterly* 57 (July 1987): 269–83.

14. Maurice B. Line, "Can Book Selection Be Improved?" *British Journal of Academic Librarianship* 1 (summer 1986): 164–65.

15. Kathleen M. Heim, "Social Scientific Information Needs for Numeric Data: The Evolution of the International Data Archive Infrastructure," *Collection Management* 9 (spring 1987): 1–53.

16. S. P. Agrawal, "Information Needs of Social Scientists," *International Library Review* 19 (July 1987): 287–99.

17. Robert N. Broadus, "Information Needs of Humanities Scholars: A Study of Requests Made at the National Humanities Center," *Library & Information Science Research* 9 (Apr.–June 1987): 113–29.

18. William McPheron et al., eds., *English and American Literature: Sources and Strategies for Collection Development*, ACRL Publications in Librarianship, 45 (Chicago: ALA, 1987); Charles W. Brownson, "Contemporary Literature," in McPheron, *English and American Literature*, 102–26; Eric Carpenter, "Collection Development for English and American Literature: An Overview," in McPheron, *English and American Literature*, 1–19; Peter V. Deelde, "Literature and Nonprint Media Resources," in McPheron, *English and American Literature*, 144–55; Richard Heinzkill, "Retrospective Collection Development in English Literature: An Overview," *Collection Management* 9 (spring 1987): 55–65, also in McPheron, *English and American Literature*, 56–81; 107. Stephen Lehmann, "Current Selection: The Role of Serial Bibliographies and Review Media," in McPheron, *English and American Literature*, 40–55; Craig S. Likness and Kathryn A. Soupiset, "Acquisitions," in McPheron, *English and American Literature*, 20–39; Michael T. Ryan, "Special Collections," in McPheron, *English and American Literature*, 181–03; Scott Stebelman, "Building Literary Reference Collections," in McPheron, *English and American Literature*, 156–80.

19. David L. Vidor and Elizabeth Futas, "The Dichotomous Collection," *Library Resources & Technical Services* 31 (July–Sept. 1987): 207–13.

20. Joseph W. Palmer, "An Inquiry into the Availability of Canadian Fiction in U. S. Libraries with Special Attention to the Influence of Reviews," *Library Acquisitions: Practice & Theory* 11, no. 4 (1987): 283–95; Yasuko Makino, "East Asian Art Materials: Toward Solving Problems of Collection Development and Management," *Art Documentation* 6 (fall 1987): 103–5.

21. Catherine Monnin, "Inspired Collection: Selecting and Purchasing Inspirational Materials for Adults and Young Adults in a Public Library," *Ohio Library Association Bulletin* 57 (Apr. 1987): 17–19; Roman Iwaschkin, "Non-provision," *New Library World* 88 (July 1987): 125–26.

22. Robert M. Gorman, "Selecting New Right Materials: A Case Study," *Collection Building* 8, no. 3 (1987): 3–8.

23. Jane C. Heiser, "Libraries, Literacy and Lifelong Learning: The Reference Connection," *The Reference Librarian* 16 (winter 1986): 109–24.

24. Mary Biggs and Victor Biggs, "Reference Collection Development in Academic Libraries: Report of a Survey," *RQ* 27 (fall 1987): 67–79.

25. Jean S. Johnson, "Collection Management for Off-Campus Library Services," *Library Acquisitions: Practice & Theory* 11, no. 1 (1987): 75–84; Glen J. Kelley, "The Development of Acquisitions and Collection Services for Off-Campus Students in Northwest Ontario: An Important Library Collection Development Issue or Merely an Issue of a More Efficient Materials Handling and Delivery System?" *Library Acquisitions: Practice & Theory* 11, no. 1 (1987): 47–66; 180. Martha Whitehead, "Collection Development for Distance Education at the University of British Columbia Library," *Library Acquisitions: Practice & Theory* 11, no. 1 (1987): 67–74.

26. Richard Landon, "Embracing the Flood: Questions About Collecting Twentieth-Century Non-Literary Works," *Rare Books & Manuscripts Librarianship* 2 (fall 1987): 81–93.

27. Samuel Streit, "Acquiring Rare Books by Purchase: Recent Library Trends," *Library Trends* 36 (summer 1987): 189–211; Inalea Weathers, "Special Collections in Public Libraries: Enhancing Community Service," *Wilson Library Bulletin* 61 (May 1987): 23–25.

28. S. Olajire Olanlokun and H. S. Issah, "Collection Development in an African Academic Library During Economic Depression: The University of Lagos Library Experience," *Library Acquisitions: Practice & Theory* 11, no. 2 (1987): 103–12. M. C. Obiagwu, "Foreign Exchange and Library Collections in Nigeria," *Information Development* 3 (July 1987): 154–60.

29. M. H. C. Du Preez, "Purchase Costs and Budget Control," *Mousaion* 5, no. 1 (1987): 66–74.

30. Jeffrey Gatten et al., "Purchasing CD-ROM Products: Considerations for a New Technology," *Library Acquisitions: Practice & Theory* 11, no. 4 (1987): 273–81.

31. Linda Stewart, "Picking CD-ROMs for Public Use," *American Libraries* 18 (Oct. 1987): 738–40.

32. Ruth Webb, "The $5000 Video Collection," *Library Journal* 112 (May 15, 1987): 34–40.

33. Barry Bratton et al., "Selection and Acquisition of Audiovisual Materials by Health Professionals," *Bulletin of the Medical Library Association* 75 (Oct. 1987): 355–61.

34. H. F. Cornelius, "AV in Australian Academic Libraries," *Australian Academic & Research Libraries* 18 (June 1987): 93–102.

35. Barbara Elleman, "Current Trends in Literature for Children," *Library Trends* 35 (winter 1987): 413–26.

36. Patricia F. Beilke and F. J. Sciara, *Selecting Materials for and about Hispanic and East Asian Children and Young People* (Hamden, Conn.: Library Professional Publications, 1986).

37. Claudia Berni, Elisabetta Forte, and Barbara Mussetto, "Il servizio bibliotecario scolastico: Caratteristiche e politica degli acquisti," *Bollettino d'informazioni* 26 (July 1986): 307–9.

38. Betty Kemp, ed., *School Library and Media Center Acquisitions Policies and Procedures,* 2d ed. (Phoenix: Oryx, 1986).

39. Lucy Shelton Caswell, "Grief and Collection Development," *Library Acquisitions: Practice & Theory* 11, no. 3 (1987): 195–99.

40. Edward P. Miller, "International Library Exchanges," *Library Acquisitions: Practice & Theory* 11, no. 1 (1987): 85–90.

41. Roswitha Poll, "Zur Praxis von Tausch und Kauftausch: die verschwiegenen Wege der Literaturerwerbung," in Yorck A. Haase and Alexandra Habermann, eds., *Zur Internationalität wissenschaftlicher Bibliotheken/76. Deutscher Bibliothekartag in Oldenberg 1986.* Zeitschrift für Bibliothekswesen und Bibliographie Sonderheft, 44 (Frankfurt am Main: Klostermann, 1987), 116–34.

42. Joachim-Felix Leonhard, "Der Schriftentausch der Deutschen Forschungsgemeinschaft: Erwerbung Grauer and spezieller Literatur als zentrale Aufgabe üt überregionaler Literaturversorgurg," in Haase and Habermann, eds., *Zur Internationalität wissenschaftlicher Bibliotheken/76,* 135–45.

43. Elizabeth Futas and David L. Vidor, "What Constitutes a 'Good' Collection?" *Library Journal* 112 (Apr. 15, 1987): 45–74.

44. Quentin L. Burrell, "A Third Note on Aging in a Library Circulation Model: Applications to Future Use and Relegation," *Journal of Documentation* 43 (Mar. 1987): 24–45; J. P. Warwick, "Duplication of Texts in Academic Libraries: A Behavioural Model for Library Management," *Journal of Librarianship* 19 (Jan. 1987): 41–52.

45. Maxine K. Rochester, "The ABN Database: Sampling Strategies for Collection Overlap Studies," *Information Technology and Libraries* 6 (Sept. 1987): 190–96.

46. Elliot Palais, "Use of Course Analysis in Compiling a Collection Development Policy Statement for a University Library," *Journal of Academic Librarianship* 13 (Mar. 1987): 8–13.

47. Michael R. Gabriel, "Online Collection Evaluation, Course by Course," *Collection Building* 8, no. 2 (1987): 20–24.

48. JoAnn Bell et al., "Faculty Input in Book Selection: A Comparison of Alternative Methods," *Bulletin of the Medical Library Association* 75 (July 1987): 228–33.

49. Joe A. Hewitt and John S. Shipman, "Cooperative Collection Development among Research Libraries in the Age of Networking: Report of a Survey of ARL Libraries," *Advances in Library Automation and Networking* 1 (1987): 189–232.

50. Joseph J. Branin, "Issues in Cooperative Collection Development: The Promise and Frustration of Resource Sharing," in June L. Engle and Sue O. Medina, eds., *Issues in Cooperative Collection Development: Papers Presented at the SOLINET Resource Sharing and Networks Support Program, March 11, 1986* (Atlanta, Ga.: Southeastern Library Network., 1986), 1–38.

51. Sue O. Medina, "Cooperative Collection Management on a Statewide Basis," in Engle and Medina, eds., *Issues in Cooperative Collection Development*, 67–79; Sue O. Medina, "Network of Alabama Academic Libraries: An Emerging State Network," *The Southeastern Librarian* 37 (summer 1987): 41–45.

52. Lee Pike, "Cooperative Collection Development Program in a Multitype Library Environment," in Engle and Medina, eds., *Issues in Cooperative Collection Development*, 55–66.

53. S. R. Korale, "Resource-Sharing: The HELLIS Experience in Sri Lanka," *Information Development* 3 (Oct. 1987): 214–19.

54. Benjamin Amon and Marcel Lajeunesse, "Les bibliothèques universitaires en Afrique de L'Ouest francophone: problèmes et perspectives," *Libri* 37 (June 1987): 109–25; Charles B. M. Lungu, "Resource-Sharing and Self-Reliance in Southern Africa," *Information Development* 3 (April 1987): 82–86.

55. Paul Kaegbein, "National Collection Building in the Federal Republic of Germany," *Journal of Academic Librarianship* 13 (May 1987): 81–85.

56. Wolfgang Kehr, "Facts and Trends in Academic and Research Libraries (FRG)," *Libri* 37 (June 1987): 90–93.

57. Eva Tornier, "Gezielter Bestandaufbau und Kontinuierliche Bestandsüberwachung in den Bibliotheken der DDR," *Der Bibliothekar* 40 (Sept. 1986): 388–93.

58. Peter Allison, "Stalking the Elusive Grey Literature," *College & Research Libraries News* 48 (May 1987): 244–46.

59. Christine Hasemann, "Graue Literatur: Beispiele für Kooperation," *Zeitschrift für Bibliothekswesen and Bibliographie* 33 (Nov./Dec. 1986): 417–27.

60. Association of Research Libraries, *NCIP: Means to an End*, minutes of the 109th Meeting, Oct. 22–23, 1986 (Washington, D.C.: The Association, 1987).

61. David H. Stam, "Development and Use of the RLG Conspectus," in Association of Research Libraries, *NCIP*, 7–10.

62. Robert C. Miller, "NCIP in the United States," in Association of Research Libraries, *NCIP*, 11–13.

63. Marianne Scott, "NCIP in Canada," in Association of Research Libraries, *NCIP*, 14–18; Marianne Scott, "The National Plan for Collections Inventories," *Canadian Library Journal* 44 (Oct. 1987): 289–90.

64. Anthony W. Ferguson, Joan Grant, and Joel Rutstein, "Internal Uses of the RLG Conspectus," in Association of Research Libraries, *NCIP*, 21–25; reprinted in *Journal of Library Administration* 8 (summer 1987): 35–40.

65. Millicent D. Abel, "The Conspectus: Issues and Questions," in Association of Research Libraries, *NCIP*, 26–30.

66. Jeffrey Horrell, "The RLG Conspectus and the NCIP Project: A Means to a Beginning," *Art Documentation* 6 (fall 1987): 106–7.

67. Stephen Hanger, "Collection Development in the British Library: The Role of the RLG Conspectus," *Journal of Librarianship* 19 (Apr. 1987): 104.

68. Ann Matheson, "The Planning and Implementation of Conspectus in Scotland," *Journal of Librarianship* 19 (July 1987): 141–51.

69. David Henige, "Epistemological Dead End and Ergonomic Disaster? The North American Collections Inventory Project," *Journal of Academic Librarianship* 13 (Sept. 1987): 209–13.

70. Hendrick Edelman and Karen Muller, "A New Look at the Library Market," *Publishers Weekly* 231 (May 29, 1987): 30–35; reprinted in *Show-Me Libraries* 38 (Sept. 1987): 15–23.

71. Corrie Marsh, "'Déja Vu All Over Again?' Book Marketing and Selection Update: A Forum for Librarians, Publishers and Wholesalers," *Library Acquisitions: Practice & Theory* 11, no. 4 (1987): 347–55.

72. Lenore Clark, "Materials Costs and Collection Development in Academic Libraries," in Sul H. Lee, ed., *Pricing and Costs of Monographs and Serials: National and International Issues*, Journal of Library Administration Monographic Supplement, 1 (New York and London: Haworth, 1987), 97–109.

73. Ulrich Montag, "Erwerbungsarbeit und internationaler Buchmarkt," *Zeitschrift für Bibliothekswesen und Bibliographie* 33, no. 6 (1986): 428–46.

74. Rebecca R. Martin, "Special Collections: Strategies for Support in an Era of Limited Resources," *College & Research Libraries* 48 (May 1987): 241–46.

75. Jasper G. Schad, "Fairness in Book Fund Allocation," *Collection & Research Libraries* 48 (Nov. 1987): 479–86.

76. G. G. Allen and Lee Ching Tat, "The Development of an Objective Budget Allocation Procedure for Academic Library Acquisitions," *Libri* 37 (Sept 1987): 211–21; Larraine M. Lane, "The Relationship between Loans and In-House Use of Books in Determining a Use-Factor for Budget Allocation," *Library Acquisitions: Practice & Theory* 11, no. 2 (1987): 95–102.

77. Kent Hendrickson, "Pricing from Three Perspectives: The Publisher, the Wholesaler, the Library," in Lee, *Pricing and Costs of Monographs and Serials,* 1–12.

78. Leonard Schrift,, "Truth in Vending," in Lee, *Pricing and Costs of Monographs and Serials,* 27–35; George W. Bauer, "Mountains and Molehills: How University Presses Determine Book Prices and How Those Prices Relate to Library Budgets," in Lee, *Pricing and Costs of Monographs and Serials,* 47–52; Dana Alessi, "Books across the Waters: An Examination of United Kingdom Monographic Pricing," in Lee, *Pricing and Costs of Monographs and Serials,* 37–46.

79. Rolf Griebel, "Preisindizes und Haushaltsplanung," in Haase and Habermann, *Zur Internationalität wissenschaftlicher Bibliotheken,* 99–115.

80. Denis Pallier, "Le coût de la documentation: Politiques d'acquisition et allocations de crédits; essai de comparaison internationale," *Bulletin des bibliothèques de France* 31, no. 5 (1986): 486–92.

81. John Fletcher, "Inflation Indexes for Academic Library Purchases," *Library Association Record* 89 (Aug. 1987): 400–1.

82. Christian M. Boissonnas, "Differential Pricing of Monographs and Serials," in Lee, *Pricing and Costs of Monographs and Serials,* 67–78.

83. Hermann Josef Dörpinghaus, "Gespaltene Preise bei ausländischen Verlagen am Beispiel der Preis- and Vertriebspolitik von Yale University Press und Masson," *Zeitschrift für Bibliothekswesen and Bibliographie* 33 (July/Aug. 1986): 237–46.

84. J. Periam Danton, "University Library Book Budgets, 1860, 1910, and 1960," *Library Quarterly* 57 (July 1987): 284–302.

85. Karen A. Schmidt, "The Acquisitions Process in Research Libraries: A Survey of ARL Libraries' Acquisitions Departments," *Library Acquisitions: Practice & Theory* 11, no. 1 (1987): 35–44.

86. Christian M. Boissonnas, "The Cost Is More Than That Elegant Dinner: Your Ethics Are at Steak," *Library Acquisitions: Practice & Theory* 11, no. 2 (1987): 145–52; Scott R. Bullard, "The Ethics of Working with Vendors: A Report on the RTSD RS Acquisitions Librarians/ Vendors of Library Materials Discussion Group," *Library Acquisitions: Practice & Theory* 11, no. 4 (1987): 373–75; Wanda V. Dole, "Librarians, Publishers, and Vendors: Looking for Mr. Goodbuy," *Library Acquisitions: Practice & Theory* 11, no. 2 (1987): 125–34; Edward J. Lochman, "Is the Customer Always Right; or, Wait a Minute, Don't You Want My Business? (Publishing Policies and Their Impact on Markets)," *Library Acquisitions: Practice & Theory* 11, no. 2 (1987): 121–24; Sally W. Somers, "Vendor/Library Relations: A Perspective," *Library Acquisitions: Practice & Theory* 11, no. 2 (1987): 135–38.

87. Ruth H. Miller and Martha W. Niemeier, "Vendor Performance: A Study of Two Libraries," *Library Resources & Technical Services* 31 (Jan.–Mar. 1987): 60–68.

88. Corrie Marsh, "The Business of Library Acquisitions: A Consumer Action Model," *Library Acquisitions: Practice & Theory* 11, no. 2 (1987): 161–63.

89. Gary J. Rossi, "Library Approval Plans: A Selected Annotated Bibliography," *Library Acquisitions: Practice & Theory* 11, no. 1 (1987): 3–34.

90. Jennifer Cargill, "The Approval Connection: Pricing the Ordering Alternatives," in Lee, *Pricing and Costs of Monographs and Serials,* 13–25; Siegfried Feller, "Die amerikanische Erwerbungspraxis: Approval Plans," in Haase and Habermann, *Zur Internationalität wissenschaftlicher Bibliotheken,* 146–54.

91. Jane Maddox, "Are the Gods Listening?" *Library Acquisitions: Practice & Theory* 11, no. 3/4 (1987): 209–13.

92. Scott A. Smith, "Linking Approval Plans and Automated Library Acquisitions Systems," *Library Acquisitions: Practice & Theory* 11, no. 3 (1987): 215–16; Nancy J. Gibbs, "LC MARC Approval Tapes at Auburn University," *Library Acquisitions: Practice & Theory* 11, no. 3 (1987): 217–19.

93. Thomas E. Nisonger, "Cost Analysis of the LIBRIS II Automated Acquisitions System at the University of Texas at Dallas Library," *Library Acquisitions: Practice & Theory* 11, no. 3 (1987): 229–38.

94. Zahiruddin Khurshid, "DOBIS/LIBIS Acquisitions Subsystem in Operation at King Fahd University of Petroleum and Minerals," *Library Acquisitions: Practice & Theory* 11, no. 4 (1987): 325–34.

95. Katherine Blauer, "BISAC Implementation at OCLC," *Library Acquisitions: Practice & Theory* 11, no. 4 (1987): 363–66; Scott R. Bullard, "Standards for Automated Acquisitions Systems: BISAC and SISAC Considerations," *Library Acquisitions: Practice & Theory* 11, no. 4 (1987): 357–58; Amy Miller, "Vendor's View of Library Automation Standards," *Library Acquisitions: Practice & Theory* 11, no. 4 (1987): 359–61; Sally W. Somers, "Standards! Standards! Standards! Experiences with Standards at the University of Georgia Libraries," *Library Acquisitions: Practice & Theory* 11, no. 4 (1987): 367–72.

96. Helen M. Shuster, "A Versatile dBase III+ Acquisitions Program at Worcester Polytechnic Institute," *Library Acquisitions: Practice & Theory* 11, no. 3 (1987): 241–53; David J. Nuzzo, "A Reasonable Approach to Out-of-Print Procurement Using dBase II or dBase III." *Library Acquisitions: Practice & Theory* 11, no. 2 (1987): 165–80.

BIBLIOGRAPHY

Abel, Millicent D. "The Conspectus: Issues and Questions." In Association of Research Libraries, *NCIP,* 26–30.

Agrawal, S. P. "Information Needs of Social Scientists." *International Library Review* 19 (July 1987): 287–99.

Agyei-Gyane, L. "The Development and Administration of the Africana Collection in the Balme Library, University of Ghana, Legon." *Libri* 37 (Sept. 1987): 222–38.

Alessi, Dana. "Books across the Waters: An Examination of United Kingdom Monographic Pricing." In Lee, *Pricing and Costs of Monographs and Serials,* 37–46.

Allen, G. G., and Lee Ching Tat. "The Development of an Objective Budget Allocation Procedure for Academic Library Acquisitions." *Libri* 37 (Sept. 1987): 211–21.

Allison, Peter. "Stalking the Elusive Grey Literature." *College & Research Libraries News* 48 (May 1987): 244–46.

Alt, Martha S. and Richard D. Shiels. "Assessment of Library Materials on the History of Christianity at Ohio State University: An Update." *Collection Management* 9 (spring 1987): 67–77.

Amon, Benjamin and Marcel Lajeunesse. "Les bibliothèques universitaires en Afrique de L'Ouest francophone: problèmes et perspectives." *Libri* 37 (June 1987): 109–25.

Association of College and Research Libraries, Audiovisual Committee, "Guidelines for Audiovisual Services in Academic Libraries." *College & Research Libraries News* 48 (Oct. 1987): 533–36.

Association of Research Libraries. *NCIP: Means to an End.* Minutes of the 109th Meeting, Oct. 22–23, 1986. Washington, D.C.: The Association, 1987.

Bastiampillai, Marie Angela, and Peter Harvard-Williams. "Subject Specialization Re-Examined." *Libri* 37 (Sept. 1987): 196–210.

Bauer, George W. "Mountains and Molehills: How University Presses Determine Book Prices and How Those Prices Relate to Library Budgets." In Lee, *Pricing and Costs of Monographs and Serials,* 47–52.

Beilke, Patricia F., and F. J. Sciara. *Selecting Materials for and about Hispanic and East Asian Children and Young People.* Hamden, Conn.: Library Professional Publications, 1986.

Bell, JoAnn, et al. "Faculty Input in Book Selection: A Comparison of Alternative Methods." *Bulletin of the Medical Library Association* 75 (July 1987): 228–33.

Berni, Claudia, Elisabetta Forte, and Barbara Mussetto. "Il servizio bibliotecario scolastico: Caratteristiche e politica degli acquisti." *Bollettino d'informazioni* 26 (July 1986): 307–9 .

Biggs, Mary, and Victor Biggs. "Reference Collection Development in Academic Libraries: Report of a Survey." *RQ* 27 (fall 1987): 67–79.

Blauer, Katherine. "BISAC Implementation at OCLC." *Library Acquisitions: Practice & Theory* 11, no. 4 (1987): 363–66.

Bobick, James E., comp. *Collection Development Organization and Staffing in ARL Libraries.* SPEC Kit 131. Washington, D.C.: Association of Research Libraries, 1987.

Boissonnas, Christian M. "The Cost Is More Than That Elegant Dinner: Your Ethics Are at Steak." *Library Acquisitions: Practice & Theory* 11, no. 2 (1987): 145–52.

_____. "Differential Pricing of Monographs and Serials." In Lee, *Pricing and Costs of Monographs and Serials,* 67–78.

Branin, Joseph J. "Issues in Cooperative Collection Development: The Promise and Frustration of Resource Sharing." In Engle, *Issues in Cooperative Collection Development,* 1–38.

Bratton, Barry, et al. "Selection and Acquisition of Audiovisual Materials by Health Professionals." *Bulletin of the Medical Library Association* 75 (Oct. 1987): 355–61.

Broadus, Robert N. "Information Needs of Humanities Scholars: A Study of Requests Made at the National Humanities Center." *Library & Information Science Research* 9 (Apr.–June 1987): 113–29.

Broderick, J. C. "The Cost of a Bad Book." *Scholarly Publishing* 18 (Jan. 1987): 83–88.

Brown, Charlotte. "Deaccessioning for the Greater Good." *Wilson Library Bulletin* 61 (Apr. 1987): 22–24.

Brownson, Charles W. "Contemporary Literature." In McPheron, *English and American Literature,* 102–26.

Bryant, Bonita. "The Organizational Structure of Collection Development." *Library Resources & Technical Services* 31 (Apr.–June 1987): 111–22.

Bullard, Scott R. "The Ethics of Working with Vendors: A Report on the RTSD RS Acquisitions Librarians/Vendors of Library Materials Discussion Group." *Library Acquisitions: Practice & Theory* 11, no. 4 (1987): 373–75.

_____. "Highlights of the Collection Management/Selection for Public Libraries Discussion Group." *Library Acquisitions: Practice & Theory* 11, no. 3 (1987): 221–22.

_____. "Highlights of the Publisher/Vendor/Library Relations Committee Meeting." *Library Acquisitions: Practice & Theory* 11, no. 3 (1987): 227–28.

_____. "Standards for Automated Acquisitions Systems: BISAC and SISAC Considerations." *Library Acquisitions: Practice & Theory* 11, no. 4 (1987): 357–58.

Burrell, Quentin L. "A Third Note on Aging in a Library Circulation Model: Applications to Future Use and Relegation." *Journal of Documentation* 43 (Mar. 1987): 24–45.

Caldiero, Wendy A. "The Selection and Use of Children's Audiovisual Materials in Public Libraries." *Catholic Library World* 57 (Mar./Apr. 1986): 212–15.

Campbell, Douglas G. and Barbara J. Fahey. "The Browsing Collection: A Lab for Library Science

Students." *Journal of Education for Library and Information Science* 27 (spring 1987): 298–301.

Carbonne, Pierre. "Coûts de gestion et tableau de bord." *Bulletin des bibliothèques de France* 31, no. 5 (1986): 476–79.

Cargill, Jennifer. "The Approval Connection: Pricing the Ordering Alternatives." In Lee, *Pricing and Costs of Monographs and Serials,* 13–25.

_____. "Bottom Line Blues: Preparing Library Budgets." *Wilson Library Bulletin* 61 (June 1987): 31–33.

Carpenter, Eric. "Collection Development for English and American Literature: An Overview." In McPheron, *English and American Literature,* 1–19.

Caswell, Lucy Shelton. "Grief and Collection Development." *Library Acquisitions: Practice & Theory* 11, no. 3 (1987): 195–99.

Chamberlin, Carole E. "Fiscal Planning in Academic Libraries: The Role of the Automated Acquisitions System." *Advances in Library Administration and Organization* 6 (1986): 141–52.

_____. "The Impact of Institutional Change: Opportunities for Acquisitions." *Library Acquisitions: Practice & Theory* 11, no. 2 (1987): 153–59.

Clark, Lenore. "Materials Costs and Collection Development in Academic Libraries." In Lee, *Pricing and Costs of Monographs and Serials,* 97–109.

Clark, Mae M., and Leona Wise. "RTSD/RS Gifts and Exchange Discussion Group." *Library Acquisitions: Practice & Theory* 11, no. 3 (1987): 205–6.

Cogswell, James A. "The Organization of Collection Management Functions in Academic Research Libraries." *Journal of Academic Librarianship* 13, no. 5 (1987): 268–76.

Cornelius, H. F. "AV in Australian Academic Libraries." *Australian Academic & Research Libraries* 18 (June 1987): 93–102.

Cubberley, Carol W. "Organization for Collection Development in Medium Sized Academic Libraries." *Library Acquisitions: Practice & Theory* 11, no. 4 (1987): 297–323.

Curt, Anne. "A propos de PDC." *Bulletin des bibliothèques de France* 31, no. 2 (1986): 154–63.

Curtis, Robert. "Classical Music on CD's: Creating and Controlling the Collection." *Collection Building* 8, no. 3 (1987): 12–16.

Daly, Sister Sally. "Happiness Is Good Selection Techniques." *Catholic Library World* 58: (Mar./Apr. 1987) 226–28, 31.

Danton, J. Periam. "University Library Book Budgets, 1860, 1910, and 1960." *Library Quarterly* 57 (July 1987): 284–302.

Daum, Patricia B. "Recession: A Challenge for Special Librarians." *Canadian Library Journal* 6 (Oct. 1987): 299–302.

Deelde, Peter V. "Literature and Nonprint Media Resources." In McPheron, *English and American Literature,* 144–55.

Dole, Wanda V. "Librarians, Publishers, and Vendors: Looking for Mr. Goodbuy." *Library Acquisitions: Practice & Theory* 11, no. 2 (1987): 125–34.

Dörpinghaus, Hermann Josef. "Gespaltene Preise bei ausländischen Verlagen am Beispiel der Preis- and Vertriebspolitik von Yale University Press und Masson." *Zeitschrift für Bibliothekswesen and Bibliographie* 33 (July/Aug. 1986): 237–46.

Dorst, Tom. "Statewide Cooperative Collection Development Project." *Illinois Libraries* 69 (Jan. 1987): 17–18.

Dubois, Henry J. "No Room at the Inn: Media Collections and University Libraries." *College & Research Libraries News* 48 (Oct. 1987): 530–32.

Du Preez, M. H. C. "Purchase Costs and Budget Control." *Mousaion* 5, no. 1 (1987): 66–74.

Edelman, Hendrick, and Karen Muller. "A New Look at the Library Market." *Publishers Weekly* 231 (May 29 1987): 30–35. Reprinted in *Show-Me Libraries* 38 (Sept. 1987): 15–23.

Elleman, Barbara. "Current Trends in Literature for Children." *Library Trends* 35 (winter 1987): 413–26.

Elstein, Rochelle S. "Mapping the Landscape: Analysis and Evaluation of Art Libraries' Collections." *Art Documentation* 6 (summer 1987): 66–67.

Engle, June L., and Sue O. Medina, eds. *Issues in Cooperative Collection Development: Papers Presented at the SOLINET Resource Sharing and Networks Support Program, March 11, 1986.* Atlanta, Ga.: Southeastern Library Network, 1986.

Evans, G. Edward. *Developing Library and Information Center Collections.* 2d ed. Library Science Text Series. Littleton, Colo.: Libraries Unlimited, 1987.

Feller, Siegfried. "Die amerikanische Erwerbungspraxis: Approval Plans." In Haase and Habermann, *Zur Internationalitat wissenschaftlicher Bibliotheken,* 146–54.

Ferguson, Anthony W., Joan Grant, and Joel Rutstein. "Internal Uses of the RLG Conspectus." In Association of Research Libraries, *NCIP,* 21–25. Reprinted in *Journal of Library Administration* 8 (summer 1987): 35–40.

Fletcher, John. "Inflation Indexes for Academic Library Purchases." *Library Association Record* 89 (Aug. 1987): 400–401.

Fouts, Judi. "Report on the Business of Acquisitions Regional Institute." *Library Acquisitions: Practice & Theory* 11, no. 3 (1987): 255–66.

Futas, Elizabeth and David L. Vidor. "What Constitutes a 'Good' Collection?" *Library Journal* 112 (Apr. 15, 1987): 45–74.

Gabriel, Michael R. "Online Collection Evaluation, Course by Course." *Collection Building* 8, no. 2 (1987): 20–24.

Gatten, Jeffrey, et al. "Purchasing CD-ROM Products: Considerations for a New Technology." *Library Acquisitions: Practice & Theory* 11, no. 4 (1987): 273–81.

Gibbs, Nancy J. "LC MARC Approval Tapes at Auburn University. " *Library Acquisitions: Practice & Theory* 11, no. 3 (1987): 217–19.

Gleaves, Edwin W. "Carter and Bonk Revisited: A Review of Recent Collection Development Literature." *Collection Management* 9 (spring 1987): 79–85.

Gorman, Robert M. "Selecting New Right Materials: A Case Study." *Collection Building* 8, no. 3 (1987): 3–8.

Griebel, Rolf. "Etatsituation der wissenschaftlichen Bibliotheken 1987." *Zeitschrift für Bibliothekswesen and Bibliographie* 34 (July/Aug. 1987): 276–82.

———. "Preisindizes and Haushaltsplanung." In Haase and Habermann, *Zur Internationalität wissenschaftlicher Bibliotheken,* 99–115.

Haase, Yorck A., and Alexandra Habermann, eds. *Zur Internationalität wissenschaftlicher Bibliotheken/76. Deutscher Bibliothekartag in Oldenberg 1986.* Zeitschrift für Bibliothekswesen and Bibliographie Sonderheft, 44. Frankfurt am Main: Klostermann, 1987.

Hamaker, Charles. "Caveat Emptor: Foreign Imprints in the U.S. Marketplace—Tips for New Selectors." *RTSD Newsletter* 12 (fall 1987): 48–49.

Han, Jean C. "The Exchange Program with the People's Republic of China at the East Asiatic Library, University of California at Berkeley." *Library Acquisitions: Practice & Theory* 11, no. 4 (1987): 341–45.

Hanger, Stephen. "Collection Development in the British Library: The Role of the RLG Conspectus." *Journal of Librarianship* 19 (Apr. 1987): 89–107.

Hasemann, Christine. "Graue Literatur: Beispiele für Kooperation." *Zeitschrift für Bibliothekswesen and Bibliographie* 33 (Nov./Dec. 1986): 417–27.

Hayden, Ron. "If It Circulates, Keep It." *Library Journal* 112 (June 1, 1987): 80–82.

Heim, Kathleen M. "Social Scientific Information Needs for Numeric Data: The Evolution of the International Data Archive Infrastructure." *Collection Management* 9 (spring 1987): 1–53.

Heinzkill, Richard. "Retrospective Collection Development in English Literature: An Overview." *Collection Management* 9 (spring 1987): 55–65. Also in McPheron, *English and American Literature,* 56–81.

Heiser, Jane C. "Libraries, Literacy and Lifelong Learning: The Reference Connection." *The Reference Librarian* 16 (winter 1986): 109–24.

Hendrickson, Kent. "Pricing from Three Perspectives: The Publisher, the Wholesaler, the Library." In Lee, *Pricing and Costs of Monographs and Serials,* 1–12.

Henige, David. "Epistemological Dead End and Ergonomic Disaster? The North American Collections Inventory Project." *Journal of Academic Librarianship* 13 (Sept. 1987): 209–13.

Hewitt, Joe A. "Education for Acquisitions and Serials Librarianship: The Students' View." *Library Acquisitions: Practice & Theory* 11, no. 3 (1987): 185–94.

Hewitt, Joe A., and Shipman, John S. "Cooperative Collection Development among Research Libraries in the Age of Networking: Report of a Survey of ARL Libraries." *Advances in Library Automation and Networking* 1 (1987): 189–232.

Hicken, Mandy. "Stack Management." In Ray Prytherch, ed. *Handbook of Library Training Practice.* Aldershot: Gower, 1986, 341–82.

Holter, Charlotte. "Selecting Books for Young Adults: A Considerable Responsibility." *Catholic Library World* 57 (Jan./Feb. 1986): 170–71.

Horrell, Jeffrey. "The RLG Conspectus and the NCIP Project: A Means to a Beginning." *Art Documentation* 6 (fall 1987): 106–7.

Iwaschkin, Roman. "Non-provision." *New Library World* 88 (July 1987): 125–26.

Johnson, Jean S. "Collection Management for Off-Campus Library Services." *Library Acquisitions: Practice & Theory* 11, no. 1 (1987): 75–84.

Johnson, R. D. "The College Library Collection." *Advances in Librarianship* 14 (1986): 143–74.

Josslin, Daniel, and Patricia A. Tarin. "Sources of Spanish-Language Books." *Library Journal* 112 (July 1987): 28–31.

Kaegbein, Paul. "National Collection Building in the Federal Republic of Germany." *Journal of Academic Librarianship* 13 (May 1987): 81–85.

Kehr, Wolfgang. "Facts and Trends in Academic and Research Libraries (FRG)." *Libri* 37 (June 1987): 85–108.

Kelley, Glen J. "The Development of Acquisitions and Collection Services for Off-Campus Students in Northwest Ontario: An Important Library Collection Development Issue or Merely an Issue of a More Efficient Materials Handling and Delivery System?" *Library Acquisitions: Practice & Theory* 11, no. 1 (1987): 47–66.

Kemp, Betty, ed. *School Library and Media Center Acquisitions Policies and Procedures.* 2d ed. Phoenix: Oryx, 1986.

Khurshid, Zahiruddin. "DOBIS/LIBIS Acquisitions Subsystem in Operation at King Fahd University of Petroleum and Minerals." *Library Acquisitions: Practice & Theory* 11, no. 4 (1987): 325–34.

Korale, S. R. "Resource-Sharing: The HELLIS Experience in Sri Lanka." *Information Development* 3 (Oct. 1987): 214–19.

Kreyche, Michael. "Use of Approval Plans with Automated Acquisitions: The RTSD RS Automated Acquisitions/In-Process Control Systems Discussion Group." *Library Acquisitions: Practice & Theory* 11, no. 3 (1987): 207–8.

Krzys, Richard. "Collection Development Courses." In John F. Harvey and Frances Laverne Carroll, eds. *Internationalizing Library and Information Science Education* New York: Greenwood, 1987, 201–14.

Landon, Richard. "Embracing the Flood: Questions About Collecting Twentieth-Century Non-Literary Works." *Rare Books & Manuscripts Librarianship* 2 (fall 1987): 81–93.

Lane, Larraine M. "The Relationship between Loans and In-House Use of Books in Determining a Use-Factor for Budget Allocation." *Library Acquisitions: Practice & Theory* 11, no. 2 (1987): 95–102.

Laughrey, Edna. "Acquisitions Costs: How the Selection of a Purchasing Source Affects the Cost of Processing Materials." In Lee, *Pricing and Costs of Monographs and Serials,* 53–65.

Lee, Sul H., ed. *Pricing and Costs of Monographs and Serials: National and International Issues.* Journal of Library Administration Monographic Supplement, 1. New York: Haworth, 1987.

Lehmann, Stephen. "Current Selection: The Role of Serial Bibliographies and Review Media." In McPheron, *English and American Literature,* 40–55.

Leonhard, Joachim-Felix. "Der Schriftentausch der Deutschen Forschungsgemeinschaft: Erwerbung Grauer and spezieller Literatur als zentrale Aufgabe üt überregionaler Literaturversorgurg." In Haase and Habermann, *Zur Internationalität wissenschaftlicher Bibliotheken*, 135–45.

Likness, Craig S. and Kathryn A. Soupiset. "Acquisitions." In McPheron, *English and American Literature*, 20–39.

Line, Maurice B. "Can Book Selection Be Improved?" *British Journal of Academic Librarianship* 1 (summer 1986): 160–66.

_____. "The Total National Resource: Reflections on Document Provision and Supply in New Zealand." *New Zealand Libraries* 45 (Sept. 1986): 45–49.

Lochman, Edward J. "Is the Customer Always Right; or, Wait a Minute, Don't You Want My Business? (Publishing Policies and Their Impact on Markets)." *Library Acquisitions: Practice & Theory* 11, no. 2 (1987): 121–24.

Losee, Robert M. "A Decision Theoretic Model of Materials Selection for Acquisition." *Library Quarterly* 57 (July 1987): 269–83.

Lungu, Charles B. M. "Resource-Sharing and Self-Reliance in Southern Africa." *Information Development* 3 (Apr. 1987): 82–86.

Maddox, Jane. "Are the Gods Listening?" *Library Acquisitions: Practice & Theory* 11, no. 34 (1987): 209–13.

Makino, Yasuko. "East Asian Art Materials: Toward Solving Problems of Collection Development and Management." *Art Documentation* 6 (fall 1987): 103–5.

Marsh, Corrie. "The Business of Library Acquisitions: A Consumer Action Model." *Library Acquisitions: Practice & Theory* 11, no. 2 (1987): 161–63.

_____. "'Déja Vu All Over Again?' Book Marketing and Selection Update: A Forum for Librarians, Publishers and Wholesalers." *Library Acquisitions: Practice & Theory* 11, no. 4 (1987): 347–55.

Martin, Rebecca R. "Special Collections: Strategies for Support in an Era of Limited Resources." *College & Research Libraries* 48 (May 1987): 241–46.

Mastejulia, Robert. "Publisher Policies and Their Impact on the Market." *Library Acquisitions: Practice & Theory* 11, no. 2 (1987): 139–44.

Matheson, Ann. "The Planning and Implementation of Conspectus in Scotland." *Journal of Librarianship* 19 (July 1987): 141–51.

McKinin, Emma Jean. "A CATLINE SDI for the Reference Department: Collection Development and Current Awareness Tool." *Bulletin of the Medical Library Association* 75: (Oct. 1987) 362–65.

McPheron, William, et al., eds. *English and American Literature: Sources and Strategies for Collection Development*. ACRL Publications in Librarianship, 45. Chicago: ALA, 1987.

Medina, Sue O. "Cooperative Collection Management on a Statewide Basis." In Engle, *Issues in Cooperative Collection Development*, 67–79.

_____. "Network of Alabama Academic Libraries: An Emerging State Network." *The Southeastern Librarian* 37 (summer 1987): 41–45.

Miller, Amy. "Vendor's View of Library Automation Standards." *Library Acquisitions: Practice & Theory* 11, no. 4 (1987): 359–61.

Miller, Edward P. "International Library Exchanges." *Library Acquisitions: Practice & Theory* 11, no. 1 (1987): 85–90.

Miller, Robert C. "NCIP in the United States." In Association of Research Libraries, *NCIP*, 11–13.

Miller, Ruth H. and Martha W. Niemeier. "Vendor Performance: A Study of Two Libraries." *Library Resources & Technical Services* 31 (Jan.–Mar. 1987): 60–68.

Monnin, Catherine. "Inspired Collection: Selecting and Purchasing Inspirational Materials for Adults and Young Adults in a Public Library." *Ohio Library Association Bulletin* 57 (Apr. 1987): 17–19.

Montag, Ulrich. "Erwerbungsarbeit und internationaler Buchmarkt." *Zeitschrift für Bibliothekswesen und Bibliographie* 33, no. 6 (1986): 428–46.

Moody, Marilyn. "Social Security Administration Publications." *Collection Building* 8, no. 2 (1987): 46–50.

Morton, Bruce. "The Depository Library System: A Costly Anachronism." *Library Journal* 112 (Sept. 15, 1987): 52–54.

Natoli, Joseph. "Textual Studies and the Selection of Editions." In McPheron, *English and American Literature*, 127–43.

Naylor, Richard J. "The Efficient Mid-Size Library: Comparing Book Budget to Population to Collection Size." *Library Journal* 112 (Feb. 15, 1987): 119–20.

Neary, Sharon. "International Library Development: Grassroots Project Works." *Canadian Library Journal* 44 (Oct. 1987): 281–86.

Nisonger, Thomas E. "Cost Analysis of the LIBRIS II Automated Acquisitions System at the University of Texas at Dallas Library." *Library Acquisitions: Practice & Theory* 11, no. 3 (1987): 229–38.

Nuzzo, David J. "A Reasonable Approach to Out-of-Print Procurement Using dBase II or dBase III." *Library Acquisitions: Practice & Theory* 11, no. 2 (1987): 165–80.

O'Connor, Thomas F. "Collection Development in the Yale University Library 1865-1931." *The Journal of Library History* 22 (spring 1987): 164–89.

Obiagwu, M. C. "Foreign Exchange and Library Collections in Nigeria." *Information Development* 3 (July 1987): 154–60.

Olanlokun, S. Olajire, and H. S. Issah. "Collection Development in an African Academic Library During Economic Depression: The University of Lagos Library Experience." *Library Acquisitions: Practice & Theory* 11, no. 2 (1987): 103–12.

Palais, Elliot. "Use of Course Analysis in Compiling a Collection Development Policy Statement for a University Library." *Journal of Academic Librarianship* 13 (Mar. 1987): 8–13.

Pallier, Denis. "Le coût de la documentation: Politiques d'acquisition et allocations de crédits; essai de comparaison internationale." *Bulletin des bibliothèques de France* 31, no. 5 (1986): 486–92.

Palmer, Joseph W. "An Inquiry into the Availability of Canadian Fiction in U.S. Libraries with Special Attention to the Influence of Reviews." *Library Acquisitions: Practice & Theory* 11, no. 4 (1987): 283–95.

Pike, Lee. "Cooperative Collection Development Program in a Multitype Library Environment." In Engle, *Issues in Cooperative Collection Development*, 55–66.

Poll, Roswitha. "Zur Praxis von Tausch and Kauftausch: die verschwiegenen Wege der Literaturerwerbung." In Haase and Habermann, *Zur Internationalität wissenschaftlicher Bibliotheken*, 116–34.

Rochester, Maxine K. "The ABN Database: Sampling Strategies for Collection Overlap Studies." *Information Technology and Libraries* 6 (Sept. 1987): 190–96.

Rossi, Gary J. "Library Approval Plans: A Selected Annotated Bibliography." *Library Acquisitions: Practice & Theory* 11, no. 1 (1987): 3–34.

Rutledge, John, and Luke Swindler. "The Selection Decision: Defining Criteria and Establishing Priorities." *College & Research Libraries* 48 (Mar. 1987): 123–31.

Rutstein, Joel S. "The Present and Future Withering Away of Collection Development." *Colorado Libraries* 12 (Sept.) 1986: 43–44.

Ryan, Michael T. "Special Collections." In McPheron, *English and American Literature*, 181–203.

Schad, Jasper G. "Fairness in Book Fund Allocation." *Collection & Research Libraries* 48: (Nov 1987) 479–86.

Schmidt, Karen A. "The Acquisitions Process in Research Libraries: A Survey of ARL Libraries' Acquisitions Departments." *Library Acquisitions: Practice & Theory* 11, no. 1 (1987): 35–44.

Schon, Isabel, et al. "Books in Spanish for Young Readers in School and Public Libraries: A Survey of Practices and Attitudes." *Library & Information Science Research* 9 (Jan.–Mar. 1987): 21–28.

Schrift, Leonard. "Truth in Vending." In Lee, *Pricing and Costs of Monographs and Serials,* 27–35.

Scott, Marianne. "NCIP in Canada." In Association of Research Libraries, *NCIP*, 14–18.

_____. "The National Plan for Collections Inventories." *Canadian Library Journal* 44 (Oct. 1987): 289–90.

Shuster, Helen M. "A Versatile dBase III+ Acquisitions Program at Worcester Polytechnic Institute." *Library Acquisitions: Practice & Theory* 11, no. 3 (1987): 241–53.

Simonot, Genevieve. "Paris-Texas: Analyse de la politique de développement des collections aux Etats-Unis et en France." *Bulletin des bibliothèques de France* 31, no. 2 (1986): 142–45.

Smith, Scott A. "Linking Approval Plans and Automated Library Acquisitions Systems." *Library Acquisitions: Practice & Theory* 11, no. 3 (1987): 215–16.

Sohn. Jeanne. "Collection Development Organizational Patterns in ARL Libraries." *Library Resources & Technical Services* 31 (Apr.–June 1987): 123-34.

Somers, Sally W. "Standards! Standards! Standards! Experiences with Standards at the University of Georgia Libraries." *Library Acquisitions: Practice & Theory* 11, no. 4 (1987): 367–72.

_____. "Vendor/Library Relations: A Perspective." *Library Acquisitions: Practice & Theory* 11, no. 2 (1987): 135–38.

Spicer, Claudia A. "An Inventory for the '80s." *Collection Building* 8, no. 3 (1987): 16–18.

Stam, David H. "Development and Use of the RLG Conspectus." In Association of Research Libraries, *NCIP,* 7–10.

Stebelman, Scott. "Building Literary Reference Collections." In McPheron, *English and American Literature*, 156–80.

Stewart, Linda. "Picking CD-ROMs for Public Use." *American Libraries* 18 (Oct 1987.): 738–40.

Stillings, Craig. "North Alabama Union List of Serials." In Engle, *Issues in Cooperative Collection Development*, 39–53.

Streit, Samuel. "Acquiring Rare Books by Purchase: Recent Library Trends." *Library Trends* 36 (summer 1987): 189–211.

Tarin, Patricia A. "Books for the Spanish-Speaking: Sí se puede." *Library Journal* 112 (July 1987): 25–28.

Thomas, Lawrence. "Tradition and Expertise in Academic Library Collection Development." *College & Research Libraries* 48 (Nov. 1987): 487–93.

Tolliver, Barbara. "Collection Development: Problems and Opportunities." *Catholic Library World* 58 (Mar./Apr. 1987): 223–25, 236.

Tornier, Eva. "Gezielter Bestandaufbau und Kontinuierliche Bestandsüberwachung in den Bibliotheken der DDR." *Der Bibliothekar* 40 (Sept. 1986): 388–93.

Tyckoson, David A. "On the Conference Circuit." *Technicalities* 7 (Aug. 1987): 1, 9–10.

Vidor, David L., and Elizabeth Futas. "The Dichotomous Collection." *Library Resources & Technical Services* 31 (July–Sept. 1987): 207–13.

Warner, Marnie, and Kathleen Flynn. "Legal Collections in Small and Medium-Sized Public Libraries." *Collection Building* 8, no. 2 (1987): 25–33.

Warwick, J. P. "Duplication of Texts in Academic Libraries: A Behavioural Model for Library Management." *Journal of Librarianship* 19 (Jan. 1987): 41–52.

Weathers, Inalea. "Special Collections in Public Libraries: Enhancing Community Service." *Wilson Library Bulletin* 61 (May 1987): 23–25.

Webb, Ruth. "The $5000 Video Collection." *Library Journal* 112 (May 15, 1987): 34-40.

Whitehead, Martha. "Collection Development for Distance Education at the University of British Columbia Library." *Library Acquisitions: Practice & Theory* 11, no. 1 (1987): 67–74.

Williams, Roy. "Weeding an Academic Lending Library Using the Slote Method." *British Journal of Academic Librarianship* 1 (summer 1986): 147–59.

Winkel, Lois. "Developing Collections to Service Children: The Tools of the Trade." *Catholic Library World* 57 (Jan./Feb. 1986): 172–77.

Wise, Leona L. "RTSD/RS Gifts and Exchange Discussion Group." *Library Acquisitions: Practice & Theory* 11, no. 4 (1987): 339–40.

Wortman, William A. "Collection Management, 1986." *Library Resources & Technical Services* 31 (Oct.–Dec. 1987): 287–305.

Yaple, Henry M. "People in Hell Want Ice Water, Too." *Library Acquisitions: Practice & Theory* 11, no. 3 (1987): 223–26. [A discussion of concerns about cost increases.]

23 SELECTION FOR PRESERVATION

A MATERIALISTIC APPROACH

Ein wirklich historisches Denken muss die eigene
Geschichtlichkeit mitdenken.
—Hans-Georg Gadamer[1]

Because decisions to preserve library materials affect the quality and composition of library collections, such decisions clearly must be made in consultation with collection development staff. To date, however, very little effort has been made to describe the processes and criteria of preservation selection from the perspective of collection development. This is partially because preservation has in most libraries only recently acquired the status of a fully legitimate library operation deserving coordination with other library functions, but also because some of the values that underlie selection for preservation are alien to those that inform current collection development, as I will try to show in this paper.

The fundamental preservation problem facing collection development is, as Gordon Williams put it ten years ago, that, while "everyone will agree that not everything needs to be preserved forever," there is "far less agreement . . . on exactly which books [and other materials] need not be preserved."[2] Dan Hazen, therefore, whose 1982 article remains far and away the best treatment of preservation selection, sees it as the primary responsibility of collection development in the preservation process to make item-by-item preservation selection decisions on the basis of criteria similar (but not identical) to the criteria used for the selection of current materials.[3]

The extent to which the function posited by Hazen is valid will be considered in the course of this paper. One must, in any event, agree with Hazen that the most productive approach to the topic of the interface between collection development and preservation is from the standpoint of selection decision making. Therefore, I will first define the location of collection development in the preservation decision process. While many detailed descriptions of preservation programs are now available, it will be useful for any future study of these programs, or for the creation of a program where none has previously existed, to attempt to reduce the activity of decision making for preservation to a minimal model, which might then be adapted to different organizational situations. Second, once the location of collection development in the decision-making process has been determined, I can then turn around, so to speak, and examine the activity of preservation from this perspective. In order to clarify from the standpoint of collection development the basic functions of preservation and their relationship to each other and to determine where the particular mode of microfilming fits into the whole scheme, I will make some suggestions for a rudimentary typology of preservation. Finally, using the characteristics of preservation that emerge from this typology, I can begin to speculate on the obstructions

This article first appeared in *Library Resources & Technical Services* 30, no. 4 (Oct./Dec. 1986): 341–53.

to large-scale cooperative preservation efforts and offer some suggestions for the qualities that a cooperative plan must contain to overcome such impediments.

Throughout this paper, the term *microfilming* will be used to refer to the best method of inexpensive and efficient reformatting generally available. If another method of reformatting becomes broadly available that is more inexpensive or efficient or will result in a more durable or accessible product, that new method should certainly be adopted, and what I have to say in this paper with respect to microfilming will be valid for such a new method as well.

THE DECISION CYCLE

It is a basic purpose of all human communication to make a text available in some material form long enough for that text to have some meaning assigned to it by someone other than the author. If that meaning is judged for whatever reason to be of some special significance, the length of time the text is available can be extended to afford the opportunity for further evaluation. The decision to reproduce a spoken text in written form, the decision to publish a written text, the decision to include a publication in a library collection—all of these extend the text's availability. By the time a document reaches a point at which a library must decide to preserve it through microfilming or any other means, the text of that document has been subject to a series of decisions, beginning with the expression of the text in phonic or graphic form, all of which have resulted in the material extension of the text's accessibility. The extreme discomfort of preservation selection derives in no small part from the realization that a negative decision (i.e., a decision not to preserve) represents a reversal—and in many cases a permanent reversal—of a series of positive "preservation" decisions made throughout the history of the text. Not to preserve is therefore always to silence a voice, which, in the opinion of a number of people in the past (authors, editors, publishers, librarians), has had something to say significant enough to warrant extended consideration.

The decisions made at any stage in the history of a text to extend its availability are clearly of two general types: (a) should the text be made further available, and, if so, (b) by what material means? These decisions are, needless to say, distinguishable but not separable. The minimal decision cycle in the library's preservation operation continues to conform to this pattern, as depicted in figure 1.

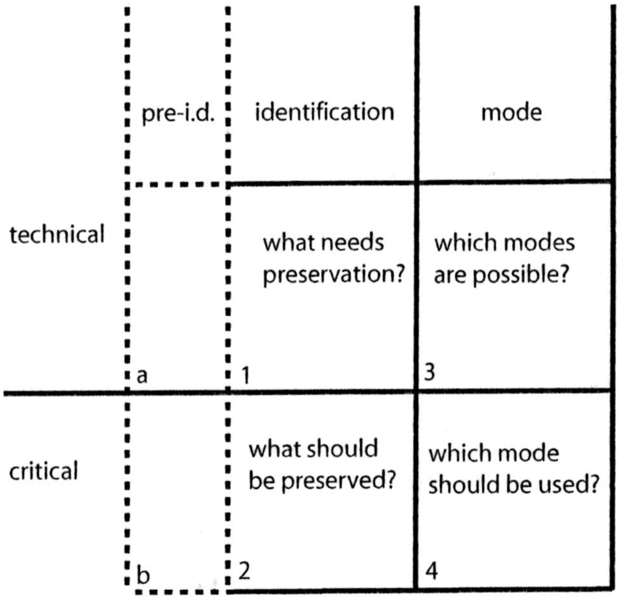

The two fundamental decisions that must be made in all cases of preservation—identification for preservation and determination of the mode of preservation—are, moreover, invariably two-dimensional, involving both technical and critical considerations. In each instance, the critical decisions can be made only subsequent to and on the basis of the technical decisions; it is, in fact, the essential purpose of the technical decisions in this process to define the options available for the critical decisions.

The first decision that must be made in this cycle of decision making is this: Which items in the col-

	pre-i.d.	identification	mode
technical		what needs preservation?	which modes are possible?
	a	1	3
critical		what should be preserved?	which mode should be used?
	b	2	4

FIGURE 1. The Decision Cycle

lection are physically in need of preservation? Which will not last the decade? or the year? or another circulation? Which will fall apart in marking before they can even be put on the shelf? This is a technical decision based on a knowledge and experience of such matters as printing, binding, and paper chemistry. Only after that set of materials in need of preservation has been identified on the basis of technical criteria (step 1) can the subset of materials that should in fact be preserved be isolated (step 2).

It should be noted that, especially in larger collections, the first technical decision may need to be preceded by a preidentification phase, which would consist of a critical decision (step b) as to which segments of the collection should be surveyed in order to identify items in need of preservation. This preidentification critical decision may, moreover, also be preceded by a preidentification technical decision (step a) concerning, for example, which segments of the collection are most likely to contain the highest proportion of disintegrating materials.

Once decisions concerning identification have been made, the proper mode of preservation must be considered. The technical questions to be answered at this point (step 3) are these. Of the modes of preservation available which are possible for the materials identified and what are the projected costs for each mode? The standard options have been outlined in a number of publications, perhaps most clearly in Gay Walker's chapter of Carolyn Morrow's *Preservation Challenge*.[4] With respect to microfilm, there are also a number of other formal considerations, which have been delineated by Pamela Darling, concerning the suitability of microfilm for certain types of materials.[5] Once the technical experts have determined the options, it is the responsibility of the critical decision makers to determine from among the modes available the one that will as nearly as possible balance cost with projected use.

It should also be noted that technical decisions in the cycle not only provide the options for the following critical decisions but also can affect earlier critical decisions. If, for example, the technical determination is made in step 3 that the only practical method of preservation is restoration, then the decision made in step 2 to preserve that item may be cancelled if the value of the item does not justify the cost of such treatment.

This very simplified decision cycle for preservation applies, I would expect, in virtually all cases for printed materials. In smaller libraries the critical and technical decisions may be made by the same person, while in larger libraries preservation experts will be entrusted with the technical decisions, and different collection development staff will usually be assigned responsibility for many of the critical decisions.

It is also possible, and in some cases highly desirable, for the critical decisions to be macrodecisions.[6] It may be that in a given project aimed at a discrete collection segment, a single decision can be made in step 2 that all items identified to be in need of preservation within that segment should in fact be preserved. Or in step 4, the single decision could be made, for example, that all materials determined in the previous (technical) step to be conducive to microfilming should indeed be microfilmed.

TOWARD A TYPOLOGY OF PRESERVATION

The fundamental question, from the standpoint of collection development, remains why certain items should survive while others should not, i.e., how to respond to the need for a system of "planned deterioration" for printed materials.[7] Until we can answer that question in a consistent and generally acceptable fashion, we have very little chance of establishing standards for preservation selection in individual libraries, let alone of handing over to the twenty-first century a true research collection, i.e., one that consists, to use Mosher's word, of a "community" of documentation rather than a random assortment.[8]

Let me suggest, therefore, a rudimentary typology of preservation based upon three different and, to my mind, equally legitimate answers to the question of why certain categories of library materials deserve preservation. See figure 2. This typology can be summarized as follows.

Class 1 Preservation

We must begin by admitting that certain library materials need to be preserved in order to protect their capital value. Special or unique items, e.g., rare books (and manuscripts),

	Class 1	Class 2	Class 3
object	high capital value	high use value	low use/ future research
primary mode	restoration	replace/ repair	microform
decision locus	local	local	regional/ national
decision type	macro	micro	macro

FIGURE 2. Typology of Preservation

must be preserved if the library is not to forfeit a considerable investment tied up in a relatively small number of documents. The purpose of what I will call class 1 preservation, therefore, is to preserve materials or groups of materials that have a high economic value. Emphasis on the economic value is not to deny, of course, that such materials have research value. Certainly they do, but the decision to preserve these materials must be made on the basis of their economic rather than their research value; for there are, after all, many other materials with potential research value moldering throughout the library, and to define special collections as having greater research value, and therefore as being more worthy of preservation, than main stacks collections would be highly problematic—especially, as I will explain shortly, at this particular time in the history of valuation.

Because the artifactual worth forms much of the basis of the capital value of many of the objects of class 1 preservation, its primary mode is clearly restoration. I am assuming that the microfilming of special collection materials is probably exceptional and would usually be done only to produce working copies of the originals or to save materials so totally decrepit that their content is jeopardized.

Class 1 preservation cannot, however, be limited to the type of documentation found in special collections. There is another type of material that does fit (albeit with some squeezing) into class 1 and which is often conducive to microfilming—especially if mass deacidification is not an option. Level-five collections (as defined by the Conspectus) can also be of significant capital value, if for no other reason than for the amount of labor that has been invested in their development.[9] In such collections the special value or uniqueness often lies in the combination or comprehensiveness of the materials rather than in any single item by itself. The capital (and research) value of such a collection, in other words, exceeds the combined value of its individual parts. Individual pieces of such collections must be preserved, therefore, if the capital value of the whole is to be protected.

Critical decision making in class 1 preservation is usually of the macro variety and, at least in the case of special collections, should require very little input from collection development staff. All materials of significant capital value in special collections must be preserved, and the order of their preservation will normally be determined by the technical estimate of the degree of deterioration in combination with the amount of the capital value. In the case of level-five collections, however, collection development will have an important role in what we defined above as the preidentification stage of critical decision making. Once the parameters of the level-five collection have been defined by a bibliographer, however, the macrodecision will usually be made to preserve all of the items within the collection segment in need of preservation. It should also be the responsibility of the bibliographer to identify for preservation any stray materials, such as any classified outside of the relevant collection segment, which the bibliographer would define as being part of or intimately related to the collection.

Finally, class 1 preservation is always a local decision-making operation; it is mandated by local constituencies and is intended to serve (for the most part) local needs. Since the materials are to a great extent unique (either individually or in combination with each other), and since the primary criterion for class 1 preservation is economic rather than bibliographical, cooperation among institutions is not usually an option.

CLASS 2 PRESERVATION

At the opposite end of the bibliographic spectrum from the materials targeted in class 1 preservation are those to be identified for class 2 preservation. Class 2 preservation consists of higher use items that are currently in demonstrable demand for curriculum and research purposes. A major source of information about such material is circulation, and the need for preservation of such materials often derives from overuse. It is in class 2 decisions that the classical studies of use patterns, such as those by Trueswell or Fussier and Simon, are most applicable.[10] Christinger Tomer has devised a statistical method for identifying candidates for this kind of preservation, based on date of publication (as an indicator of physical condition) and date of last circulation (as a measure of frequency of use).[11] From a less quantitative perspective, the criteria developed by Hazen, which include the note that "some priority should be attached to the materials people actually use," would appear to be aimed, in my opinion, largely at this type of preservation.[12]

The objective of class 2 preservation, then, is to preserve materials currently being used, or very likely to be used as projected on the basis of what is currently being used. It is in class 2 preservation, moreover, that bibliographers have the most important role to play in the preservation process, for the knowledge amassed by bibliographers as to the current needs and activities of users and the current trends in the subject are precisely the criteria that must be applied to class 2 preservation selection decisions. Class 2 preservation is, in fact, really only an extension of or supplement to the core building and maintenance done by most selectors in most libraries. It is, in a manner of speaking, simply current selection by other means. Because it also clearly involves item-by-item selection (microdecisions), it would seem to correspond to Hazen's view of preservation selection.

Because of the high use of class 2 materials, the primary mode of preservation tends to be replacement. If copies or reprints are not available, then bound photocopies within the limits permitted by copyright are probably the most preferable mode. Microfilm can, of course, be used for class 2 preservation, and I expect it is used occasionally for some core serials. For the most part, however, use of microfilm for class 2 preservation occurs, in my opinion, only when the appropriateness of the item for class 2 is in some doubt—when, in other words, the utility of the item has been projected more on the basis of probability than observation. The parameters of a core (or even of a canon) are always fuzzy, so that there is a tendency for class 2, which aims at high-use items, to blend into what we will shortly define as class 3, the class directed at low-use items and which does indeed take microfilm as its primary mode of preservation.

Like class 1, true class 2 preservation is activated exclusively by local values. Decisions to preserve are based directly on the demonstrated needs of current local clientele. Unlike class 1 items, however, most class 2 materials are being preserved simultaneously at many different institutions. Such duplication of preservation is, moreover, thoroughly justified by high use. Cooperation is once again, therefore, usually not an option, because such material must be available in-house.

CLASS 3 PRESERVATION

The most problematic category of preservation is the third class, which has as its function to maintain for posterity lower-use research materials. Because it consists of less frequently used materials, class 3 preservation has microfilm (or its equivalent) as its main mode of preservation.

Although there is clearly a great deal of class 3 preservation being done at local institutions throughout the country, local needs are not the main motivation for class 3. Indeed, the clientele for whom this material is being preserved has not yet, for the most part, arrived on the scene. Because of the absence of direct local motivations—which are to a great extent satisfied by class 2 and to a lesser degree by class 1 preservation—and because of the magnitude of the problem, class 3 preservation is the exclusive source of cooperative preservation projects. To complete this equation, therefore, if the three classes defined here provide something approaching a sufficient typology of preservation, then a primary use of microfilm as a mode of preservation is for projects that usually require and deserve coordination among libraries. For a library to engage in a large-scale preservation microfilming effort without such coordination would be, in my opinion, a very questionable undertaking.

While selection criteria for classes 1 and 2 are, as we have seen, relatively easy to define, the criteria for class 3 present significant difficulties. Why preserve this material, anyway? Just what is it that posterity is not going to be able to do if it lacks access to this documentation? Will whatever posterity could do with access to this material tomorrow be of sufficient value to justify the considerable expenditure of resources today necessary to prepare that access?

The purpose of large-scale, coordinated preservation is not merely to help the future understand the past, but also to provide the future with the ability to understand itself—to supply a ground of knowledge upon which the future can build and against which the future can contrast and thus identify and define itself. Orwell was quite right: who controls the past controls the future. In this sense, it is certainly we who control the future because the future will only be able to understand and define itself in relation to what we give it. This responsibility requires that we devise effective and reliable methods to supply the future with the best possible collection—as defined, of course, by our own values at this time.

The most appropriate publications for preservation must always be selected on the basis of the values in place—or, if you prefer, the "dominant ideology"—at the time of the decision. There is absolutely no escaping this requirement—not in the past and not now. We have no alternative but to make our selection decisions for class 3 preservation on the basis of the late twentieth-century values, which inform all of our decisions. The only problem is that late twentieth-century values are thoroughly permeated by a highly developed and all-encompassing network of ethical and epistemological relativism.

We are all products of an age, a nation, and a profession that has become increasingly unwilling to accept or to apply absolutes. The vital role of libraries in the opposition to political censorship is indicative of this position. The Library Bill of Rights is a noble document, and it expresses eloquently the ethical relativism and humanistic tolerance that characterize our era and profession—but as a determinant of values for any discriminating activity such as preservation selection, it leaves us completely helpless.

Closely related to this ethical position is the epistemological relativism that so clearly pervades contemporary thought. Kuhn's analysis of scientific revolutions, Patrick Wilson's theory of research quality as consensus, the historicity of phenomenology and the textuality of post-structuralism, the rejection of positivism even by Western Marxism, the increasing acceptance of the centrality of interpretation in the social sciences—all of these (and many other) current and extremely influential concepts and trends render highly unlikely the possibility of developing a broadly acceptable and stable scale of values, which would be restrictive enough to permit the final rejection of certain library materials.[13]

American research libraries in the late twentieth century have embraced and promoted such relativistic trends. There is no doubt in my mind that this is a major reason research collections have been increasingly driven by an ideal of inclusiveness. The Library of Congress is considered the greatest library in the country: it is not just a coincidence that it is also the largest. Quantity is quality in the research library, and this perspective has evolved, I would maintain, primarily because of our inability to define or measure bibliographical quality in any other terms.

Another obvious manifestation of this syndrome is our attitude toward weeding—which, from a critical point of view, is simply preservation done in reverse. While much has been written on the methods and values of weeding, research libraries, as Curley and Broderick realistically note, "will rarely weed, aware that what seems superfluous today may contain the essence of our times for the researcher of tomorrow."[14] The reason for such a reluctance to weed is that we lack at this time the epistemological apparatus to distinguish a level of quality or veracity that would clearly permit a decision to reject or retain. In the absence of an absolute measure, any statement has potential value, and any statement is thus worthy of retention. One wonders whether there has ever been an age so monumentally ill equipped to devise a system of planned deterioration. This, from the standpoint of collection development, is the ultimate problem of class 3 preservation.

TOWARD A COORDINATED PROGRAM FOR CLASS 3 PRESERVATION

There are many and varied preservation programs in operation throughout the country today. Some of these are cooperative and as such are aimed at class 3 materials. But there remains, partially for reasons I have just described, a clear lack of a general strategy linking these programs. Indeed, it is becoming increasingly likely that the major threat to the systematic preservation of library materials will turn out to be not an excess of acidity in paper but rather a shortage of coordination among libraries. How is such coordination to be achieved?

A successful coordinated program for class 3 preservation must satisfy certain general requirements:

First, it must provide scholars of the future with access to some kind of representative collection of documentation.

Second, it must be economically feasible and practicable; a library must be able to afford to take on a regionally or nationally coordinated class 3 responsibility in addition to accommodating its local responsibilities for class 1 and 2 preservation.

Third, it must be politically acceptable, i.e., it must not strain faculty-library relations at the institutional level, nor must it place undue pressure on relations among research libraries.

Fourth, it must be structured in such a way that it will permit, but not depend for its success on, indefinite expansion, so that more and more materials can be preserved as time and resources become available.

Fifth, it must be in operation relatively soon.

To these requirements we might add the excellent summary recommendation of Margaret Child that we "should not agonize too much over the fine points of definition of scope, but should begin to deal with the most easily grasped portion of the problem in an organized way as soon as possible."[15]

One view of the problem of valuation in preservation selection is represented in figure 3. Let the vertical axis represent the scale of values in effect and the horizontal axis some division of the collection, such as by subject. Because we are operating under severe time constraints, it is clear that we should want to proceed in the diagram horizontally, i.e., we want to preserve all of the most valuable materials on all subjects first, then the second most valuable, and so on. In the cases of class 1 and class 2 preservation, these values (capital value and current use value respectively) are relatively definable, so that a horizontal process is feasible in local institutions. When we attempt to implement a program at a regional or national level for class 3 preservation, however, we find it impossible, because, as I have tried to explain above, we have not succeeded in defining a uniform scale of values. It has therefore frequently been the practice in cooperative preservation projects to proceed vertically, i.e., to select a subject (perhaps with formal limitations such as format or imprint) and to try to preserve everything (within those limitations) on that subject found in the collections of the participating institutions down to some vague point (the dotted line) below which items are no longer of sufficient value to be preserved. Clearly, the risk of such a procedure is that, whatever scale of values is being used, materials of less value (according to that scale) in one subject are being preserved, while materials of greater value (according to the same scale) in another subject are being permitted to disintegrate.

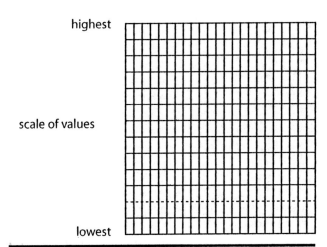

FIGURE 3. Cooperative Preservation Planning

There is, in my opinion, only one practical method for a large-scale cooperative preservation program that has any chance of success and that is to begin to build the program not around subjects but rather exclusively around subject collections in place. We must agree, in other words, to define the qualification of a document for class 3 preservation solely by virtue of its current inclusion in a designated collection of record. Systematic class 3 preservation of this type would thus result in a stringing together of different subject collections in different libraries into a single cooperative collection. Although each subject collection at each institution is obviously built in response to local needs, each collection will also, if it is a research collection (Conspectus level-4) built by competent bibliographers, represent the scholarship on the subject in a relatively balanced and unbiased manner. Each bibliographer is, after all, subject to and struggling with the same ethical and epistemological relativism described above. Any research level subject collection is by necessity representative of a variety of trends and biases, and therefore should be acceptable as the minimally adequate subject segment of a cooperatively preserved collection. Material in such a designated subject collection would be preserved by the holding institution, and material on the subject not in that collection would be left (for the time being) at risk. This would provide us with an initial, practicable, and (procedurally and critically) achievable method of "planned deterioration" for printed materials.

The first step in such a plan should be to identify in a general fashion the strengths of collections by subject throughout the region or country. This is, of course, precisely the purpose of the Conspectus, so this should present few difficulties. We need to identify strong research collections through this method, but not special collections aimed at inclusiveness. (These special level-five collections will, in any case, probably survive through class 1 preservation.)

The second step would be for preservation specialists to determine a ratio of deterioration among subjects and then to annotate the Conspectus accordingly. It does not matter that collections at different institutions are deteriorating at different rates. Such a ratio of deterioration by subject would presumably hold for all institutions, even though the rates of deterioration may vary. (Use a code like a = probable large percentage of materials on this subject are deteriorating; b = moderate percentage; c = small percentage.) Using also the latest shelflist data, it should then be possible to gain some idea of the extent of the problem in each general subject area.

Finally, this information should be used to assign as equitably and systematically as possible responsibility for preservation of particular subject collections among cooperating institutions. For each subject area, a strong (level-4) collection should be identified, which will serve as the collection of record. It would then be the responsibility of that institution to monitor this collection and to microfilm all deteriorating materials before they are lost. All cooperating institutions should accept the past work of the different bibliographers who have built the particular subject collections of record as informed and the resulting collections as sufficiently representative to satisfy many of the needs of future scholarship.

A shared bibliographic database with the capacity to identify items that have been preserved, such as RLIN and, in the near future, OCLC, is clearly essential for such a cooperative class 3 program, since it will permit the library of record to avoid preserving items it holds that are already preserved elsewhere. In many cases such preservation elsewhere will have been the result of class 2 decisions, especially those, mentioned above, involving items microfilmed because they fall on the fuzzy border between classes 2 and 3.

Let me emphasize that such a method would require the preservation of all materials in the designated subject collection of record identified as being in need of preservation. Never mind the current bibliographer's current evaluation of those materials. Such an evaluation, in fact, should not be solicited. Never mind the opinion of faculty or other experts as to which items are eternally significant and which are worthless. A certain amount of the collection may be trash, but it is our duty to pass that on in a representative collection, because a certain quantity of the reality the collection is to represent consists of what currently looks like trash. Let posterity decide it is trash. The only way to recognize quality material is, in any case, to have some trash with which to contrast it.[16]

Such a method of dividing responsibility among a large number of institutions could be implemented fairly quickly and would not place significant financial strain on any single institution—especially if the information on collection sizes, strengths, and the ratios of deterioration by subject are figured into the planning and if a shared database is available. Serious political problems with current users should not arise, because the identification of especially relevant documents (in the judgment of users) should always be accommodated as part of class 2 preservation. Clearly what would stand most in the way of such a plan and what has impaired our ability to establish such programs in the past is our reluctance to abandon in such circumstances the principles of current collection building. We must recognize that we cannot preserve cooperatively using the same values and procedures that we use to build a current local collection. We cannot approach a coordinated class 3 preservation project as if it were simply an expanded version of class 2 local preservation. Even if there were time for bibliographers to evaluate every item on every subject in a variety of libraries in the same way that bibliographers make current selection decisions—which there obviously isn't—we nevertheless demonstrably lack the criteria to make those judgments in a coordinated fashion at this time.

Coordinated class 3 preservation decisions must therefore be administrative decisions relating to material and which, in the absence of known users and trends, are best regulated by a material system of values. Let us return to figure 3. To initiate a cooperative class 3 preservation project, let the horizontal axis represent not subjects, but rather subject collections in place (i.e., a different subject collection in each library). Let the value system in the vertical column then be the rate of material decomposition, so that the most rapidly disintegrating items will then receive the highest value. In this way we can achieve a kind of horizontal parity by having all institutions (each responsible for a different subject) proceed vertically in a coordinated fashion according to a relatively measurable set of values. The dotted line in this case will separate materials disintegrating (above the line) from those not disintegrating (below it).

Once such a designated collection has been brought to a condition of stability, i.e., once all items in the collection in need of preservation have been preserved and a mechanism is in place to ensure that all items in future need of preservation will be preserved, a second phase of the program, which can be expanded indefinitely, can be undertaken to identify and preserve subject materials not contained in the designated collections of record. If we never attain such an advanced phase, however, (and I am somewhat doubtful that we ever would) we can still be certain that such a program would safeguard a minimally adequate representative research collection for the future.

In conclusion, let us return to the original question: why undertake class 3 preservation? Perhaps in the effort to answer how to go about it, we have also managed to formulate a rationale. For the past four thousand years, civilization has found classes 1 and 2, for the most part, adequate. Now it is necessary to introduce a new kind of preservation, what I have been calling class 3. It is necessary not because we have more library materials than ever before, nor because their rate of disintegration is faster than ever before, nor even because there now are better and more accurate methods of preservation. The reason for undertaking large-scale coordinated class 3 preservation is that the values by which we live and work demand it. That very system of values that makes it so difficult to decide what to preserve provides us at the same time with the moral and epistemological imperative to secure for the future a balanced and representative collection, one that will provide posterity—in the same way that we provide current users—the opportunity for evaluation and for the acceptance and rejection of ideas embodied in library materials. We are, in a sense, obligated to confront and solve the complexities of cooperative class 3 preservation as much for ourselves as for the readers of the future who will rely on our judgment. The sooner we get on with it, therefore, the better for them—and the better for us.

REFERENCE NOTES

1. Hans-Georg Gadamer, *Wahrheit und Methode: Grundzüge einer philosophischen Hermeneutik,* 2d ed. (Tübingen: Mohr, 1965), 283.

2. Gordon R. Williams, "Objectives of a National Preservation Program" in *A National Preservation Program: Proceedings of the Planning Conference* (Washington, D.C.: Library of Congress, 1980), 29.

3. Dan C. Hazen, "Collection Development, Collection Management, and Preservation," *Library Resources & Technical Services* 26 (Jan.–Mar. 1982): 6–10.

4. Gay Walker, "Preserving the Intellectual Content of Deteriorated Library Materials" in *The Preservation Challenge: A Guide to Conserving Library Materials,* Carolyn Clark Morrow, ed. (White Plains, N.Y.: Knowledge Industry, 1983), 101–16.

5. Pamela W. Darling, "Microforms in Libraries: Preservation and Storage," *Microform Review* 5 (Apr. 1976): 94–95.

6. Hazen, "Collection Development, Collection Management, and Preservation," 6–7. See also Hendrik Edelman, "Selection Methodology in Academic Libraries," *Library Resources & Technical Services* 23 (winter 1979): 37.

7. Margaret Child, "Deciding What to Save," *The Abbey Newsletter* 6, no. 4 (Aug. 1982): suppl. 2.

8. Paul Mosher, keynote address delivered at the Collection Management and Development Institute, Trinity University, San Antonio, Tex., 15 May 1985.

9. The Conspectus, as most collection development librarians are aware, is a tool, developed originally by the Research Libraries Group (RLG) and now in use in many North American research libraries, to rate subject collections on a scale of 0 (out of scope) to 5 (comprehensive). See Nancy E. Gwinn and Paul H. Mosher, "Coordinating Collection Development: The RLG Conspectus," *College & Research Libraries* 44 (Mar. 1983): 128–40.

10. See, for example, Richard L. Trueswell, "Some Behavioral Patterns of Library Users: The 80/20 Rule," *Wilson Library Bulletin* 43 (Jan. 1969): 458–61; Herman H. Fussier and Julian L. Simon, *Patterns in the Use of Books in Large Research Libraries* (Chicago: Univ. of Chicago Pr., 1969).

11. Christinger Tomer, "Identification, Evaluation, and Selection of Books for Preservation," *Collection Management* 3 (spring 1979): 34–54.

12. Hazen, "Collection Development, Collection Management, and Preservation," 8.

13. Thomas S. Kuhn, *The Structure of Scientific Revolutions,* 2d ed. rev. (Chicago: Univ. of Chicago Pr., 1970); see also Gerald Doppelt, "Kuhn's Epistemological Relativism: An Interpretation and Defense" in *Relativism: Cognitive and Moral,* ed. Jack W. Meiland and Michael Krausz (Notre Dame, Ind.: Univ. of Notre Dame Pr., 1982), 113–46; Patrick Wilson, "Second-Hand Knowledge: An Inquiry into Cognitive Authority. Contributions in Librarianship and Information Science," 44 (Westport, Conn.: Greenwood, 1983), 81–121; Daniel Bell, "The Turn to Interpretation: An Introduction," *Partisan Review* 51 (1984): 217.

14. Arthur Curley and Dorothy Broderick, *Building Library Collections,* 6th ed. (Metuchen, N.J.: Scarecrow, 1985), 308–309.

15. Child, "Deciding What to Save," 2.

16. See Daniel Boorstin's remark in *A National Preservation Program,* 72: "But a larger epistemological concern—and one reason why I think this subject [i.e., preservation selection] is of cosmic importance—is that we are always tending to second guess the future, to think we know what's trash and what isn't."

24 THE LANGUAGE
OF THE LEVELS

REFLECTIONS ON THE COMMUNICATION OF COLLECTION DEVELOPMENT POLICY

The collection development policy, as a means to express and systematize guidelines for collection building, fulfills three basic functions: the referential, the generative, and the rhetorical. The division of the policy into subject categories, and the use of "collection levels" (such as those defined in the ALA Guidelines for Collection Development) *to rank the collection and the collecting effort for each subject, serves these three functions well. More work needs to be done, however, on defining collection levels and the collecting effort to which they refer. These definitions may be more easily achieved if we begin to view the collection levels as designating varying degrees of two opposing collection strategies: inclusion and exclusion.*

If we understand policies simply as "guides to carrying out an action," then there are normally as many selection policies in a library as there are selectors, for each selector necessarily develops, over time, a set of personalized guidelines upon which to base selection decisions.[1] Such policies are usually vague and unarticulated. On the rare occasions when they are written, they are of necessity expressed from the specialized viewpoint of the individual selector. The values upon which such policies are based and the goals toward which they are directed vary, therefore, from one selector to another.

It is the task of the collection development policy to specify, consolidate, coordinate, and adjust such separate selection policies in order to promote the development of a collection that will, as a whole, best respond to the needs of current and future clientele. This task is accomplished by bringing about the translation of the various selection policies into a single language, making adjustments in the individual policies to fit the general collection plan, and then stitching these adjusted policies together into a unified document. While the translation and consolidation reduce the disparity among individual selection policies, it should be noted that such disparity can never—and probably should never—be eliminated entirely. The separate segments of the collection development policy must remain the personal responsibilities and products of individual selectors.

The primary objective of the collection development policy, therefore, is to unify or focus expression concerning the current state and future direction of the collection. If we are to determine how policy works and how to use policy for purposes of collection planning, we need first to understand its operation as a system of communication. This paper is an attempt to move us a step closer to such an understanding. It begins with an examination

This article first appeared in *College & Research Libraries* 50, no. 5 (Mar. 1986): 140–49. An earlier version of this paper was read at the RTSD Collection Management and Development Institute, Trinity University, on May 16, 1985 of the general functions of collection development policy, and then turns to a more detailed dissection of the policy's standard structure.

POLICY FUNCTIONS

Although the functions of collection development policy can be described or defined from a variety of administrative, bibliographical, or epistemological perspectives, the collection policy as a communications device intended to transfer information about the development of a collection fulfills at least three fundamental functions. First, it provides a description of the collection's current state, development, and desired direction. This is the policy's *referential* function. Second, the policy serves the selector, if only inferentially, as a method or instrument to transform the collection from its current to its desired condition. This is the policy's *generative* function. Finally, the policy also acts as an argument that there is a systematic collection plan in effect, and that such a plan is worth pursuing. This is the policy's *rhetorical* function. The referential function is primary; the generative and rhetorical functions derive from the referential function. Let us take a closer look at these three functions.

Like any document, the collection policy fulfills its referential function through the application of a conventionalized system of signs. A sign is a "cultural unit" that "is defined inasmuch as it is *placed* in a system of other cultural units which are opposed to it and circumscribe it."[2] In other words, meaning derives from the relationships among signs. Because such relationships take place entirely within a system, moreover, that system is, to use Umberto Eco's cumbersome term, *auto-clarificatory*, i.e., "capable of checking itself entirely by its own means."[3] The only way to learn the reference or meanings of the signs of which a sign system (such as a language) is composed, therefore, is to make use of that system, contrast its constituent signs with each other, and arrive at an understanding of how those signs relate among themselves.

The core of the standard collection development policy for larger libraries, and increasingly for smaller libraries, consists of a series of subject categories.[4] The current collection strength, current collecting intensity, and the desired collecting intensity for each subject category are then ranked according to a scale of "collection levels."[5] These components will be examined in detail when the problem of structure is discussed. The subject categories and collection levels serve as specialized sign systems, the constituent signs of which can only be understood by using those systems and, through such use, contrasting the signs within each system to each other. The referentiality and the effect of the collection policy derive from the use of these systems in conjunction with each other. The collection policy is, therefore, ultimately a self-validating network of relationships; the key to making, writing, and using collection policy is to understand how its constituent elements interrelate.

Turning to the generative function, we should recognize that a successful policy is one that supplies the means to generate, over time, a collection with certain desired properties. The policy must also provide the selector with some insight into the method of achieving such a desired collection state. As a consequence, the collection policy must not only refer to the current and the desired states of the collection but should permit the selector to infer how to transform the collection from the current to the desired state. This complex and problematic area of collection policy has received little attention. Nevertheless, it is clear that a policy that does not fulfill a generative function will have little effect.

Closely linked to the referential and generative functions is the rhetorical function. The purpose of rhetoric is persuasion. The targets are the three audiences of collection policy identified by Eric Carpenter.[6] First, the policy should show faculty and students that the reasons the library contains certain materials and not others are part of a rational, consistent, publicly announced plan. Second, the institutional administration should be led by the policy to recognize that optimum use is being made of materials funding, and that requests for increased funding derive from a process of sustained and systematic planning. Third, the library's consortia partners should also be moved by the policy to view the collection development operation as stable and reliable, and to accept the possibility of entering into mutually advantageous agreements with clearly defined goals. Within the library the policy fulfills its rhetorical function by demonstrating to selectors that there is indeed a consciously controlled, library wide collection development system in effect that defines the parameters of their responsibilities.

These three fundamental functions of collection policy are closely related and interdependent. The generative function clearly relies upon the rhetorical function, for merely to provide a method is no guarantee that it will be used. The selector must receive from the policy not simply direction but also the impetus to take that direction into account. Regardless of how thoroughly the selector is convinced of its merit or utility, this direction cannot be followed unless it is intelligible. This is achieved through the network of relationships established by the policy's referential function.

POLICY STRUCTURE

Over the past two decades, as collection development has become a recognized and distinct library operation, an increasingly standardized structure for collection policy has evolved.[7] The components of this structure have been summarized and canonized in the ALA *Guidelines*, and have been most ably amplified by Charles Osburn.[8] In its standard form the policy includes introductory material on general objectives, divisions of subject responsibility, and duplication. A glance at the anthology of policies compiled by Elizabeth Futas will confirm the variety and significance of such information.[9] Indeed, the "analysis of mission, clientele and programmatic objectives is a vital prelude to the detailed subject analysis of collection policy."[10] The heart of the policy remains, however, the segmentation of the collection into subjects, and the rating of the quality of each subject segment according to the system of collection levels.[11] It is to this central component of collection policy that attention needs to be directed.

The core structure consists of two parts: (a) the matrix that is formed by the intersection of the subject classes and three collection aspects, i.e., current collection strength, current collecting intensity, and desired collecting intensity and (b) the collection levels that serve as a scale for rating the collection aspects for each subject. See figure 1.

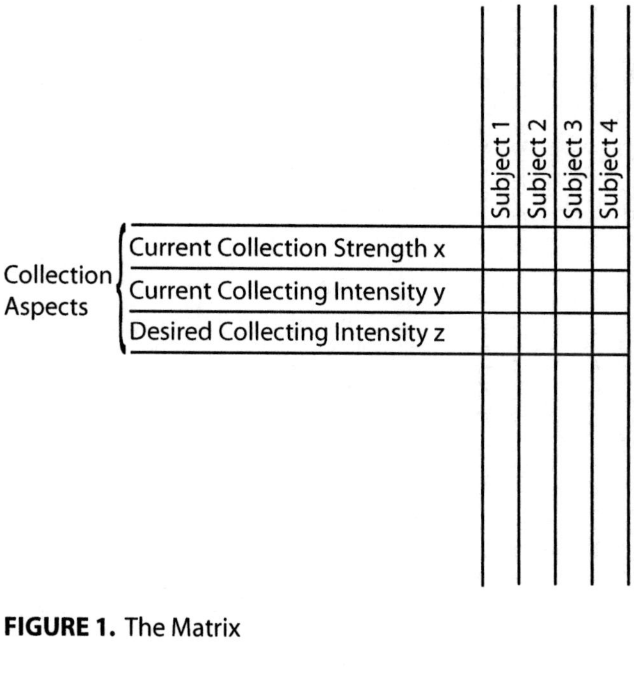

Let us begin with an examination of the matrix. Although the collection aspects usually form the vertical columns, and the subject classes the horizontal rows, I have tilted this

FIGURE 1. The Matrix

formation on its side in figure 1 because I feel this enhances our understanding of the relationships among the components of the matrix.

Collection policies traditionally categorize subjects according to standard disciplines. It is now becoming common to subdivide these general subjects into smaller topical subjects. The subject classification system to be used and the detail of subject breakdown depend upon such factors as the size and scope of the collection, the publishing rate in the subjects collected, the extent to which the policy is to serve as a basis for cooperation with other libraries, and the sophistication of the policy users.

While a policy without subject categories is not unthinkable, a policy without some kind of collection classification is. In rare cases when a library unit is more concerned with the physical content than the intellectual content of its collection, classification by format could be preferable. It is also conceivable that a policy for some very narrowly defined special collections could be based on imprint or even date of publication. Policies of larger university libraries are usually divided by topical subject, and then further subdivided by categories such as format, geography, or chronology. In any case, the value of classification is not only that it divides the collection into manageable units and creates the opposition necessary for the policy to achieve an appropriate level of reference, but also that it permits reference to segments of the collection without detailed knowledge of the composition of these segments. This is, of course, the distinctly bibliographical use of subject categories.

At the user level subjects are normally understood as subject matter, i.e. as topics of documents. On the bibliographical level, however, that relationship is inverted: subjects are not primarily concepts to which library materials refer, but rather concepts that refer to library materials. Subjects are systems of reference already in place; as such, they function as cumulative titles that permit us to refer not only to groups of materials already held but also to groups of materials that have not yet been created. To be sure, such a prospective application of subject categories depends for its success upon the creativity of the selectors who must determine which concrete titles fit into which abstract categories. This is one reason why it is possible for two libraries with identical collection policies to build different collections.

The other component of the matrix consists of the three collection aspects. Let us label these aspects, following Berkeley, x, y, and z.[12] Each of these aspects is to be rated for each subject according to the collection levels. The first (x) is what the Research Libraries Group (RLG) calls "estimated collection strength," and which the ALA *Guidelines* refer to as "collection density." This represents the current condition of the collection. The second (y), called "current collecting intensity" is the level at which the collection is currently being built. While collection strength is an indication of the level of the subject collection in place, current collecting intensity is a reference to the level at which the collection is presently being developed. The third aspect (z) is what the *Guidelines* label the "desirable level of collecting."[13] The latter category represents the actual "policy judgment."[14] This occurs because policies, as George Steiner and John Miner put it, "are means to ends and, as such, explain what people should do as contrasted with what they are doing."[15] Thus y is a statement of what x is evolving into, while z represents a projection of what x should be evolving into. Z is, therefore, the collecting objective. The distance of the library from its objective is represented by the difference between z and y, for once the level of y has become the level of z, the library is in the process of transforming x into z. We are consequently justified in labeling z the "desired collecting intensity."

Some policies, such as Stanford's or Northwestern's contain only a value for z, while others, such as Berkeley's and the recent Brown policy include values for both x and z.[16] Berkeley established values for y as well, but these were apparently deleted as out-of-date before the final draft of the policy was completed.[17] The policy presently being developed by the University of Oklahoma contains values for x, y, and z. There is, in any case, still some disagreement over the relationship between y and z. In my experience some policymakers seem either to confuse these separate concepts or to think of the term "current collecting intensity" as generally what is being strived for rather than what is actually being achieved.

Before turning to an analysis of the collection levels, something needs to be said about the mechanics of filling in the matrix. This work is normally undertaken by the selector responsible for that subject segment of the collection to which the matrix is referring. Assuming that the selector understands the collection levels—no easy task, as we will see in a moment which procedure should the selector follow to apply those values to the collection aspects in order to fill out the matrix?

It is sometimes recommended that the collecting intensity or y be established first, then the estimated collection strength or x.[18] While this is doubtless a practicable method, it fails to take into account the fundamental relationships between x and y. Row x is a string of signs that refers in its cumulation to the current condition of the collection. It is an encrypted description of the collection, using the code of the collection levels. Clearly it must entail some kind of collection evaluation, or a series of evaluations. Whatever method of evaluation is applied, however, the selector must begin by using the evaluation to establish the level at which the collection on a particular subject should be located. This first step is without a doubt the most difficult. It is essentially a matter of expressing the results of the evaluation in the language of the collection levels. In order to do this, the selector completing the matrix must learn the language of collection levels: he or she must decide what the levels symbolize with respect to the particular collection segment. As in any encryption, decryption, or translation process, the first step is necessarily tentative. Gradually, however, contexts are established and judgments can be based increasingly on consistency. Once one cell in row x is filled in, therefore, it can be opposed and compared to another cell in row x, and so forth. As one proceeds to complete row x, cells filled in earlier will need to be altered in order to conform. Eventually, however, the entire row will form a consistent whole, expressed in the language of the collection levels as a "self-clarificatory" system thoroughly understood by the selector as it relates to the particular collection for which the selector is responsible.

This method of playing off the whole and the part against each other is, of course, a classical concept of interpretation, the so-called hermeneutic circle. In interpreting a text, the whole must reflect its individual parts, and each part must be consistent with the whole. The only problem is that, if one can only understand the whole through the parts and the parts through the whole, there would be no place to start. The solution to this dilemma has traditionally been the so-called "hermeneutic leap." The interpreter must simply begin at some point with some tentative interpretation, and as the interpreter progresses through the text, constantly gauging the parts by the whole and vice versa, and eventually arrives at a self validating interpretation.[19] This is also the only reliable method to establish a systematic description of collection strength using the language of the collection levels. A primary purpose of row x, then, is to provide the selector with the possibility and the opportunity to learn the language of the collection levels.

The next step is to complete row y. From the standpoint of interpretation, this is much easier than completing row x, because the code has, so to speak, already been broken. While row x is filled out horizontally (in figure 1), row y should initially be compared with the cell above it in row x. In each case the selector needs simply to ask: Given those qualities of the collection as signified by the language of the collection levels in row x, how are my current selections affecting those qualities?

The final step in filling out the matrix is the completion of row z, which involves the actual formulation of policy. This row is best completed by the collection development officer working with the selector who completed rows x and y. (The collection development officer is the administrator responsible for the library's overall collection policy. This person may also serve as a selector.) Thus rows x and y supply data that contribute to the policy decisions to be represented in row z.

Other data needed in making such policy decisions (in addition, obviously, to a full assessment of the bibliographic needs of current and future clientele) are the qualities of other collections expressed in the same language so that collection sharing agreements can be established. This is, of course, the rationale behind the Conspectus: it assists policy-making in that it provides an intelligible indication of whether the qualities of collections in other libraries might make possible an arrangement whereby libraries can rely on each other's collections for certain subjects.[20] It should be noted, however, that such descriptions of collections in other libraries using the same language of collection levels will not help the individual selector to learn that language; having access to policies of other libraries will not, in other words, assist the selector to complete row x, because the selector is not normally acquainted with the detailed characteristics of those collections in other libraries. The selector cannot, therefore, know how the levels refer to the collection qualities of other libraries. One purpose of the verification studies in RLG has been to provide its members with some insight into the characteristics of each other's collections in order to assist in the completion of the Conspectus.

The collection development officer needs a general understanding of the language of the collection levels, both to ensure that the language is being used consistently and to understand the collection policies of other libraries. But as in the case of selection, the collection development officer must rely upon the special knowledge and integrity of the selector. The collection development officer makes policy by deciding whether the current collecting intensity, as expressed in row y, should be raised, lowered, or left the same in row z. The collection development officer must assume that the values expressed in rows x and y are accurate, but need not know precisely how the value in rows x and y refer to the detailed qualities of the collection. Indeed, the collection development officer cannot have such precise and detailed knowledge without having participated in the evaluation and language learning achieved by the selector in completing row x.

This is why the collection development policy represents the fusion of a series of individual selection policies. The language of the levels permits communication because we have agreed among ourselves that the signs composing that language stand for certain abstract collection attributes. However, each selector in using such signs to describe a collection will necessarily understand those signs differently from other selectors. Ambiguity deriving from individuality of use is common to most languages; the language of the collection levels is no exception.

The collection development officer normally knows only the abstract definitions of the collection levels such as appear in the *Guidelines* and makes policy accordingly. But the selector must carry out that policy. When the collection development officer determines that the library needs to develop a four-level collection, say, in fluid mechanics, the selector must decide what that means. This is not simply in the sense of abstract definitions but from the standpoint of actual titles. The selector is able to do this because he or she has already learned the meaning of the language of the collection levels with respect to the particular collection by completing row x in the policy. Without that knowledge, the plans represented in row z would mean very little.

All meaning derives from relationships: If you don't know where you are, you don't know where you are going, because where you are going is understandable only in relation to where you are. Z (where you want to go) and y (where you are going) are only understandable as relationships to x. This is why x is an essential part of any policy. The inclusion of x is, moreover, vital not only for referential purposes but also for the fulfillment of the policy's generative function. Only by including *x*, and only by using the same language to describe *x* as is used to describe *y* and *z*, does the method of transforming the collection from *x* to *z* become conceivable and expressable for the selector.

THE COLLECTION LEVELS

The levels of A–E in the ALA *Guidelines,* used in part by the RLG and the Association of Research Libraries as 5–0, are fast becoming the standard means to describe collections.[21] The levels have been the source of controversy, because they have been designed for academic libraries, or more specifically, for large research collections.[22] Smaller libraries have adapted the definitions to their needs by subdividing the two- and three-levels where the bulk of their collections fall. Subdividing can be useful. Care must be taken, however, to ensure that the divisions between the broader collection levels (especially between levels two and three) remain intact. Otherwise these adaptions may create separate languages. When this happens the levels can no longer serve as a means of communication among libraries.

In spite of the criticism and the adaptations and permutations of the levels, to my knowledge there has been no effective challenge to the use of levels to formulate collection development policy. The essential question, therefore, is not how the levels are being adjusted but rather to what the levels refer or what they permit us to scale.

Let us examine the collection levels as a scale. The primary function of all scales is representational: the relationships among the calibrations on the scale are intended to represent the relationships among the properties of the scaled object.[23] But some scales are clearly more representational than others. Using the traditional classification of scales as defined by S. S. Stevens, it is apparent that the collection levels constitute an ordinal scale that "presupposes a natural rank—ordering of objects with respect to some property."[24] The collection levels as an ordinal scale, therefore, must rank order some property of collections. But what is this property?

It is a mistake to imagine that the property we are seeking is equivalent to what we have been referring to as the collection aspects. This would tell us nothing. We do well to recall that much of the language we use to talk about information consists of metaphor.[25] This is especially true of collection development in which we rely heavily on such metaphors as *density, intensity, strength, breadth, depth,* and *scope.* These metaphors stand for a multitude of inferred qualities that we never seem to delineate. Just what do we mean by a strong collection? Is it a collection that approaches the unattainable comprehensive collection? Or is it the one that users agree is the most useful? Or is it one that librarians define as the strongest on the basis of evaluation—and if so, which method of evaluation?

It is apparent that the collection levels on an ordinal scale must represent some quantitative relationships. Because the levels are often considered to be progressively inclusive—a four-level collection, for example, is often thought to contain within it a three-level collection—such a quantitative relationship among levels is unavoidable. The range of the scale also presupposes quantitative relationships, because the scale runs from a condition of trying not to collect anything on a subject to one of trying to collect everything on a subject. The levels represent distances from those extremes.

To view the collecting levels merely as successive stages of a continuum or merely as an ordinal scale, however, restricts our ability to perceive their full range of referentiality. One can conceive of the collection levels with the two ends of the scale understood not so much as stable points like top and bottom or strong and weak but rather as strategic directions toward which selection efforts can progress. Such a directional view implies that the levels need not be separate and distinct but can overlap. These two directions are labeled inclusive and exclusive in figure 2. Both the inclusive and the exclusive goals are absolutes and are unattainable in reality. If one cannot build a comprehensive collection, one cannot also for the same or similar reasons build a zero-level collection.

Probably the most significant characteristic of the collection directed toward the inclusive objective is the increasing blur between quantity and quality. For research collections, quantity eventually becomes quality. In the language of Hegel, there is a *nodal line*, i.e., "a point in . . . quantitative change in which Quality changes."[26] When a collection increases in size beyond a certain critical mass, the collection's quality also improves—at least from the inclusive perspective. It is, moreover, important to recall that the use of collection levels for policy purposes has until recently been restricted to large research libraries where quality is necessarily viewed in a relatively quantitative fashion. This is why we may be inclined to view the collection levels as primarily quantitative.

As we move toward the exclusive goal, the distinction between individual items becomes increasingly important. Quality is defined to a great extent by use. Eventually, at the far end of the exclusive direction, demonstrably high use becomes the sole basis for selection. Exclusively oriented collections thus place the main emphasis on use value, while inclusively oriented collections subscribe to a system that may be viewed as something closer to exchange value. This does not mean that utility is not important for large libraries. In libraries as in commerce, use value is a precondition for the consumption of products by the public. It is only toward the inclusive end of the scale that the individual documents held by a library become increasingly interchangeable as members of the theoretical class of all materials on the subject that the comprehensive level symbolizes.

The dichotomy between inclusion and exclusion also affects collection assessment. For collections inclined toward exclusion, use and user studies, or some types of citation analysis, probably provide the most effective method of evaluation. For collections aimed at inclusion, more quantitative methods of assessment would be more effective such as shelf-list counts or the list-checking method.[27] RLG relies heavily on the list-checking method for its verification studies.

The exclusion-oriented collection emphasizes currency and depends—or should depend—on weeding. The policy of such an exclusively directed collection should therefore provide special guidelines for deselection. The inclusively oriented collection emphasizes historicity and requires guidelines applicable to retrospective selection and preservation.

The orientation of the collection also affects language, format, date of publication, and place of publication. These are all special features of documents and become increasingly important toward the exclusive end of the scheme. The more one moves toward that end, the more useful these qualities become as excluding devices. On the other hand, the closer one moves to the inclusive end, the less vital these matters become. As one approaches the ideal state of absolute comprehensiveness only found in special collections, one acquires material on the subject regardless of when or where it was published, or of the format or language in which it was published.

A final advantage to taking a more dichotomous view of the collection levels is the insight that it may permit into another dimension of collection value: the degree of selection effort involved in building different kinds of collections. Part of the reason for making policy is to know the amount of total resources—including the work of selectors—required for collection building. This is necessary because part of the value of anything produced for the consumption of others must be determined by the labor needed for its production.

The *b*-axis in figure 2, represents collection effort. It is possible to construct a 2+ collection with macrodecisions alone. By developing a vendor profile, designating relevant subjects and standard publishers, a 2+ collection can be built more or less automatically. As one moves toward *either* end of the scale, however, collection effort increases. The labor intensity of selection becomes greater in approaching the inclusive end, because the selector expends ever greater energy in searching out material not easily available or widely known. As one approaches the exclusive end, labor intensity also increases as the selector must have more rigorous criteria to justify avoiding selection and for predicting that a given item will have high use.

By taking such a two-dimensional view of the collection level as depicted in figure 2, it is possible to factor into collection policy a more unified reference to the cost in human resources. One can then consider axis *a* as representing the materials costs, and axis *b* as representing the personnel costs necessary for collection building.

CONCLUSION

It is clear that to view the collection levels merely from the standpoint of what they denote as an ordinal scale severely limits our ability to understand the full extent of the policy's content. While the levels may denote quantitative distinctions, they connote much more concerning the relative values and methods that effect the development of different types of collections. Ultimately, it is the connotations that contribute most substantially to the policy's essential functions. By mastering the connotations of the collection levels the selector can use the levels to refer to the special qualities of the appropriate collection segment. By means of such connotations the selector is also encouraged to draw conclusions about the processes necessary to transform a collection from one state to another. Even the rhetorical function is served in this way, because in establishing such connotations the selector is obliged to invest time and thought, and this participation should contribute to the selector's acceptance of the value of the policy. If we intend, therefore, to improve our understanding of the use and potential of collection policy, it is essential that we devote more attention to unraveling the complex and subtle network of relationships that constitute the policy as a system of communication.

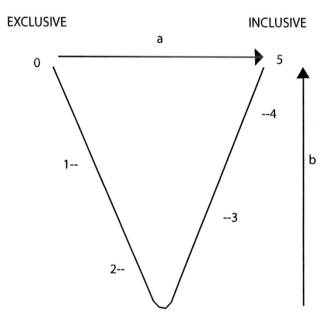

FIGURE 2. The Collection Levels

REFERENCE NOTES

1. George A. Steiner and John B. Miner, *Management Policy and Strategy: Text, Reading and Cases* (New York: Macmillan, 1977), 24.

2. Umberto Eco, *A Theory of Semiotics,* Advances in Semiotics (Bloomington, Ind.: Indiana Univ. Pr., 1976), 73.

3. Ibid., 68.

4. Elizabeth Futas, ed., *Library Acquisition Policies and Procedures,* 2d ed. (Phoenix: Oryx, 1984), 435.

5. David L. Perkins, ed., *Guidelines for Collection Development* (Chicago: ALA, 1979), 3–5, defines five collection levels: A (Comprehensive), B (Research), C (Study), D (Basic), and E (Minimal).

6. Eric J. Carpenter, "Collection Development Policies: The Case For," *Library Acquisitions: Practice and Theory* 8 (1984):44.

7. Marion L. Buzzard, "Writing a Collection Development Policy for an Academic Library," *Collection Management* 2 (winter 1978): 323.

8. *Guidelines*, 1–8; Charles B. Osburn, "Planning for a University Library Policy on Collection Development," *International Library Review* 9 (Apr. 1977): 209–24.

9. *Library Acquisition Policies and Procedures*, 435.

10. Sheila T. Dowd, "The Formulation of a Collection Development Policy Statement," in *Collection Development in Libraries: A Treatise*, ed. Robert D. Stueart and George B. Miller, Jr. (Greenwich, Conn: JAI Pr., 1980), 73.

11. Charles B. Osburn, "Some Practical Observations on the Writing, Implementation, and Revision of Collection Development Policy," *Library Resources & Technical Services* 23 (winter 1979): 10.

12. Dorothy A. Koenig, "Rushmore at Berkeley: The Dynamics of Developing a Written Collection Development Policy Statement," *The Journal of Academic Librarianship* 7 (Jan. 1982): 346.

13. Perkins, *Guidelines for Collection Development*, 7.

14. Dowd, "The Formulation of a Collection Development Policy Statement," 78; Koenig, "Rushmore at Berkeley," 346.

15. Steiner and Miner, *Management Policy*, 25.

16. Paul H. Mosher, *The Libraries of Stanford University: Collection Development Policy Statement* (Stanford, Calif.: Stanford Univ. Libraries, 1980); Richard L. Press, *An Acquisition Policy for the Northwestern University Library Evanston Campus*, rev. ed. (Evanston, Ill.: Northwestern Univ. Library, 1972); Dorothy Koenig and Sheila Dowd, *Collection Development Policy Statement*, prelim. ed. (Berkeley, Calif.: The General Library, Univ. of California, 1980); *Brown University Library Collection Development Policy* (Providence, R.I.: Brown Univ. Library, 1984).

17. Koenig, "Rushmore at Berkeley," 346.

18. Jutta Reed-Scott, *Manual for the North American Inventory of Research Library Collections* (Washington, D.C.: Assn. of Research Libraries, 1985), 35.

19. Richard E. Palmer, *Hermeneutics: Interpretation Theory in Schleiermacher, Dilthey, Heidegger, and Gadamer*, Northwestern University Studies in Phenomenology & Existential Philosophy (Evanston, Ill.: Northwestern Univ. Pr., 1969), 87.

20. Nancy E. Gwinn and Paul H. Mosher, "Coordinating Collection Development: The RLG Conspectus," *College & Research Libraries* 44 (Mar. 1983): 136–37.

21. *RLG Collection Development Manual*, 2nd ed (Stanford: The Research Libraries Group, 1981), 2-1–2-2. RLG level 5 is equivalent to level A (Comprehensive) in the ALA *Guidelines*, RLG level 4 is equivalent to ALA level B (Research), etc. See also Reed-Scott, *Manual*, 14–16.

22. Rose Mary Magrill and Doralyn J. Hickey, *Acquisitions Management and Collection Development in Libraries* (Chicago: ALA, 1984), 25.

23. See Ernest W. Adams, "Measurement Theory," in *Current Research in Philosophy of Science*, ed. Peter D. Asquith and Henry E. Kyburg, Jr. (East Lansing, Mich.: Philosophy of Science Assn., 1979), 208.

24. S. S. Stevens, "On the Theory of Scales of Measurement," *Science* 103 (7 June 1946): 677–80; Karel Berka, "Scales of Measurement: A Critical Analysis of the Concept of Scales and of their Function in the Theory of Measurement," in *Language, Logic, and Method*, ed. Robert S. Cohen and Marx W. Wartofsky, Boston Studies in the Philosophy of Science, 31 (Dortrecht: Reidel, 1983), 18.

25. See Patrick Wilson, "Second-hand Knowledge: An Inquiry into Cognitive Authority" in *Contributions in Librarianship and Information Science*, 44 (Westport, Conn.: Greenwood, 1983), 3–10.

26. *Hegel's Science of Logic,* trans. W. H. Johnston and L. G. Struthers (New York: Macmillan, 1929), 387.

27. The best current synopsis of evaluation methods is Paul H. Mosher, "Quality and Library Collections: New Directions in Research and Practice in Collection Evaluation," *Advances in Librarianship* 13 (1984): 211–38.

25 THE CITATION AS INTERTEXT

TOWARD A THEORY OF THE SELECTION PROCESS

A model is needed to depict how individual selection decisions are made. This paper presents such a model based upon a typology of contexts according to which citations (in the sense of references) are understood and used for selection. Three contexts are defined: the "syntagmatic context" within the citation itself, the "contexts of supplementation" provided by the selection source, and the "contexts of resolution" derived from the selector's experience of the collection, the clientele, and the subject.

Selection is difficult to describe. Although the standard textbooks on collection development offer much detailed prescription as to how library materials should be selected, descriptions of the selection process itself—what actually occurs when selectors select—tend to consist for the most part of superficial and self-evident generalities. The explanation is that selection is always a private, cognitive activity that does not submit to precise observation or delineation. Yet if we are ever to understand how bibliography operates and what collection development is about, some extended and systematic description of selection—no matter how tentative—must somehow be posited. The only answer would appear to be a hypothetical model that can represent the selection process and serve as a basis for future description and discussion. The construction of such a model is the purpose of this paper.

While the model I will propose is designed to describe book selection in academic libraries, it is sufficiently broad to be applied—or at least adapted without much difficulty—to the selection of other types of materials in other kinds of libraries. Our aim will be to elucidate microdecisions, i.e., item-by-item selection, rather than macrodecisions, not because the latter are less significant but rather because they are derivative: macrodecision criteria consist for the most part of abstractions drawn from previous microdecision experiences.[1] The model will center on the smallest meaningful unit of bibliography—the citation. Let us define *citation* as any string of natural-language signs that refers to or represents, regardless of its textual location, a particular information source or set of sources.[2] All selection must reduce ultimately to the manipulation of such texts that stand for other texts. To a great extent, therefore, our task will be to explain how citations are understood and used for selection purposes. Let us begin by noting briefly some special properties of the citation.

IMPLICIT AND EXPLICIT CITATION

Reference to previously encountered texts is integral to the production of any document:

This article first appeared in *Library Resources & Technical Services* 28, no. 2 (Apr./Jun. 1984): 109–19.

In very large measure, most books are about previous books. This is true at the level of the semantic code: writing persistently refers to previous writing. Explicit or implicit citation, allusion, reference are essential means of designation and proposition.[3]

Steiner's distinction between explicit and implicit citation deserves attention. We have recently become especially sensitive in library science to the applications of explicit citation to research and collection management. We have developed complicated statistical techniques that permit us to exploit with some apparent success the scholarly penchant for acknowledging direct textual origins and sources in published works.[4] There is, however, much more citation buried in any work than the explicit variety recorded in footnotes and rearranged in Garfield's remarkable indexes. As Barthes has expressed it:

Every text, being itself the intertext of another text, belongs to the intertextual, which must not be confused with a text's origins: to search for the "sources of" and "influence upon" a work is to satisfy the myth of filiation. The quotations from which a text is constructed are anonymous, irrecoverable, and yet *already read:* they are quotations without quotation marks.[5]

To make sense of a text, in other words, is always to refer implicitly and for the most part unwittingly to texts one has previously experienced. "The 'I' which approaches the text is already itself a plurality of other texts."[6] The reader is very much the product of the texts he or she has come upon before; an individual's ability not only to understand but also to evaluate and make other decisions about newly encountered documents (or other utterances) depends upon his or her reference to such personal textual experience.

A citation is also a text, and its understanding depends upon the reader's referring, in turn, to other texts previously encountered and comparing and opposing those texts to the natural-language text of the citation. It is, therefore, to those other texts—to be found for the most part outside of the citation—that the selector must constantly turn wittingly and unwittingly in order to carry out his or her responsibilities. The citation, like any text, must function as an intertext: its use by the selector depends, in other words, upon the contexts in which the selector finds or puts it, for "any entity," and thus also any sign, is defined relatively, not absolutely, and only by its place in the context."[7] Decisions as to both the meaning of the citation and the appropriateness of the cited document for inclusion in the collection will be made, therefore, on the basis of such contexts, and it is to the definition of these contexts that the remainder of this article will be devoted. In my view there are three general categories: the syntagmatic context, the contexts of supplementation, and the contexts of resolution. These categories are represented in figure 1.

THE SYNTAGMATIC CONTEXT

Although most of the contexts affecting (and effecting) the selection decision exist external and in opposition to the citation, we must begin by recognizing the essential play of contexts that occurs within the citation itself. The citation, while perhaps not qualifying as a sentence, does nevertheless consist of a closed string of signs—primarily proper names and numbers—that represent certain qualities of the cited document. Convention dictates not only which qualities are selected for representation but also the order of their arrangement in the citation. Within such a closed, conventionalized construct, any element necessarily functions as the intertext of its neighbors. This is the relationship defined by Saussure as syntagmatic.[8]

At the most basic bibliographic level, then, there exists a contextual relationship within any citation that permits the understanding and use of one element to be defined or influenced by another. (This relationship is represented in figure 1 by the lines between the components of the citation.) Thus my assumptions about the nature of a treatise, say, on the history of the Jewish mercantile tradition will be different if I am expecting the citation to conclude "Zurich, 1982" and I find instead "Berlin, 1942." My judgment will similarly influenced if a document purporting to examine the philosophical foundations of the Enlightenment turns out to consist of seven pages rather than the seven hundred pages I was anticipating from the title. Another example of the use of the syntagmatic context is the tendency to draw conclusions—usually totally unfounded—about an unknown publisher on the basis of the place of publication encountered previously in the citation.

The syntagmatic context, as we are defining it here, is thus based upon nothing more than the realization that any part of the citation can influence and be influenced by the citation as a whole.

THE CONTEXTS OF SUPPLEMENTATION

Citations used for selection are extracted from a variety of sources, most of which overlap notoriously in their coverage. One source is normally preferred over another because of the extent to which it provides or constitutes a supplementary context for the citations it contains. It is to these contexts that we now need to turn our attention. They can be divided into two general types that we will call direct and indirect supplementation

Direct supplementation most frequently serves to increase the selector's knowledge of the subject matter of the document cited. Such supplementary information may consist of a classification according to some standard system, or it may include subject headings as will be found in national bibliographies, for example, or in such sources as LC proof slips. This direct supplementation provides a special context that facilitates and complements the synoptic function of the cited title. At the same time we must admit, however, that classification of any kind tends also to close off or limit further speculation as to the potential qualities of the subject matter. Direct supplementation can therefore also have a negative

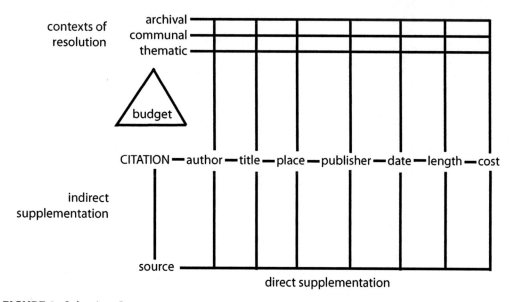

FIGURE 1. Selection Context

effect on selection decisions. All tools employing classification, including especially our library catalogs, are powerful and subtle censorship devices that exclude all but a few of the subjects considered in the document. It is for this reason that in some cases we will want to use for selection a variety of sources that do overlap and provide independently the same type of direct supplementary data.

Further direct supplementation to the synopsis of subject matter in the citation may be supplied by annotations (as are found in subject bibliographies), and reviews (either in standard review sources like *Publisher's Weekly* or scholarly journals. Yet direct supplementations need not always serve to improve our knowledge of the subject matter. Notes in a catalog, for example, may supplement the date information in the citation by identifying the document as a reprint. Antiquarian catalogs are especially rich in this kind of direct supplementation, frequently including essential information on the document's physical or publishing history.

In all cases we must bear in mind, however, that these data remain, from a bibliographical point of view, supplementary. Anything outside of the citation has bibliographical significance only as context. Even the document itself, which serves as a context of supplementation when an approval plan is used for selection, is an addendum to the citation and is not necessarily, as has been recently maintained, "the best possible source of information" for a selection decision.[9] Having the document in hand may provide a good context for the selector's determination of the subject matter, but the selector's decision as to the significance and appropriateness of the document for the collection will depend far more heavily upon other contexts of supplementation, as well as other varieties of contextual data that we still have to define. The document itself is only one more context, and it itself must still be understood within other contexts. Indeed, it is a purpose in this article to emphasize that the understanding and use of any text always depends on what is not in it—on other texts, on contexts. Thus while the document itself can serve as one useful context to the citation, it plays no privileged role in the selection decision precisely because its bibliographical value—like its literary or historical value—will depend upon the environment or context in which it is placed.

The other general type of supplementation provided by selection sources we will label indirect supplementation. While direct supplementation, as we have seen, increases the selector's understanding of individual components of the citation, such as the title or the date, indirect supplementation tends normally to increase or influence our estimate of the citation as a whole and thus our conclusions about the cited document. The context provided by indirect supplementation derives from the material in the source not directly linked to the particular citation being considered, i.e., from the other citations listed as well as the purpose and quality of the source itself. Thus it is possible to infer from a citation in a national bibliography no special quality except the country of publication. A citation in a packet of vendor slips implies a conscious act of selection by a vendor based on his interpretation of a prearranged profile. A citation in a core list such as *Books for College Libraries* or a citation drawn from citation studies of core journals also provides a context from which the selector can infer certain qualities of the cited documents.

In some rare cases, moreover, the indirect supplementation can be used as the sole foundation for a selection decision. If, for example, an American library collects contemporary fiction, then that library will almost certainly select a novel reviewed on the front page of the *New York Times Book Review* regardless of who wrote the novel, where it was published, what it is about, or even what the review says about it. The decision is made on the basis of the citation context with little regard at all for any information contained in the citation itself. Another example is provided by the use in research libraries of book reviews in core journals covering scholarly subjects: the citation's status in such cases comes not so much from the direct supplementation of the conclusions in the review as from the indirect circumstance that the document represented by the citation was reviewed in such an important journal.

Indirect supplementation can also add to the selector's view of the accessibility of the cited document. Published library catalogs, the National Union Catalog, or national databases such as RLIN or OCLC are also used as sources for selection—although frequently after the citation has already been found in another source. Routine interlibrary cooperation, to the extent that it is practicable, depends initially upon relating citations for works under consideration to the larger supplementary context of multilibrary catalogs or databases.

We must, finally, not overlook the indirect supplementation provided when the source of the citation is a library user. The character and legitimacy of the user can and frequently does in such cases supplement indirectly the selector's understanding and use of the citation. In extreme situations the nature of the citation can be totally eclipsed by the status of the requester, for bibliography, like any other human activity, must often be carried out within a political context.

THE CONTEXTS OF RESOLUTION

While the syntagmatic context and the contexts of supplementation are represented by discrete texts fairly easily discernible on a case-by-case basis, the third and most unique context category upon which selection depends belongs primarily to the selector and is not immediately available for general scrutiny. These contexts of resolution, as I will call them, are at once the most crucial to selection and the most elusive, for while their presence pervades the selection process, their individual qualities are ultimately visible only as mirrored in their product—the collection. The realization that selection as a branch of librarianship, consists of "the exercise of choice and judgment," the charge that selection is an art rather than a craft, or the suspicion that subjectivity in selection is unavoidable—these conclusions follow logically from the fact that the suitability of the cited document is finally determined on the basis of a context that can only be privately assembled and applied.[10]

The contexts of resolution are a set of three interrelated and competing contexts: the archival, the communal, and the thematic.[11] (I have arranged these in the schematic vertically above the linear citation.) The archival context is equivalent to the selector's knowledge of what is already in the collection. The communal context is the selector's understanding of the research needs and interests of the clientele. The thematic context is the selector's awareness of what is being (or has been) published on the subject. Like all texts, these have their origins in individual experience and, since no two individuals have ever had the same combinations of experience, no two selectors can ever operate with exactly the same contexts of resolution. Also, like all other texts, these are constantly evolving as the selector gradually increases his or her experience of what the collection consists of, what the users are concerned with, and what the subject is developing into.

The final selection decision is, therefore, normally made by relating the linear components of the citation, as influenced by each other (i.e., syntagmatically) and as supplemented directly and indirectly by the source, to the contexts of resolution. (This process is symbolized in the schematic by those points at which the vertical lines from the citation and the horizontal lines extending from the three contexts of resolution intersect or connect.) The configuration of such connections will, of course, vary radically from one citation to another. Some of the connections will not be made at all, others will be of minor—or merely supportive—importance in the decision, while a few will play a major role in judging the document's appropriateness. A simplified, generalized example of a selection decision might therefore proceed as follows: "While this subject is currently in fashion (title in thematic context), I will not select it because none of my constituency is currently working on it (title in communal context); and even if I am wrong on that account and someone is working on this subject, that individual would probably want a newer document (date in communal context); above all I feel justified in not ordering this document in any case because it is published by a vanity press and except in highly unusual cases we do not by policy collect vanity press publications (publisher in archival context.)" There are, needless to say, a vast variety of combinations of connection and emphasis. Often a major connection will cancel out the less significant connections, while at other times minor connections can gang up on a major connection, obstruct its authority, and bring about the opposite selection decision.

Why, then, do certain connections within these contexts of resolution have greater influence on the selection decision than others? In the first place this influence can proceed from inferences drawn from the syntagmatic context or from supplementation supplied by the selection source. But this variant significance that we note in these contextual connections has another origin as well: the inevitable weighting in different situations of the three contexts. Depending upon such factors as the goals of the library, the nature of the subject, the status of the subject within the library, and the predilections of the individual selector, the three contexts will be prioritized. One context will always take precedence over the other two. There are, in other words, archival and thematic and communal libraries and subjects and selectors. While such weighting is inevitable, however, the contexts are in my experience seldom if ever exclusive. All three will play a role in virtually all selection: one will normally tend to dominate, but its dominance will be tempered by the other two.

Probably the clearest example of the dominance of the archival context in selection decisions will be found in a special collections department. While special collections selectors will obviously take into account the state of the subject under consideration and the patterns of use in the library, their primary consideration in selection will normally be—and should normally be—what is already in the collection. The communal context, on the other hand, becomes dominant in smaller academic libraries, small or medium public libraries, and in the development of working collections in larger academic libraries. Finally, research collections are produced for the most part by giving primary emphasis to the thematic context: the selector's concern is to construct a collection that reflects what is occurring (in the sense of what is being or has been published) in the subject.

The origins of the selector's experience, from which such contexts of resolution evolve, also vary considerably depending upon the emphasis given in selection to one context over the others. The individual selector, in other words can and normally will attempt to mold or control his own experience. If the archival context plays less of a role in selection than the other contexts—as will be the case, for example, in the building of smaller academic collections—experience from which that context derives will tend to consist for the most part of the previous selection decisions made by that particular selector. The more weight given the archival context, the more systematized its construction will be, frequently in the form of written policy, and the greater the concern to measure the accuracy of selection decisions through some form of collection evaluation. It is a quality of the archival perspective, moreover, that the results of evaluation tend to be used as the primary basis for the formulation of collection policy. The patterns of previous development—regardless of whether they have evolved from accident or design—provide a powerful foundation for decisions on future development. Strong areas of a collection built with archival emphasis will continue to be strengthened, while weaker areas will continue to be ignored.

Like the archival context, the communal context can be developed either casually or intensively, depending on the degree of significance ascribed to that context in the selection process. If it is considered less important, the communal context will evolve piecemeal as a result of day-to-day contact with users. If it is understood as having greater significance, it will develop through systematic and aggressive use and user studies. In extreme forms of communal context dominance, the users themselves can become the selectors, at which point the archival and thematic considerations become increasingly suspect and suppressed. The purpose of the communal context is to respond to the needs of the users, and in such extreme forms easily discernible user actions—normally in the form of circulation—will tend to define those needs to a large extent. Evidence of the dominance of the communal context will be found not only in the recent user-defined selection approaches in Baltimore and in the radical rationalism of Dennis Dickinson but also in Gore's vision of the Alexandrian menace, as well as in the infamous Pitt study.[12]

The thematic context derives its origin from exposure to publishing trends. Like the other two contexts, the attention given to the development of the thematic context also depends on the significance attributed to it in the selection process. If it is seen as less significant, the selector will develop it in the course of routine selection by noting generally in selection sources which subjects are being treated. If, on the other hand, the thematic context is to play a dominant role in selection, then the selector will actively endeavor to increase his exposure to the main trends in the subject by, among other things, more reading of the secondary subject literature.

Of the three contexts, the thematic is the one that is most susceptible to charges of accepting the fallacy of comprehensiveness. The purpose of the library from the thematic perspective, however, is not to collect everything on the subject (which is neither possible nor desirable), but rather to acquire a judiciously selected representation of not only the topics that are being publicly considered but also in the proportion they are being so considered. Thus while the library clearly does not seek comprehensiveness, it does attempt to maintain generally the same proportions between subject areas that a theoretically comprehensive collection might maintain. While the communal context, moreover, is intended to provide the selector with the capacity and the responsibility to *respond* to the needs of the clientele, the thematic context is intended rather primarily to *create* such needs—needs that the library may or may not be able to satisfy. In some cases information needs will be generated that no library can satisfy, and the user will consequently be obliged to discover or invent such information for himself.

The thematic context is predicated to a great extent upon the assumption that the user should make his or her own selections from among library holdings.[13] If different points of view and approaches have been published, then the user must have the opportunity to make a choice among them. And selection always entails rejection. From the communal perspective, therefore, there must always be a certain amount of wastage in any thematically developed collection. We must recall, however, that to decide not to use a book is to use it. For the researcher to decide that nothing but trash has been published for the last five years in his subject, that trash must be available in the library to be identified as such.

The thematic context is especially important in the university library because it forms the basis for an unwritten contract between the faculty and the library. The faculty has increasingly abrogated its responsibility for selection on the assumption, I believe, that the library will continue to provide a representative collection that the faculty can use to determine the current condition of the various subjects treated at the institution. This approach represents a significant difference between the way research collections used to be built by the faculty and the way they are currently built by subject selectors.

It should also be noted that in a collection development effort dominated by the thematic context, deselection and preservation become especially problematic. In collections or subjects where the communal or archival contexts dominate, such decisions are relatively straightforward. The communally dominated library preserves items people are using (i.e., borrowing) and weeds the rest. The archivally dominated library will normally avoid much weeding and will preserve what it defines as its collections of distinction. In the thematically dominated library, however, the selectors have trained themselves—frequently with considerable difficulty—to suspend judgment. By operating according to a system that leaves to the user the responsibility for evaluating the quality of individual documents, selectors deny themselves an easily accessible scale of value that could serve as a basis to determine what to keep and what to discard, what to preserve and what to allow to disintegrate. This is an especially alarming situation since clearly most of the preservation must be done by larger research libraries, the building of which is primarily thematically oriented. The solution to this situation has been either to abandon the thematic approach in favor either of the archival method of preserving strong collections or the communal-eclectic method of preserving whatever turns up in circulation requiring repair. The other alternative has been to maintain the thematic perspective as much as possible but to diffuse its effects through interinstitutional cooperation.

The final ingredient in our description of the selection process must inevitably be the budget. Clearly the budget does figure conspicuously in any selection decision, but just as clearly it should not be used as a basis for selection. Its purpose should rather be to regulate the extent to which such contexts of resolution are applied. Generally speaking, this regulation is accomplished in the course of routine selection by allowing the opposition between the three contexts to become increasingly equal and thus to restrict each other. The better the budget, in other words, the more one context can achieve dominance and be more fully implemented. The tighter the budget, however, the more the selector must allow the contexts to play against each other, suppressing the excesses of the dominant one. In thematically dominated selection, for example, the selector will base cutbacks on the communal criterion that no one is doing research on the subject in his or her institution. Conversely, in a communally based selection situation, reduction can be made using the thematic criterion that a particular area of the subject is not receiving much attention generally, and that material on that subject should be of less interest to specific scholars at the institution.

CONCLUSIONS

Although the contexts of resolution are, as we have seen, weighted, and although that weighting can be consciously adjusted by the selector, nevertheless, these contexts remain in their aggregate both unique to the individual selector and self-justifying. Written policies may, of course, be used to provide some regulation and coordination among selectors, but such policies no matter how detailed must still always be interpreted by each selector on the basis of his or her personal experience at the time of each selection decision. While it is possible to establish certain guidelines that can be more or less mechanically applied on the basis of information discernible in the citation and in the surrounding supplementary data provided directly or indirectly by selection sources, there can be no final, impartial, objective determination as to precisely what belongs in a particular collection and what does not; for every citation remains from the standpoint of every individual a single intertext in a vast network of personal and constantly evolving contexts that influence decisively the citation's meaning and significance.

This is not to purport, of course, that selection is chaotic. Contexts overlap greatly between individuals, so that most instances of selection invite little dispute. But overlap is not coincidence, and creativity and interpretation must therefore not only be accepted but also respected and even encouraged as essential to the conduct of effective and responsible selection.

REFERENCE NOTES

1. Hendrik Edelman, "Selection Methodology in Academic Libraries," *Library Resources & Technical Services* 23 (winter 1979): 37.

2. It has recently become fashionable to distinguish *references* from *citations* so that the "number of references a paper has is measured by the number of items in its bibliography as endnotes and footnotes, etc., while the number of citations a paper has is found by looking it up in some sort of citation index and seeing how many other papers mention it" (Derek J. De Solla Price, "Citation Measures of Hard Science, Soft Science, Technology and Nonscience," in *Communicating among Scientists and Engineers*, ed. Carnot E. Nelson [Lexington, Mass.: Heath, 1970], 7). I have preferred not to adopt this convention because the word *citation* has a well-established and specific meaning, while the term *reference* should be reserved for more general uses, including the primary activity of the citation.

3. George Steiner, "After the Book?" in his *On Difficulty and Other Essays* (New York: Oxford Univ. Pr., 1978), 190.

4. Robert N. Broadus, "The Applications of Citation Analyses to Library Collection Building," *Advances in Librarianship* 7 (1977): 299–335.

5. Roland Barthes, "From Work to Text," trans. Josue V. Harari, in *Textual Strategies*, ed. Josue V. Harari (Ithaca: Cornell Univ. Pr., 1979), 77.

6. Roland Barthes *S/Z*, trans. Richard Miller (New York: Hill & Wang, 1974), 10.

7. Louis Hjelmslev, *Prolegomena to a Theory of Language*, trans. Francis J. Whitfield (Madison: Univ. of Wisconsin Pr., 1969), 45.

8. Ferdinand de Saussure, *Course in General Linguistics*, trans. Roy Harris (London: Duckworth, 1983), 121–23. Throughout the discussion I have omitted reference to the other relationship posited by Saussure, the "associative" or what we now call the paradigmatic. To the extent that the paradigmatic implies the facility to establish some form of lexical meaning, its presence does not require special note since I am assuming that the selector can understand the natural language of which the citation is composed. To the extent that the paradigmatic is understood as the "axis of opposition," i.e., that sense is made of signs by opposing them to other signs in the language, the "contexts of resolution" that I formulate in the latter half of this paper are intended to serve precisely that function in the selection process.

9. Jean Boyer Hamlin, "The Selection Process," in *Collection Development in Libraries: A Treatise*, vol. 1, eds. Robert D. Stueart and George B. Miller Jr. (Greenwich, Conn.: JAI Pr., 1980), 199.

10. Paul H. Mosher, "Collection Evaluation in Research Libraries: The Search for Quality, Consistency and System in Collection Development," *Library Resources & Technical Services* 23 (winter 1979): 23.

11. Dan C. Hazen, in his "Collection Development, Collection Management and Preservation," *Library Resources & Technical Services* 26 (Jan.–Mar. 1982): 7–8, has carefully posited "five distinct but interrelated factors" as the basis for collection development decisions: (a) "academic activity or user demand," (b) "historical precedent," (c) "volume and cost of materials," (d) "availability of alternatives to purchase," and (e) "discipline-specific models of access to information." While I would certainly endorse the particular significance of these five factors, I believe (as apparently does Hazen) that they are, nevertheless, very different kinds of knowledge which will be used differently in selection decisions. Hazen's factors a, b, and e correspond roughly to the communal, archival, and thematic contexts, respectively, that I am formulating. Hazen's factor d I would relegate to—in my nomenclature—the contexts of supplementation. Finally, as I will note at the end of this paper, I believe the budget should be viewed not as a criterion for selection but rather as an influence upon the relative extent to which selection criteria are acted upon.

12. Nora Rawlinson, "Give 'Em What They Want," *Library Journal* 106 (Nov. 15, 1981): 2188–90. See also the response by Murray C. Bob, "The Case for Quality Book Selection," *Library Journal* 107 (Sept. 15, 1982): 1707–10; Dennis W. Dickinson, "A Rationalist's Critique of Book Selection for Academic Libraries," *Journal of Academic Librarianship* 7 (July 1981): 138–43; Daniel Gore, "Farewell to Alexandria: The Theory of the No-Growth, High Performance Library," in *Farewell to Alexandria: Solutions to Space, Growth, and Performance Problems of Libraries*, ed. Daniel Gore (Westport, Conn.: Greenwood, 1976), 164–80; Allen Kent and others, *Use of Library Materials: The University of Pittsburg Study* (New York: Dekker, 1979).

13. William A. Katz, *Collection Development: The Selection of Materials for Libraries* (New York: Holt, 1980), 107–108.

Printed in the United States
40872LVS00002B/1-92

9 780838 983614